Public Sector Financial Management

This series brings together cutting edge research in public administration on the new budgeting and accounting methodologies and their impact across the public sector, from central and local government to public health care and education. It considers the need for better quality accounting information for decision-making, planning and control in the public sector; the development of the IPSAS (International Public Sector Accounting Standards) and the EPSAS (European Public Sector Accounting Standards), including their merits and role in accounting harmonisation; accounting information's role in governments' financial sustainability and crisis confrontation; the contribution of sophisticated ICT systems to public sector financial, cost and management accounting deployment; and the relationship between robust accounting information and performance measurement. New trends in public sector reporting and auditing are covered as well. The series fills a significant gap in the market in which works on public sector accounting and financial management are sparse, while research in the area is experiencing unprecedented growth.

More information about this series at
http://www.palgrave.com/gp/series/15782

Hassan Ouda

Practice-Relevant Accrual Accounting for the Public Sector

Producers' and Users' Perspectives

with contribution from Susana Jorge

palgrave
macmillan

Hassan Ouda
Department of Accounting and Finance
Faculty of Management Technology
German University in Cairo
Cairo, Egypt

with contribution from
Susana Jorge
Faculty of Economics
University of Coimbra
Coimbra, Portugal

Public Sector Financial Management
ISBN 978-3-030-51594-2 ISBN 978-3-030-51595-9 (eBook)
https://doi.org/10.1007/978-3-030-51595-9

This Palgrave Macmillan imprint is published by the registered company Springer Nature Switzerland AG.
The registered company address is: Gewerbestrasse 11, 6330 Cham, Switzerland

I would like to dedicate this book to my professors:
Professor Aad Bac, Tilburg university, The Netherlands
Professor Klaus Lüder, Speyer University, German
Professor Rowan Jones, Birmingham University, UK
Professor James L. Chan, University of Illinois, USA
Professor Jan van Helden, Groningen University, The Netherlands
Professor June Pallet, Canterbury University, New Zealand
Drs. Kees Horden, Erasmus University Rotterdam, The Netherlands
Dr. Bert Bettonvil, Tilburg University, The Netherlands

Foreword

The Comparative International Governmental Accounting Research (CIGAR) network, which has existed for more than 30 years now, has witnessed lively debates about accrual accounting adoption in the public sector. Various issues have been discussed: is accrual accounting, as invented for the business sector, applicable to the public sector; if so, which adaptations are required to align them to the specifics of the public sector; and, how accrual accounting, which has often replaced cash accounting, can be implemented successfully? International standard-setting developments, such as IPSAS and more recently EPSAS, have impacted these debates.

This book provides important contributions to these debates. It discusses a wide variety of themes, but for me three themes stand out. First, whether we need specific accounting principles and rules for the recognition and measurement of heritage assets, such as monuments, which are different from assets with earning capacity in the private sector? Second, how do public sector accounting principles and rules need to be adapted for giving insight into the fiscal sustainability of the government? And third, how can we identify a match between needs of users, such as politicians and governmental managers, and the preferences of producers of accounting information, such as standard-setters, accountants, and auditors? An overarching philosophy which underlies discussions about these themes is that public sector accounting research should become more practice-relevant.

This book by Hassan Ouda and Susana Jorge is not a neutral review of public sector accounting themes in general and accrual accounting adoption in particular. It is predominantly normative. Hassan Ouda, as the main author of the book, is a passionate scholar and practitioner with strong ideas and opinions. But that also makes this book valuable to many people with an interest in public sector accounting, both academics and practitioners. It encourages us to think about the issues raised in the book and to engage ourselves in debates with others.

This book also presents an agenda for future research. An intriguing question for future investigations regards the fit between user needs and producer preferences, as discussed in Chaps. 6 and 7 of the book. In practice we are often faced with different goals of users and producers of public sector accounting information. Producers have their professional standards and pretend to know what proper accounting information should be. Users require information for solving problems, for legitimizing certain actions, or for serving their political agenda. Then a match or fit may be unlikely. Also learning processes as propagated in the book are not likely to take place. So, the ideas in this book are focused on achieving consensus between demanders and suppliers of information. But a clash between both, at the least, can be understandable. Future research needs to investigate the circumstances under which either a match or a mismatch between the supply and demand sides of accounting information can be expected. This is a challenging and also an important research question.

University of Groningen
Groningen, The Netherlands

Jan van Helden

Preface

The overall objective of this book is to develop a practice-relevant accrual accounting for the public sector, which on the one hand recognizes the specific characteristics of the public sector in comparison to the private sector, and on the other hand gives voice to both producers and users of public sector accounting. The adoption of accrual accounting in the public sector has started since three decades. The world of public sector accounting practice regards it as self-evident progress; yet, they consider it a problematic reform. This is because the adoption of accrual accounting in the public sector is based on the one-size-fits-all model, applying conventional accrual accounting principles developed for the private sector to public sector entities without taking into consideration that public sector entities and assets are different in purpose and essence. Actually, when an accounting method is introduced into a new environment, it is naïve to assume that by assembling the components of a system the desired or officially intended outcome will be achieved. Despite that, there is a long-standing academic argument for using accrual accounting in the public sector; yet it is noted that some necessary adjustments for adopting accrual accounting in the public sector are missed.

Accordingly, this book has attempted to deal with and tackle these necessary adjustments. This could be the starting point for making accrual accounting more practice-relevant for the public sector entities. The first part of this book focuses on the necessary developments from the producers' perspective. The main focus of this part is on reshaping the application of accrual accounting principles and assumptions to fit the context of public sector entities. This part also focuses on developing a practice-relevant holistic accounting approach for governmental capital assets that is based on developing and reshaping the assets recognition criteria. In this part, there is also a suggestion for a sustainable accounting approach for reporting on long-term fiscal sustainability. This approach is based on developing the accounting bases and measurement focus and expanding the scope of government financial reporting and the indicators of long-term fiscal sustainability. Besides, a reconsideration of the scope of general-purpose financial reporting from an accountability perspective is done by Susana Jorge.

The second part of the book outlines the necessary developments and adjustments from the users' perspective. Thus, the main focus is on developing a dynamic model for making public sector accrual accounting more user practice-relevant. On top of that a theory of accounting information usefulness is developed and presented. The theory explains how cognitive aspects do influence the use/nonuse of accounting information by the politicians. The last chapter provides some final remarks and underlines many "outstanding issues." It expresses the deep belief that there is a lot of work that needs to be done to make the public sector accrual accounting more practice-relevant from both producers' and users' perspectives.

The value of this book relies on its outstanding objective and approach along with its challenging goals. The available books are either textbooks for teaching or collections of mainly descriptive country studies. All the chapters in this book add to current knowledge in the emerging research area on making accrual accounting more practice-relevant for the public sector. This would be of interest to academics, researchers, policy-makers, public managers, international organizations, and standard-setters who are involved in, or are responsible for, reforming the public sector accounting.

German University in Cairo
New Cairo, Egypt

Hassan Ouda

CONTENTS

About the Authors

Hassan Ouda is a Professor of Accounting at Faculty of Management Technology, German University in Cairo (GUC), Egypt. His research interests include public sector accounting and budgeting reform, particularly in relation to implementation of accrual accounting and budgeting, performance-based budgeting, and performance audit in the public sector. He is an international expert in public sector accounting and budgeting reform and has been advising for many years the governmental organizations through the managerial and technical changes required to achieve greater value, accountability, transparency, and performance. Since March 2013, he has been appointed as a member of International Public Sector Accounting Standards Committee-ICGFM-USA. Since 2015, he has been the editor of *International Journal on Government Financial Management* (USA). In June 2015, he was appointed as a board member of International Comparative Government Accounting Research (CIGAR). He developed (2001 and 2004) the *Basic Requirements Model (BRM) for successful implementation of accrual accounting in the public sector*. The BRM has been used by the United Nations in 2005 to determine the key success factors of the adoption of full accrual accounting in United Nations Organizations. In 2010, he developed *A Prescriptive Model for Successful Transition to Accrual Accounting in Central Government*. In 2014, he developed the *Practical Accounting Approach for Heritage Assets: An Alternative Reporting Model for the NPM Practices*. In 2016, he developed the *Holistic Practical Accounting Approach for Governmental*

Capital Assets. In 2019, he was the key player in Drafting the Unified Public Finance Law in Egypt.

He has published more than 80 articles in international journals, book chapters in international books, and papers in the proceedings of international conferences. He earned his Ph.D. in Public Sector Accounting Reform from Tilburg University and his M.Sc. in Accountancy and Business Economics from Erasmus University Rotterdam, The Netherlands.

Susana Jorge is Senior Lecturer at the Faculty of Economics, University of Coimbra (Coimbra, Portugal) and is affiliated with the Research Center in Political Science – CICP (Braga, Portugal). Her fields of expertise are public sector accounting and financial reporting, with special focus on local government; transparency; local financial management; relationship between governmental accounting and national accounts; reforms in public sector accounting, and IPSAS. Her academic research has been published in a variety of journals including *Public Money and Management*, *International Journal of Public Administration*, *Public Management Review*, *International Review of Administrative Sciences*, *Accounting in Europe*, *Journal of Comparative Policy Analysis*, *Revista de Contabilidad*, *The Electronic Journal of e-Government*, *Journal of Applied Accounting Research*, and *Journal of Public Budgeting, Accounting & Financial Management*. She is currently Chair of the Executive Board of the research network Comparative International Governmental Accounting Research (CIGAR), and member of the Academic Advisory Group of the International Public Sector Accounting Standards Board (IPSASB-AAG).

Abbreviations

AARF	Australian Accounting Research Foundation
AASB	Australian Accounting Standards Board
ACCA	Association of Chartered Certified Accountants
AICPA	American Institute of Certified Public Accountants
AIRD	Accounting Information Research Department
AIUT	Accounting Information Usefulness Theory
ASB	Accounting Standards Board
CF&B	Cash Flow & Balances
CFR	Consolidated Financial Reporting
CFR	Current Financial Resources
CFT	Cognitive Fit Theory
CICA	Canadian Institute of Chartered Accountants
CIPFA	Chartered Institute of Public Finance and Accountancy
DfS	Design for Sustainability
DOD	Department of Defense
EPSAS	European Public Sector Accounting Standards
FASAB	Federation Accounting Standards Advisory Board
FASB	Financial Accounting Standards Board
FRC	Financial Reporting Council
FRS	Financial Reporting Standard
GAAP	Generally Accepted Accounting Principles
GASB	Governmental Accounting Standards Board
GDP	Gross Domestic Product
GGS	General Government Sector
GPFR	General-Purpose Financial Reporting
GRI	Global Reporting Initiative
HA	Heritage Assets

IASB	International Accounting Standards Board
IFAC	International Federation of Accountants
IFRS	International Financial Reporting Standards
IIRC	International Integrated Reporting Council
IMF	International Monetary Fund (IMF)
IPSAS	International Public Sector Accounting Standards
IPSASB	International Public Sector Accounting Standards Board
NCGA	National Committee on Governmental Accounting
ND	Net Debt
NFD	Net Financial Debt
NFW	Net Financial Worth
NPFM	New Public Financial Management
NPM	New Public Management
NW	Net Worth
NZSA	New Zealand Society of Accountants
OBR	Office for Budget Responsibility
OECD	Organisation for Economic Co-operation and Development
PBEs	Public Benefit Entities
PFI	Private Financial Initiative
PFM	Public Financial Management
PNW	Positive Net Worth
PSND	Public Sector Net Debt
RPG	Recommended Practice Guideline
SAC-4	Statement of Accounting Concepts-4
SCT	Social Cognitive Theory
SFFAS	Statement of Federal Financial Accounting Standards
SNFW	Sustainable Net Financial Worth
SNW	Sustainable Net Worth
TER	Total Economic Resources
TFR	Total Financial Resources
TSER	Total Sustainable Economic Resources
TSFR	Total Sustainable Financial Resources
WB	World Bank

List of Figures

List of Tables

CHAPTER 1

Introduction

Research in public sector accounting should ultimately fulfill a practical purpose and should aim at improving the public sector accounting practice. While the academics (e.g., CIGAR scholars) have exerted great effort in the last three decades to develop public sector accounting, these efforts are still of little value to the public sector accounting practice. This is because their efforts were not mainly directed towards improving the public sector accounting practice, but they were simply directed to describe or understand, analyze, or critique it. Similar to what has been claimed by Choudhury (1986) for the management accounting research, public sector accounting research is also relevant to practice when it helps practitioners to understand their organizations and improve practices, and when it contributes to a theoretical body of knowledge that is beneficial to effective organizational change in the future. Accordingly, public sector accounting research should be redirected to focus on creating better practices and developing the public sector accounting as an academic discipline. While the movement towards New Public Management (NPM) has required the reforming of public sector accounting through the adoption of accrual accounting in the public sector (Hood 1995; Ball and Grubnic 2007), Lapsley et al. (2009) have argued that despite the limited evidence available on the efficacy of an accrual accounting system, the world of public sector accounting practice regarded the adoption of accrual accounting as self-evident progress; they, however, consider it a 'problematic' reform.

H. Ouda, *Practice-Relevant Accrual Accounting for the Public Sector*, Public Sector Financial Management,
https://doi.org/10.1007/978-3-030-51595-9_1

It is a problematic reform because the adoption of accrual accounting in the public sector has been based on a one-size-fits all model, which applies conventional accrual accounting principles, developed for the private sector, to public sector entities without taking into consideration that public sector entities and assets are differentiated in purpose and essence. It is also a problematic reform because public sector accounting scholars, standard setters, and professional bodies did not reshape the application of accrual accounting principles and assumptions (which were originally designed for measuring net income in the private sector) to fit the context of public sector accounting practice and to consider the specific nature of public sector entities. In fact, public sector accounting scholars, standard setters, and professional bodies did not develop more practice-relevant recognition and measurement criteria for specific public capital assets. Furthermore, as a result of a wider range of potential users that General Purpose Financial Reporting (GPFR) by public sector entities are expected to serve, the scope of financial statements in the public sector should be expanded to include financial and nonfinancial information, whether this information may be presented in the notes to financial statements or in separate reports included in the GPFR. Reporting such information is necessary for governments to discharge their obligations to be accountable—that is, to account for, and justify the use of, the resources raised from or on behalf of constituents (IFAC 2013).

In addition, the financial reporting of public sector entities needs to be expanded to provide information about financial commitments that can have an impact on the sustainability of service delivery. Accordingly, the new set of financial statements should include all items that will affect the fiscal sustainability of governments in the future; for example, the financial statement might be supplemented by separate statements of future and contingent liabilities, statements of commitments, and a "trust assets" statement that includes heritage assets in physical units. Furthermore, one of the common reasons given for the adoption of accrual accounting in the public sector is the discharge of accountability. However, there is an argument in the literature that strongly debates whether the requirement for public sector entities to provide financial statements based on private sector Generally Accepted Accounting Practices (GAAP) impacts positively or negatively on public sector accountability outcomes (see, for example, Barton 1999; Carnegie and West 2005; Wild 2013; Micallef and Peirson 1997; Cooper and Owen 2007). The discharge of accountability obligations requires the provision of information about the entity's management of resources entrusted to it for the delivery of services to constituents and others. Given the way in which the services provided by public sector entities are funded (primarily by taxation revenues or other non-exchange transactions) and the dependency of service recipients on the provision of those services over the long term, the discharge of accountability obligations will also require the provision of information about such matters as the entity's service delivery achievements during the reporting period, and its capacity to continue to provide services in future periods.

1 Accrual Accounting and Its Practice-Relevance for the Public Sector

In fact, when an accounting method is introduced into a new environment, "it is naïve to assume that by simply assembling the components of a system that desired or officially intended outcome will be achieved" (Hodges 2013). Hodges has further argued that the long-standing academic argument for using accrual accounting in the public sector (Taussing 1963) appears to have missed some necessary adjustments. The general finding is that mimicry of private sector techniques can be imposed and apparently complied with but that their assimilation into the culture of the public sector, if it is achieved at all, will take a considerable period of time and require a considerable change that makes it suitable for the public sector entities that are differentiated in purpose and essence. Moreover, Mellett et al. (2009) argue that although the adoption of accrual accounting in the public sector requires some necessary adaptation, public sector accounting policies start from the private sector's GAAP and change only where it is necessary to match them with the different environment of the public sector; such amendments have been relatively few in practice. The lack of such amendments/adjustments and the differences between the public and private sectors give rise to trouble for practitioners/producers. Accordingly, the following question can be raised:

What are the necessary adaptations/adjustments that are required for making accrual accounting more practice-relevant for public sector entities?

This book provides a starting point for developing a more practice-relevant version of accrual accounting to fit the context of public sector entities and improve public sector accounting practices, thus helping producers (which include two circles of producers of accounting information: (1) inner circle practitioners/preparers of financial statements such as the employees in an accounting department, controllers, and internal audit office; and (2) outer circle such as standard setters, professional bodies, and academics) to understand the nature of governmental entities and how to apply accrual accounting to the public sector. Therefore, the final aim of this book is to open the door for developing a new version of accrual accounting that is initially designed for public sector entities and not just a modified version of commercial accrual.

The topic of practice-relevance of accrual accounting for the public sector from both producers' and users' perspective has been considered as a fascinating research topic for the last two decades. Although this research has resulted in publications in several accounting journals, it would be a good time to reflect on that topic and bring the necessary adjustments together to provide a cohesive big picture of the practice-relevance of accrual accounting for the public sector.

Accordingly, the particular benefits offered by this book and the needs that it aims to satisfy are as follows:

First: Making public sector accrual accounting more practice-relevant should be approached from two perspectives: the users' and the producers'. This is because public sector entities and assets are differentiated in purpose and essence, which in turn require public sector academics, standard setters, professional bodies, and practitioners to find practical solutions for the challenging accrual accounting issues that cause problems for practitioners and to challenge the design of public sector accounting to better fit into users' practices and to meet the diverging needs of different users (e.g., politicians, public managers, oversight bodies, and citizens).

Second: Reshaping the application of accrual accounting principles and postulations to fit the public sector accounting practice is an important aspect for making public sector accrual accounting more practice-relevant. It has been noticed that the last three decades have witnessed standard setters, academics, and practitioners direct their efforts to force public sector entities' information into business-reporting frameworks (Carlin 2005; Mack and Ryan 2006), instead of really thinking about reshaping the application of accrual accounting principles, assumptions, and concepts to make them more practice-relevant for public sector entities. Laughlin

(2008) also argues that "some of the [private sectors] underlying concepts and standards need reshaping to allow them to fit the context of PBEs [Public Benefit Entities]." While the International Public Sector Accounting Standards Board (IPSASB) (and its predecessor) has issued the IPSASs (International Public Sector Accounting Standards) to be applied to the public sector entities and has developed a Conceptual Framework for General Purpose Financial Reporting by Public Sector Entities (IPSASB 2014), both IPSASs and the conceptual framework have not considered the reshaping of accrual accounting principles and postulations to allow them to fit the context of public sector entities and to make them more practice-relevant from the producers' perspective.

Some accrual accounting principles and assumptions (postulations) can be applied equally to both public and private sectors. However, given public sector specificities, some others can only be applied to the public sector after making some modifications; and others need total reshaping for the public sector. What are the accrual accounting principles and assumptions that should be reshaped? How can they be reshaped? What is the impact of reshaping the application of these principles and assumptions on the practice? Chapter 2 addresses the reshaping of the application of these principles and assumptions from the producers' perspective, which is necessary for improving public sector accounting practice.

Third: In addition to the reshaping of the accrual accounting principles and assumptions, the recognition of governmental capital assets in the financial statements is an important issue, which has not been fully resolved. The public sector accounting literature in the last 30 years has shown that reporting of the governmental capital assets has become a highly problematic issue for the public sector entities holding those assets, as there is no consensus about which capital assets should be included in the balance sheet and which ones should be excluded from the balance sheet. While some studies have focused on the recognition of some specific assets such as heritage assets and defense assets (Barton 1999, 2005; Hooper and Kearins 2005; Ouda 2014; Anessi-Pessina et al. 2019), another study has taken a holistic approach for the treatment of capital assets (Christiaens et al. 2012). However, these studies did not resolve the problem from the practitioners' perspective and they are not consistent with the assets recognition criteria determined by IPSAS 16 &17. In addition, these studies did not consider the impact of reporting governmental capital assets in economic values on the Net Worth and Statement of Financial Performance. How far should the accounting recognition of governmental capital assets go under the full accrual accounting? Are the current recognition criteria enough to include or to exclude the governmental capital assets? Do the current recognition criteria for governmental capital assets require a reshaping to fit the context of public sector entities? Does the reshaping of the recognition criteria require new recognition attributes? Chapter 3 tackles these questions from multiple theoretical angles and practical experience of pioneer countries to gain a comprehensive understanding of what should be recognized as assets without leading to the exaggeration of the net worth.

Fourth: Nowadays, different users and stakeholders of public sector entities' reports require information that goes beyond financial and budgetary information, as traditionally included in the GPFR. There is an overall demanding for wider accountability concerning different issues. Accordingly, Chap. 4 addresses different forms of extending public sector entities' and governments' reporting to embrace other types of (nonfinancial) information, namely performance reporting, sustainability, integrated and popular reporting, and public value reporting. The aim is to highlight how the combinations of these perspectives in public sector entities' reporting may foster the discharge of accountability towards citizens and other stakeholders.

Fifth: One fundamental topic is the public sector accounting and government's fiscal sustainability and how public sector accounting can contribute to measuring and reporting on the long-term fiscal sustainability. In addition to the traditional role of government accounting in satisfying traditional users' needs and the specific politicians' needs, government accounting is currently required to furnish information about the fiscal sustainability of governmental entities that indicates the ability of a government to meet current and future obligations when they become due, and to continue providing services to the public in current and future periods. Accordingly, the satisfaction of different users' needs requires public sector accountants to maintain a traditional accrual accounting system, which produces cost-based financial statements that are basically constrained by GAAP and directed towards satisfying the decision-making, accountability, compliance, and stewardship objectives. In addition, public sector accountants are required to take the initiative and think outside the box and innovate additional accounting and financial reporting systems, which may not be guided by current accounting policies and regulations and are directed towards providing the accounting information needs of long-term fiscal sustainability. Is accrual-based financial reporting providing practice-relevant accounting information required for reporting on government's long-term fiscal sustainability? Can the Net Worth and Intergenerational Equity provide the best measures for long-term fiscal sustainability? To what extent can public sector accounting go beyond the traditional accounting reporting and provide information for reporting on long-term fiscal sustainability? Should the scope of public sector financial reporting be expanded to include both backward- looking (past) activity and forward-looking (future) activity? Do accounting bases need to be developed to be able to report on long-term fiscal sustainability? Chapter 5 tackles these questions drawing on optimal distinctiveness professional guidelines and guidance (e.g., IPSASB 2013; FASAB 2008, 2015) and other theoretical frameworks from the public sector accounting literature.

Sixth: While the previous chapters have focused on the practice-relevance of accrual accounting issues from the producers'/practitioners' perspective, it is also fundamental to address the practice-relevance of public sector accrual accounting from the users' perspective. This requires the public sector accounting scholars to use the Practice-Oriented Co-design Approach that integrates the efforts of accounting researchers, practitioners, consultants, users, and standard-setting bodies together to produce a practice-relevant public sector accrual accounting and financial reporting system that considers the diverse needs of different users and enhances the actual use of accounting information by the politicians. In addition, co-design makes users act as experts of their own experience by actively involving them in all design decisions and these decisions should be taken within the context of the users, their needs, and their environment. In addition, the users' perspective requires that public sector accounting should start a new era that shifts its concentration from attempting to fit users and their needs into the design process to challenging the design process to better fit into users' practice. *How can the Practice-Oriented Co-design Approach be used to develop a dynamic model aiming at designing a practice-relevant public sector accrual accounting and financial reporting system that satisfies the diverging needs of different users?*

Chapter 6 addresses this question by exploring a method for insight generation of a practice-relevant public sector accrual accounting and financial reporting system. This method uses a Practice-oriented Co-design Approach aiming at conceptualizing a dynamic model for designing an accrual accounting and financial reporting system that can produce practice-relevant financial information, which takes into account the diverging needs of different stakeholders and can be used and appreciated by politicians and other users.

Seventh: Chapter 7 should be seen as complementary to Chap. 6. While Chap. 6 focuses on making public sector accounting and financial reporting more user-practice-relevant through the Practice-oriented Co-design Approach, Chap. 7 focuses on developing a theory that aims at producing practice-relevant accounting information for the governing politicians by making such accounting information more specific to the task to be performed, to the problem to be solved, to the challenges to be coped with, and/or to the matter at hand *('task fit')*. To date, however, the public sector accounting literature appears to have arrived at few conclusions with regard to the rationale underlying the lack of actual use of accounting information by the politicians. The public sector accounting literature has yet to articulate in a coherent way the relationship between the producers (supply side) and the users (demand side) of accounting information that can enhance the actual use of accounting information by the politicians and public managers. If the use of accounting information is to be considered in a comprehensive and coherent way, taking into consideration both the producers and the users of accounting information, a theory of information matching between the producers and the users is needed. The accounting literature does not currently provide such a theory; nor does it promise one in the near future. The aim of this chapter is to fill this important gap by developing a theory that explains the matching relationship between the producers and the users of accounting information and a match between the accounting information provided in each stage of the policy decision-making processes and the accounting information required for each stage. The notion is that the actual use of accounting information and hence its usefulness will be enhanced when there is a cognitive fit (matching) between the accounting information provided by the producers in each stage and that information required by the user for each stage. *How do cognitive aspects influence the use/nonuse of accounting information by the politicians?*

In addition, Chap. 7 discusses how the developed theory can be applied to practice. In order to fulfill this purpose, this chapter considers the policy decision-making process and its five stages identified by Lasswell (1956) and Howlett and Ramesh (2003): agenda-setting; policy formulation; decision-making; implementation; and evaluation. It is assumed that the usefulness of accounting information and its actual use will be enhanced when it is specific to the problems the users face in each stage (Ouda and

Klischewski 2019). Therefore, this theory will show that matching of cognition of both the producers and users, through the learning alignment and continuous information use audit and hence the formation of consistent mental representations that emphasize the same type of information, will enhance the usefulness of accounting information and its actual use by making the accounting information more specific to the problems the users face in each stage.

Finally, Chap. 8 concludes the book by discussing implications for scholars, standard-setting bodies, and practitioners. It suggests a number of directions for future research that hopefully inspire future research and researchers to develop a more practice-relevant version of accrual accounting that is initially designed for the public sector and not just a modified version of the commercial accrual accounting.

References

Anessi-Pessina, E., Caruana, J., Sicilia, M., & Steccolini, I. (2019). Heritage: The Priceless Hostage of Accrual Accounting. *International Journal of Public Sector Management, 33*(2/3), 285–306.

Ball, A., & Grubnic, S. (2007). Sustainability Accounting and Accountability in the Public Sector. In J. Unerman, J. Bebbington, & B. O'Dwyer (Eds.), *Sustainability Accounting and Accountability* (pp. 243–265). UK: Routledge.

Barton, A. (1999). Public and Private Sector Accounting—The Non-Identical Twins. *Australian Accounting Review, 9*(2), 22–31.

Barton, A. D. (2005). The Conceptual Arguments Concerning Accounting for Public Heritage Assets: A Note. *Accounting, Auditing & Accountability Journal, 18*(3), 434–440.

Carlin, T. (2005). Debating the Impact of Accrual Accounting and Reporting in the Public sector. *Financial Accountability & Management, 21*(3), 309–336.

Carnegie, G., & West, B. (2005). Making Accounting Accountable in the Public Sector. *Critical perspectives on Accounting, 16*, 905–928.

Choudhury, N. (1986). In Search of Relevance in Management Accounting Research. *Accounting and Business Research, 17*(65, Winter), 21–32.

Christiaens, J., Rommel, J., Barton, A., & Everaert, P. (2012). Should All Capital Goods of Governments be Recognized as Assets in Financial Accounting? *Baltic Journal of Management, 7*(4), 2012.

Cooper, S., & Owen, D. (2007). Corporate Social Reporting and Stakeholder Accountability: The Missing Link. *Accounting, Organizations and Society, 32*, 649–667.

Federal Accounting Standards Advisory Board (FASAB). (2008, September). Reporting Comprehensive Long-Term Fiscal Projections for the U.S. Government. *Exposure Draft.*

Federal Accounting Standards Advisory Board (FASAB). (2015). *Statement of Federal Financial Accounting Standards 36: Comprehensive Long-Term Projections for the U.S Government.* Version 14 (06/15). Retrieved from www.fasab.gov/fiscal-sustainability-reporting-sffas-36/.

Hodges, R (2013). Accountability and Accounting for PPPs. Chap. 18 in P. de Vries & E. Yehoue (Eds.), *The Routledge Companion to Public Private Partnerships.* Washington DC: Routledge.

Hood, C. (1995). The New Public Management in the 1980s: Variations on a Theme. *Accounting, Organizations and Society, 20*(2/3), 93–103.

Hooper, K. C., & Kearins, K. N. (2005). Knowing the Price of Everything and the Value of Nothing: Accounting for Heritage Assets. *Accounting, Auditing and Accountability Journal, 62*(4), 181–184.

Howlett, M., & Ramesh, M. (2003). *Studying Public Policy: Policy Cycles and Policy Subsystems.* Toronto: Oxford University Press.

IFAC. (2013). *Compliance Responses and Action Plans.* New York: IFAC [online]. Retrieved from http://www.ifac.org/aboutifac/membership/compliance-program/compliance-responses.

IPSASB. (2013). *Reporting on the Long-Term Sustainability of Public Sector Entity's Finances.* Recommended Practice Guideline No. 3.

IPSASB. (2014). *The Conceptual Framework for General Purpose Financial Reporting by Public Sector Entities.*

Lapsley, I., Mussari, R., & Paulsson, G. (2009). On the Adoption of Accrual Accounting in the Public Sector: A Self-Evidence and Problematic Reform. *European Accounting Review, 18*(4), 719–723.

Lasswell, H. D. (1956). The Political Science of Science. *American Political Science Review, 50*(4), 961–979.

Laughlin, R. (2008). A Conceptual Framework for Accounting for Public-Benefit Entities. *Public Money and Management, 28*(4), 247–254.

Mack, J., & Ryan, C. (2006). Reflection of the Theoretical Underpinning of the General-Purpose Financial Reports. *Accounting, Auditing, and Accountability Journal, 109*(4), 592–612.

Mellett, H., Marriott, N., & Macniven, L. (2009). Devolution, Accruals Accounting and Asset Management in NHS Wales. *Financial Accountability & Management, 25*(4), 434–450.

Micallef, F., & Peirson, G. (1997). Financial Reporting of Cultural, Heritage, Scientific and Community Collections. *Australian Accounting Review, 7*(13), 31–37.

Ouda, H. (2014). Towards a Practical Accounting Approach for Heritage Assets: An Alternative Reporting Model for the NPM Practices. *Journal of Finance and Accounting, 2*(2), 19–33.

Ouda, H., & Klischewski, R. (2019). Accounting and Politicians: A Theory of Accounting Information Usefulness. *Journal of Public Budgeting, Accounting and Financial Management, 31*(4), 496–517.

Taussing, R. (1963). Governmental Accounting: Fund Flow or Service Cost. *Accounting Review, 38*(3), 562–567.

Wild, S. (2013). Accounting for Heritage, Cultural and community Assets- An Alternative Metrics from a New Zealand Maori education Institution. *Australasian Accounting Business and Finance Journal (AABFJ), 7*(1), 3–22.

PART I

The Producers' Perspective

CHAPTER 2

Reshaping the Application of Accrual Accounting Principles and Postulations to Fit the Context of Public Sector Entities

1 Introduction

The transition to accrual accounting has been the most notable reform of government accounting in the last three decades for many countries. The last three decades have seen standard-setters, academics, and practitioners direct their efforts to force public sector entities' information into business reporting frameworks (Ball 1994; IFAC 1998, 2000, 2004, 2006; Carlin 2005; Mack and Ryan 2006; Nagendrakumar 2017; Rakhman and Wijayana 2019), instead of really thinking about reshaping the application of accrual accounting principles, assumptions, and concepts to make them more practice-relevant for public sector entities. Laughlin (2008) also argues that "some of the [private sector] underlying concepts and standards need reshaping to allow them to fit the context of Public Benefit Entities (PBEs).

While the International Public Sector Accounting Standards Board (IPSASB) (and its predecessor) has issued the International Public Sector Accounting Standards (IPSASs) to be applied to public sector entities and has developed a Conceptual Framework for General Purpose Financial Reporting by Public Sector Entities (IPSASB 2014), both IPSASs and the conceptual framework have scarcely considered the reshaping of accrual accounting principles and postulations to allow them to fit the context of public sector entities and to make them more practice-relevant from the practitioners' perspective.

H. Ouda, *Practice-Relevant Accrual Accounting for the Public Sector*, Public Sector Financial Management,
https://doi.org/10.1007/978-3-030-51595-9_2

This is not only true for IPSASB, given that other public sector accounting standard-setting bodies have not tackled this issue either (see, for example, GASB-USA, FRC-UK, and CICA-Canada). For example, while the Financial Reporting Council—FRC-UK (2005) has attempted to develop a conceptual framework for the public sector entities in its *Statement of Principles for Financial Reporting—Proposed Interpretation for Public Benefit Entities*, the clarification of accrual accounting principles and postulations and how they can be applied to the public sector have not been properly considered.

Some of the principles and postulations on which accrual accounting is based have been regarded for many years as an obstacle in the way it is adopted in the public sector. These principles and postulations need further clarification as to how they can be applied to the public sector. Others, including the International Monetary Fund and the World Bank (World bank 2010), see accrual accounting as a means of improving accountability and transparency on the part of governments, particularly since the sovereign debt crisis, and as an essential component of improved Public Financial Management (PFM). IFAC also sees accrual accounting as a way of providing better information for decision-making by governments themselves, and by investors or fund providers.

This chapter discusses how the principles and postulations associated with accrual accounting might or might not be applied to the public sector, recognizing the similarities between the public and private sectors, and exploring the differences. Furthermore, it makes propositions about how some of these principles and postulations can be reshaped so that they can be properly applied to the public sector realm.

2 Accrual Accounting Principles and Postulations

At the time of writing, the International Accounting Standards Board (IASB) is consulting on its revision to its Conceptual Framework for Financial Reporting. The IPSASB published its Conceptual Framework for General Purpose Financial Reporting by Public Sector Entities in 2014 (IPSAB 2015). While both conceptual frameworks deal with the qualitative characteristics, the IPSASB makes no distinction between fundamental and enhancing qualitative characteristics, as shown in Table 2.1.

Table 2.1 Qualitative characteristics underlying international standards

IASB	*IPSASB*
Fundamental qualitative characteristics	Relevance
Relevance	Faithful representation
Faithful representation	Understandability
Enhancing qualitative characteristics	Timeliness
Comparability	Comparability
Verifiability	Verifiability
Timeliness	
Understandability	

Source: Author

The IPSASB Conceptual Framework also includes three constraints on information included in general purpose financial reports: materiality, cost–benefit, and balance between the qualitative characteristics. The IASB refers only to cost constraints.

Although the two Boards developed their conceptual frameworks independently, both address the same qualitative characteristics, and both discuss the elements in financial statements, their recognition and measurement, and the presentation of information, thereby subsuming within them the generally accepted accounting principles, which have traditionally been accepted as the basis for accrual accounting:

Matching
Recognition
Conservatism
Consistency
Full disclosure
Objectivity
Materiality

Both conceptual frameworks briefly discuss the characteristics of the reporting entity, and assume that the entity preparing the financial reports is a going concern—two of the generally accepted postulations (going concern and accounting entity). Neither conceptual framework discusses the third postulation of a stable unit of measurement: these are dealt with at standards level (IAS 21, *The Effects of Changes in Foreign Exchange Rates* and IPSAS 4, *The Effects of Changes in Foreign Exchange Rates*).

Some accrual accounting principles and assumptions (postulations) can be applied equally to both public and private sectors. However, given public sector specificities, some others can only be applied to the public sector after making some modifications; and others need total reshaping for the public sector. The focus of the remainder of this chapter will be on those accrual accounting issues that led to a conceptual challenge/difference and need to be reconsidered in terms of creating new concepts, recognition criteria, and standards, namely, matching, recognition, consistency, conservatism, and going concern. In other words, the main focus will be on the challenging issues that may cause problems for the practitioners and represent a fundamental departure from a commercial framework.

3 Conceptual Challenges: Accrual Accounting Principles

3.1 Matching Principle

The matching principle is designed for measuring net income in the private sector. Measuring net income requires the identification of both revenues and the expenses for generating those revenues. This process of identifying revenues and expenses to generate it is called matching. The essence of the matching principle is to compare that the thing generated with what was taken to generate it (Van Peursem 2006; Bergmann et al. 2019). Ingram et al. (1991) argue that matching of costs and revenues refers to the simultaneous or combined recognition of revenues and expenses that result directly and jointly from the same transactions or other events. The New Zealand Society of Accountants (NZSA) stated that "under accrual accounting, expenses and revenues are recognized as they are incurred or earned (rather than as money is paid or received) and recorded in the financial statements of the period to which they relate. Results for the period are determined by matching expenses with the related revenues" (NZSA 1987, para 4.2 (a)). This means that the application of the matching principle in the private sector is based on a cause-and-effect relationship between reported expenses and reported revenues. Therefore, the direct link between revenues and expenses is a prerequisite in order to apply the matching principle (Ouda 2007). However, the direct link between revenues and expenses is often missing in the public sector; public sector entities do not generally aim at making profit but at serving the public interest by providing public goods and services. The revenues, mainly from taxes, are generated through a political process, not as a result of expenditures made by the public sector entities. If, therefore, one attempts to match expenses to resources inflows, this will present a dilemma (Van Peursem 2006). This means that the inflows accrued through political means cannot be reasonably matched to expenses accrued from payouts for what Rutherford (1992) terms «self-sustaining operations». Private sector enterprise is self-sustaining whereas public sector entities transfer, collect, or distribute wealth and support a public good. In addition, Van Peursem (2006) has concluded that, unfortunately, alternatives to a traditional matching of revenues with expenses do not offer themselves up. It makes little sense to match politically derived resources (taxes, grants, and contributions) to internally managed expenses and where outputs may be nonfinancial. The following problem therefore remains: How can one achieve relevance in netting politically driven resources against managerially driven expenses? In fact, applying the matching principle without making the necessary adjustments represents a dilemma for the practitioners in the public sector entities, therefore we, as public sector accounting scholars, should find a solution for this dilemma. Laughlin (2008) argues that "some of the [private sector] underlying concepts and standards need reshaping to allow them to fit the context of public benefit entities." In doing so, we should take into consideration that the public sector entities and assets are differentiated in purpose and essence. While private firms exist in an environment of competition, equity return, and decision-usefulness, and their reporting requirements reflect this, the profit motive also explains user interest in statements of 'income', and in the accumulated earnings that can be returned to owners (Van Peursem 2009), the situation is entirely different in the public sector as

> [g]overnments ... are elected by citizens to make collective decisions on their behalf to provide those goods and services which cannot readily be provided by private firms, and those for social welfare purposes. (Barton 2005, pp. 141–142)

And in standards, public sector entities are reporting entities whose primary objective is to provide goods or services for a community or a social benefit (NZICA 2007c, para. 8.2).

Accordingly, the opponents of adoption of accrual accounting in the public sector have concluded that the matching principle cannot generally be properly applied to governmental organizations (Monsen and Nasi 1997; Wynne 2008). *But is this correct?*

3.1.1 How to Adapt the Matching Concept to the Public Sector Realm?

Conceptual Approach

As a result of the differences in objectives between public sector entities and private sector firms, the application of the matching principle should be reshaped to fit the context of public sector entities. *Basically, for governmental entities the net annual measure is of the net resources consumed to provide services during the year and the net accumulated figure is a measure of unconsumed economic resources* (IFAC 1991, p. 16). In this context, Ouda (2003) has suggested *the conceptual approach*, which assumes that the matching principle can be applied to the public sector entities to match resources consumed during the accounting period with services and goods provided (and usefulness accomplished) during the same accounting period or to match outputs with the associated costs. In this way, the conceptual approach does not aim at measuring the net income; instead, it measures the efficiency of governments in using available public resources. However, the operationalization of the conceptual approach through the financial statements has revealed that it is not possible to gauge efficiency from the financial statements, since one has to determine whether the outcomes (the policy objectives, for example) have been delivered (Ouda 2007). If they have been delivered, then one can ask whether they could have been delivered as effectively for a lower cost—which is the efficiency point. However, it is difficult (even impossible) to prove the conceptual approach from the financial statements, as they indicate neither the level nor the quality of the goods and services which have been provided. Accordingly, I think that the conceptual approach is only right to the extent that the accruals accounts show the resources consumed in providing the services. That is, the inputs are matched against the outputs in financial reporting terms but the inputs and outputs are not matched against the outcomes (Ouda 2007). This conclusion leads us to agree with Guthrie (1998): "it has been argued that the changes from the use of cash based statements to accrual based statements reflect a focus on an efficient and effective output and outcome (National Commission of Audit NCA 1996, Australia). This fails to recognize the reality that accounting statements are themselves focused on inputs. Outcomes are no more easily measured via the use of accrual financial reporting than cash based reporting and are usually determined on the basis of separate surveys, for example of customer satisfaction or the state of health or education (Guthrie 1998)."

Similar to the conceptual approach, Van Peursem (2009) suggested *a Conceptual Public Benefit Entities (PBE) Reporting Framework* where he replaced the traditional Statement of Income by two statements: The Statement of Net Expenses and the Statement of Service Efficiency (see Fig. 2.1). The Statement of Net Expenses includes operating expenses matched only with commercial/earned revenues, to distinguish between earned revenue and non-earned (political) revenue. The non-earned (non-commercial) revenue is included in a Statement of Net Inflows, which is equivalent to the commercial Cash Flow Statement. In using this title, there is a desire to convey the idea that Net Inflows are not equivalent to Net Income (Van Peursem 2009). The Statement of Service Efficiency is used to match costs to nonfinancial enhancements (outputs). The Statement of Service Efficiency compares nonfinancial enhancements (outputs) to managed costs (inputs), and holds public sector entities to account for their productivity in proportion to the outflows employed in reaching them. Van Peursem (2009) further notes:

> While the ending balance from the Statement of Service Efficiency, being in ratio form, cannot be carried forward as would Net Income, it does not need, as equity, to represent accumulated earnings in the PBE sector. The Statement of Service Efficiency's contribution is in disclosing a PBE proxy for managerial efficiency, which is of value to the reader presumably no less than its equivalent (Net Income) is of value to commercial report users.

To avoid repetition, the same criticism directed at Ouda's conceptual approach can also be directed at the Van Peursem's Statement of Service Efficiency. As earlier noted, efficiency cannot be measured from the financial statements as this requires matching outputs with inputs and fails to recognize the reality that accounting statements are themselves focused on inputs (Guthrie 1998). In addition, the conceptual framework of Van Peursem (2009) (Fig. 2.1) gives rise to considerable confusion for practitioners as it distinguishes the commercial revenue from noncommercial revenue and both revenues are included in different statements, which makes the application of matching principles to public sector entities more difficult. In fact, he did not provide practical solutions on how the

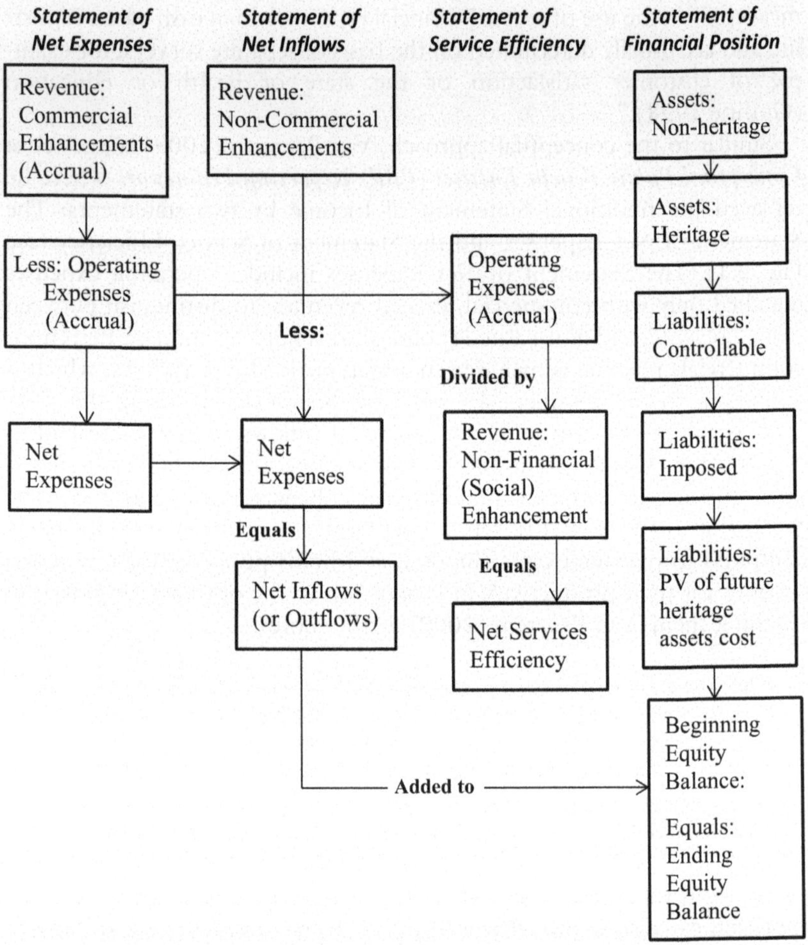

Fig. 2.1 Conceptual PBE reporting framework. (Source: Van Peursem (2009))

matching principle can properly be applied to public sector entities but, rather, made the situation more complicated for the public sector practitioners.

To assist practitioners in applying the matching principle to the public sector entities and due to the difficulties inherent in the operationalization of both Ouda's conceptual approach and Van Peursem's conceptual framework, there is an urgent need to reshape the application of the matching principle in a practical way in order to justify the adoption of accrual accounting with its matching principle in public sector entities.

Practical Approach: Timing Relationship

The cornerstone of the practical approach, which was developed by Ouda (2007) is that the adoption of accrual accounting in the public sector will allow for the measurement of the total cost of providing services on an aggregated basis, and also allow for more accurate cost measurement of specific programs and activities. The total costs include not only the cost of goods and services produced or purchased and paid for during the accounting period but also the cost of using long-lived assets (e.g., depreciation and cost of capital) and other noncash costs. Accrual accounting means that the actual cost will be recognized in the year in which it occurs. It is stated in the Consolidated Financial Statements of the New South Wales Public Sector 1996–1997 that "*expenses are recognized when incurred and are reported in the financial year to which they relate.*" In addition, Ouda (2007) argued that in government, matching would be central to calculating intergenerational equity, that is, to show that there are sufficient revenues collected in this period to cover all costs, whether actual outlays or promised outlays.

Consequently, we see that the matching principle can be used to allow for the total costs of one period to be charged to the operating statement in the period in which they are incurred and matched with the total revenues (whether levied through the sovereign power or earned through the operations) related to the same period.

The practical approach takes into consideration the specific nature and characteristics of the public sector in comparison with the private sector and it proposes that the matching of revenues with expenses of a certain fiscal year should be based on a **Timing Relationship** instead of an **Exchange Relationship (cause–effect)** (Ouda 2007). This is based on the fact that "governments generally use resources from a variety of sources to pay for a variety of services. The "matching" relationship that normally exists between resources provided and services received is a timing relationship (that is, both occur during the fiscal year) rather than an exchange relationship" (GASB 1987). This is consistent with the Universality Principle of budgeting, where all revenues are used to finance all expenditure without allocating revenues to particular items of spending as no relationship exists between revenues and expenditures. So, in the context of lacking a direct link between revenues and expenses, the matching principle can be used in the public sector to show the accrual-based surplus (or deficit) of revenues over expenses. This is a useful measure of whether a government has managed to meet current expenses from current revenues, and whether its net resource position has increased or decreased. Thus, comparing revenues with total expenses helps in assessing the inter-period/intergenerational equity (i.e., whether current revenues are sufficient to cover the costs of programs and services provided in the current period).

In reality, application of the matching principle in the public sector, based on a timing relationship, not only measures the intergenerational equity but also assists in demonstrating intergenerational fairness by charging the costs incurred in production of the usefulness to the period in which this usefulness will be consumed. Bac (1989, 2000) stated that *"good allocation and sound inter-generationally neutral government financing demands that the cost of government activities will be so divided over time that cost will be attributed to the period in which the usefulness of such activities and the referred assets will be consumed."* This means that

> *[c]osts incurred should be—attributed to—the period of consumption of the usefulness.*

In this context, the matching principle means that both services and costs incurred in providing those services have to be recognized in the same reporting period in order to assure that current taxpayers are paying for the services that they receive and not passing those costs on to future generations. This assists in ensuring an equitable distribution of expenses between generations and that the long-term position of the government remains sound (Bartos 2000). So in order to operationalize the practical approach (the timing relationship), I use the financial statements of the New Zealand government to show how accrual accounting with its matching principle is applied to the public sector. These are Statement of Financial Performance (operating statement), Statement of Movements in Equity, and Statement of Financial Position, for the year ended 30 June 2014 (see the following statements).

Generally, expenses can be provided in the Statement of Financial Performance in one of two ways (IPSAS 1, paras 111–113): the first is referred to as the nature of expense method. Expenses are aggregated in the statement of financial performance according to their nature (depreciation, purchases of materials, transport costs, wages, salaries, etc.), and are not reallocated among various functions within the entity. The second is referred to as the functional method of expense classification, which classifies expenses according to the programs or purpose for which they were made (health, education, defense, etc.). This presentation often provides more relevant information to the users than the classification of expenses by nature. The Statement of Financial Performance of the New Zealand government uses the classification of expenses by nature; this is in addition to providing an analysis of expenses according to the functional method. The Statement of Financial Performance of the New Zealand government can show to what extent the New Zealand government has managed to meet the total expenses of one period from the total revenues related to the same period and whether the government actions have added to the net worth of the state, and whether the current generation has increased or decreased the worth of what is left for the next generation. It is evident from the Statement of Financial Performance of the New Zealand government that total expenses have been covered by total revenues earned at the same period and the government has achieved a surplus (positive operating balance) of NZ$ 2946 million, which means that the government actions have improved the net worth of the state and intergenerational equity. Thus, identifying a surplus or deficit each year would, over time, enable a conclusion to be reached about whether a government is eroding, enhancing, or maintaining the net worth.

Statement of Financial Performance as of 30 June 2014

<u>*Forecast*</u>			<u>*Actual*</u>	
Budget 2013 $m	*Budget 2014 $m*		*30 June 2014 $m*	*30 June 2013 $m*
		<u>Revenue</u>		
61,773	61,380	Taxation revenue	60,879	58,134
5296	5383	Other sovereign revenue	5450	5172
67,069	66,763	Total sovereign revenue	66,329	63,306
17,080	16,432	Sales of goods and services	16,472	16,713

(continued)

(continued)

Forecast			*Actual*	
Budget 2013 $m	*Budget 2014 $m*		*30 June 2014 $m*	*30 June 2013 $m*
3588	3160	Interest revenue and dividends	3175	2939
3867	3622	Other revenue	3420	3697
24,535	23,214	Total revenue earned through operations	23,067	23,349
91,604	**89,977**	**Total revenue (excluding gains)**	**89,396**	**86,655**
		Expenses		
23,485	23,394	Transfer payments and subsidies	23,360	22,708
20,172	20,488	Personnel expenses	20,484	19,935
4640	4644	Depreciation and amortization	4872	4812
37,608	36,527	Other operating expenses	35,553	36,163
4516	4461	Interest expenses	4400	4358
3215	3283	Insurance expenses	3501	3031
461	77	Forecast new operating spending	–	–
(600)	(660)	Top-down expense adjustment	–	–
93,497	92,214	Total expenses (excluding losses)	**92,170**	**91,007**
(140)	(210)	Minority interests share of operating balance before gains and losses	(159)	(62)
(2033)	(2447)	Operating balance before gains and losses (excluding minority interests)	(2933)	(4414)
1748	3604	Net gains/(losses) on financial instruments	4820	7270
443	1590	Net gains/(losses) on non-financial instruments	540	3706
2191	**5194**	**Total gains/(losses)**	**5360**	**10,976**
200	259	Net surplus from associates and joint ventures	360	395
–	(33)	Minority interests share of net gains/losses	21	(32)
358	2973	Operating balance (excluding minority interests)	2808	6925
		Operating balance allocated between:		
358	2973	Operating balance (excluding minority interests)	2808	6925
140	243	Minority interests share of operating balance	138	94
498	**3216**	**Operating balance (including minority interests)**	**2946**	**7019**

Source: The New Zealand Treasury

Statement of Financial Position as of 30 June 2014

Forecast			*Actual*	
Budget 2013 $m	*Budget 2014 $m*		*30 June 2014 $m*	*30 June 2013 $m*
		<u>Assets</u>		
15,244	11,108	Cash and cash equivalents	11,888	14,924
18,070	17,873	Receivables	17,480	19,883
44,713	47,870	Marketable securities, deposits, and derivatives in gain	48,457	44,000
18,176	19,672	Share investments	20,596	17,359
25,312	24,611	Advances	24,756	22,613
1321	1158	Inventory	1099	1140
2061	2267	Other assets	2510	2295
112,627	112,264	Property, plant, and equipment	116,306	109,833
9642	10,021	Equity accounted investments	10,071	9593
2837	2841	Intangible assets and goodwill	2920	2776
505	13	Forecast for new capital spending	–	–
(330)	(395)	Top-down capital adjustment	–	–
250,178	**249,303**	**<u>Total assets</u>**	**256,083**	**244,416**
		<u>Liabilities</u>		
4897	5072	Issued currency	4964	4691
12,360	11,952	Payables	11,294	11,160
1553	1802	Deferred revenue	1962	1714
112,201	103,058	Borrowings	103,419	100,087
35,902	34,900	Insurance liabilities	35,825	37,712
11,766	10,732	Retirement plan liabilities	10,885	11,903
6317	6320	Provisions	6955	7138
184,996	**173,836**	**Total liabilities**	**175,304**	**174,405**
65,182	**75,467**	**Total assets less total liabilities**	**80,779**	**70,011**
		Net worth		
6230	13,344	Taxpayer funds	13,300	10,862
55,831	56,648	Property, plant, and equipment revaluation reserve	62,225	57,068
(64)	40	Other reserves	43	141
61,997	70,032	Total net worth attributable to the crown	75,568	68,071
3185	5435	Net worth attributable to minority interests	5211	1940
65,182	**75,467**	**Total net worth**	**80,779**	**70,011**

Statement of changes in net worth for the year ended 30 June 2014

Forecast				*Actual*		*Total*	
Budget	*Budget*			*Taxpayer*	*Reserves*	*Minority*	*Net*
2013	*2014*			*Funds*		*Interest*	*Worth*
$m	*$m*			*$m*	*$m*	*$m*	*$m*
498	3216	Operating balance		2808	–	138	2946
–	(351)	Net revaluations		–	5386	9	5395
(59)	(119)	Transfers to/(from) reserves		229	(229)	(2)	(2)
–	(3)	(gains)/losses transferred to the statement of financial performance		–	(43)	–	(43)
47	3	Other movements		(22)	(55)	2	(75)
486	**2746**	**Total comprehensive income**		**3015**	**5059**	**147**	**8221**
175	(542)	Gain/(loss) on government share offers		(577)	–	–	(577)
1325	3300	Increase in minority interest from government share offers		–	–	3308	3308
(74)	(48)	Transactions with minority interests		–	–	(184)	(184)
65,182	**75,467**	**Net worth as of 30 June 2014**	**28**	**13,300**	**62,268**	**5211**	**80,779**

Finally, one can conclude that the matching principle can generally be applied, whether to the private or the public sector, based on the following two relationships:

- ***Exchange Relationship*** to measure net income ***(private sector)***
- ***Timing Relationship*** to measure the surplus (or deficit) of revenues over expenses, and hence to measure the inter-period/intergenerational equity ***(public sector)***

So the practitioners in the public sector can apply the matching principle based on the timing relationship—not to measure the net income, but to measure the accrual-based surplus or deficit. If it is a surplus, then the government has enhanced the net worth and the current generation has borne its own burden as well as providing support to the next generations.

If it is a deficit, then the current generation is shifting its burden to the next generations and the government has eroded the net worth.

3.2 Recognition Principle

The revenue recognition principle is an accounting principle that requires revenue to be recorded only when it is earned. This means that revenues or income should be recognized when the services or products are provided to customers regardless of when the payment takes place. While the private sector receives its revenues from exchange transactions, public sector entities receive a large portion of their revenues through non-exchange transactions, referred to in IPSAS 23 as taxes and transfers. Transfers include intergovernmental grants, entitlements, subsidies, and other financial assistance, and private donations. In addition, governments provide financial assistance to other governmental and nongovernmental entities. Therefore, the government's decision with respect to the timing of the recognition of non-exchange transactions in the financial statements can have significant impact on the reported results and financial position and on the users' ability to compare information across governments and over time.

Despite IPSASB having issued IPSAS 23 of non-exchange transactions, there is a lack of a uniform guidance in accounting standards on when to report these transactions. This has resulted in making the situation more difficult for the practitioners who need to report these transactions and for users (internal and external) to understand the financial statements and to make their decisions. Therefore, there is a need to develop a practice-relevant approach that can assist the practitioners. The main aim of this section is to make an attempt to develop a practice-relevant approach for the recognition of revenues (including exchange and non-exchange transactions) in the public sector context.

3.2.1 Theoretical Background: Recognition Principle

Unlike the private sector, governments obtain their inflows from different sources, and this, in turn, makes the recognition problems in case of the adoption of accrual accounting more difficult since diversity of sources will require different recognition points. The following are the main categories of inflows to governments (IFAC 1996, para. 69):

(1) Revenues derived from exchanges in a manner similar to the private sector. These include revenues from sales of goods or services, dividends, interest, and gains arising from the sale of assets.
(2) Revenues derived from the use of sovereign powers; these include a large variety of direct and indirect taxes, duties, fees, and fines. These revenues are called non-exchange revenues. These are
    - Income tax
    - Fringe benefits tax
    - Sales tax
    - Value-added tax
    - Payroll tax
    - Property tax
    - Capital gains tax
    - Stamp and credit duties
    - Death/estate duties
    - License tax
    - Road-user charges and motor vehicle fees
    - Lives
    - Fines
(3) Other non-exchange transfers such as grants or donations from other governments, from supranational authorities, or from the private sector.
(4) Financing inflows, notably borrowings.
(5) Custodial receipts. These include taxes collected as agent for another government, contributions towards pension and welfare funds, and other receipts collected as agent for another entity.

As mentioned earlier, governments raise revenues from both exchange transactions and non-exchange transactions. Due to the fact that exchange transactions are entirely different from non-exchange transactions, the revenue recognition of both transactions requires different accounting approaches. Therefore, the recognition principle, similar to the matching principle, needs to be reshaped to fit the context of public sector entities. In order to be able to discuss the reshaping of the recognition principle, we will present in the following section the revenue recognition from different standard-setting bodies' perspectives.

3.2.2 Revenue Recognition from Different Standard Setting Bodies' Perspectives

The main issue in accounting for revenue is to determine when the revenue should be recognized in the financial statements of public sector entities. IPSAS 9, para 33—Revenue from Exchange transactions determines two main criteria for the recognition of revenues. Revenue is recognized when it is probable that (1) future economic benefits or service potential will flow to the entity, and (2) these benefits can be measured reliably. While these two criteria are applicable to both exchange and non-exchange transactions, the accounting for revenue arising from non-exchange transactions is entirely different from the revenue arising from exchange transactions in terms of basis and timing of recognition.

Revenue Arising from Exchange Transactions

Exchange transactions are transactions in which each party receives and gives up essentially equal values. In order to suggest the accounting treatment of revenue arising from exchange transactions, the use of ASB-GRAP 9, IPSAS 9, IFRS 15, and AASB 15 can assist in determining when the revenues arising from exchange transactions should be recognized. The focus here is on the revenue arising from exchange transactions and events as follows:

- The sale of goods
- The rendering of services
- The use by others of entity assets yielding interest, royalties, dividends, or similar distributions

Goods include goods produced by the entity for sale such as publications or purchased for resale, for example, merchandize or land. According to IPSAS 9 and GRAP 9 (2014), rendering of services involves the performance by the entity of an agreed task over an agreed period of time. Rendering of services by governmental entities for which revenue is received in exchange can be one of the following examples: management of toll roads, management of water facilities, or provision of housing. Also the use by others of entities' assets gives rise to revenue in the form of interest: charges for the use of cash or cash equivalents or amounts due to the entity; royalties: charges for the use of long-term assets of the entity, for example, patents and copyrights; and dividends or similar distributions: distributions of surpluses to holders of equity investments in proportion to their holdings of a particular class of capital (IPSAS 9 and GRAP 9, para. 28–33).

While IFRS 15 focuses only on contracts with customers for goods and services supplied in the ordinary course of operations, IPSAS 9 and GRAP 9 base the revenue recognition on the type of transaction, for example, whether revenue relates to the provision of goods, services, interest, royalties, or dividends. Although they share the two main criteria of revenue recognition, there are specific conditions related to each transaction and event that should be satisfied to consider whether the revenue arising from the exchange transaction can be recognized or not, as follows:

- *Sale of goods*

Revenue from the sale of goods shall be recognized when all the following conditions have been satisfied (IPSAS 9 and GRAP 9, para 28):

(a) The entity has transferred to the buyer the significant risks and rewards of ownership of the goods.
(b) The entity retains neither continuing managerial involvement to the degree usually associated with ownership nor effective control over the goods sold.
(c) The amount of revenue can be measured reliably.
(d) It is probable that the economic benefits associated with the transaction will flow to the entity.
(e) The costs incurred or to be incurred in respect of the transaction can be measured reliably.

- *Rendering of services*

While the recognition of revenue arising from the sale of goods depends on transferring the significant risks and rewards of ownership of goods to the customer, the revenues associated with the rendering of services shall be recognized by reference to the stage of completion of the transaction at the end of the reporting period. The outcome of a transaction can be estimated reliably when all the following conditions are satisfied (IPSAS 9 and GRAP 9 para. 19):

(a) The amount of revenue can be measured reliably.
(b) It is probable that the economic benefits associated with the transaction will flow to the entity.

(c) The stage of completion of the transaction at the end of the reporting period can be measured reliably.
(d) The costs incurred for the transaction and the costs to complete the transaction can be measured reliably.

- *Interest, royalties, and dividends*

For interest, royalties, and dividends, revenue shall be recognized on the following bases (IPSAS 9 and GRAP 9, paras 33–34):

(a) Interest shall be recognized on a time proportion basis that takes into account the effective yield on the asset.
(b) Royalties shall be recognized on an accrual basis in accordance with the substance of the relevant agreement.
(c) Dividends shall be recognized when the shareholder's right to receive payment is established.

Despite the use of different approaches for the recognition of revenues arising from exchange transactions in the public sector, these approaches are not entirely different from those used in the private sector. For example, the risk and rewards approach used by IPSAS 9 and GRAP 9 is, to a great extent, consistent with the performance obligations approach used by IFRS 15. A performance obligation is a promise to transfer goods or services to another party. However, in identifying performance obligations associated with a contract under IFRS 15, the main focus is on identifying distinct goods and services. A good or service is distinct when the following criteria are met (IFRS 15, para. 15.27):

- The customer can benefit from the good or service on its own or together with other readily available resources.
- The entity's promise to transfer the good or service to the customer is separately identifiable from other promises in the contract.

So, once the distinct goods and services are identified, the performance obligations can also be identified. Accordingly, a public sector entity using the IFRS framework recognizes revenue when performance obligations are satisfied by transferring the promised goods or services to the customer. Similarly, under IPSAS 9 and GRAP 9, revenue is recognized for goods when risks and rewards of ownership are transferred or when services are provided. ASB-UK (2015) concluded that while the process followed by the two approaches is different, the effect on revenue recognition may be similar. In addition, the Australian Accounting Standards Board has also issued AASB 1058 (2016)—Income of Not-for-Profit (NFP) Entities, which also requires the application of the performance obligations approach to exchange transactions. The core principle under AASB 15 (2014) is that an entity recognizes revenue at an amount that reflects the consideration to which the entity expects to be entitled in exchange for transferring goods or services to a customer. AASB 15 also stated that for performance obligation to exist with respect to an NFP entity, the promise to transfer a good or service must be sufficiently specific to be able to determine when the obligation is satisfied. So application of the performance obligation approach is more consistent with exchange transactions.

Revenue from Non-Exchange Transactions

Non-exchange transactions (including taxes and transfers) are revenues not directly derived from incurring costs and an entity will receive resources and provide no or nominal consideration directly in return (IPSAS 23, para 9). In other words, non-exchange revenues are politically, not economically, driven (Van Peursem 2006). While exchange transactions are, to a great extent, similar to the transactions in the private sector, non-exchange transactions are different from the private sector in respect of the approach that a practitioner will need to take to ensure appropriate recognition and measurement. For example, when should tax revenues be recognized and measured? While it may be probable that a government is entitled to revenue at the time a taxpayer earns income subject to taxation, it may not be possible to measure the amount of the tax revenue until some later point—for example, at the end of the income year, when tax returns are filed or when tax is assessed (IFAC 1996). Furthermore, there may be a considerable time lag between the point at which the transaction which gives rise to the revenue takes place and the point at which the amount can reliably be estimated. For example, there may be a lag between when sales tax is collected by a vendor and the time it is accounted for by the government.

To overcome the problem associated with the recognition of non-exchange transactions, IPASAB issued IPSAS 23—Revenue from Non-exchange transactions (including taxes and transfers) (IPSASB 2006, 2018)—to tackle this problem. IPSAS 23 tackles the requirements for the recognition, measurement, and disclosure of revenue from non-exchange transactions. It develops an assets–liabilities approach, which requires entities to recognize revenue when an inflow of resources is recognized as an asset, to the extent that a liability or a contribution from owners is also not recognized. IPSAS 23 states in paragraphs 44 to 48 the following recognition and measurement criteria for revenue from non-exchange transactions:

a. An inflow of resources from a non-exchange transaction recognized as an asset shall be recognized as revenue, except to the extent that a liability is also recognized in respect of the same inflow.
b. As an entity satisfies a present obligation recognized as a liability in respect of an inflow of resources from a non-exchange transaction recognized as an asset, it shall reduce the carrying amount of the liability recognized and recognize an amount of revenue equal to that reduction.
c. Revenue from non-exchange transactions shall be measured by the amount of increase in net assets recognized by the entity as on the date of initial recognition of assets arising from the non-exchange transactions.

And if an inflow of resources satisfies the definition of the contributions from owners, it is not recognized as a liability or revenue.

According to IPSAS 23, the assets and liabilities approach should be based on the control-based model. Control of an asset arises when the entity has the ability to exclude or regulate the access of others to the benefits of an asset and when the entity can use or otherwise benefit from the asset in pursuit of its objectives. However, exercising of a regulatory role by governments over some activities such as pension funds does not necessarily mean that such regulated items meet the definition of an asset or satisfy the criteria for recognition as an asset in government financial statements. Therefore, in many cases, the entity will need to establish enforceability of its control of resources before it can recognize an asset (IPSAS 23, para 32). This is due to the fact that if the entity does not have an enforceable claim to resources, it cannot exclude or regulate the transferor's access to those resources.

Besides IPSAS 23, the Australian Accounting Standard Board has released an Exposure Draft (ED) 260 in 2015. This draft has been partially driven by a range of concerns with the current standard, AASB 1004 contributions (AASB 1004), and the issuance of AASB 15—Revenue from

Contracts with Customers (AASB 15). Unlike the IPSAS 23, the ED 260 considers not only the control-based model for the recognition of the non-exchange transactions but also the enforceable right to receive funds. Therefore, ED 260—Part B, has distinguished between two non-exchange transfers:

- **Voluntary transfers**:
  - Donations, including identifiable donation components of contracts with customers
  - Other transactions with donation elements such as where the fair value of assets acquired by the public sector entity significantly exceeds the consideration paid
  - Grants in relation to which specific performance obligation has not been identified
  - Appropriations to government department and agencies
- **Compulsory transfers**: taxes, rates, and fines

The revenue recognition is determined by an assessment of when the control of funds passes to the public sector entity (control-based model) for voluntary transfers or when the entity has an enforceable right to receive funds (compulsory transfers). Therefore, voluntary transfers would usually be recognized on receipts of funds, and compulsory transfers would usually be recognized when the underlying "taxable event" occurs.

So both control-based model and enforceable right to receive funds based on the occurrence of taxable events are consistent with the assets and liabilities approach. For taxes, the enforceable right to receive funds is based on the occurrence of the underlying "taxable event." As examples of the occurrence of taxable events, we can use the New Zealand and Australian experience as follows.

New Zealand: the recognition points of major nonreciprocal revenues are summarized in Table 2.2.

Australia: The bases of recognition for major types of taxation revenue are summarized in Table 2.3.

In addition to the aforementioned public sector accounting standard-setting bodies, the USA-GASB (1998) issued Statement No. 33—Accounting and Financial Reporting for Non-exchange Transactions (GASB 33). The main focus is on the timing of the recognition of

Table 2.2 Tax revenues and recognition point

Revenue type	*Revenue recognition point*
Source deductions (PAYE)	When an individual earns income that is subject to PAYE
Residents' withholding tax	When an individual is paid interest or dividends subject to deduction at source
Fringe benefits tax (FBT)	When benefits are provided that give rise to FBT
Provisional tax	Payment due date
Terminal tax	Assessment filed date
Goods and services tax	When the liability to the crown is incurred
Excise duty	When goods are subject to duty
Road user charges and motor vehicle fees	When payment for the fees or charges is made
Stamp and credit card duties	When the liability to the crown is incurred
Other indirect tax	When the debt to the crown arises

Source: New Zealand Treasury

Table 2.3 Tax revenues and basis of recognition

Major type of taxation revenue	*Basis of revenue recognition*
Income tax from individual (PAYE, PPS, provisional tax)	Recognized on earnings of taxpayers during the reporting period where such amounts can be reliably measured and are expected to be collected
Company tax and superannuation fund tax	Recognized on company income for the reporting period
Sales tax and withholding tax	Recognized on defined sales and other relevant activities occurring during the reporting period
Fringe benefits tax	Recognized on fringe benefits provided to employees during the reporting period
Excise duty	Recognized when goods are distributed for home consumption
Customs duty	Recognized when imported goods are distributed for home consumption

Source: Australian Treasury

non-exchange transactions—that is, *when* should governmental entities recognize the non-exchange transactions in the financial statements?

Statement No. 33 (para 7) identifies four classes of non-exchange transactions based on shared characteristics that affect the timing of recognition as follows:

- *Tax revenues*: result from assessments imposed on exchange transactions (i.e., income taxes, sales taxes, and other assessments on earnings or consumption).
- *Non-exchange revenues*: result from assessments imposed on nongovernmental entities, including individuals, other than assessments on exchange transactions (i.e., property taxes; fines and penalties; and property forfeitures, such as seizures and escheats).
- *Non-exchange transactions*: occur when a government at one level provides resources to a government at another level and requires the recipient to use the resources for a specific purpose (i.e., federal programs that state or local governments are mandated to perform).
- *Non-exchange transactions*: result from legislative or contractual agreements, other than exchanges, entered into willingly by two or more parties to the agreement (i.e., certain grants, certain entitlements, and private donations).

GASB Statement No. 33 has determined the timing of recognition of the four classes of non-exchange transactions under both accrual accounting and modified accrual accounting. It assumes the timing of recognition should be the same whether the accrual or modified accrual basis is used (paras 29 and 30). However, under the modified accrual basis, revenues should only be recognized when the recognition criteria are met and the revenues are available. "Available" means that the government has collected the revenues in the current period or expects to collect them soon enough after the end of the period to use them to pay liabilities of the current period (GASB Statement No. 33, paras 29–30). According to this Statement, the timing of revenues recognition is outlined as follows (paras 16,17,18, 19, and 20):

– ***Derived tax revenues***

Revenues are recognized when the underlying exchange transaction occurs. Resources received before the underlying exchange has occurred should be reported as deferred revenues (liabilities).

– ***Imposed non-exchange revenues***

Revenues are recognized in the period when use of the resources is required or first permitted by time requirements (e.g., for property taxes, the period for which they are levied; and for other than property taxes, in the period when an enforceable legal claim has arisen), or at the same time as the assets, if the government has not established time requirements. Resources received or recognized as receivable before the time requirements are met should be reported as deferred revenues.

- ***Government-mandated non-exchange transactions and voluntary non-exchange transactions***

Revenues are recognized when all applicable eligibility requirements are met. According to GASB Statement No. 33, the eligibility requirements comprise one or more of the following (para 19):

a. *Required characteristics of recipients.* The recipient (and secondary recipients, if applicable) has the characteristics specified by the provider. For example, under a certain federal program, recipients are required to be states and secondary recipients are required to be school districts.
b. *Time requirements.* Time requirements specified by enabling legislation or the provider have been met. For example, the period when the resources are required to be used (sold, disbursed, or consumed) or when use is first permitted or has begun, or the resources are being maintained intact, as specified by the provider.
c. *Reimbursements.* The provider offers resources on a reimbursement (expenditure-driven) basis and the recipient has incurred allowable costs under the applicable program.
d. *Contingencies* (applies only to voluntary non-exchange transactions). The provider's offer of resources is contingent upon a specified action of the recipient and that action has occurred. For example, the recipient is required to raise a specific amount of resources from third parties or to dedicate its own resources for a specified purpose and has complied with those requirements.

After reviewing the accounting professional literature regarding the revenue recognition in the public sector from different international and national standard-setting bodies' points of view, it is obvious that these bodies disagree not only about the accounting approach used but also on the classification itself of non-exchange transactions. For example, in Australia, non-exchange transactions are classified as voluntary transfers and compulsory transfers, while in the USA, they are classified into four groups as stated earlier. It can therefore be concluded that there is a lack of unified guidance of accounting on revenues arising from both exchange and non-exchange transactions, even if within these several classifications might be admitted. This makes the matter more difficult for the practitioners; therefore, the next section will propose a unified guidance by developing a practice-relevant approach for revenue recognition for both the exchange and non-exchange transactions, bringing together what is included in the aforementioned international and national standards.

3.2.3 A Practice-Relevant Approach for Revenue Recognition: A Practitioner's Perspective

Revenue from Exchange Transactions: Public Sector Performance Obligation Approach

Under the accrual accounting regime, assets, liabilities, revenues, and expenses arising from transactions and events must be recognized in the financial statements when they have an economic impact on the public sector entity, regardless of when the associated cash flows occur. As stated earlier, public sector entities obtain their revenues from both exchange transactions and non-exchange transactions. The accounting treatment of revenues arising from exchange transactions in the public sector is, to a reasonable extent, similar to that of the private sector. The accounting treatment of revenue in both sectors uses the same two main revenue recognition criteria:

a. Revenue is recognized when it is probable that future economic benefits will flow to the entity.
b. These benefits can be measured reliably.

In addition, there is a consensus in both sectors that these recognition criteria should be applied separately to each transaction (see IAS 18, IFRS 15, IPSAS 9, AASB 15, and GRAP 9). Revenues arising from exchange transactions and events include sale of goods; rendering of services; and the use by others of entity assets yielding interest, royalties, dividends, or similar distributions. While the two recognition criteria are applied to all revenues arising from exchange transactions and events, there are specific conditions associated with each transaction that should be satisfied so that the revenue is recognized.

For the <u>sale of goods</u>, the recognition of revenue should be based on the risks and rewards model in accordance with IPSAS 9, whereas it should be based on the control-based model in accordance with IFRS 15. For the <u>rendering of services</u>, the recognition of revenue should be based on the stage of completion of the transaction at the end of the reporting period.

The recognition of revenue by reference to the stage of completion of a transaction is often referred to as the percentage of the completion method. In this method, revenue is recognized in the accounting period in which the services are rendered. The recognition of revenue on this basis provides useful information on the extent of service activity and performance during a period. For interest, royalties, and dividends, revenue shall be recognized on the following bases (IPSAS, 9 para. 34):

(a) Interest shall be recognized on a time proportion basis that takes into account the effective yield on the asset.
(b) Royalties shall be recognized on an accrual basis in accordance with the substance of the relevant agreement.
(c) Dividends shall be recognized when the shareholders' right to receive payment is established.

It is obvious that approaches and models that have been used as a basis for the recognition of revenue arising from the exchange transactions and events (such as risks and rewards model and percentage of completion method) are to a great extent consistent with the performance obligation approach applied to the private sector based on IFRS 15. According to IFRS 15, the revenue should be recognized when an entity transfers control of goods or services to the customer for the amount to which the entity expects to be entitled. Consequently, the recognition of revenue with respect to the performance obligation approach is based on the control-based model, not on the risks and rewards model. The question is: can the performance obligation approach also be applied to the public sector? IPSASB (2016) has considered the extent to which the performance obligation approach can be applied to revenue and expense transactions (both exchange and non-exchange) in the public sector. The IPSASB noted that the performance obligation approach in IFRS 15 only relates to contracts for good and services with customers. Accordingly, it does not cover the accounting treatment of other exchange transactions such as the use by others of the entity's assets yielding interest, royalties, dividends, or similar distributions. Therefore, the IPSASB suggested that the performance obligation approach should be broadened to include the other exchange transactions with performance obligations. Such transactions include those that meet the criteria in IFRS 15 and transactions out of the scope of IFRS 15 that contain performance obligations. Moreover, the IPSASB sees that developing the performance obligation approach to be applied to the public sector needs to include noncontractual binding arrangements in the public sector, noting that specific legislative requirements can give rise to performance obligations. Furthermore, there is a need to take a broad view of the enforceability of binding arrangements, which is not just through legal means (IPSASB 2016).

However, the core concept of revenue recognition under the performance obligation approach based on IFRS 15 is that revenue is recognized when the performance obligation is settled. The settlement of a performance obligation at a point in time is considered in relation to the transfer of control over the asset that is created in fulfillment of the performance obligation. This means that the point at which control over the asset is transferred coincides with the point in time that a performance obligation can be considered to have been fulfilled. This establishes the control-based revenue recognition model employed by IFRS 15. However, within the public sector entities, the nature of certain transactions may make it difficult to distinguish whether a performance obligation is settled over a period of time or at a point in time (ASB 2015, para. 4.2.4). Accordingly, most of the standard-setting bodies in the public sector such as ASB (FRC)-UK and IPSASB (GRAP 9 and IPSAS 9) prefer the use of the risks and rewards model, where the revenue from the sale of goods is only recognized when the risks and rewards related to an asset are transferred to the customer. Therefore, *the transfer of risks and rewards can be considered in IFRS 15 to be a subset in evaluating the transfer of control over an asset*. As such, it is considered that the control-based model of IFRS 15 might result in a later point of revenue recognition in the public sector entities (ASB 2015), which can create confusion in practice from the practitioner's standpoint. Therefore, we suggest that the development of the public sector performance obligation approach should be based on the risks and rewards model or at least to consider the latter as a subset of the control-based model.

Taking into account that the IFRS 15 performance obligations approach is only appropriate where there are identifiable, specific, and enforceable performance obligations in a contract with a customer for the provision of goods or services, the development of a Public Sector Performance Obligations Approach will need to consider how to interpret these requirements in a public sector context—for example, by looking at how performance obligations are expressed in binding and non-legally binding arrangements and considering how public sector entities can demonstrate enforceability. Furthermore, there may be a need to consider how the transfer of risks and rewards might continue to be used as a proxy for the transfer of control.

This means that the development of the Public Sector Performance Obligation Approach for exchange transactions should be based on the following:

1. Identifying which goods or services are distinct and should hence be accounted for as a separate performance obligation. This can be facilitated by focusing on
   a. Transactions with performance obligations stipulated in both IFRS 15 and AASB 15 such as sales and service provision
   b. Transactions with performance obligations but not included in IFRS 15 and AASB 15, such as interest and royalties
2. When considering the large volume of customers of public sector entities, it is envisaged that the use of the control-based model would be onerous to the point of becoming impracticable; therefore, the satisfaction of the performance obligation should be based on the transferring of significant risks and rewards of promised goods or services to a customer.
3. Enforceability should be considered as a key aspect of the Public Sector Performance Obligation Approach for legal and equivalent binding arrangements.

Considering the aforementioned adaptations of the IFRS 15 criteria will result in improving reporting of revenue from exchange transactions within the public sector. However, given the current level of maturity of accounting practice in the public sector it is considered that the public performance obligation approach should be simplified to remove the complexities provided in IFRS 15.

Revenue from Non-Exchange Transactions: Assets–Liabilities Approach

While the performance obligation approach can be modified to be applied to the revenues arising from exchange transactions, some accounting standard bodies argue (such as AASB 15 and IPSASB-CP August, 2017) that the performance obligation approach can be applied to both exchange and non-exchange transactions by using both IFRS 15 and AASB 15. In other words, they call for using a single revenue recognition model. Some others, such as ASB, argue that while it is possible to extract certain principles from the approach in IFRS 15 and apply them to non-exchange transactions, it is difficult to apply (a single model) the model "as is" to non-exchange transactions. This is because (ASB 2015, para. 4.6)

(a) Non-exchange transactions often arise from statutory rather than contractual arrangements, which makes the initial step in the IFRS 15 difficult to apply. So the single model as provided would therefore not cater for a significant portion of revenue in the public sector, and it would need to be adjusted accordingly.
(b) Non-exchange transactions are not executory in nature in that they do not require performance by both parties to the transaction. For the model in IFRS 15 to accommodate revenue from non-exchange transactions it will require amendment to facilitate the recognition of revenue where no party to the arrangement has yet performed, and where legislation or its equivalent is the driver rather than the contract.
(c) The model in IFRS 15 requires the identification of a customer. Unlike the private sector, the nature of transactions in the public sector entities often prevents the identification of a specific customer. Moreover, the goods and services provided by the public sector entities are determined by their legislative mandate to a wide range of people/entities and they are also provided collectively rather than individually. Accordingly, the customer of these services and the portion of the services provided to individual customers cannot always be identified.

In addition to the aforementioned, under IFRS 15, the event that gives rise to the initial recognition of a transaction is usually based on one party to the arrangement having performed in terms of the arrangement. In contrast, the event that gives rise to the recognition of non-exchange transactions is often the occurrence of an event, for example, a taxable event, or breach of a law. Because the recognition of transactions in IFRS 15 is driven by performance by parties and the satisfaction of performance obligations, the initial recognition of transactions and the recognition of revenue under IFRS 15 is unclear for many non-exchange transactions.

Moreover, IPSASB (2015) agreed that a performance obligation approach cannot be applied to transactions that are not subject to performance obligations, and that these transactions would need to be dealt with separately. Given all these concerns, the non-exchange transactions should be treated differently from the exchange transactions and the IFRS 15, in its current form, would not be appropriate for application to revenue from non-exchange transactions (ASB 2015).

Furthermore, non-exchange transactions entail the public sector entity receiving resources, either free of charge or for nominal consideration that is considerably lower than prevailing market prices. The transaction or arrangement that governs the transfer of the resources, irrespective of whether it is statutory or contractual, gives one party to the transaction or arrangement a right to receive the resources (ASB 2015).

Consequently, the recognition principle should be reshaped to enable public sector entities to recognize revenues resulting from non-exchange transactions. The performance obligation approach, whether based on the control-based model or on the risks and rewards model, is unlikely to be valid for application to the non-exchange transactions. There should be a new approach that can recognize the revenues that are politically and not economically driven—in other words, revenues derived from the use of sovereign powers.

Therefore, standard-setting bodies (such as IPSASB, ASB, and GASB) agreed on the application of the assets–liabilities approach to the public sector entities for the recognition of revenues arising from non-exchange transactions. The assets–liabilities approach with respect to recognition of revenues works as follows (GRAP 23 (2014) and IPSAS 23):

1. Determine if the entity can recognize an asset from a non-exchange transaction.
2. Identify the stipulations attached to the transaction or arrangement and determine whether they give rise to conditions or restrictions.
3. Recognize revenue to the extent that an asset is recognized, and any present obligation is satisfied (i.e., to the extent that conditions are met).
4. Measure revenue at the amount of the increase in net assets recognized by the entity.

In addition, IPSAS 23.44 and GRAP 23.43 mention that "[a]n inflow of resources from a non-exchange transaction recognized as an asset shall be recognized as revenue, except to the extent that a liability is also recognized in respect of the same inflow."

This means that under the assets–liabilities approach, described in IPSAS 23 and GRAP 23, the starting point of the revenue recognition is determining whether an arrangement gives the right to receive resources that would meet the definition of an asset. Once the right to receive resources is confirmed, the public sector entity is required to determine whether it controls such a resource and meets the definition of an asset. This is confirmed by IPSAS 23.32 and GRAP 23.27 as they state that "[a]n entity will recognize an asset arising from a non-exchange transaction when it gains control of resources that meet the definition of an asset and satisfy the recognition criteria."

Gaining the control of an asset means that the public sector entity has the ability to exclude or regulate the access of others to the benefits of an asset (IPSAS 23.32 and GRAP 23.27). It is evident that GRAP 23 and IPSAS 23 employ a control-based model for the recognition of assets arising from non-exchange transactions. Once an entity confirms the existence of the right to an asset, and that it has the ability to control such an asset, it will recognize an asset in accordance with IPSAS 23 and GRAP 23 and either a liability or a revenue as the counter entry (ASB 2015).

However, based on the experiences of some countries (such as Australia and the USA), the control-based model alone is not enough to cover the recognition of all revenues resulting from the non-exchange transactions.

For example, Australian AASB 15 distinguishes between two non-exchange transfers: ***(a) Voluntary transfers*** including items such as donations, grants, and appropriations, where the recognition of revenues arising from these transactions should be based on the use of a control-based model; and ***(b) Compulsory transfers*** such as taxes, rates, and fines, where the revenues would be recognized when the public sector entity has an enforceable legal claim to receive funds and the underlying taxable event occurs.

In the USA, as noted earlier, GASB 33 distinguishes four classes of non-exchange transactions: derived tax revenues, imposed non-exchange revenues, government-mandated non-exchange transactions, and voluntary non-exchange transactions. As is obvious from the literature (discussed in Sect. 3.2.2), the four classes of non-exchange transactions are recognized using different approaches. Some classes of revenue are recognized based on the occurrence of the taxable event and the existence of an enforceable legal claim, as in the case of derived tax revenues. In some other cases, such as imposed non-exchange revenues, the recognition is divided into two cases: in case of the property tax, revenue is recognized in the period in which the property taxes are levied; while in other than property taxes, such as fines and penalties, the revenue is recognized in the period when an enforceable legal claim has arisen. This means that the recognition of property taxes is based on the control-based model, whereas other than property taxes are based on the arising of enforceable legal claim and the occurrence of the underlying taxable event. So it could be inferred that in addition to the control-based model, the enforceable legal claim and occurrence taxable event are also essential elements for the recognition of the revenue resulting from the non-exchange transactions.

As is obvious from the aforementioned discussion, the application of the recognition principle needs to be reshaped to fit the context of public sector entities, particularly for non-exchange transactions. Moreover, reshaping the application of the recognition principle should take into consideration the specificities of public sector entities and what they do compared to the private sector business entities. The recognition of revenues resulting from non-exchange transactions is different to a great extent from that arising from exchange transactions. Accordingly, to help practitioners, this section concludes by suggesting a practice-relevant approach for the recognition of revenues arising from both the exchange and non-exchange transactions.

The contribution of the practice-relevant approach to the current literature is as follows: (a) it requires that the development of the performance obligation approach for exchange transactions in the public sector be based on the risks and rewards model or at least consider the risks and rewards model as a proxy for the transfer of control. This is due to the fact that the performance obligation approach described in IFRS 15 requires the identification of a customer, whereas the nature of transactions in the public sector often precludes the identification of a specific customer. The goods and services rendered by public sector entities are determined by their legislative mandate to a wide range of people/entities. These goods and services are also often provided collectively rather than individually (ASB 2015). (b) Taking the public sector specificities into consideration, it emphasizes the significance of enforceability and considers it a key aspect of the Public Sector Performance Obligation Approach for legal and equivalent binding arrangements. (c) It requires that the performance obligation approach should be broadened to include other exchange transactions with performance obligations such as the use by others of an entity's assets yielding interest, royalties, dividends, or similar distributions. This is because the performance obligation approach presented in IFRS 15 is only related to contracts for goods and services with customers. (d) For non-exchange transactions, it emphasizes the fact that the assets–liabilities approach should not be based only on the control-based model, but also includes the enforceable legal claim and the occurrence of the taxable event. Accordingly, taking the contribution of the practice-relevant approach into consideration will simplify the use of the performance obligation approach and remove its complexities highlighted by the IFRS 15 and facilitate the application of the assets–liabilities approach by classifying the non- exchange transactions into voluntary transfers and compulsory transfers; and using not only the control-based model but also the enforceable legal claim and the occurrence of the taxable event. Finally, the practice-relevant approach—as depicted in Fig. 2.2—has attempted to cater for the wide variety of transactions and circumstances prevalent in the public sector.

3.3 Consistency Principle

The consistency principle refers to the use of similar accounting procedures by a single accounting entity from period to period and the use of similar measurement concepts and procedures for related items within the statements of an entity for a single period (Hendriksen 1982; Franklin et al. 2019). In fact, the consistency principle requires a persistent application by an entity of any selected accounting policies and principles, period after period. As a result, a user of the entity's financial statements may assume that in keeping its records and in preparing its statements, the entity used the same procedures used in previous years (Larson and Pyle 1987; Franklin et al. 2019). The use of the consistency principle is important because, if different accounting procedures and principles are used, it will be difficult for the user to discern the effects on the entity, from period to period, caused by external factors such as changes in economic conditions. In addition, it will be difficult for the user to separate the fluctuations caused by internal and external economic factors.

While the use of the consistency principle in a business enterprise is necessary, its use in the public sector is imperative. For instance, it has been stated that the matching principle can be used in the public sector to show the surplus (or deficit) of revenues over expenses (see Sect. 3.1). As long as the rules of recognizing expenses and revenues have been established and are applied in accordance with the principle of consistency, the variations in the surplus or deficit over years can provide important information about the impact of fiscal policies. In addition, the use of the consistency principle in the public sector can provide the user with a reliable

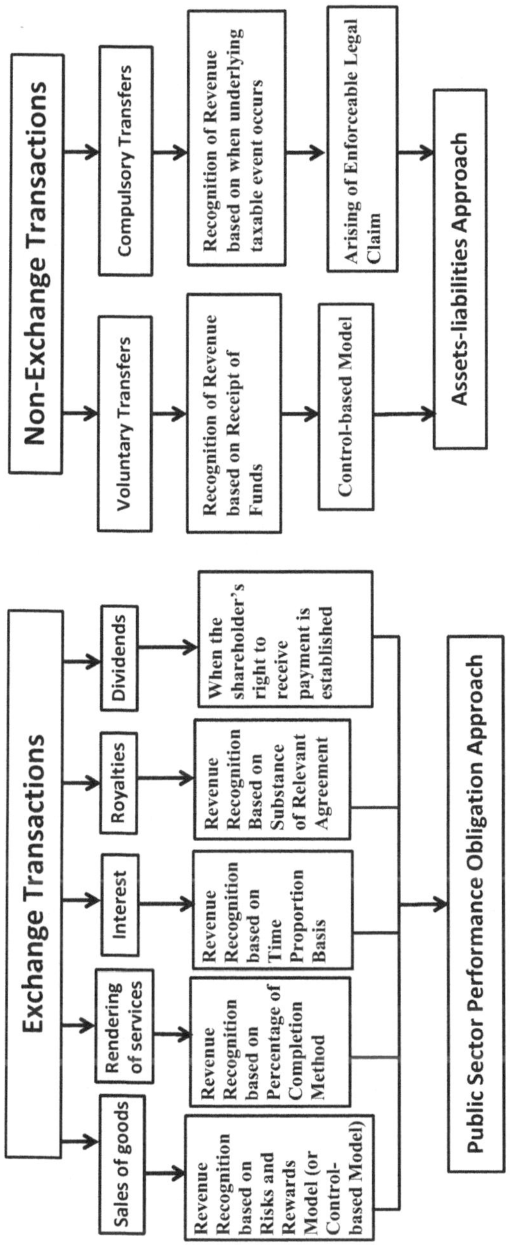

Fig. 2.2 Practice-relevant approach for the revenues recognition in the public sector. (Source: Author)

measure of net worth, period after period. The user can measure and judge the impact of government actions on whether those actions have deteriorated or improved net worth. Without the use of consistent accounting policies, the public sector entities can easily affect the net worth, for example, by valuing its assets at historical cost in some periods and at current cost in other periods. Consequently, it will make the comparison of net worth from period to period meaningless. Similarly, the use of the consistency principle will provide a reliable measure for intergenerational equity, period after period. Also, without the use of the consistency principle, the true and fair view about the financial position of the government can be distorted.

Furthermore, preparing the consolidated accrual statements for the whole government will require the adoption of accrual accounting by the public sector entities. One significant issue that arises from the use of accrual accounting for the consolidated statements of the government as a whole is the ***meaning of any reported deficit***. A deficit under accrual accounting would reflect the fact that the government had not used its compulsory revenue-raising powers sufficiently to cover all costs; for example, it would indicate the extent to which emerging liabilities are not being funded (Shand 1989). It could also mean that a government had not kept a tight rein on its costs.

In contrast, a deficit under cash accounting indicates the net borrowing requirement to fund current cash outlays.

However, the main problem with consolidated financial statements emerges when separate legislative powers exist within the government and especially when these powers have not resulted in uniform accounting policies for similar transactions and other events in similar circumstances. If public sector entities use accounting policies other than those adopted in the consolidated financial statements for similar transactions and events in similar circumstances, the deficit included in the consolidated accrual statements would not indicate the right meaning of the government deficit. For instance, under accrual accounting the public sector entities should disclose the amount of the unfunded liability for superannuation commitments. While some of the public sector entities can treat it as a liability on their balance sheet, other entities can only show the amount of liability as a parenthetical note. Then, the varying treatment for the accumulated liability will affect the reported deficit or surplus. Therefore, the adoption of accrual accounting for such consolidated statements would need to be accompanied by careful explanations and appropriate modifications to the way financial information might otherwise be displayed (Shand 1989). In addition, if governmental entities use accounting policies other than those used in the consolidated financial statements for similar transactions and events in similar circumstances, appropriate adjustments should be made to their financial statements when they are used in preparing the consolidated accrual statements.

In general, in order to avoid the ambiguity about the meaning of the reported deficit, there should be consistent accounting policies for the government as a whole and they should be used in preparing the consolidated accrual statements. If there is a deviation from the use of the consistent accounting policies in preparing the consolidated accrual statements, this should be disclosed in the notes that accompany the consolidated accrual statements. What makes this disclosure important is that there are inevitably problems attached to the interpretation of government financial statements, whether consolidated or not. As stated earlier, liabilities (e.g., unfunded pensions) are much more under the discretionary control of the government than would ever be the case for private sector decision-makers (Heald and Georgiou 2000; Franklin et al. 2019). Furthermore, future tax revenues, which will be the means for meeting these liabilities as they mature, are not capitalized, thereby increasing the difficulty of interpreting the meaning of the government deficit.

Thus, the development of uniform accounting policies and using them on a consistent basis (consistency principle) for the government as a whole is an essential step in providing a true and fair view of the government deficit. So in order to avoid the misinterpretation of reported deficit, the public sector entities' financial statements and the consolidated financial statements for the government as a whole should be prepared and presented on consistent accounting policies. Consequently, the use of unified accounting policies and procedures and application of the consistency principle in the public sector is necessary for better interpretation of any reported deficit, for analyzing and evaluating the impact of fiscal policies, for comparing years, for measuring trends and discerning the effects on the governmental entity caused by either external or internal factors.

3.4 *Conservatism Principle*

The conservatism principle (also named by some as 'prudence' principle) is sometimes expressed simplistically as "recognize all losses but anticipate no profits" (Larson and Pyle 1987; Franklin et al. 2019). This principle is generally used to indicate that accountants should report the lowest of several possible values for assets and revenues and the highest of several possible values for liabilities and expenses. It also implies that expenses should be recognized sooner rather than later and that revenues should be recognized later than sooner (Hendriksen 1982; Bergmann et al. 2019; Franklin et al. 2019). So, recognize no gains until they happen but record all possible losses even before they take place.

Unlike the private sector, the recognition of revenues in the public sector is more difficult, since diversity of sources, as discussed in the previous sections, will require different recognition criteria. The conservatism principle holds that some degree of risk is involved in the collection of these revenues. Hence, it may be unwise to treat these revenues in the financial statements of public sector entities as fully collectable. Historical data may support the fact that, over the past several years, public sector entities had only been successful in collecting a certain percentage of these revenues. Applying the conservatism principle in this case would be to state the value of the probable collection of revenues based on this objective information. In general, public sector accountants should also avoid the use of subjective judgement in making estimates for financial statements. In this instance, there is some support both for the use of historical trends and for taking a more conservative view.

Furthermore, unlike the private business sector, the public sector entities own different types of physical assets such as infrastructure assets and heritages assets. Most of these assets are, to a large extent, difficult to measure reliably; and the realization of the value increases of these assets will also be difficult. Overstating the value of assets can result in overstating the probable asset base of the public sector entity or government. Therefore, recording the value of these assets should be based on historical data and a conservative or prudent view. In other words, I would say that in a context full of particularities such as the public sector, it might sometimes not be so easy to apply conservative principle as it is applied to the private sector. For example, to assess impairment losses of assets requires different criteria than in business, because there is no market value; also historical cost might not be known. Another example would be that most receivables might come from taxpayers, whose probability of non-receiving might be more difficult to assess than that from regular clients in a company. Also, making estimates of revenue to accrue is not as easy as in a business, again due to the main type of revenue—taxes, whose estimates depend on macroeconomic conditions. Consequently, it can be concluded that the conservatism principle needs to be reshaped to take into account the specificities of the public sector entities and these specificities make the conservatism principle more applicable to public sector accounting. This means that proper allowance should be made for all known and foreseeable losses and liabilities; income should only be included where there is a reasonable certainty of it arising (Green Paper 1994). Thus, pessimism is assumed to be better than optimism in financial reporting of the public sector entities and governments.

4 Conceptual Challenges: Accrual Accounting Postulations

Of the three accrual accounting postulations (going concern, stable unit of measure, and accounting entity), the going concern postulation seems to be the only one that gives rise to debate on how it can be applied to the public sector. This section, therefore, focuses on reshaping the application of the going concern postulation.

4.1 Going Concern

The going concern postulation means that the accounting entity will continue in operation long enough to carry out its existing commitments. In other words, the accounting entity will exist for a time period sufficient to justify the deferral process inherent in business organization accrual accounting (Ingram et al. 1991; Franklin et al. 2019; Bergmann et al. 2019).

While some governments have already adopted accrual accounting, some others are still using cash accounting. "*One of the fundamental flaws in the argument for cash accounting is that it assumes that government is not a going concern*" (Hardman 1982; Ouda 2006). Certainly, the apparent ownership of government operations may change periodically with the election of a new government; however, the business, management, assets, and clientele of government continue more or less unchanged through successive governments. Moreover, the going concern postulation means that it is expected that the 'business' will remain in operation at least as long as the longest useful life of any of its resources or obligations. Simply, this assumption is more applicable to the public sector due to the very long life of many physical assets and long-term liabilities in comparison with the business enterprises. In other words, it is more likely that the going concern postulation in the public sector is linked to the ongoing nature of government. For example, while in the private sector the going concern may be at risk when sales decrease and companies start to default financially, in the public sector and government, as long as the government keeps the power to raise taxes, and the citizens and the economy as a whole support the burden of those taxes, the going concern is assured.

Governmental entities are also expected to continue providing services in the future as a consequence of ***a political decision*** and then making the appropriations available. The UK Government Financial Reporting Manual stated that for nontrading entities in the public sector, the anticipated continuation of the provision of a service in the future, as evidenced by inclusion of financial provision for that service in published documents, is normally sufficient evidence of ***going concern***. This also means that the continuation of the governmental entities is not only based on ***an economic decision but also on a political decision***.

The nature of governmental activity, unlike the private sector, means that consideration of going concern needs to be focused on more broadly. IPSAS 1 argued that there may be circumstances where the usual going concern tests of liquidity and solvency appear unfavorable, but other factors suggest that the entity is nonetheless a going concern. For example:

a. In assessing whether a government is a going concern, the power to levy rates or taxes may enable some entities to be considered as a going concern even though they may operate for extended periods with negative net assets/equity.
b. For an individual entity, an assessment of its statement of financial position on the reporting date may suggest that the going concern assumption is not appropriate. However, there may be multiyear funding agreements, or other arrangements, in place that will ensure the continued operation of the entity.

Consequently, the major difference in the interpretation of the going concern postulation between the private business sector and the public sector is that in the private sector the going concern depends on an economic assessment and decision that may be based on the financial statements, whereas in the public sector, it depends on a political assessment and decision and the financial statements may or may not assist in this decision. A state enterprise, which is considered politically essential, may be retained despite making huge losses. Therefore, the going concern assumption in the public sector should be reshaped to consider the political assessment and decision alongside the economic assessment and decision in determining whether public sector entities are considered as going concern or not. The assumption that a government is not a going concern cannot be justified, due to the fact that the going concern assumption is based on different criteria in the public sector, that is, political rather than financial factors.

5 Conclusion

As a consequence of the discussion of the accrual accounting principles and the going concern postulation, it could be inferred that the application of some accrual accounting principles and postulations should be reshaped to allow them to fit the context of the public sector entities and governments overall.

This chapter discussed and provided some suggestions for these adaptations.

Taking into consideration the specific nature of the public sector activities in comparison with the private business sector activities, the **matching** of revenues with expenses of a certain fiscal year should be *based on a timing relationship instead of an exchange relationship*. This is because governments generally use resources from a variety of sources to pay for a variety of services. Consequently, the matching relationship that normally exists between resources provided and services received is a timing relationship (that is, both occur during the fiscal year) rather than an exchange relationship.

Reshaping the application of the **recognition** principle should take into consideration the specificities of public sector entities compared to private business sector entities, since the recognition of revenues resulting from exchange transactions is to a great extent different from that of non-exchange transactions. Accordingly, to facilitate the matter for practitioners a practice-relevant approach was suggested for the recognition of revenues arising from exchange transactions and non-exchange transactions which is based on different approaches and models. The practice-relevant approach made clear that the performance obligation approach used in the private business sector can be used for exchange transactions but only after making some amendments which are required to simplify it and to remove the complexities highlighted in IFRS 15. Furthermore, these amendments are needed to facilitate appropriate application of that approach, from the practitioners' perspective, in the public sector. Moreover, non-exchange transactions require a different approach to the recognition of revenues, which is the assets–liabilities approach using the control-based model, enforceable legal claim, and the occurrence of the taxable event.

The development of consistent accounting policies and their use on a consistent basis (**consistency** principle) for the government as a whole is an essential step towards providing a true and fair view of the government deficit. Moreover, the use of unified accounting policies and procedures and the application of the consistency principle in the public sector are necessary for better interpretation of any reported deficit, for analyzing and evaluating the impact of fiscal policies, for comparing years, for measuring trends, and for discerning the effects on the governmental entity caused by either external or internal factors.

Due to the fact that public sector entity obtains its revenues (inflows) from different sources, which, in turn, requires different recognition points, and because it owns different types of assets that are difficult to measure reliably and the realization of the value increases of these assets will also be difficult, this makes the **conservatism** principle more applicable to public sector accounting. This also requires that the application of the conservatism principle should be reshaped to fit the context of the public sector entities.

Finally, it can be inferred that the application of **going concern** postulation needs to be reshaped, as its application in the public sector is based not only on economic factors but also on political factors.

References

AASB 15. (2014). *Revenue from Contracts with Customers*. Australian Accounting Standard Board, Commonwealth of Australia.

ASB South Africa. (2015, March). *Impact of IFRS 15 Revenue from Contracts with Customers on Revenue in the Public Sector*. Accounting Standard Board, Issued by the Board.

ASB-UK. (2005, August). *Statement of Principles for Financial reporting, Proposed Interpretation for Public Benefit entities*. Accounting Standards Board, UK.

Bac, A. (1989). *Overheids Accountancy, Bijzonder Genoeg*. Leiden: Stenfert Kroese.

Bac, A. (2000). Commentary (for the 5th CIGAR Workshop—Speyer October, 2000): *Accounting for Capital Assets: The IPSAS Approach and the Main Issues*.

Ball, I. (1994, November 2). Initiatives in Public Sector Management and Financial Management: The New Zealand Experience. In A. Anderson (Ed.), *Financieel beheer, verslaggeving en prestatiemeting bij de Rijksoverheid*. Symposium verslag, Circustheater Scheveningen, 10127/1.

Barton, A. D. (2005). The Conceptual Arguments Concerning Accounting for Public Heritage Assets: A Note. *Accounting, Auditing & Accountability Journal, 18*(3), 434–440.

Bartos, S. (2000, November 13–14). *Implementing Accruals*. OECD International Accrual Accounting and Budgeting Symposium, Paris.

Bergmann, A., Fuchs, S., & Schuler, C. (2019). A Theoretical Basis for Public Sector Accrual Accounting Research: Current State and Perspectives. *Public Money & Management, 39*(8), 560–570.

Carlin, T. (2005). Debating the Impact of Accrual Accounting and Reporting in the Public Sector. *Financial Accountability & Management, 21*(3), 309–336.

Franklin, M., Graybeal, P., & Cooper, D. (2019). *Principles of Accounting: Volume 1 Financial Accounting*. Houston, TX: OpenStax Rice University.

GASB. (1987). *Concepts Statement No.1 of the Governmental Accounting Standards Board: Objectives of Financial Reporting*.

GASB. (1998). *GASB 33 "Accounting and Financial Reporting for Non-Exchange Transaction"*. Governmental Accounting Standards Series, No. 165-B.

GRAP 23. (2014). *Revenue from Non-Exchange Transactions*. National Treasury, Republic of South Africa, Published by Department National Treasury.

GRAP 9. (2014). *Revenue from Exchange Transactions*. National Treasury, Republic of South Africa, Published by Department National Treasury.

Green Paper. (1994, July). *Better Accounting for Taxpayer's Money—The Government Proposals—Resource Accounting and Budgeting in Government*. Presented to Parliament by the Secretaries of Treasury by Command her Majesty, London.

Guthrie, J. (1998). Application Accrual Accounting in the Australian Public Sector—Rhetoric or Reality? *Financial Accountability and Management, 14*(1), 1–19.

Hardman, D. (1982). *Government Accounting and Budgeting*. New York: Prentice-Hall of Australia PTY LTD.

Heald, D., & Georgiou, G. (2000). Consolidation Principles and Practices for the UK Government Sector. *Accounting and Business Research, 30*(2), 153–167.

Hendriksen, E. (1982). *Accounting Theory* (4th ed.). Homewood, IL: Richard D. Irwin, INC.

IFAC. (1991). *Financial Reporting by National Governments*. Issued by the International Federation of Accountants, Study 1.

IFAC. (1996). *Definition and Recognition of Revenues*. Study 9.

IFAC. (1998). *Guideline for Governmental Financial Reporting*. Exposure Draft.

IFAC. (2000). *Government Financial Reporting: Accounting Issues and Practices*. May Study 11.

IFAC. (2004, January). *Revenue from Non-Exchange Transactions (Including Taxes and Transfers.* Invitation to Comment (ITC), p. 70.

IFAC. (2006). *Exposure Draft 29: Revenue from Non-Exchange Transactions (Including Taxes and Transfers).*

In IFRS 15. IFRS 15 Revenue from Contracts with Customers.

Ingram, R., Petersen, R., & Martin, S. (1991). *Accounting and Financial Reporting for Governmental and Nonprofit Organizations.* Basic Concepts, McGRAW-HILL, INC.

IPSAB. (2015). *Handbook of International Public Sector Accounting Pronouncements.* 2015 Edition, Volume I-Including IPSAS 9 and IPSAS 23, Published by IFAC.

IPSASB. (2006). *Revenue from NON-EXCHANGE Transactions.* Toronto: IPSASB.

IPSASB. (2014). *The Conceptual Framework for General Purpose Financial Reporting by Public Sector Entities.*

IPSASB. (2015). *Handbook of International Public Sector Accounting Pronouncements.* 2015 Edition, Volume I-Including IPSAS 9 and IPSAS 23, Published by IFAC.

IPSASB. (2016). *Handbook of International Public Sector Accounting Pronouncements.* Volume 1.

IPSASB. (2017, August). *Accounting for Revenue and Non-Exchange Expenses.* Consultation Paper.

IPSASB. (2018). *Handbook of International Public Sector Accounting Pronouncements.* Volume 1.

Larson, K., & Pyle, W. (1987). *Fundamental Accounting Principles.* Homewood, IL: Irwin.

Laughlin, R. (2008). A Conceptual Framework for Accounting for Public-Benefit Entities. *Public Money & Management, 28*(4), 247–254.

Mack, J., & Ryan, C. (2006). Reflection of the Theoretical Underpinning of the General-Purpose Financial Reports. *Accounting, Auditing, and Accountability Journal, 109*(4), 592–612.

Monsen, N., & Nasi, S. (1997). *The Contingency Model Reconsidered: On the Definition of Government Accounting Innovations.* Paper published at the 6th Biennial CIGAR Conference, Milan.

Nagendrakumar, N. (2017). Public Sector Accounting and Financial Reporting Reforms: Public Entities Perspectives, Sri Lanka. *International Journal on Governmental Financial Management, XVII*(1), 17–34.

New Zealand Institute of Chartered Accountants (NZICA). (2007c). *IAS 1 Presentation of Financial Statements.* Wellington: NZICA.

New Zealand Society of Accountants (NZSA). (1987). *Public Sector Accounting Statement No. 1: Determination and Disclosure of Accounting Policies for Public Sector Service Oriented Activities.* Wellington: NZSA.

Ouda, H. (2003). Accrual Accounting in the Government Sector: Background, Concepts, Benefits and Costs. *ICGFM-Public Fund Digest, 111*(2), 52–73.

Ouda, H. (2006, February). Cash Accounting and the Backwardness of Government Accounting and Related Systems. *Public Fund Digest, 6*(1), 55–65. Washington, DC: The International Consortium on Governmental Financial Management (ICGFM).

Ouda, H. (2007, February). Accrual Accounting Principles and Postulations in the Public Sector: Rhetoric or Reality. *Public Fund Digest, 7*(1). Washington, DC: The International Consortium on Governmental Financial Management (ICGFM).

Rakhman, F., & Wijayana, S. (2019). Determinants of Financial Reporting Quality in the Public Sector: Evidence from Indonesia. *The International Journal of Accounting, 54*(3), 1950009.

Rutherford, B. (1992). Developing a Conceptual Framework for Central Government Financial Reporting, Intermediate Users and Direct Control. *Financial Accountability and Management, 8*(4), 265–280.

Shand, D. (1989). Public Sector Accounting Standards-Progress and Implementation in Australia. In J. Guthrie, D. Shand, & L. Parker (Eds.), *Contemporary Readings in Accounting and Auditing*. Sydney: Harcourt Brace Jovanovich.

Van Peursem, K. (2006, October). *Public Benefits Vs Private Entities: A Fresh Look at Accounting Principles*. Working Paper Series, Management School, the University of Waikato, Number 89.

Van Peursem, K. (2009). Conceptual Framework for PBE Reporting: A Meaningful Basis for 'Sector Neutrality'. *Financial Reporting Regulation and Governance, 2009*(8), 1.

World Bank. (2010). *Public Financial Management Reform in the Middle East and North Africa: An Overview of Regional Experience*. Part II- Individual Country Cases, Report No. 55061-MNA.

Wynne, A. (2008). Accrual Accounting for the Public Sector—A Fad That Has Had Its Day? *International Journal on Governmental Financial Management, VIII*(2), 117–132.

CHAPTER 3

Towards A Practice-Relevant Holistic Accounting Approach for Governmental Capital Assets: An Alternative Reporting Model for the NPM Practices

1 Introduction

The past three decades have witnessed radical reforms in the public administration system of many developed and developing countries. These reforms are characterized by managerial freedom, market-driven competition, businesslike service delivery, value-for-money, result-based performance, client orientation, and a pro-market culture. These aspects of the administrative reforms have been described collectively as New Public Management (NPM) (Hood 1991, Keany and Hays 1998; Kaganova and Nayyar-stone 2000; Kickert 1997; Haque 2002; Kelly 1998; Ball and Grubnic 2008; Pollit and Bouckaert 2011; Bonini 2014; Lacovino et al. 2017; Klenk and Reiter 2019). The NPM was the umbrella for many public sector financial management reforms (which are called New Public Financial Management (NPFM)) such as public sector accounting reform (transition to accrual accounting), budgeting reform, enhancing public accountability and better governance, and so on. Similar to the profit sector, the adoption of accrual accounting in the public sector has entailed that all governmental capital assets should be identified and valued. This can assist the public sector entities in preparing their balance sheets. In contrast to the profit sector, where most of accounting standards regulate the capital assets in a similar way, the identification, valuation, and recognition of the capital assets in the public

H. Ouda, *Practice-Relevant Accrual Accounting for the Public Sector*, Public Sector Financial Management,
https://doi.org/10.1007/978-3-030-51595-9_3

sector are not easy tasks since these assets have existed for decades and have been acquired in different ways. Therefore, the identification, recognition, and valuation process of these assets are still the issue of many unresolved questions and debates (Ball 1994; Correia 2005; IFAC 2013; Christiaens 2004, 2012; Ouda 2005, 2015; Aversano et al. 2019).

Within the NPM and NPFM realm, governments have become more responsible for efficient and effective public assets management. This entails the existence of responsible and accountable governments, oriented towards overseeing the welfare of all citizens as a precondition for efficient public assets management (Ouda 2007; Grubišić et al. 2008; Aversano et al. 2020). For efficient public asset management, there should be an accounting and reporting system that facilitates the accounting and accountability of governmental capital assets, which can lead at the end to better governance of those assets. However, prior literature in the past three decades has shown that reporting of governmental capital assets has become a highly problematic issue for the public sector entities holding those assets, as there is no consensus about which capital assets should be included in the balance sheet and which ones excluded from it (Pallot 1990; Carnegie and Wolnizer 1995; Barton 1999, 2005; Hooper and Kearins 2005; Christiaens et al. 2012; Wild 2013; Ouda 2014, 2016; IPSASB 2014, 2017; Ellwood 2018; Aversano et al. 2020; De Wolf et al. 2020). This is due to the fact that public sector entities have distinct types of capital assets that are not comparable to those of the private sector, such as heritage assets and defense assets. Based on the NPM practices, public sector entities are required to report to stakeholders on a model disclosing the economic values of all assets under their control. In other words, the NPM philosophy requires the public sector entities to attribute economic values to governmental capital assets including heritage and defense assets, and produce annual financial statements prepared on an equivalent basis to the corporate model (Wild 2013). The argument of attributing economic values to governmental capital assets raises the question of whether it is appropriate to view all governmental capital assets through a similar lens. Most of the heritage assets and defense assets are not used to generate revenue for the government but are operated to provide cultural, social, and national security benefits to the country. Therefore, it is misleading and inappropriate to include these assets together with other assets that generate economic benefits on the government's balance sheet. While there exists an extensive prior literature focused on how heritage and defense assets might be accounted for and whether the heritage assets are sufficiently different to merit different treatment (IPSASB 2010, 2014,

2017; De Wolf et al. 2020), there is little that addresses the reporting of heritage and defense assets from an alternative, financial and nonfinancial perspective (Wild 2013).

Moreover, the capitalization of specific assets such as heritage assets can have different effects on the net worth of different countries, as these effects will differ according to the volume of heritage assets that are owned by each country. For example, the city of Luxor in Egypt hosts one-third of all the monuments and antiquities of the world (heritage assets). Therefore, the capitalization of all heritage assets in Egypt will lead to the exaggeration of net worth, which indicates that Egypt has many positive economic/financial resources while it is suffering from big amounts of public debt and budget deficit. Furthermore, if heritage assets have no financial value to the governmental entity, then it is misleading to match them against the liabilities. They are not resources which can be used to generate cash for the discharge of liabilities, and their inclusion in a balance sheet is misleading to the management and creditors (Carnegie and Wolnizer 1995; Hone 1997).

Accordingly, the following questions have been raised:

- ***How far should the accounting recognition of governmental capital assets go under the full accrual accounting?***
- ***Are the current recognition criteria enough to include or to exclude the governmental capital assets?***
- ***Do the current recognition criteria for governmental capital assets require a reshaping to fit the context of public sector entities?***
- ***Does the reshaping of the recognition criteria require new recognition attributes?***

Consequently, the methodology used in this chapter is based on a critical analysis of relevant literature, including the promulgations of accounting standard-setting agencies and related organizations. Hence, it will critically analyze the doctrines and the ideologies of the NPM model, challenging its assumptions that private sector financial reporting requirements based on GAAP are appropriate to account for all government capital assets including heritage and defense assets. While the NPM model believes in the one-size-fits-all application of GAAP to entities and assets differentiated in their purpose and essence (Hooper and Kearins 2005), I will propose a Practice-Relevant Holistic Reporting Model based on an alternative metric for the recognition and measurement of governmental capital assets, centered on a framework that suggests a set of broad stakeholder-driven social, legal, cultural, and national security, rather than only economic values for reporting governmental capital assets. In particular, the chapter argues against the NPM assumption that reporting all government capital assets including the heritage and defense assets held by public sector entities in economic terms improves accountability in those entities.

The chapter's contribution to the literature is twofold: First, the chapter attempts to provide a practical solution for the unresolved issue in the past three decades, where there is a lack of a practice-relevant holistic approach in which the recognition of governmental capital assets is examined. Consequently, the chapter attempts to develop a Practice-Relevant Holistic Accounting Approach for governmental capital assets. The development of this approach has resulted in developing two new recognition criteria and five recognition attributes that have been used to develop three sub-approaches for the accounting treatment of governmental capital assets. Second, it contributes to a deeper understanding of the specific characteristics of governmental capital assets compared to the private sector and provides insight into the development of practice-relevant recognition criteria and attributes that take into consideration the specific nature of the governmental capital assets.

2 New Public Management Practices

Hood (1995) argues that the accountability paradigm of the public administration system put heavy stress on two cardinal doctrines: The first was to keep the public sector sharply distinct from the private sector; the second was to maintain buffers against political and managerial discretion. On the contrary, the basis of the accountability paradigm of the NPM lay in reversing or removing differences between the public and the private sector. Accordingly, Hood (1995, p. 96) identified seven doctrinal components of the NPM:

1. Unbundling of the public sector into corporatized units organized by product
2. More contract-based competitive provision, with internal markets and term contracts
3. Stress on private sector styles of management practice
4. More stress on discipline and frugality in resource use
5. More emphasis on visible hands-on top management

6. Explicit formal measurable standards and measures of performance and success
7. Greater emphasis on output control

Doctrine 3, which stresses on the private sector styles of management practices, is of fundamental importance for this chapter, as one possible implication of stressing private-sector styles of management practices is the use of private sector accounting norms. The NPM philosophy is based on the assumption that public sector entities regardless of prior orientation would be more efficient and effective if run like their private sector counterparts (Hooper and Kearins 2005). Based on the NPM doctrine 3 that entails the adoption of the private sector accounting system (accrual accounting), all public sector entities have been required to attribute economic values to governmental capital assets including the heritage and defense assets, and to produce annual financial reports prepared on an equivalent basis to the corporate model (Wild 2013). The need to prepare financial reporting similar to the corporate model stems from the fact that managers in the public sector entities badly need reliable financial data that can assist them in the decision-making process and in using the available resources efficiently.

In point of fact, I agree with Hooper and Kearins (2005) that we do not deny that managers of public sector entities need good management (including a good accounting system) to be efficient and effective in achieving their goals. However, the one-size-fits-all mode of application of private sector GAAP to entities and assets differentiated in their purpose and essence is considered as managerial overreach according to Hooper and Kearins (2005). Primarily, public sector entities need an accounting system that takes into consideration the distinctive nature and characteristics of governmental capital assets such as heritage assets, natural resources, military assets, and community assets. Secondly, one of the common themes for both management and accounting changes in the public sector is the discharging of accountability. Accountability is closely associated with the NPM and the adoption of accrual accounting in the public sector since enhanced accountability has been one of the explicit aims of all management and accounting reforms. The purely instrumental NPM view of accountability—one that focuses on results—will promote accountability mechanisms that pay close attention to the purpose of the public action (Martin 1997). However, there is an argument in the literature strongly debating whether the requirement for public sector entities to provide financial statements based on the private sector GAAP affects positively or negatively on public sector accountability outcomes (see, for example, Barton 1999; Carnegie and West 2005; Wild 2013; Micallef and Peirson 1997; Cooper and Owen 2007).

3 The Transition from Cash Accounting to Accrual Accounting

As a result of using the cash-based accounting system by most governments, the governmental entities have traditionally accounted for capital assets in a way that reflects the financing required to meet their costs rather than their pattern of use (Rutherford 1992). Accordingly, there are no assets adjustments because the accounts are not concerned with recording usage, only with the fact that cash has been paid for acquisition of those assets. Therefore, no information can be provided about the investment in the total assets and no subsequent accounts are taken of whether the assets are still in use, whether they have reached the end of their useful life, or whether they have been sold (Ouda 2005).

On the contrary, in the private sector where accrual accounting is in use, all fixed assets acquired are included in the balance sheet and written down progressively over their useful lives by means of charges in the operating statement for depreciation which reflects the costs of using up the assets (Rutherford 1992; Franklin et al. 2019). Thus, the transition to accrual accounting in the public sector requires the governmental entities to identify and value their assets to be able to prepare the balance sheets. However, the main problem of identification and recognition of governmental capital assets is that in order to record the assets the governmental entity has to not only know what assets it owns but must also put a value on them, even if the value is their historic cost. Therefore, if no assets register exists which records the values, the task of taking an inventory of fixed assets and valuing them might be a huge and expensive one (Jones and Pendlebury 1984; Bergmann et al. 2019). In fact, most governments hold many lists describing the physical aspects of their capital assets. In the absence of regular financial reporting of capital assets, those listings are seldom complete or up-to-date. To reestablish physical records of long-lived government assets where these have been neglected is a daunting and expensive task which is a major obstacle to any proposal to extend asset recognition. So, the lack of accurate, relevant, and detailed information about governmental capital assets can be considered as an obstacle in adopting sound public sector governance. Furthermore, it can be inferred that the use of the traditional government accounting system did not yield all the information needed for asset management purposes. However, accrual accounting, coupled with improved financial management information systems, can provide comprehensive and timely information that is necessary. These approaches require the maintenance of complete and accurate asset registers and regular revaluations and appraisals of asset holdings. Unlike the private sector, governments own different capital assets, which can be classified as follows (IFAC 2000 Study 11, Christiaens et al. 2012):

a. **Businesslike governmental assets**:
   - *Capital assets—Property, plant, and equipment (PP&E)*
b. **Non-businesslike governmental assets (specific governmental assets):**
   - ***Capital assets—Infrastructure assets.*** Examples of these assets: sewer systems; road networks including bridges, kerbs, channels, and footpaths; water supply systems; drainage systems; communication networks; flood control works; power supply systems; and recreation reserves
   - ***Capital assets—Heritage assets.*** Examples of these assets: monuments; art and museum collections; wilderness; battlefields; and buildings designated for preservation
   - ***Capital assets—Defense assets.*** Examples of these assets: military hardware; and defense equipment such as tanks, planes, and military airport
   - ***Capital assets—Community assets.*** Examples of these assets: parks; and historic buildings
   - ***Capital assets—Natural resources.*** Example of these resources: forests; farmland; fish stocks; water for electricity generation; petroleum; and mineral deposit.

While the adoption of accrual accounting in the public sector has entailed that all governmental capital assets should be recognized in the balance sheet, the public sector accounting literature did not present a practical accounting solution for the recognition of governmental capital assets in the balance sheet. Accordingly, the recognition of governmental capital assets has become a highly problematic issue for the public sector entities holding those assets and remains an unresolved issue.

4 Accounting for Governmental Capital Assets from General and Specific Perspectives

This section will address the accounting for governmental capital assets from general and specific perspectives. First, Sect. 4.1 will present the literature related to accounting for all governmental capital assets (general perspective) and Sect. 4.2 will deal with the literature of accounting for specific assets such as heritage assets (specific perspective). Both perspectives will present the points of view of both the antagonists and the protagonists whether they are academics or professional standard-setting bodies.

4.1 General Perspective

This section sheds light on the important differences surrounding the debate of recognition of the governmental capital assets. Reviewing the public sector accounting literature has shown that there are massive heterogeneous points of view concerning the recognition of governmental capital assets among the protagonists and antagonists, whether they are researchers or standard-setting bodies. Actually, there are some supporters for the recognition of all governmental capital assets (including infrastructure, community assets, defense assets, heritage assets, and land under the road) on the balance sheet and they assume that they do not differ largely from the other assets (Rowles 1991; Micallef and Peirson 1997). Moreover, they are in the view that representation faithfulness is not possible without assigning monetary value. They believe, for instance, that heritage assets are commercially quantifiable even though they may not be for sale. The argument that collections cannot be measured in financial terms because they do not have financial attributes has merit but could equally apply to most types of assets; the question could be asked as to whether land necessarily has financial attributes. Rowles (1991) extends the criteria of recognition and measurement to argue that all assets have the same characteristics. In turn, he deals with several arguments:

- Sunk costs may apply to plant as well as heritage assets.
- Both plant and heritage assets may have no market value but such costs are recoverable through social purpose and such purpose is hardly distinguishable from the commercial purpose in that both focus on the economic benefit or service potential.
- Heritage assets are often not indivisible.
- Lack of a market value and lack of economic life are problems which many assets other than heritage assets share.
- That heritage assets have infinite life is untrue and applies only to land.

Moreover, Rowles (1992) argues that government departments and agencies controlling environmental, cultural, and historical assets will need to value and include them, as well as their capital assets, in their financial statements. Furthermore, other assets that do not fit readily into a definition of capital, such as monuments, works of art, historical relics, and collections of artistic and cultural works are included (Rowles 1992; Stanton and Stanton 1997). So the inclusion of the governmental capital assets such as heritage assets rests on the conclusion that, for accounting purposes, they cannot be readily distinguished from other physical assets (Rowles 1992), and they meet the asset definition test contained in the Statement of Accounting Concepts 4 (SAC 4) (Rowles 1992). Furthermore, Rowles et al. (1998) are in the view that recognition of capital assets such as infrastructure assets, community assets, heritage assets, and land under the roads is necessary because they provide useful information for economic decision-making. They further argue that accrual accounting information is needed to judge whether or not the government operates efficiently. Accordingly, recognition in general purpose financial reporting is the first step in discharging accountability and improving public assets management and, hence, leading to good governance of governmental assets.

From the good governance and assets management point of view, Walker et al. (2000, 2004) emphasize the importance of recognition of infrastructure assets as capital assets in general purpose financial reporting. They based their views on the fact that infrastructure assets require important decisions in terms of maintenance, repair, and assets management; therefore they adopt a user perspective and suggest to combine supplementary financial with nonfinancial disclosure (e.g., concerning the physical state of infrastructure and it will cost to maintain, repair, or upgrade them) (Christiaens and Rommel 2008). Moreover, Anthony (1994) has suggested a new approach where capital assets financed by loans or debts had to be reported as assets and the related debt had to be reported as a liability. This approach is consistent with the so-called system of debt charge accounting that had been used by the British local government for many years but was abandoned around the mid-1990s.

In addition to the protagonists for capitalizing all governmental capital assets, there are also several antagonists (Mautz 1988; Pallot 1990, 1992; Carnegie and Wolnizer 1995, 1996, 1999; Barton 1999, 2000, 2002; Carnegie and West 2004). Accordingly, the public sector accounting literature has shown that there is no consensus between the protagonists and antagonists about a unified accounting approach for government capital assets. This can lead us to see what the situation of international and national standard-setting bodies is.

International standard-setting bodies such as IPSASB have issued IPSAS 17, which focuses mainly on the accounting treatment for PP&E so that the users of financial statements can discern information about an entity's investment in PP&E and the changes in such investment (Christiaens 2004). Moreover, IPSAS 17 has also stated in paragraph 21 that infrastructure assets meet the definition of PP&E and should be accounted for in accordance with IPSAS 17. However, IPSAS 17 does not require an entity to recognize specific governmental capital assets. In other words, it does not discuss, for example, whether heritage assets should be capitalized or not. Moreover, IPSASB (2014) has issued a Conceptual Framework (CF) for General Purpose Financial Reporting by Public Sector entities. The CF has identified the recognition criteria for the assets that should be recognized in the financial statements. The recognition criteria are as follows:

- An item satisfies the definition of an element.
- An item can be measured in a way that achieves the qualitative characteristics and takes account of constraints on information in GPFRs.

The CF states in Para. 6.3 that all items that satisfy the recognition criteria are recognized in the financial statements. In some circumstances, an IPSAS may also specify that, to achieve the objectives of financial reporting, a resource or obligation that does not meet the definition of an element is to be recognized in the financial statements provided it can be measured in a way that meets the qualitative characteristics and constraints.

So, according to the IPSASB-CF all items that satisfy the recognition criteria should be included in the financial statements without differentiating specific assets such as heritage assets from other governmental capital assets.

In New Zealand, the standard-setters had issued FRS-3 in May 2001 and revised it in November 2001 and February 2002, requiring all public sector entities to account for all governmental capital assets (including heritage assets) as they would any other item of PP&E and depreciate such assets based on estimates of useful life. These assets are to be valued on the same basis as other physical noncurrent assets of an entity (NZSA 1993; New Zealand Treasury 2003). The standard-setters in Sweden are in the view that the acquisition of all governmental capital assets is capitalized like other assets. The Australian Accounting Standards AAS27, AAS29, AAS31, and SAC4 (AARF 1990, 1992, 1993, 1996) were prepared by the Australian Accounting Research Foundation (AARF) and advocate the recognition of all governmental capital assets (including heritage assets) in Australian government financial statements (Rowles 1992;).

In the USA the Federation Accounting Standards Advisory Board (FASAB) has divided the governmental capital assets into two subgroups. The first subgroup includes general PP&E. According to FASAB, this subgroup is considered as comprising assets which are recognized in the balance sheet and depreciated in the income statement. The motivation for the recognition here is that these assets are used to provide general government services and goods, or are used in business-type activities and hence are not considered as unique assets. The second subgroup includes stewardship assets comprising (a) National defense PP&E: these assets are not recognized as capital assets. FASAB requires that expenditures on the acquisition, construction, reconstruction, or improvement of these assets be expensed in the period incurred. (b) Heritage assets: these assets are not recognized as capital assets and have no depreciation. (c) Stewardship assets: these assets are not recognized as capital assets and have no depreciation (FASABs, SFFAS 29 (2005, par. 19). So it can be inferred that the national and international standard-setters are in line with the protagonists and antagonists that there is no consensus about a unified accounting approach for all governmental capital assets. Accordingly, we agree with Christiaens et al. (2012) that until now there is a lack of a general approach where the recognition of all kinds of governmental capital goods are examined.

While there is a consensus among the international and national standard-setters and academic about the recognition of PP&E and infrastructure assets, there is no consensus about whether specific assets such as heritage and defense assets should be recognized as capital assets in the balance sheet. Therefore, the next sections address some specific assets such as heritage (specific perspective) assets and Sect. 7 will address a holistic approach for all governmental assets (general/holistic perspective).

4.2 *Specific Perspective: Accounting for Heritage Assets*

4.2.1 *Relevant Literature and International Practices*

While the past three decades have witnessed some efforts over how heritage assets might be accounted for, and whether heritage assets are sufficiently different to merit different treatment, there is a lack of consistency and uniformity in accounting treatment for heritage assets among the countries that have already adopted full accrual accounting in their public sector (such as New Zealand, UK, Australia, USA, and Canada). Consequently, several authors are in the view that the accounting for heritage assets would seem to be more problematic and is subject to different treatment by different countries and standard-setting bodies. Some of these authors do not consider the heritage assets as assets and hence they should not be capitalized. Barton (2000) argues that heritage assets do not satisfy the concepts of assets because of their public goods nature, that is, they are for the benefits of the public and are not for sale. They are provided to the public on a noncommercial basis and are funded primarily from non-exchange revenues (e.g., taxation, fines). Moreover, they are not maintained for income generation but for other purposes such as cultural, educational, recreational, and other community purposes (Barton 2000). Furthermore, Barton (2000) argues that the inclusion of heritage assets in the statement of financial position of an entity would distort its representational faithfulness to readers. Therefore, he proposed that heritage assets should be treated as trust assets and this requires that the heritage assets be kept separate from government operating assets. Barton (2000) explains the trusteeship approach to accounting for heritage assets as follows: The government holds the heritage assets in trust for present and future generations and has a responsibility to protect and preserve them. The costs of protecting and maintaining them should be borne by each generation as they enjoy the benefits from them. As trust assets, public heritage assets should not be included in the government's own statement of assets and liabilities. They should not be regarded as financial resources and be available to meet its financial commitments. In trust accounting, the trustee is obliged to keep trust assets separate from his/her own assets and to report them separately.

Actually, Barton is not the only author who backs this direction; there are other authors who are in line with him. Carnegie and Wolnizer (1999) are of the opinion that because public heritage assets cannot be or should not be sold, there is an argument that they should not be included in governments' (or other managing entities') statements of financial position. Carnegie and Wolnizer (1995, 1996) also argue that if heritage facilities have no financial value to the entity, then it is misleading to match them against its liabilities. They also agree with Barton that heritage assets are not resources which can be used to generate cash for the discharge of liabilities, and their inclusion in a statement of financial position is misleading to the management and creditors. Carnegie and Wolnizer (1999) believe that not-for-profit public collections should not be recognized for financial reporting purposes. Furthermore, they argue that collections in the public domain are prized for their cultural, heritage, scientific, and educative qualities and that those attributes cannot be quantified in monetary terms. Besides, Carnegie and Wolnizer (1995) are in the view that taking into consideration the characteristics and nature of heritage assets, it can be inferred that they can absorb wealth but not for generating it in financial terms. It would be more appropriate to classify them as liabilities, or alternatively to call them facilities and keep them separate from other assets.

Similarly, Mautz (1988) is also in the view that heritage assets might be accounted for as liabilities of the government because of the negative cash flow streams they incur in their use and maintenance, and the inability to sell them. Barton (2000) argues that such assets in commercial firms would not be retained, as they would be a drain on the firm's resources; rather firms would sell them. Other studies develop further arguments for not including heritage assets in financial statements, because of the different roles that heritage assets fulfill compared with normal commercial assets. Mautz (1988) argues that they should be differentiated, and proposes that they be called "facilities." Likewise, Pallot (1990) is of the opinion that heritage assets should be kept separate from other assets and proposes that they be called "community assets." Pallot (1990, 1992) based her proposal on making a distinction between public sector assets used for community purposes and commercial assets as she believes that public sector assets differ in fundamental respects from commercial assets. One of these respects is related to the assets ownership rights, as she classifies asset ownership rights into the following:

a. The right to manage
b. The right to the benefits
c. The right to dispose of the property

Of course, the government has the right to manage, but the right to the benefits rest with the public, and the right of the government to dispose of the property is not an unfettered one. Furthermore, Pallot distinguishes between physical assets as input to a productive process and assets which service the public directly. When the assets are inputs, they are used up in the productive process, except for land. This is true of commercial assets. However, when the assets provide services directly to the public, their use does not necessarily use up the asset—viewing a work of art does not damage the item. Based on the aforementioned reasons, heritage assets differ from the commercial assets and they should be kept separate from other assets. Moreover, other studies argue for not recognizing the heritage assets in the balance sheet. Ström (1997) argues that even though market values exist or can be estimated, developing the market values may outweigh the benefits, especially in volatile markets. Also, Littrell and Thompson (1998) propose that opportunity cost or replacement cost is a relevant measure. However, because heritage assets are different due to their unlimited life or uniqueness, their replacement cost is zero and should be excluded.

In addition to the opponents, there are some supporters of the recognition of heritage assets in the balance sheet (Rowles 1991; Micallef and Peirson 1997) who are in the view that representation faithfulness is not possible without assigning monetary value. They believe that heritage assets are commercially quantifiable even though they may not be for sale. The argument that collections cannot be measured in financial terms because they do not have financial attributes has merit but could equally apply to most types of assets; the question could be asked as to whether land necessarily has financial attributes. Unlike the opponents, Rowles 1992) assumes that heritage assets do not differ largely from other assets, which means that he acknowledges their recognition as assets in the statement of financial position of governments. He argues that government departments and agencies controlling environmental, cultural, and historical assets will need to value and include them, as well as their capital assets, in their financial statements. Also, other assets that do not fit readily into a definition of capital, such as monuments, works of art, historical relics, and collections of artistic and cultural works, are included (Rowles 1992; Stanton and Stanton 1997). So the inclusion of heritage asset items rests on the conclusion that, for accounting purposes, they cannot be readily distinguished from other physical assets (Rowles 1992), and they meet the asset definition test contained in the Statement of Accounting Concepts 4 (SAC 4) (Rowles 1992).

The aforementioned discussion, including both opponents and supporters, makes clear that there is no consensus about whether or not heritage assets can be properly accounted for, and whether or not they should be accounted for. This can lead us to see what the situation is of national and international standard-setting bodies with respect to accounting for heritage assets.

International standard-setting bodies such as IFAC-IPSASB have issued IPSAS 17, which focuses mainly on the accounting treatment for PP&E so that the users of financial statements can discern information about an entity's investment in its PP&E and the changes in such investment (Christiaens 2004). However, IPSAS 17 does not require an entity to recognize heritage assets. In other words, it does not discuss whether heritage assets should be capitalized or not. In paragraph 9 of IPSAS 17, it is stated that some assets are described as "heritage assets" because of their cultural, environmental, or historical significance. It describes the disclosure requirements in paragraphs 88–94, where it requires the governmental entities to make disclosures about recognized assets. Accordingly, the entities that recognize heritage assets are required to disclose in respect of those assets such matters as the measurement basis used; the depreciation method used, if any; the gross carrying amount; the accumulated depreciation at the end of the period, if any; and a reconciliation of the carrying amount at the beginning and end of the period showing certain components thereof.

In addition, IFAC-IPSASB started in 2006, as it issued a Consultation Paper (CP) about *"Accounting for Heritage Assets Under the Accrual Accounting Basis of Accounting,"* which identifies a number of matters relating to the treatment of heritage assets set out in the UK Accounting Standards Board Discussion Paper entitled *"Heritage Assets: Can*

Accounting Do Better" (UK-ASB 2006). The CP dealt with the definition of heritage assets and whether the heritage assets meet the asset definition, and discussed in detail the two proposed approaches to accounting for heritage assets: A full capitalization approach and a non-capitalization approach. However, the CP (2006) did not resolve the problem of recognition of heritage assets and IPSASB postponed further work on heritage assets until after the completion of its Conceptual Framework for General Purpose Financial Reporting by Public Sector Entities (CF). Since then, the IPSASB did not publish anything related to accounting for heritage assets till 2017, when IPSASB published the CP titled *Financial Reporting for Heritage in the Public Sector*. In fact, the CP-IPSASB (2017) proposed that heritage be recognized and measured in financial statements.

IPSASB has already received feedback from different parties about the CP and is currently developing an Exposure Draft (ED) on the subject (IPSASB 2020; De Wolf et al. 2020).

It can be inferred that while IPSASB started with different projects to develop accounting and disclosure requirements for heritage assets a long time ago, it did not issue a specific IPSAS related to accounting for heritage assets up till now.

The Australian Accounting Standards AAS27, AAS29, AAS 31, and SAC4 (AARF 1990, 1992, 1993, 1996) were prepared by the Australian Accounting Research Foundation (AARF) and advocates the inclusion of heritage assets in Australian government financial statements (Rowles 1992;). Similarly, In New Zealand, the standard-setters had issued FRS-3 in May 2001 and revised it in November 2001 and February 2002, requiring all reporting entities, including central and local government agencies, to account for heritage assets as they would any other item of PP&E and depreciate such assets based on estimates of useful life. Heritage assets are to be valued on the same basis as other physical non-current assets of an entity. FRS-3 requires subsequent revaluations of these assets, provided that fair value is used. The standard-setters in Sweden are in the view that acquisition of heritage assets are capitalized like other assets and retrospective capitalization is permissible but is rarely used.

In the UK, FRS 15 requires all tangible fixed assets to be recognized and capitalized including heritage assets. A number of entities in the museum and galleries sector report amounts for their total holding of heritage assets in the balance sheet. However, many public benefit entities have only capitalized subsequent acquisitions of heritage assets since the adoption of FRS 15 in 2001. This means that the UK used a mixed approach where the recently acquired heritage assets are recognized and capitalized and similar heritage assets that have been acquired for many years remain off-balance. In addition, in the UK the standard-setters made a distinction between operational heritage assets and nonoperational heritage assets. Heritage assets are those assets that are usually irreplaceable, that are intended to be preserved in trust for future generations. Operational heritage assets are those assets used for purposes in addition to the maintenance of national heritage (e.g., heritage building with office space, parkland). Operational assets will be capitalized whereas nonoperational heritage assets will not be capitalized. Nonoperational heritage assets include museum and gallery collections, other works of art, national archives; as well as archeological sites, ruins, burial sites, monuments, and statues.

In the USA, the Financial Accounting Standard Board (FASB) encourages retrospective capitalization of art collections, while acknowledging that the cost of retrospective capitalization is often likely to exceed the incremental benefits to users (FAS 116). Conversely, the FASAB requires expenditures on the acquisition, construction, reconstruction, or improvement of heritage assets to be expensed. A separate standard details disclosure requirements from a stewardship perspective.

The international standard-setting bodies are in line with the opponents and supporters that there is no consensus about a unified accounting approach for heritage assets and whether or not heritage assets can properly be accounted for and whether or not they should be accounted for. In fact, the lack of unified accounting treatment for heritage assets among the standard-setting bodies contradicts fundamental accounting requirements that reported information should reflect qualitative characteristics of consistency, relevance, comparability, and verifiability, and should faithfully represent what it claims to represent, in order to be useful to stakeholders (Wild 2013; Ellwood 2018).

4.2.2 *Accounting Approaches for Heritage Assets*

While the debate on accounting for heritage assets under accrual accounting has been continuing for more than two decades, there is no definitive or legal definition of heritage assets and there is no consensus about a unified or better accounting treatment for heritage assets. The lack of consensus among the standard-setting bodies, opponents, and supporters can raise the following questions: *Do heritage assets meet the definition of assets?*

Can heritage assets be considered as a separate class of assets rather than a separate class of PP&E? Generally, in order to include an item in the balance sheet, this item should follow two steps, which are identified in IASB and IPSAS 1, 16 and 17 as follows: (a) *whether the item meets the definition of an asset*; (b) *whether the item satisfies the recognition criteria*.

The International Accounting Standards Board (IASB) (formerly known as IASC) defines an asset in the following way: "an asset is a resource controlled by the enterprise as a result of past events and from which future economic benefits are expected to flow to the enterprise (IASB 1989, Para. 49). The IASB definition refers only to future economic benefits. However, the PSC-IFAC, in common with other public sector standard setters, sees that the definition of an asset needs to incorporate both economic benefits and service potential. IPSAS 1 Presentation of Financial Statements, paragraph 6, defined assets as follows: Assets are resources controlled by an entity as a result of past events and from which future economic benefits or service potential are expected to flow to the entity. While this definition is generally valid for governmental capital assets, heritage assets are defined as assets with historic, artistic, scientific, technological, geophysical, or environmental qualities that are held and maintained principally for their contribution to knowledge and culture and this purpose is central to the objectives of the entity holding them (UK-ASB 2006). Also, IPSAS 16 & 17 and IPSASB-CF (2014) identified two criteria that can be used for determining when an asset should be recognized: *(a) It is probable that future economic benefits or service potential associated with the asset will flow to the entity; and (b) The cost or fair value of the asset to the entity can be measured reliably.*

Do Heritage Assets Meet the Definition of Assets?

The accounting literature has made clear that there are different standpoints about whether the heritage assets meet the definition of an asset or not. On the one hand, Stanford (2005) sees that the IPSAS definition of assets as "*resources controlled by an entity as a result of past events and from which future economic benefits or service potential are expected to flow to the entity* appears sufficiently wide to comprise most of the items commonly referred to as "heritage assets." On the other hand, he is in the view that if the entity has no intention to use the asset for operational purposes, put it on display, or use it for cultural or educational purposes, it is questionable whether such assets are likely to give rise to service potential and therefore whether they should be capitalized. On the contrary, the UK

Accounting Standards Board issued FRS 30, Heritage Assets in 2009 (hereafter ASB-FRS 30). The ASB-FRS 30 considers that, conceptually, heritage assets are assets. They are central to the purpose of an entity such as a gallery or a museum: without them, the entity cannot function. An artifact held by the Egyptian Museum might be realizable for cash and it might generate income indirectly through admission charges. However, the most important thing is that the museum needs the artifact in order to function as a museum. The artifact is held and maintained to serve some purposes such as educational and cultural or it can be preserved for future display or for academic or scientific research. The ASB-FRS 30 has further argued that the future economic benefits associated with the artifact are primarily in the form of its service potential rather than cash flows.

Accordingly, the ASB-FRS 30 is in the view that by virtue of the service potential they provide, heritage assets meet the definition of an asset; that is, they provide rights or other access to future economic benefits controlled by an entity as a result of past transactions or events. Consequently, it can be inferred that heritage assets meet the definition of assets as they can provide future economic benefits in the form of service potential and they are held and maintained principally for their contribution to knowledge and culture and this purpose is central to the objectives of the entity (e.g., Museum) holding them.

Can Heritage Assets Be Considered as a Separate Class of Assets Rather Than a Separate Class of Property, Plant, and Equipment?

Heritage assets are one of the public sector assets that have been subjected to a diversity of concepts, terminology, and classification. Some authors called heritage assets community assets (e.g., Pallot 1990, 1992), although the community assets include some assets that are not essentially pure heritage assets such as urban parks and sports-grounds; public infrastructural assets; national parks; public road and rail systems. Basically, community assets are a broad term and we need to distinguish heritage assets from those community assets that can be for sale and used for economic purposes, for example, many of the national parks in Egypt have been used for other purposes such as building houses for youths. Therefore, pure heritage assets (such as museum and gallery collections, other works of art, national archives; and archeological sites, ruins, burial sites, monuments, and statues) should be distinguished from other community assets (such as national parks; and public road and rail systems). Heritage assets cannot be replaced or sold due to the existence of legal, social, or cultural restrictions. Thus, I consider them as **Restricted Assets**. However, some other authors consider heritage assets as public goods/public facilities (Barton 2000; Mautz 1988). The term public goods is also a broad term as most of the public sector assets can be considered as public goods. For instance, public roads are public goods and archeological sites are also public goods. While public roads are used for facilitating the daily life of the public and can be used for economic purposes, they are different from heritage assets, which are mainly held for their contribution to knowledge and cultural purposes (such as works of art, history books, and national archives). Moreover, public roads could be replaced or changed. For example, some public roads in Egypt have been changed/cancelled due to the need for expanding the constructed area of some cities and, hence, the government has constructed a new public road outside the city. In addition, most of the authors forget one essential point, which **is the period of time** that needs to pass before considering any asset as a heritage asset. In fact, many countries are setting some time conditions for considering any asset as a heritage asset. For example, the Egyptian government considers any public asset as a heritage asset if it has existed for more than 100 years. According to Egyptian Law no. 117 of 1983 as amended by law no. 3 of 2010, "[a]ny real-estate or chattel is considered an antiquity whenever it meets the following conditions:

- To be the product of Egyptian civilization or the successive civilizations or the creation of art, sciences, literature, or religion that took place on the Egyptian lands since the pre-historic ages and during the successive **historic ages till before100 years ago**.
- To be of archeological or artistic value or of historic importance as an aspect of the different aspects of Egyptian civilizations or any other civilization that took place on the Egyptian lands.
- To be produced and grown [] on the Egyptian lands and of a historical relation thereto and also the mummies of human races and beings contemporary to them are considered like any antiquity which is being registered in accordance with this law."

Actually, the three aforementioned conditions are sufficient to consider heritage assets as a separate class of assets rather than a separate class of PP&E. The heritage assets should be the product of the country's civilization, should take place on the country's land, and should have existed for more than 100 years. They must be of archeological or artistic value or of historic importance and they must be produced and grown on the country's land. In addition, it can be argued that the cost of most of the assets that have existed for more than 100 years has already depreciated. Therefore, when these assets transfer to heritage assets, there should be no book values as their values have already depreciated during the last 100 years. Furthermore, most of the accounting standard-setters have discussed a number of specific characteristics which can enhance the aforementioned argument in considering heritage assets as a separate class of assets rather than a separate class of PP&E. The following is a list of these characteristics:

- They are often irreplaceable and their value may increase over time even if their physical condition deteriorates.
- They are rarely held for their ability to generate cash inflows or sale proceeds and there may be legal or social obstacles to using them for such purposes.
- They are protected, kept unencumbered, cared for, and preserved.
- It may be difficult to estimate their useful lives, which in some cases could be several hundred years and they may incur high costs to maintain them.
- Their value in cultural, environmental, educational, and historical terms is unlikely to be fully reflected in a financial value based purely on a market price.
- They are often described as inalienable, that is, the entity cannot dispose of them without external consent.

Accordingly, it can be inferred that heritage assets are accounted for as a distinct category of assets because their value is unlikely to be fully reflected in a financial value or price. Many are unique, meaning their value may increase rather than depreciate, even if the physical condition deteriorates. In addition, heritage assets may incur high costs of maintenance and their life might be measured in hundreds of years. Moreover, heritage assets are restricted assets as there may be legal, cultural, or social obstacles to sell or dispose of them.

Current Accounting Approaches for Heritage Assets

The accounting literature for heritage assets has proposed different options for accounting these assets under accrual accounting as follows:

- Full capitalization of both new acquisitions and retrospectively acquired items
- Capitalization of new acquisitions with no recognition of heritage assets acquired before the adoption of accrual accounting
- A non-capitalization approach and expensing of heritage items
- Provision of extensive information through disclosure

– ***Full capitalization of both new acquisitions and retrospectively acquired items***

According to the full capitalization approach (where an entity can obtain reasonable current values for the majority), heritage assets values should be reported in the balance sheet (ASB 2006). This approach would require each public sector entity to recognize and capitalize heritage assets, including those acquired in previous and recent accounting periods, in the balance sheet where information on cost or value is available. One merit of this approach is that this would ensure a consistent accounting treatment for previously and recently acquired heritage assets. In addition, the full capitalization of heritage assets will assist in informing the funders and financial supporters about the value of assets held, reporting on stewardship of the assets by the owner entity and informing the decision-makers about whether resources are being used appropriately (ASB 2006). Moreover, if heritage assets are not capitalized, the balance sheet will not provide a complete picture of an entity's financial position. For this reason, it is better to report heritage assets in the balance sheet where information is available on cost or value rather than leave these assets out of the balance sheet. The ASB-FRS 30 considers that the best financial reporting is achieved when heritage assets are reported as tangible assets at values that provide useful and relevant information on the balance sheet date. Thus, the ASB-FRS 30 observes that the current valuation will be more useful than historical cost, although it is acknowledged that there may be difficulties in obtaining valuations for heritage assets. In fact, most accounting standard-setting bodies prefer that heritage assets should be reported at current value rather than at historical cost. This is due to the fact that many heritage assets were acquired sometime in the past; the passage of time and the subsequent changes in market values—where they exist and which can be unpredictable—mean that the historical cost is not a useful guide to their value. This means that over time the historical cost will not be useful and relevant for reporting heritage assets.

- ***Capitalization of new acquisitions with no recognition of heritage assets acquired before the adoption of accrual accounting***

This approach has been used in the UK in 2001 when public-benefits entities adopted the FRS 15. This approach aims at capitalizing the newly acquired heritage assets and not capitalizing similar heritage assets that have been acquired in the past (before the adoption of accrual accounting). This approach is known as a mixed approach. Some claim that this approach appears to have some practical advantages in that reliable cost information is readily available for recent purchases and there is no requirement for retrospective valuation where cost information might not be available (ASB 2006). However, this approach suffers from some shortcomings as follows: *Inconsistent treatment of similar assets*: within the same class of assets two accounting policies (capitalization and non-capitalization approach) are applied. For instance, a gallery or a museum may own two similar heritage assets, of which one may have been acquired some time ago and is not capitalized in the balance sheet, whereas the other might have been acquired recently and has been capitalized at market value. The different accounting treatments can lead to confusion with respect to the statement of financial position and statement of the financial performance of the gallery or the museum. *Subsequent expenditure*: Inconsistent accounting treatment will lead to different treatment for subsequent expenditure. For instance, the restoration costs that may extend the life of a historical building should be capitalized. However, if these costs were related to a historical building not capitalized, then these costs would be expensed. Accordingly, the inconsistent treatment has led to different treatment for the same costs for similar assets. In addition, the capitalization of some assets and not capitalizing of other assets will lead to incomplete financial information. Therefore, the adoption of this approach will lead to different accounting problems and will not solve the dilemma of accounting for heritage assets.

- ***Non-capitalization approach and expensing of heritage items***

Under this approach, the public sector entities are not allowed to capitalize heritage assets whether those assets were acquired recently or in the past. This would ensure that an accounting policy is applied consistently to all heritage assets. In addition, the adoption of this approach will avoid the aforementioned problems under the mixed approach. However, the main problem of applying this approach is that it will lead to the distortion of the performance statement since the acquisition of a heritage asset will be recorded as an expense in the performance statement. In fact, this could be seen to misrepresent the substance of the transaction in that an asset has been acquired and has not been consumed. This distorts the level of reported expenses and does not properly reflect financial performance (ASB 2006). Moreover, reporting the full proceeds from the disposal of heritage assets as income in the performance statement is also distorting (ASB 2006). In an attempt to avoid this distortion, it is proposed that under a non-capitalization approach the acquisition and disposal of heritage assets should be presented separately from the statement of financial performance. This is the main aim of the last option, which is the disclosure approach.

- ***Provision of extensive information through disclosure (disclosure approach)***

A disclosure approach agrees with the non-capitalization approach in that public entities would not be required to capitalize heritage assets acquired in the past or during the current period. Instead, public entities should provide sufficient disclosure on the reasons for not adopting the capitalization approach, the nature and number of heritage assets held, the purpose for their preservation, and financial on acquisitions and disposals within the reporting period (Stanford 2005). Unlike the non-capitalization approach, under a disclosure approach it is proposed to segregate heritage asset transactions (such as acquisitions, disposals, and major restoration costs) from the income and expenditure account (performance statement) for the reporting period. IFAC and Stanford (2005) are in the view that the presentation of acquisition of a heritage asset as an expense would be wrong as an asset has been acquired which has not been consumed. This distorts the level of reported expenses and does not properly reflect financial performance. The proposes that heritage asset transactions should be presented in a separate statement clearly distinguished from financial performance. It is considered that this approach will provide users with a clearer picture of heritage asset transactions for the reporting period. However, while the disclosure approach attempted to avoid the distortion of the performance statement, it did not avoid the disadvantages of the non-capitalization approach and did not provide an appropriate accounting approach for heritage assets. While it proposed to segregate heritage asset acquisition, disposal, and major restoration costs from the income and expenditure account for the reporting period, it remained silent on how to account for not capitalizing heritage assets and how to treat the revenues or costs related to heritage assets. Besides, it did not provide information on the format and shape of the separate statement. Accordingly, it can be inferred that the aforementioned four approaches did not provide a unified and appropriate accounting approach and the accounting for heritage assets remains an unresolved problem.

5 Critical Analysis of the NPM Ideologies and Current Accounting Approaches for Heritage Assets

It was obvious from the discussion of current accounting approaches that there has been considerable variability and inconsistency in the accounting treatment applied to heritage assets. Starting with full capitalization of heritage assets, non-capitalization of heritage assets and expensing them in the statement of financial performance, it ended with the provision of extensive information through disclosure. In fact, these current accounting approaches have been based on the NPM ideologies and its assumption that all public sector entities have been required to attribute economic values to governmental capital assets including heritage assets, and to produce annual financial reports prepared on an equivalent basis to the private sector model. Basically, the NPM ideologies and assumptions did not consider the impact of full capitalization of heritage assets on the net worth of a country (e.g., Egypt) and full expensing of heritage assets on the distortion of the performance statement. In order to discuss this impact, we should take into consideration some points: for example, history and culture of nations are not for sale; the volume of heritage assets owned by each country and its impact on the net worth; and usefulness of accounting information to the stakeholders. In addition, we assume that there is available information on cost or value of heritage assets. Taking the aforementioned points into account and studying the situation of a country like Egypt can demonstrate to what extent the full capitalization approach can affect the net worth in Egypt. Egypt hosts different types of heritage assets such as

- Pharaonic antiquities
- Greco-Roman antiquities
- Islamic-Coptic antiquities
- Recent antiquities

In fact, the city of Luxor in Egypt hosts one-third of the monuments and antiquities of the whole world (Pharaonic heritage assets only). So if we add the other Pharaonic antiquities in other cities and the Greco-Roman antiquities, Islamic-Coptic antiquities, and Recent antiquities, we find that Egypt possesses around two-thirds of heritage assets of the whole world. Assume that there is available information on the value or cost of two-thirds of heritage assets; the question is: How much will be the amount of two-thirds of heritage assets? Actually, nobody can imagine how much this amount will be. But presumably it will be trillions of dollars. So if these heritage assets are capitalized in the balance sheet of the Egyptian government, nobody can imagine the volume of the positive net worth. Therefore, the full capitalization of all heritage assets in Egypt will lead to the exaggeration of the net worth, which can give an indication that Egypt has huge positive economic/financial resources (net worth). As a matter of fact, this is untrue as Egypt is suffering from a big amount of public debt and budget deficit. The question here is: In spite of assuming that the information on cost or value of heritage assets is available, can the Egyptian government dispose of/sell those heritage assets and use them to match the liabilities? Based on the aforementioned assumption that the history and culture of nations are not for sale, no Egyptian government has dared/attempted to do that before. Then, the question is: What is the benefit of having financial values that cannot be matched against liabilities, cannot be used to repay debts, or to cover the budget deficit? Furthermore, what is the usefulness of the inclusion of such information in the financial statements for the stakeholders? Therefore, the inclusion of such information will mislead the fair presentation of the actual financial position of the government and the reliability of financial information. Basically, heritage assets are held and maintained principally for their contribution to knowledge and culture of the present and future generations.

Consequently, it could be inferred that while the information on cost or value of heritage assets is available and the heritage assets meet the definition of an asset and the two recognition criteria, the inclusion of heritage assets in the balance sheet (***where there are restrictions on their disposal*** and hence cannot be matched against the liabilities) is misleading to the stakeholders. Thus, the current accounting approaches for heritage assets fail to provide information that meets the fundamental qualitative characteristics of financial reporting (Wild 2013), which comprises *Relevance, Faithful Representation, Understandability, Comparability, Timing, Verifiability.*

Thus, it cannot be claimed that the current approaches satisfy the information needs of the stakeholders and provide information that is useful for decision-making.

In addition, the NPM assumptions claim that reporting all heritage assets held by public sector entities in economic terms improves accountability in those entities. There are some supporters for this assumption, for example, Micallef and Peirson (1997) argue that it is necessary for public sector entities to provide financial statements, and for heritage and cultural assets to be assigned economic values, in order to effectively evaluate management accountability. Moreover, the provision of information about heritage assets controlled by those entities is necessary to make informed assessments about the allocation of public funds and to assess whether the value of the assets controlled by those entities has been eroded, improved, or retained (Wild 2013; Ellwood 2018).

However, are against that assumption, as they are in the view that for heritage assets in local government, it may not be clear whether they are economic resources, as it may not be clear whether they are of the entity or indeed exactly what the entity is. Also dismisses the utility of imposing an economic value on cultural assets as being merely "an accounting fiction." Barker (2006) argues that heritage assets, which are held for future generations for cultural, historic, aesthetic, or ecological reasons, and are highly unlikely to be traded at any time in the future should not be valued. If there is cost associated with them, the cost should be expensed as incurred and nonfinancial information should be given to account for the stewardship of the guardian entity. The nonfinancial information can be considered as an example of the opportunity for cross-disciplinary deliberation to determine the most appropriate accountability form for the heritage assets. For example, a virtual tour of the heritage assets would be a better mechanism for accountability with the possibility of interrogation of the guardians online than trying to force a numerical value on them (Barker 2006). Accordingly, the assignment of economic values to heritage assets is not the only way to enhance and discharge accountability for heritage assets. The disclosure of heritage assets in physical units is appropriate and necessary for the proper discharge of an entity's accountability for its heritage assets.

6 A Practical Accounting Approach for Heritage Assets Under Accrual Accounting

It is obvious from the aforementioned that the NPM reporting model, which believes in a one-size-fits-all application of GAAP to entities and assets differentiated in their purpose and essence (Hooper and Kearins 2005), is less appropriate for public sector heritage assets. As argued in this chapter, public sector heritage assets are different in their purpose and essence in comparison with regular assets and, therefore, they require an accounting treatment that takes into account their specific nature and characteristics, which will provides suitable accounting information that can satisfy the stakeholders' needs and be useful for decision-making. Accordingly, there is a need to move to a new reporting model that differentiates the heritage assets from other assets and recognizes that they should be accounted for separately from administrative assets of the government. Actually, the NPM—current accrual accounting approaches concerning the capitalization or not of heritage assets—has focused on whether information on cost or value of heritage assets is available or not. If it is available, then heritage assets should be capitalized and if it is not available, then heritage assets should not be capitalized regardless of whether heritage assets can be sold/disposed of and can be matched against the liabilities or not. The current accrual accounting approaches do not take into consideration whether there are **legal, cultural, or social restrictions** or not on the disposal of heritage assets. Moreover, they do not recognize the consequences of the capitalization and non-capitalization of heritage assets on the net worth and the performance statement respectively. They can lead to an exaggeration of net worth if a country like Egypt, which possesses at least one-third of worldwide heritage assets, has capitalized all its heritage assets. They can also lead to distorting the performance statement if the Egyptian government has not capitalized the heritage assets and expensed them in the account of revenue and expenditures. Therefore, in order to improve the quality of financial reporting of governmental entities and to overcome the exaggeration of net worth and distortion of the statement of financial performance and to provide suitable information for decision-making and stakeholders needs, there is an urgent need to develop a new accounting approach that focuses on consistent and transparent accounting treatment for heritage assets. As a response to this, the **Practical Accounting Approach for Heritage Assets** has been developed by Ouda (2013, 2014). The proposed Practical Accounting

Approach considers the specific nature and characteristics of the heritage assets and is based on the following assumptions:

- History and culture of nations are not for sale.
- The main task of accounting and accountants is not to mislead the stakeholders but to assist them in making the right decision and to inform them what the benefits are of capitalization of heritage assets that cannot be matched against liabilities.
- The issue is not to focus only on the technical side of accounting for heritage assets but also on reliability, relevance, credibility, verifiability, and comparability of accounting information that is included in the financial statements and its usefulness to different stakeholders.
- The legal, cultural, and social restrictions on the heritage assets are considered as barriers at their disposal. Therefore, these restrictions should be considered when deciding on whether heritage assets should be capitalized or not.
- For governmental entities to avoid the exaggeration of net worth or distortion of the statement of financial performance, the main issue is not only whether information on cost or value of heritage assets is available or not, but also whether heritage assets can be disposed of and matched against liabilities or not.
- Where information on cost or value of heritage assets is available and heritage assets can be sold/disposed of (no legal, cultural, and/or social restrictions on those assets—**Unrestricted Assets**) and matched against liabilities, they should be capitalized. (This I might call **Assets–Liabilities Matching Approach**).
- Where information on cost or value of heritage assets is not available or is available but cannot be sold or considered as financial resource that can be matched against liabilities due to legal, cultural, and/or social restrictions on the disposal of heritage assets (**Restricted Assets**), they should not be capitalized. (This I might call **Non-Assets–Liabilities Matching Approach**).
- Heritage assets are custodial in nature and the government is the custodian.

6.1 *The Practical Approach*

Based on the aforementioned assumptions, the practical approach takes into consideration whether there are legal, cultural, and/or social restrictions on the disposal of heritage assets or not. If there are legal, cultural, and/or social restrictions on the disposal of heritage assets **(Restricted Heritage Assets)**, then the capitalization of heritage assets will be misleading to the management and creditors because they are not legally accessible by them. If there are no legal, cultural, and/or social restrictions on the disposal of heritage assets and the information on cost and value of heritage assets is available, then the capitalization of heritage assets will not lead to misleading of the stakeholders as they can be matched against the liabilities **(Unrestricted Heritage Assets)** (Ouda 2013, 2014). In addition, the practical approach recognizes the consequences of the accounting treatment of heritage assets on the net worth and performance statement and its impact on the reliability of financial information provided in the financial statements. Consequently, The Practical Approach has been based on the following two sub-approaches (Ouda 2013, 2014):

- **Assets–Liabilities Matching Approach**: Capitalize if the information on cost or value of heritage assets is available and heritage assets can be disposed of, and hence be matched against liabilities **(Unrestricted Heritage Assets)**.
- **Non-Assets–Liabilities Matching Approach**: Do not capitalize if the information on cost or value is not available or is available but the heritage assets cannot be disposed of, and hence cannot be matched against liabilities **(Restricted Heritage Assets)**.

6.1.1 Assets–Liabilities Matching Approach

Under this approach, heritage assets are considered legally, culturally, and socially **unrestricted assets**. The information on their cost or value is available and they can be matched against the liabilities. Accordingly, they should be capitalized in the balance sheet at current value. An obvious example of heritage assets that can follow this approach in Egypt is the heritage presidential palaces. Due to the financial problems after the January 25 Revolution, many Egyptian economists argued that these problems can be solved through the disposal of many of the presidential palaces in Egypt which are not in use. Actually, this option had already been applied in Tunisia in 2012 as a solution to their financial problem after the revolution. The adoption of the Assets–Liabilities Matching Approach does not require completely new accounting standards. Different accounting standards have been developed and can be used by this approach such as UK-ASB-FRS 11, 15, and 30 and the Accounting Guideline GRAP 103 of the Republic of South Africa.

However, for these accounting standards to be consistent with the practical approach, there should be some amendments to these standards, for instance, UK-ASB-FRS 30 required that heritage assets be reported in the balance sheet where information on cost or value is available. The Assets–Liabilities Matching Approach agrees with this context. And it should clearly be stated that there are no legal, cultural, and/or social restrictions on the disposal of heritage assets, and hence they can be matched against the liabilities. After making this amendment, this approach can follow the aforementioned Accounting Standards. According to FRS 30 an entity should report heritage assets as tangible assets and recognize/measure these assets in accordance with FRS 15. Tangible fixed assets are subject to the requirements set out in paragraphs 19 to 25 (FRS 30). Herein, there should be some amendments *(**in italic and bold**)* as follows.

Recognition and Measurement

19. Where information is available on the cost or value of heritage assets ***and the heritage assets can be disposed of and matched against the liabilities***, (1) they should be presented in the balance sheet separately from other tangible fixed assets; (2) the balance sheet or the notes to the accounts should identify separately those classes of heritage assets being reported at cost and those at valuation; and (3) changes in the valuation should be recognized in the statement of total recognized gains and losses, except for impairment losses that should be recognized in accordance with paragraph 24.

20. Where assets have previously been capitalized or are recently purchased, information on their cost or value will be available. Where this information is not available, and cannot be obtained at a cost which is commensurate with the benefits to users of the financial statements, the assets will not be recognized in the balance sheet ***and should be treated in accordance with the Non-Assets–Liabilities Matching Approach***.

21. Valuations may be made by any method that is appropriate and relevant.

22. There is no requirement for valuations to be carried out or verified by external valuers; nor is there any prescribed minimum period between valuations. However, where heritage assets are reported at valuation, the carrying amount should be reviewed with sufficient frequency to ensure the valuations remain current.

Depreciation and Impairment

23. Depreciation need not be provided on heritage assets that have indefinite lives.

24 The carrying amount of an asset should be reviewed where there is evidence of impairment, for example, where it has suffered physical deterioration or breakage or new doubts arise as to its authenticity. Any impairment recognized should be dealt with in accordance with the recognition and measurement requirements of FRS 11 '*Impairment of fixed assets and goodwill.*'

The objective of FRS 11 is to ensure that

a. Fixed assets and goodwill are recorded in the financial statements at no more than their recoverable amount.
b. Any resulting impairment loss is measured and recognized on a consistent basis.
c. Sufficient information is disclosed in the financial statements to enable users to understand the impact of the impairment on the financial position and performance of the reporting entity.

FRS 11 sets out the principles and methodology for accounting for impairments of fixed assets and goodwill. It replaces the previous approach whereby diminutions in value were recognized only if they were regarded as permanent. Instead, the carrying amount of an asset is compared with its recoverable amount and, if the carrying amount is higher, the asset is written down. Recoverable amount is defined as the higher of the amount that could be obtained by selling the asset (net realizable value) and the amount that could be obtained through using the asset (value in use). Value in use is calculated by forecasting the cash flows that the asset is expected to generate and discounting them to their present value. Where individual assets do not generate independent cash flows, a group of assets (an income-generating unit) is tested for impairment. Impairment tests are only required when there has been some indication that impairment has occurred.

Donations

25. The receipt of donations of heritage assets should be reported in the *Performance Statement* at valuation. Where, exceptionally, it is not practicable to obtain a valuation of heritage assets acquired by donation, the

reasons for this should be stated. Disclosures should also be provided on the nature and extent of significant donations of heritage assets.

6.1.2 Non- Assets–Liabilities Matching Approach

According to this approach, heritage assets are considered legally, culturally, and socially **restricted assets** and they should not be capitalized in the balance sheet but treated as **Agent Assets**, **Trust Assets**, or **Custodial Assets**. This approach agrees with Barton (2000, 2005) that the government holds the heritage assets in trust for present and future generations and has a responsibility to protect and preserve them. The costs of protecting and maintaining them should be borne by each generation as they enjoy the benefits from them. As trust assets, public heritage assets should not be included in the government's own statement of assets and liabilities. They should not be regarded as financial resources and be available to meet its financial commitments. In trust accounting, the trustee is obliged to keep trust assets separate from its own assets and to report them separately (Barton 2000). This means that the heritage assets are beyond the financial position of the government. The most obvious examples of heritage assets in Egypt that can follow this approach are the Pharaonic antiquities, Greco-Roman antiquities, Islamic-Coptic antiquities, which include museum and gallery collections, other works of art, and national archives; and archeological sites, ruins, burial sites, monuments, and statues. Consequently, each country should create an **Agent/Trust Assets Statement** where heritage assets are stated ***in physical units, not in financial values*** (Ouda 2013, 2014). The statement of trust assets should include a description of major categories (types), physical units added and withdrawn during the year, and a description of the methods of acquisition and withdrawal. In addition, an explanatory note (note disclosure) should supplement the statement of trust assets. The note disclosure related to heritage assets should provide the following (FASAB 2005):

a. A concise statement explaining how they relate to the mission of the entity.
b. A brief description of the entity's stewardship policies for heritage assets. Stewardship policies for heritage assets are the goals and principles the entity established to guide its acquisition, maintenance, use, and disposal of heritage assets consistent with statutory requirements, prohibitions, and limitations governing the entity and the heritage assets.

c. A concise description of each major category of heritage assets. The appropriate level of categorization of heritage assets should be meaningful and determined by the preparer based on the entity's mission, types of heritage assets, and how it manages the assets.
d. Heritage assets should be quantified in terms of physical units. For each major category of heritage assets (identified in c) the following should be reported:
   1. The number of physical units by major category
   2. The number of physical units by major category that were acquired and the number of physical units by major category that were withdrawn during the reporting period
   3. A description of the major methods of acquisition and withdrawal of heritage assets during the reporting period

This should include disclosure of the number of physical units transferred to and/or from the entity and the number of physical units acquired through donation. Moreover, the fair value of heritage assets acquired through donation during the reporting period should be disclosed, if known, and as material. Furthermore, heritage assets held in trust may generate revenues indirectly through ***admission charges*** and incur costs such as restoration and maintenance costs. So in order to account for the revenues and costs related to the heritage assets, each county should create a **Trust Fund (Agent Fund)** (Ouda 2013, 2014). This fund will include all the revenues and costs related to heritage assets in a country. The balance of the trust fund would be reported as either a liability or an asset in the balance sheet. If this balance is positive, then it will be considered as an asset (fund surplus) and the increase of the net worth will be called **Heritage Net Worth**. Moreover, if it is negative (fund deficit), then it will be considered as a liability and the decrease in the net worth will be called **Negative Heritage Net Worth** (Ouda 2013, 2014). The Practical Accounting Approach will be reflected in Fig. 3.1.

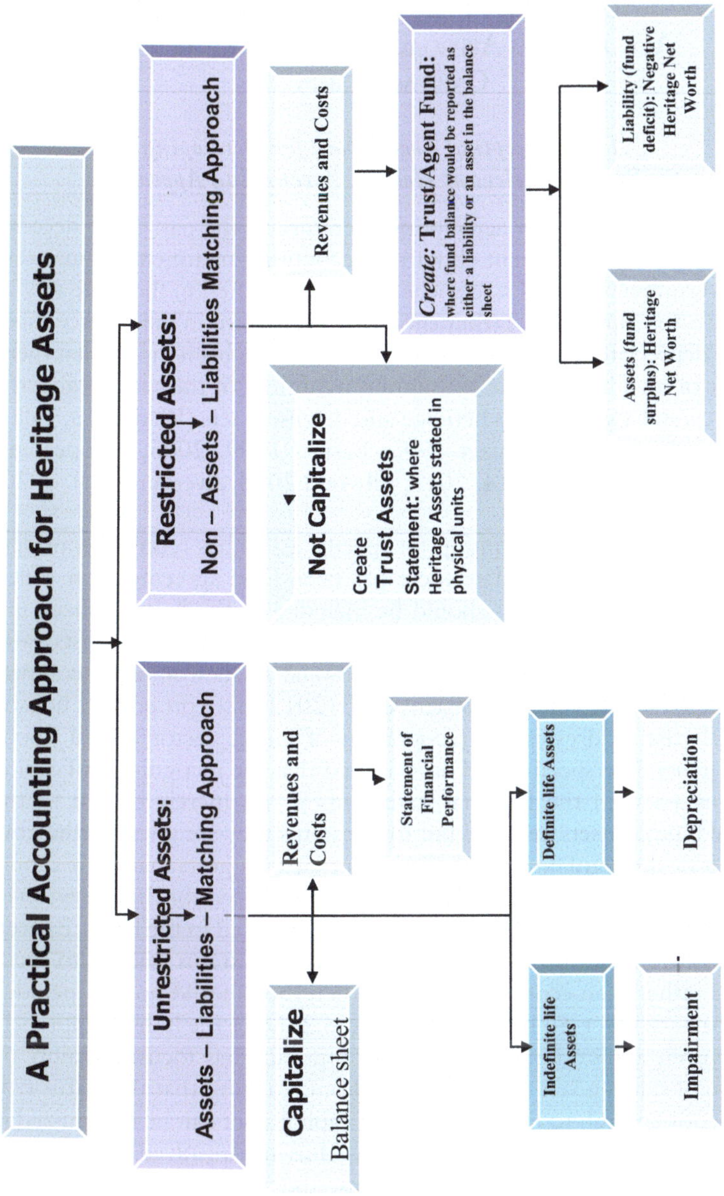

Fig. 3.1 A practical accounting approach for heritage assets. (Source: Ouda (2013, 2014))

7 Towards A Practice-Relevant Holistic Accounting Approach for Governmental Capital Assets

7.1 Conceptual Framework for Developing the Practice-Relevant Holistic Accounting Approach

Despite the public sector accounting literature in the past three decades having shown an agreement about the accounting treatment of business-like governmental capital assets where they are treated in the same way as private sector capital assets (they should be capitalized in the balance sheet and are depreciated in the income statement), it has been shown that there is a lack of unanimity of the accounting treatment of the specific governmental capital assets such as heritage and defense assets (Wild 2013; Pallot 1990; Carnegie and Wolnizer 1995; Barton 1999, 2005; Hooper and Kearins 2005; IPSASB 2014, 2017; Ellwood 2018; Aversano et al. 2020; De Wolf et al. 2020).

While the issue of accounting for specific assets has received considerable critical attention, to date there has been little agreement on which governmental capital assets should be included in the balance sheet and which ones excluded. So far, however, there has been little discussion about the recognition of governmental capital assets from a general perspective. To fill the void, Christiaens et al. (2012) have proposed a holistic approach that addresses the recognition of public sector capital goods from a general perspective and have argued that the recognition of capital goods as assets in the financial statements is not merely related to the physical type of assets involved but to the status they are given by the government or the legislator. The holistic approach suggests that if the capital good is given the status of businesslike assets and used for the provision of economic benefits, then the assets should be included in the balance sheet. On the other hand, if the assets are given a social status leading to social benefits rather than economic benefits, then they should not be included in the balance sheet. So the following Fig. 3.2 shows the holistic approach.

However, application of the holistic approach has focused mainly on the type of status given to the assets without realizing that the status type alone is not enough to decide whether a capital asset can be recognized in the financial statements or not, and has thus not resolved the problem from the practitioners' perspective because the practitioners will find that the holistic approach is inconsistent with the assets recognition criteria

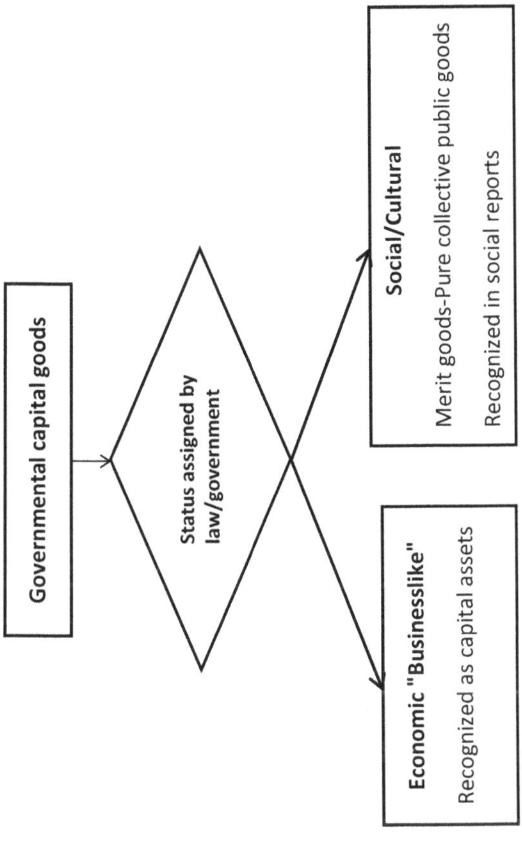

Fig. 3.2 Recognition of capital assets from a general perspective. (Source: Christiaens et al. (2012))

determined by IPSAS 16,17 and IPSASB-CF (2014). The assets recognition criteria do not focus on the type of status given to the assets but only on the flow of future economic benefits or service potential associated with the asset to the entity; and the cost or fair value of the asset to the entity can be measured reliably. Furthermore, the holistic approach does not consider the impact of reporting the governmental capital assets in economic values on the net worth and statement of financial performance. Although the holistic approach has addressed the status given to the assets, whether economic or social/cultural, it does not fully deal with all the types of status that can be given to other specific assets. For instance, there are also certain assets such as military/defense assets (such as components of weapons systems and support military missions and vessels held in preservation) which are excluded from the balance sheet because of national security reasons or because there was no output against which the costs of these items could be matched, according to information in the FASAB in the Statement of Federal Financial Accounting Standards (SFFAS—8, 11). Also, Ström (1997) supports the exclusion of defense assets from the balance sheet as he argues that future economic benefits do not occur when defense assets exist. The service potential can also be questioned because defense assets provide more of an "insurance premium" than ongoing services, thus excluding defense assets.

Consequently, the holistic approach can be modified to not only include the economic or social/cultural status but also the national security/defense status. The national security/defense status requires that defense assets be excluded from the balance sheet and disclosed in specific reports where the following information can be disclosed: the number of units of defense assets in each category of assets (this could be the number of aircraft etc.); the number of units added or withdrawn during the fiscal period; the description of the methods of acquisition and withdrawal; the condition of the defense assets; information on deferred maintenance on defense assets (SFFAS#8, 50,68,80, SFFAS#11, 10). Figure 3.3 presents the modified holistic approach.

This chapter seeks to facilitate the accounting treatment of all governmental capital assets from the practitioners' perspective. Basically, the holistic approach also aims to achieve the same objective, as Christiaens et al. (2012) argue, "that a practical consequence of applying the holistic approach is that it offers the possibility to reach clarity and general acceptance on how to deal with all kinds of capital goods in governments when applied in practice."

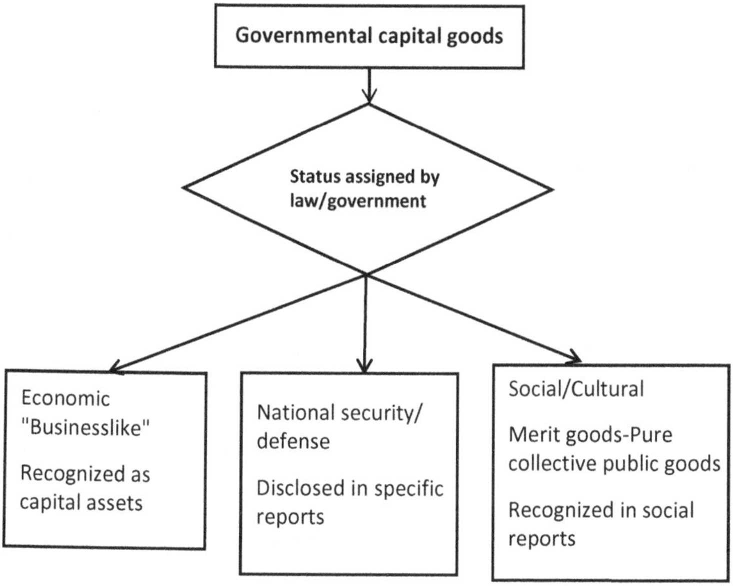

Fig. 3.3 Modified holistic approach: recognition of capital assets from a general perspective. (Source: Author)

However, application of the holistic or modified holistic approach does not resolve the problem from practitioners' perspective because the practitioners will find that the two approaches are inconsistent with the assets recognition criteria determined by IPSAS 16 &17 and IPSASB–CF (2014). An asset should be recognized in the statement of financial position when and only when

a. *It is probable that future economic benefits or service potential associated with the asset will flow to the entity.*
b. *The cost or fair value of the asset to the entity can be measured reliably.*

According to these assets recognition criteria, capital assets should be recognized in the balance sheet where information on cost or value of the capital assets is available and there are economic benefits or service potential; and they should not be recognized where the information on cost or value is not available. *So the question is: If a capital asset has been given a social/cultural status and, on the other hand, the information on cost or value of this asset is available, then should this asset be recognized?*

In fact, the answer to this question will take two perspectives: from the holistic approach perspective, so long as the asset is given social status, it should not be recognized in the balance sheet but it should be recognized in social reports; from the IPSAS recognition criteria perspective, so long as the information on the cost or value of the asset is available, it should be recognized in the balance sheet. This contradiction makes the situation for the practitioners more complicated and the governmental accounting not practice-relevant.

Furthermore, another question remains if a capital asset (e.g., heritage assets) has been given a social/cultural status and the information about its cost or value is available and this asset appears on the balance sheet: *Do the financial statements contain misleading information because there is an expectation of the ability to sell/dispose of such assets, which is unlikely for heritage assets, or does the recognition of the dollar amount of heritage assets add value to the reporting process?*

In fact, if the assets are given a social/cultural status (such as heritage assets) and the information on cost or value is available and there are cultural/social or legal restrictions on the disposal of such assets, then the capitalization of heritage assets will be misleading to the management and creditors because they are not legally accessible by them. This can be supported by the Non-Assets–Liability Matching Approach and by what is stated by SAC-4 that where assets and liabilities have been set off against each other, or where revenues and expenses have been netted off, in the presentation of those items in financial statements, those elements would nonetheless have been recognized. This means that the recognition of assets in the financial statements should only include the assets that can be disposed of and then will be matched against the liabilities. Accordingly, the inclusion of the governmental capital assets in the balance sheet that will not be matched against liabilities because there are legal, social/cultural, or defense/security restrictions on their disposal is in reality misleading. Therefore, the inconsistency between the IPSAS 16 and 17 and IPSASB-CF (2014) recognition criteria and the holistic approach can lead to the following questions:

- ***Are the current recognition criteria enough to include or to exclude the governmental capital assets?***

- ***Do the current recognition criteria for governmental capital assets require a reshaping to fit the context of public sector entities?***
- ***Does the reshaping of the recognition criteria require new recognition attributes?***

The main aim of this section is to examine to what extent the extant assets recognition criteria of governmental capital assets are sufficient and capable of increasing the reliability of general purpose financial reporting of the government and not result in misleading information to the management and creditors. Governmental capital assets are primarily used to provide services to citizens rather than to contribute to future cash flows. Unlike the private sector, they exist for serving cultural, social, defense, and economic benefits/objectives. However, the accounting literature (i.e., Carnegie and Wolnizer 1996) argues that failures in innovation in accounting assets recognition criteria possibly derive from the fact that accounting tools for the public sector (not-for-profit-oriented) have been historically borrowed from the private sector (for-profit-oriented) and often continue to be too closely tied to those schemes and logics. Argues that when an accounting method is introduced into a new environment, "it is naïve to assume that by simply assembling the components of a system that desired or officially intended outcome will be achieved." The long-standing academic argument for using accrual accounting in the public sector appears to have missed some necessary adjustments that should be available for adopting accrual accounting in the public sector. One of these adjustments is the assets recognition criteria. Actually, the assets recognition criteria are not a static thing and they should reflect the specific nature and characteristics of governmental capital assets and aim at increasing the reliability of government financial reporting.

Accounting is a service function that should aim to provide the best possible financial information to management and creditors and not to mislead them. According to the currently used assets recognition criteria in the public sector this requirement is not being met and the reason is that the definition of assets and recognition criteria is flawed. Therefore, management and external users are misinformed and misled by the inclusion of assets (such as restricted heritage assets) that will not be matched against the liabilities (Ouda 2014) or exclusion of a certain asset because it is not the result of a past "transaction or event," such as internally created assets. As providers of financial information there is a duty upon academics and practitioners to attempt to bridge this gap through reconsidering the assets definition and recognition criteria with the aim of providing reliable financial information. While this gap will never be completely bridged due to severe difficulties embedded in the specific governmental capital assets, this does not mean that this gap should be ignored and we as public sector accountants should be happy with the assets recognition criteria which have been originally established for the recognition of businesslike assets and not for the specific governmental capital assets, such as heritage assets, defense assets, and community assets.

In the private sector accounting, assets are usually defined as items that can be used to generate future cash flows. This line of reasoning does not apply to the primary characteristics of most governmental assets. To overcome this problem, the definition of assets has been redefined by the public sector accountants with reference to *Service Potential*, or according to the IPSASB, where they are defined as assets "embodying service potential" that do not generate cash flows. Public sector accountants have mistakenly assumed that adding the "potential services" to the assets definition without making a real change to the recognition criteria can solve the problem of the recognition of non-businesslike assets. This is a clear signal that it is time for a complete and fresh rethinking on the definition and recognition criteria of an asset in the public sector if we assume that financial statements should provide a faithful representation of governmental entities.

- **A Critical Review of Assets Definition and Recognition Criteria**

Although most of the governmental capital assets are different from the private sector capital assets in terms of serving cultural, social, defense, and economic benefits/objectives and do not only create cash flows, the assets definition and recognition criteria in the public sector have not yet been developed to the extent of reflecting the serving of those benefits/objectives. The first challenge in addressing the assets definition and recognition criteria is the lack of generally accepted assets definition and recognition criteria in the public sector accounting literature. Different recognition criteria are applied by national and international organizations to recognize the specific governmental capital assets. In addition, a common definition of governmental capital assets does not exist. To address this issue, the asset definition and recognition criteria are important to start with. The International Accounting Standards Board (IASB) (formerly known as IASC) defines an asset as follows: "*An asset is a resource controlled by the enterprise as a result of past events and from which future economic benefits are expected to flow to the enterprise*" (IASB 1989, Para. 49). Moreover, the Accounting Standards Board (ASB) defines assets as follows: "*Assets are rights or other access to future economic benefits controlled by an entity as a result of past transactions or events*" (ASB 1999). In addition to defines assets as follows: Assets are probable future economic benefits obtained or controlled by a particular entity as a result of past transactions or events.

While the IASB, ASB, and FASB definitions refer only to future economic benefits, the IPSASB, in common with other public sector standard setters, sees that the definition of an asset needs to incorporate both economic benefits and service potential, as defined by IPSAS 1 Presentation of Financial Statements, paragraph 6, IPSAS 16, and IPSAS 17: "*Assets are resources controlled by an entity as a result of past events and from which future economic benefits or service potential are expected to flow to the entity*". Furthermore, IPSASB-CF (2014) defines an asset as a resource presently controlled by the entity as a result of a past event.

On the other hand, other jurisdictions such as the Australian government use only the term "future economic benefits" to cover both concepts (economic benefits and service potential). It is mentioned in the *Australian Statement of Concepts No. 4, Definition and Recognition of the Elements of Financial Statements that "[t]he expression 'service potential' has been omitted from the definition and recognition criteria. It is noted in paragraph 18 of this Statement, the characteristic of future economic benefits is synonymous with the notion of service potential, a term which is used more commonly in respect of not-for-profit entities."*

Based on the definitions of IASB, IPSAS 1, 16 & 17, IPSASB-CF, and the Australian government, one can conclude that there is no consensus about the term that can be used in the definition of an asset. In addition, IASB identified two criteria that can be used for determining when assets and liabilities should be recognized. *"[A]ssets and liabilities should be recognized ... when*

(1) *[I]t is probable that increases (assets) or decreases (liabilities) in economic benefits will occur.*
(2) *[T]he amount of settlement of liabilities and the cost or other value of assets can be measured reliably.*

Also, IPSAS 1, 16, & 17 identified two criteria that can be used for determining when an asset should be recognized:

(a) *It is probable that future economic benefits or service potential associated with the asset will flow to the entity.*
(b) *The cost or fair value of the asset to the entity can be measured reliably.*

Moreover, IPSASB-CF (2014) identified the following two recognition criteria:

(a) *An item satisfies the definition of an element.*
(b) *It can be measured in a way that achieves the qualitative characteristics and takes account of constraints on information in GPFRs.*

IPSASB-CF states that all items that satisfy the recognition criteria are recognized in the financial statements.

Thus, under the IASB and IPSAS 1, 16, 17, and IPSASB-CF (2014) determining which items should be recognized in the financial statements involves the following two steps:

1. Determining whether the item meets the definition of an asset
2. Determining whether the item satisfies the recognition criteria

Herein, the question that occupies our thought is: *Are the stated criteria and assets definition, which are basically directed to the businesslike assets, relevant to or sufficient for the recognition of all governmental capital assets?*

- **Assets definition**

Actually, assets definition is still suffering from several shortcomings in the private sector and these shortcomings are also transferred to the public sector entities. While the IPSASB assets definition has attempted to overcome these shortcomings by adding the concept of "service potential" and replacing the term "enterprise" by "entity," this definition did not take into consideration the specific features and characteristics of specific governmental capital assets.

> *Assets are resources controlled by an entity as a result of past events and from which future economic benefits or service potential are expected to flow to the entity.*

The IPSASB assets definition and the required changes will be examined as follows:

- *Past events and transactions*

This condition imposes a definitional restriction on the recognition of internally created assets, particularly with respect to intangible assets such as patents and software, which are not necessarily the results of a past transaction or event. This condition can also lead to inconsistency in accounting recognition of intangible assets in financial statements. According to this condition a purchase is required for accountants to recognize an asset. The rule is that the definition recognizes and capitalizes the transaction-based or purchased patent as an asset while excluding internally created patents from the assets on the balance sheet. If both patents are expecting to generate future economic benefits, then, logically, both should be considered as assets. Argued that it is unnecessarily restrictive to exclude one of them from the balance sheet because it is not the result of a "transaction or event." So the current asset definition appears to allow some assets to be capitalized while at the same time disallowing similar assets such as internally created assets. This can show the management to be poorly informed by the absence from the balance sheet of financial information on valuable homegrown intangible assets. This will negatively impact the transparency and reliability of general purpose financial reporting of the government. The element of compulsion that the recognition of assets must result from a transaction or event now appears to be negated with respect to certain homegrown intangible assets. However, I do not call for removing this condition (as a result of a transaction or past event), as some researchers consider this condition as important to avoid assets expected to be acquired in the future being recognized as assets in the current period (Christiaens et al. 2012). Consequently, this condition must continue as an important part of assets definition but we should add ***"as a result of a transaction or past event or internally created."***

- *Flow to the entity—society/citizens*

Christiaens et al. (2012) argue that the societal benefits (service potential) do not flow back to the government as an accounting entity, but flow back to the citizens who are different entities. Because the benefits do not flow back to the government, Mautz (1988) argued that facilities providing social benefits ought to be treated as liabilities on account of the costs incurred on acquiring and maintaining them. In fact, if we assume that the main owners (principal) of the governmental entities are citizens/society/the public, then the citizens are the end objective of the economic benefits or service potential. In the private sector, the owners are the shareholders and not the citizens, therefore the economic benefits should flow back to the owners of the firm. However, the nature of public sector entities compared to the private sector entities is completely different, as they originally exist to serve the public interest and they are financed by the taxpayers/citizens. So whether the benefits flow to the governmental entity itself as an accounting entity or to the citizens as the principal, in the end they flow to the main beneficiary. This, in turn, can lead to changing the definition of an asset in the public sector by adding the following to the assets definition: ***"to flow to entity or citizens (society)."***

Based on the aforementioned discussion, the definition of an asset can be revised as follows:

> *Assets are resources controlled by an entity as a result of past events or transactions or internally created and from which future economic benefits or service potential are expected to flow to the entity or society/citizens.*

– *Future economic benefits*

Economic benefits are considered to be a problem not only for the public sector entities but also for the private sector. In the private sector, the phrase "future economic benefits" does not differentiate between future economic benefits arising from capital expenditure and those arising from deferred revenue expenditure. The latter refers to items of expenditure that are normally treated as expenses in the income statement but are treated as assets on the balance sheet instead. This is due to the fact that the benefits of such expenditure may extend to a number of years; hence, this expenditure is not charged directly to the income statement but a portion of it is charged every year to the income statement and the remaining amount at the end of the year is put as an asset in the balance sheet as deferred revenue expenditure or capitalized expenditure. Examples of such expenditure are heavy advertisement expenses paid on contract for a few years, or research and development expenses. Thus, the expenditure on advertising can create future economic benefits despite its current status as an expense rather than as an asset. In addition, economic benefits are related to the generation of cash flows, as IASB states that "the future economic benefit[] embodied in an asset is the potential contribut[or], directly or indirectly, to the flow of cash and cash equivalents to the entity". This relationship does not belong to the public sector entities, which aim to satisfy different benefits other than the generation of cash flows, such as social and cultural benefits. Therefore, the has revised the definition of an asset by adding the concept of "service potential." ITC issued by IFAC (p. 26) has distinguished service potential from future economic benefits as follows: (1) Assets that are used to deliver goods and services in accordance with an entity's objectives but which do not directly generate net **cash** inflows are often described as embodying "service potential." (2) Assets that are used to generate net cash inflows are often described as embodying "future economic benefits." So the service potential gives rise to allowing the recognition of some resources which do not generate cash flows but are held to pursue the entity mission as assets. Argued that service potential enables an entity to achieve the entity's objectives without necessarily generating net cash inflows. Examples of public sector assets that embody service potential are heritage, community, and defense assets. However, the question is: ***Does adding the concept of service potential to the definition of an asset lead to the recognition of public sector capital goods as assets in the balance sheet?***

Answering this question will lead us to address the accounting recognition criteria.

- **Recognition Criteria**

In fact, after 30 years of public sector accounting reform, public sector accountants have failed to innovate assets recognition criteria and hence they have failed to recognize and capitalize many of the specific governmental capital assets or have recognized assets (e.g., restricted heritage assets) that should not be recognized (Ouda 2014). This makes the reliability of financial statements in the public sector questionable. So, the public sector accountants are really facing a dilemma, as they are required to reshape/innovate the assets recognition criteria in a way that maintains the reliability of financial statements and at the same time should reflect the specific nature and characteristics of the specific governmental capital assets.

In order to be able to reshape/innovate the recognition criteria, we should determine the recognition attributes which will be inferred from Ouda's Practical Accounting Approach for heritage assets and Christiaens's Holistic Approach. Based on these two approaches we can determine the following five recognition attributes:

1. Status assigned to the assets
2. Type of benefits (whether economic, social/cultural, or security/defense benefits)
3. Matching (whether or not the assets can be matched against the liabilities)
4. Unrestricted assets—where there are no legal/social/cultural, or defense and security restrictions on those, and then, they can be disposed of/sold
5. Restricted assets—where there are legal/social/cultural or defense and security restrictions on those, and then, they cannot be disposed of/sold.

Based on the aforementioned recognition attributes and revised definition of assets, we can develop/reshape the recognition criteria to be suitable for the recognition of capital goods as assets. This will require adding two new recognition criteria to the original two recognition criteria stated by IPSAS 16, 17, and IPSASB-CF (2014). Accordingly, the recognition of governmental capital assets will be based on the following four criteria.

Original recognition criteria:

a. *It is probable that future economic benefits or service potential associated with the asset will flow to the entity or to the* ***citizens/society****.*
b. *The cost or fair value of the asset to the entity can be measured reliably.*

Newly developed recognition criteria:

a. *There are no legal, cultural, social, and national security/defense (or other) restrictions on the disposal of the assets (unrestricted assets).*
b. *Recognized assets should be matched against the liabilities to avoid misleading.*

The core of the newly developed criteria is that they recognize the governmental capital goods as assets in the balance sheet where the information is available on the cost or value of assets and these assets are unrestricted assets and hence they can be disposed of and matched against the liabilities.

7.2 A Practice-Relevant Holistic Accounting Approach for Governmental Capital Assets

The previous sections have demonstrated that one size does not fit all and the focused purpose of public sector entities is divergent from the logic of the private sector–style financial reporting. Furthermore, government capital assets do not appear to fit neatly into the single corporate GAAP definition of an asset. Given that the financial statements based on the NPM ideologies and assumptions do not fit the accounting treatment of specific assets such as heritage assets or of all governmental capital assets, there is an urgent need for developing an alternative reporting model for the NPM practices.

Based on the combination of the five recognition attributes, the original and newly developed recognition criteria, Ouda's Practical Accounting Approach for Heritage assets, and Christiaens's Holistic Approach, I can develop a ***Practice-Relevant Holistic Accounting Approach for governmental capital assets***. Accordingly, the cornerstones of the Practice-Relevant Holistic Accounting Approach are reflected in Fig. 3.4 (Ouda 2016).

Based on the five recognition attributes and the four recognition criteria, the following **three sub-approaches** form the CF of the Practice-Relevant Holistic Accounting Approach for governmental capital assets (Ouda 2016):

- **Economic Businesslike Assets**: Under this approach, any capital asset is given an economic businesslike status and gives rise to economic benefits; it should be capitalized in the balance sheet (Christiaens et al. 2012). Similar to businesslike assets, their expenses should be included in the statement of financial performance.

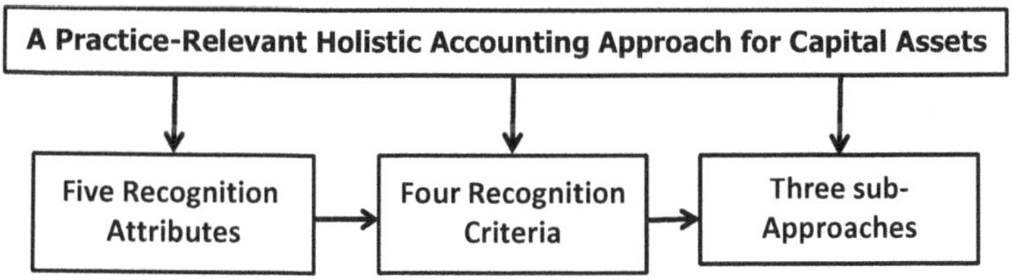

Fig. 3.4 Cornerstones of the practice-relevant holistic accounting approach. (Source: Ouda (2016))

- **Assets–Liabilities Matching Approach—Unrestricted Assets**: Under this approach, any asset is given social/cultural or defense status and gives rise to social/cultural or defense/security benefits, and is an unrestricted asset which can be disposed of and matched against the liabilities; it should be capitalized in the balance sheet (Ouda 2014, 2016). Consequently, heritage assets that are considered as legally, culturally, and socially unrestricted assets, for which information on their cost or value is available, and which can be matched against the liabilities should be capitalized in the balance sheet at current value. An obvious example of heritage assets that can follow this approach in Egypt is the Heritage Presidential Palaces. Due to the financial problems after the January 25 Revolution, many Egyptian economists argued that these problems could be solved through the disposal of many of the presidential palaces in Egypt which are not in use. In fact, this option had already been applied in Tunisia in 2012 as a solution to their financial problems after the revolution (Ouda 2014). In times of austerity, heritage assets can be sold to overcome financial problems. This was the case in the UK, as the local press reported (November 7, 2012): "Tower Hamlets Council made the difficult decision to sell the Henry Moore sculpture, Draped Seated Woman" (Ellwood and Greenwood 2014).
  Similar to heritage assets, under the assets–liability matching approach the defense assets that are legal/national security unrestricted assets and the information on their cost or value are available and can be matched against the liabilities; therefore, they should be capitalized at their current value. With respect to the revenues and expenses of heritage assets, these should be included in the statement of financial performance and we should differentiate between the indefinite and definite assets as we should calculate impairment for indefinite assets and depreciation for definite assets. Regarding defense assets, their expenses are included in the statement of financial performance.
- **Non-Assets–Liabilities Matching Approach—Restricted Assets**: Herein, such assets should not be capitalized if the information on cost or value is not available or is available but heritage assets and defense assets cannot be disposed of, and hence cannot be matched against the liabilities (Ouda 2014, 2016). According to this approach, heritage assets are considered legally, culturally, and socially restricted

assets and defense assets are also considered as legal and national security restricted assets. Therefore, they should not be capitalized in the balance sheet. But both assets are treated differently as follows: Heritage assets are treated as **Agent Assets, Trust Assets, or Custodial Assets**. Accordingly, each country should create an **Agent/Trust Assets Statement** where heritage assets stated in this statement ***in physical units, not in financial values*** (Ouda 2014). The statement of trust assets should include a description of major categories (types), physical units added and withdrawn during the year, and the methods of acquisition and withdrawal. In addition, an explanatory note (note disclosure) should supplement the statement of trust assets.

Furthermore, heritage assets held in trust may generate revenues indirectly through ***admission charges*** and incur costs such as restoration and maintenance costs. So in order to account for the revenues and costs related to heritage assets, each county should create a **Trust Fund (Agent Fund)** (Ouda 2014, 2016). This fund will include all the revenues and costs related to heritage assets in a country. The balance of the trust fund would be reported as either a liability or an asset in the balance sheet. If this balance is positive (fund surplus), then it will be considered as an asset and the increasing of the net worth will be called **Heritage Net Worth**. Moreover, if it is negative (fund deficit), then it will be considered as a liability and the decrease in the net worth will be called **Negative Heritage Net Worth** (Ouda 2014, 2016).

With respect to defense assets, each country can create defense assets statements or specific reports and disclose these assets in these statements or reports where the defense assets can either be stated in physical units (number of systems or items) or in terms of financial value. The disclosure can include the following information: the number of units of defense assets in each category of assets (this could be a number of aircraft etc.); the number of units added or withdrawn during the fiscal period; the description of the methods of acquisition and withdrawal; the condition of the defense assets; and information on deferred maintenance on defense assets (SFFAS#8, 50, 68, 80, SFFAS#11, 10). In addition, their cost will be included in the statement of financial performance. The CF of the Practice-Relevant Holistic Accounting Approach for Governmental Capital Assets will be reflected in Fig. 3.5 (Ouda 2016).

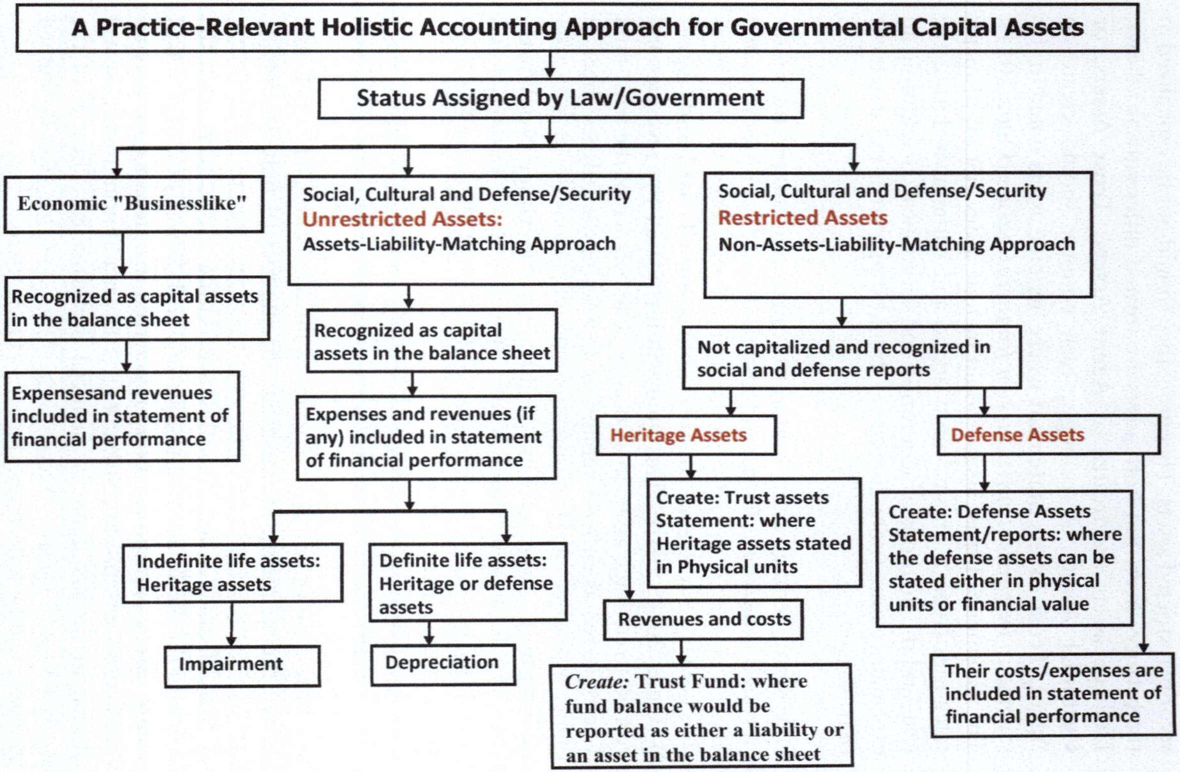

Fig. 3.5 A practice-relevant holistic accounting approach for governmental capital assets. (Source: Ouda (2016))

The Practice-Relevant Holistic Accounting Approach provides an important opportunity to advance the understanding of accounting treatment of all governmental capital assets and offers some important insights into which capital assets should be included in the balance sheet and which ones excluded.

There are several important areas where this approach makes an original contribution:

- *Developing new recognition attributes* such as status assigned to the assets; type of benefits (whether economic, social/cultural, or defense benefits); matching (whether or not the assets can be matched with the liabilities); unrestricted assets—where there are no legal/social/cultural or defense and security restrictions on those assets and accordingly they can be disposed of/sold; and finally, restricted assets—where there are legal/social/cultural or defense and security restrictions on those assets and, accordingly, they cannot be disposed of/sold.
- *Reshaping the recognition criteria by developing two new recognition criteria* and, accordingly, expanding the assets recognition criteria in the public sector to include four criteria instead of the two criteria used in the private sector:
  a. *It is probable that future economic benefits or service potential associated with the asset will flow to the entity or to the* ***citizens/society****.*
  b. *The cost or fair value of the asset to the entity can be measured reliably.*
  c. *There are no legal, cultural, social, or national security/defense (or other restrictions on the disposal of the assets (unrestricted assets).*
  d. *Recognized assets should be matched against the liabilities to avoid misleading.*
- *Developing an alternative reporting model for the NPM practices* through developing three new sub-accounting approaches to classify governmental capital assets in a more useful way and developing reporting formats that recognize the new assets classes, and avoiding misleading the management and creditors.

8 Conclusion

The improvement of governmental capital assets management and information system is a fundamental part of the NPM approach. This improvement, coupled with the idea of making public authorities accountable to act in the best interest of citizens with respect to the preservation, employment, and value enhancement of governmental capital assets, has resulted in a growing tendency to introduce accrual accounting for central and local governments, and hence to produce annual financial reports prepared on an equivalent basis to the corporate model. This means that the public sector entities are required to report to stakeholders on a model disclosing the economic values for all assets under their control. However, this chapter points out that attributing economic values to governmental capital assets raises the question of whether it is appropriate to view all governmental capital assets through a similar lens. Most of the heritage assets and defense assets are not used to generate revenue for the government but they are operated to provide cultural, social, and national security benefits to the country. Therefore, it is misleading and inappropriate to include these assets together with the other assets that generate economic benefits on the government's balance sheet. Thus, this chapter has advocated for developing an alternative reporting model that takes into account both financial and nonfinancial perspectives.

The new developed reporting model attempts to overcome the drawbacks of the corporate model by taking into consideration that public sector entities and their capital assets are differentiated in purpose and essence. Moreover, it does recognize the consequences of the capitalization and non-capitalization of specific assets such as heritage and defense assets on net worth and statements of financial performance. This has led to avoiding the exaggeration of the net worth and distortion of the performance statement. Finally, it offers the possibility to reach clarity and general acceptance on how to deal with all governmental capital assets and identify which capital assets should be included in the financial statements and which ones excluded.

As an alternative reporting model for the NPM practices, the Practice-Relevant Holistic Accounting Approach for Governmental Capital Assets has been developed. This approach has been based on three cornerstones:

(a) ***Five recognition attributes***: status assigned to the assets; type of benefits (whether economic, social/cultural, or defense benefits);

matching (whether or not the assets can be matched with the liabilities); unrestricted assets—where there are no legal/social/cultural or defense and security restrictions on those assets and, accordingly, they can be disposed of/sold; and restricted assets—where there are legal/social/cultural or defense and security restrictions on those assets and, accordingly, they cannot be disposed of/sold.

(**b**) Based on the five recognition attributes, ***two new recognition criteria*** have been developed, in addition to the ***two criteria stated** by IPSAS 16, 17 **and** IPSASB-CF* (2014*)*. The following are the two new recognition criteria:

- *There are no legal, cultural/ social and national security/defense restrictions on the disposal of the asset.*
- *Recognized assets should be matched against the liabilities to avoid the misleading.*

(**c**) Based on the new recognition criteria and the five recognition attributes, ***three sub-approaches*** are developed as follows: economic business-like assets; assets–liabilities matching approach for unrestricted assets; and non-assets–liabilities matching approach for restricted assets. Under the practice-relevant holistic accounting approach, practitioners recognize the governmental capital goods as assets in the balance sheet where the information is available on the cost or value of assets and these assets are unrestricted, and then they can be disposed of and matched against the liabilities. This, in turn, leads to avoiding the provision of misleading information to the management and creditors. Accordingly, this chapter has attempted to assist academics and practitioners in how to account for different capital assets in governmental entities in a practical way and to answer the questions raised in the introduction of this chapter.

Therefore, the main message here is that more work needs to be done if the public sector accounting researchers are to claim to having an impact on practice; therefore, they should work together with the practitioners to find practical solutions for outstanding public sector accounting issues such as the issue addressed in this chapter and stop spending their entire career just talking to other accounting researchers about their work through conferences and journals (Laughlin 2011). Otherwise, practitioners will see accounting research as a pointless exercise unless the research is deemed to be practice-relevant.

One of the most important conclusions is the recommendation of Weers (2016): "Future research should attempt to develop an alternative accounting system that categorizes government assets in a manner akin to Ouda's framework. He makes a very convincing case for at least four types of assets. Of these, only one type completely conforms to the corporate GAAP definition of an asset. The treatment of DOD (Department of Defense) property is a central point of contention and before a new reporting format can be considered, the issue of assets must be adequately addressed. It is fruitless to continue attempting to fit the government's many different types of property into a private sector accounting system and expect a new outcome."

References

Accounting Standard Board (ASB). (2006, January). *Heritage Assets Can Accounting Do Better?* Discussion paper, Accounting Standards Board, London, p. 89.

Anthony, R. N. (1994). *In Lieu of Depreciation*. Working Paper 94-067, Graduate School of Business Administration, Harvard University.

Australian Accounting Research Foundation (AARF). (1990). *Financial Reporting by Local Government*. Australian Accounting Standard AAS 27, Australian Accounting Research Foundation, Melbourne.

Australian Accounting Research Foundation (AARF). (1992). *Definition, Recognition of the Elements of Financial Statements*. Statement of Accounting Concepts SAC 4, Australian Accounting Research Foundation, Melbourne.

Australian Accounting Research Foundation (AARF). (1993). Financial Reporting by Government Departments. Australian Accounting Standard AAS 29, Australian Accounting Research Foundation, Melbourne.

Australian Accounting Research Foundation (AARF). (1996). *Financial Reporting by Government Departments*. Australian Accounting Standard AAS 31, Australian Accounting Research Foundation, Melbourne.

Aversano, N., Christiaens, J., Polcini, P., & Van Thielen, T. (2019). Does IPSAS Meet Heritage Assets' User Needs? *International Journal of Public Administration, 42*(4), 279–288.

Aversano, N., Christiaens, J., Polcini, P., & Sannino, G. (2020). Accounting for Heritage Assets: An Analysis of Governmental Organization Comment Letters on the IPSAS Consultation Paper. *International Journal of Public Sector Management, Vo., 33*(2–3), 307–322.

Ball, I. (1994, November 2). *Initiatives in Public Sector Management and Financial Management: The New Zealand Experience, Published in Arthur*

Andersen. Financieel beheer,verslaggeving en prestatiemeting bij de Rijksoverheid, Symposium verslag.

Ball, A., & Grubnic, S. (2008). Sustainability Accounting and Accountability in the Public Sector. In J. Unerman, J. Bebbington, & B. O'Dwyer (Eds.), *Sustainability Accounting and Accountability* (pp. 243–265). Abingdon: Routledge.

Barker, P. (2006). Heritage Assets: Can Accounting Do Better? *Accounting Ireland, 38*(4), 48–50.

Barton, A. (1999). Public and Private Sector Accounting—The Non-Identical Twins. *Australian Accounting Review, 9*(2), 22–31.

Barton, A. D. (2000). Accounting for Public Heritage Facilities—Assets or Liabilities of the Government? *Accounting, Auditing & Accountability Journal, 13*(2), 219–235.

Barton, A. D. (2005). The Conceptual Arguments Concerning Accounting for Public Heritage Assets: A Note. *Accounting, Auditing & Accountability Journal, 18*(3), 434–440.

Bergmann, A., Fuchs, S., & Schuler, C. (2019). A Theoretical Basis for Public Sector Accrual Accounting Research: Current State and Perspectives. *Public Money & Management, 39*(8), 560–570.

Bonini, S. (2014). "Evaluating results of public sector reforms in Rechtsstaat countries: the role of context and the role of processes in the reform of the Italian and French cultural heritage system", *International public management journal. Vol., 17*(3), 411–432.

Carnegie, G. D., & West, B. P. (2004, April 1–3). *Making Accounting Accountable in the Public Sector*. Working Paper European Accounting Conference, Prague, p. 34.

Carnegie, G., & West, B. (2005). Making Accounting Accountable in the Public Sector. *Critical Perspectives on Accounting, 16*, 905–928.

Carnegie, G. D., & Wolnizer, P. W. (1995). The Financial Value of Cultural, Heritage and Scientific Collections: An Accounting Fiction. *Australian Accounting Review, 5*(1), 31–47.

Carnegie, G. D., & Wolnizer, P. W. (1996). Enabling Accountability in Museums. *Accounting, Auditing & Accountability Journal, 9*(5), 84–99.

Carnegie, G. D., & Wolnizer, P. W. (1999). Unravelling the Rhetoric About the Financial Reporting of Public Collections as Assets. *Australian Accounting Review, 9*(1), 16–21.

Christiaens, J. (2004). Capital Assets in Governmental Accounting Reforms: Comparing Flemish Technical Issues with International Standards. *European Accounting Review, 13*(4), 743–770.

Christiaens, J., & Rommel, J. (2008). Accrual Accounting Reforms: Only for Businesslike (Parts of) Governments. *Financial Accountability & Management, 24*(1).

Christiaens, J., Rommel, J., Barton, A., & Everaert, P. (2012). Should All Capital Goods of Governments be Recognized as Assets in Financial Accounting? *Baltic Journal of Management, 7*(4), 429–443.

Cooper, S., & Owen, D. (2007). Corporate Social Reporting and Stakeholder Accountability: The Missing Link. *Accounting, Organizations and Society, 32*, 649–667.

Correia, Z. (2005). Towards a Stakeholder Model for the Co-Production of the Public Sector Information System. *IR-Information Research, 10*(3), n3.

De Wolf, A., Christiaens, J., & Aversano, N. (2020, February). Heritage Assets in the Due Process of the International Public Sector Accounting Standards Board (IPSASB). *Public Money & Management*. https://doi.org/10.1080/09540962.2020.1727114.

Egyptian Law No, 117 (1983) as Amended by Law No. 3 of 2010. *Promulgating the Antiquities, Protection Law*. Published in the official Gazette on February 14.

Ellwood, S. (2018). Accounting for What We Treasure. In A. M. Labrador & N. S. Silberman (Eds.), *The Oxford Handbook of Public Heritage Theory and Practice* (pp. 125–137). Oxford: University Press.

Ellwood, S., & Greenwood, M. (2014, April 14–16). *Accounting for Heritage Assets: Does measuring the Economic Value Kill the Cat?* Proceedings of the British Accounting and Finance Association (BAFA) 50th Annual Conference—London School of Economics and Political Science—UK.

FASAB. (2005). *Heritage Assets and Stewardship Land*. Statement of Federal Financial Accounting Standards 29, Federal Accounting Standards Advisory Board, Washington, DC.

Franklin, M., Graybeal, P., & Cooper, D. (2019). *Principles of Accounting: Volume 1 Financial Accounting*. Houston, TX: OpenStax Rice University.

Grubišić, M., Nušinović, M., & Roje, G. (2008). From Accountable Government to Public Asset Management Reform and Welfare. *Privredna kretanja iekonomska poli-tika, 18*(117, Winter), 58–117.

Haque, M. S. (2002). Structures of New Public Management in Malaysia and Singapore: Alternative Views. *Journal of Comparative Asian Development, 1*(1), 71–86.

Hone, P. (1997). The Financial Value of Cultural, Heritage and Scientific Collections: A Public Management Necessity. *Australian Accounting Review, 7*(1), 38–43.

Hood, C. (1991). A Public Management for All Seasons? *Public Administration, 69*(1), 3–19.

Hood, C. (1995). The New Public Management in the 1980s: Variations on a Theme. *Accounting, Organizations and Society, 20*(2/3), 93–103.

Hooper, K. C., & Kearins, K. N. (2005). Knowing the Price of Everything and the Value of Nothing: Accounting for Heritage Assets. *Accounting, Auditing and Accountability Journal, 62*(4), 181–184.

IASB—International Accounting Standard Board. (1989). *Framework for the Preparation and Presentation of Financial Statements.*

IFAC. (2013). *Compliance Responses and Action Plans.* New York: IFAC [online]. Retrieved from http://www.ifac.org/aboutifac/membership/compliance-program/compliance-responses.

IPSASB. (2006, February). *Accounting for Heritage Assets Under the Accrual Accounting Basis of Accounting.* Consultation Paper.

IPSASB. (2010). *IPSAS 17: Property, Plant and Equipment.* New York.

IPSASB. (2014, October). *The Conceptual Framework for General Purpose Financial Reporting by Public Sector Entities.* IFAC.

IPSASB. (2017, April). *Financial Reporting for Heritage Assets in the Public Sector.* Consultation Paper.

IPSASB. (2020, January 31). *IPSASB Work Program.* https://www.ipsasb.org/consultations-projects/work-plan:status.

IPSASB-IPSAS 16: Investment Property. New York.

Jones, R., & Pendlebury, M. (1984). *Public Sector Accounting.* London.

Kaganova, O., & Nayyar-Stone, R. (2000). Municipal Real Property Asset Management: An Overview of World Experience, Trends and Financial Implications. *Journal of Real Estate Portfolio Management, 6*(4), 307–326.

Keany, R. C., & Hays, S. W. (1998). Reinventing Government, the New Public Management and Civil Services Systems in International Perspective: The Danger of Throwing the Baby Out with the Bathwater. *Review of Public Personnel Administration, 18*(4), 38–54.

Kelly, R. M. (1998). An Inclusive Democratic Policy, Representative Bureaucracies, and the New Public Management. *Public Administration Review, 58*(3), 201–208.

Kickert, W. (1997). Public Management in the United States and Europe. In W. J. M. Kickert (Ed.), *Public Management and Administrative Reform in WESTEREN Europe* (pp. 15–39). Cheltenham: Edward Elgar.

Klenk, T., & Reiter, R. (2019). Post-New Public Management: Reform Ideas and Their Application in the Field of Social Services. *International Review of Administrative Sciences, 85*(1), 3–10.

Lacovino, N., Barsanti, S., & Cinquini, L. (2017). Public Organizations Between Old Public Administration, New Public Management and Public Governance: The Case of the Tuscany Region. *Public Organization Review: A Global Journal, 17*(1), 61–82.

Laughlin, R. (2011). Accounting Research, Policy and Practice: Worlds Together or Worlds Apart? In E. Evans, R. Burritt, & J. Guthrie (Eds.), *Bridging the Gap between Academic Accounting Research and Professional Practice* (pp. 21–30). Sydney: The Institute of Chartered Accountants in Australia.

Martin, R. (1997). Public Sector Downsizing: An Introduction. *The World Bank Economic Review, 13*(1), 1–22.

Mautz, R. K. (1988). Editorial: Monuments, Mistakes and Opportunities. *Accounting Horizons, 2*(2), 123–128.

Micallef, F., & Peirson, G. (1997). Financial Reporting of Cultural, Heritage, Scientific and Community Collections. *Australian Accounting Review, 7*(13), 31–37.

New Zealand Society of Accountants (NZSA). (1993). Infrastructural and Heritage Assets. *Accountants Journal, 72*(1), 38.

New Zealand Treasury. (2003). *Valuation Guidance for Heritage Assets.* Retrieved February 2, 2003, from www.treasury.govt.nz/valuation/cultural/default.asp.

Ouda, H. (2005). *Transition to Accrual Accounting in the Public Sector of Developed and Developing Countries: Problems and Requirements, With special focus on the Netherlands and Egypt* (p. 405). Veenendaal: Universal Press.

Ouda, H. (2007, February). Accrual Accounting Principles and Postulations in the Public Sector: Rhetoric or Reality. *Public Fund Digest, 7*(1). Washington, DC: The International Consortium on Governmental Financial Management (ICGFM).

Ouda, H. (2013, September 2–3). *A Practical Accounting Approach for Heritage Assets Under Accrual Accounting: With Special focus in Egypt.* Proceeding of the 14th Comparative International Governmental Accounting Research (CIGAR) Conference, 2013-Birmingham University, Birmingham.

Ouda, H. (2014). Towards a Practical Accounting Approach for Heritage Assets: An Alternative Reporting Model for the NPM Practices. *Journal of Finance and Accounting, 2*(2), 19–33.

Ouda, H. (2015). Making Governmental Accounting More Practice-Relevant: Practitioner's Perspective. *International Journal on Governmental Financial Management, XV(1)*, 9.

Ouda, H. (2016). Governmental Capital assets: How Far Should the Accounting Recognition of These Assets Go? *International Journal on Governmental Financial Management, XVI*(1), 24.

Pallot, J. (1990). The Nature of Public Sector Assets: A Response to Mautz. *Accounting Horizons, 4*(2), 79–85.

Pallot, J. (1992). Elements of a theoretical framework for public sector accounting. *Accounting, Auditing & Accountability Journal, 5*(1), 38–59.

Pollit, C., & Bouckaert, G. (2011). *Public Management Reform.* Oxford: Oxford University Press.

Rowles, T. (1991). Infrastructure and Heritage Asset Accounting. *Australian Accountant, 61(6), 69–74.*

Rowles, T. (1992). *Financial Reporting on Infrastructure and Heritage Assets by Public Sector Entities.* AARf Discussion Paper 17, Australian Accounting Research Foundation, Melbourne.

Rowles, T., Hutton, B., & Bellamy, S. (1998). *Accounting for Infrastructure Assets: The Case of Land Under Roads*. Annual Conference of Accounting Association of Australia and New Zealand, Adelaide.

Rutherford, B. (1992). Developing a Conceptual Framework for Central Government Financial Reporting, Intermediate Users and Direct Control. *Financial Accountability and Management, 8*(4), 265–280.

SAC-4 Statement of Accounting Concepts. *Definition and Recognition of Elements of Financial Statement*. Prepared by the Public Sector Accounting Standards Board of the Australian Accounting Research Foundation and by the Australian Accounting Standards Board.

Stanford, J. (2005, May 26–27). *Accounting for Heritage Assets: Devising a Variable Way Forward*. Paper Presented at 10th CIGAR (Comparative International Governmental Accounting Research conference), Poitiers University, Poitiers.

Stanton, P. J., & Stanton, P. A. (1997). Governmental Accounting for Heritage Assets: Economic, Social Implications. *International Journal of Social Economics, 24*(7), 988–1006.

Ström, S. (1997, April). *Accounting for Assets in Public Sector—Ifs and Hows*. Unpublished Paper, Stockholm.

Thompson, G. D. (1998). Cultural Capital and Accounting. *Accounting and Auditing and Accountability Journal, 12*(4), 394–492.

UK—Financial Reporting Standard FRS—30. (2009). *Heritage Assets, Accounting Standard Board*.

Walker, R. G., Clarke, F. L., & Dean, G. W. (2000). Options for Infrastructure Reporting. *Abacus, 1636*(2), 123–159.

Walker, R. G., Dean, G. W., & Edwards. (2004). Infrastructure Reporting: Attitudes of Preparers and Potential Users. *Financial Accountability & Management, 20*(4), 351–375.

Weers, G. (2016). *The Charitable Trust Model: an Alternative Approach for Department of Defense Accounting*. Monterey, CA: Naval Postgraduate School.

Wild, S. (2013). Accounting for Heritage, Cultural and community Assets—An Alternative Metrics from a New Zealand Maori education Institution. *Australasian Accounting Business and Finance Journal (AABFJ)., 7*(1), 3–22.

CHAPTER 4

Scope of General Purpose Financial Reporting: An Accountability Perspective

Susana Jorge

1 Introduction

Accountability, like transparency, has become one core issue of sound governance in the public sector. Although related, accountability and transparency are two different concepts, the latter regarding information availability and often being pointed as a requirement by the former (Lourenço et al. 2013).

Public sector reforms under the New Public Financial Management stream (Frederickson 1996; Pollitt 2000) have emphasized the importance of transparency as a prerequisite for accountability (Frederickson 1996; Pollitt 2000). As OECD (2001) points out, *"access to information, consultation and active participation in policy-making contributes to good governance by fostering greater transparency in policy-making; more accountability."* Therefore, the disclosure of budgetary and financial information (which can be named fiscal transparency) by public entities plays an important role since it is essential to enable citizens' and other users' judgments

"This study was conducted at the Research Centre in Political Science (UIDB/CPO/00758/2020), University of Minho/University of Évora and supported by the Portuguese Foundation for Science and Technology (FCT) and the Portuguese Ministry of Education and Science through national funds."

H. Ouda, *Practice-Relevant Accrual Accounting for the Public Sector*, Public Sector Financial Management,
https://doi.org/10.1007/978-3-030-51595-9_4

regarding the efficiency of public administrations and the proper use of the public resources that are made available to them.

The literature provides a wide range of definitions of transparency and accountability. Probably the most widely discussed concept is that of accountability, which essentially means *"the obligation to explain and justify conduct"* (Bovens 2007). Political accountability is an extremely important type of accountability within democracies, demanding transparency. Accordingly, while the concept of transparency refers to *"unfettered access by the public to timely and reliable information on decisions and performance in the public sector"* (Armstrong 2005), accountability is often defined as the obligation for public officials to report on the usage of public resources and answerability of government to the public to meet stated performance objectives (Armstrong 2005; Behn 2001; Wong and Welch 2004; Bovens 2007). In any case, these two concepts are strongly related since information access constitutes the first step of accountability processes (Meijer 2003).

For the purpose of this chapter, it is particularly interesting to consider the notion of fiscal (budgetary and financial) transparency, which can be regarded as *"an openness toward the public at large about government structure and functions, fiscal policy intentions, public sector accounts, and projections"* (Kopits and Craig 1998, p. 1, cited by Alt et al. 2006). The importance of fostering fiscal transparency on the part of public powers is clear, especially if one bears in mind the need to increase citizens' trust and, ultimately, improve the quality of democracy. In fact, in order to trust governments, citizens need to feel informed about public powers' intentions behind fiscal policy, the actual actions taken, and the long-term consequences of specific policies. Furthermore, the access to this, as well as other information within the public sector General Purpose Financial Reporting (GPFR), is also pivotal to other resource providers, such as investors and donors, to increase their trust in governing authorities and public officials, with benefits to public financial management and countries' economy overall.

Widely recognized in the literature (e.g., Piotrowski and Ryzin 2007; Caba Pérez et al. 2005, 2014), fiscal transparency is largely based on the provision of financial information to citizens and other users. Information is a basic condition to hold elected and appointed officers accountable for their actions. Effectively, accountability is exercised along the chain of principal–agent relationships (citizens, investors, and other stakeholders are principals, while politicians and public officials are the agents), implying that different needs and requirements might be at stake. Within this context, informational needs arise from the opacity of public sector entities, particularly concerning financial resources usage. Such needs call for data disclosure that would make possible for citizens and other users to realize how public entities are being efficient and effective (Pavan and Lemme 2006), underlining the importance of fiscal transparency defined as the complete disclosure of all relevant budgetary and financial information in an opportune and systematic way.

Democratic accountability requires governments to increase transparency, disclosing more budgetary and financial information to citizens and other stakeholders, promoting public expenditure scrutiny, and ultimately preventing corruption and waste of public resources. Consequently, budgetary and financial transparency, namely via disclosing GPFR, has become a pillar within public (financial) management reforms (Jorge 2019).

Within the International Public Sector Accounting Standards (IPSAS), the Conceptual Framework (CF) (IPSASB 2014, CF 1.4) underlines the role of GPFR in promoting financial transparency by governments and other public sector entities. Yet, questions can be raised about this assertion—despite the wide variety of information disclosed by the GPFR, public sector entities' accountability implies that the information be understood and useful for its users.

Usually, the GPFR comprises several types of financial and nonfinancial information. The IPSAS CF and IPSAS 1 (IPSASB 2014, 2019) explain that, apart from financial statements, the GPFR of a public sector entity includes information on service delivery activities and achievements in the current period, prospective financial and nonfinancial information (e.g., performance information, expected service delivery, and long-term consequences of current decisions), explanatory information (e.g., accounting policies), and information about compliance with legislative, regulatory, or other externally imposed regulations that affect the entity's management of resources. Still, the main focus continues to be on financial information, particularly financial statements, which in most countries is accrual-based and derived from business accounting principles and models, which essentially are the balance sheet, the income statement by nature and by function, the cash flow statement, the statement of changes in the net assets/equity, and the notes.

However, due to the importance of budgets as public policy instruments and authorizations for public spending being publicly approved, it is pivotal within the GPFR of a public sector entity or of a government to include additional information about compliance with public budgets. Comparison of budget and actual amounts (when budgets are published), either as an additional financial statement or as a budget column in the financial statements, is acknowledged as an important component of GPFR in the IPSASs, namely in IPSAS 1 and IPSAS 24 (IPSASB 2019), in order to disclose the accomplishments of the budgets finally approved. Nevertheless, while international standards endorse accrual-based accounting and reporting, in many countries budgets and budgetary reporting are still cash-based (Brusca et al. 2015).

Consequently, despite following a model that goes beyond what is comprised by the financial statements and which is generally broader than in the private sector, particularly due to budgetary reporting information (Jorge 2019), the GPFR in the public sector, especially if IPSAS-based, currently seems insufficient to allow for proper discharge of accountability.

Even if the scope of the GPFR in the public sector continues to focus on financial (and budgetary) information, there seems to be some prevalence of national roots and traditions in public sector reporting over international harmonization. Some countries/governments find the system they have in practice adequate for national policy-making, decision-making, and accountability, in order to increase trust and legitimize their activities (Manes-Rossi et al. 2016). Furthermore, some conflict seems to arise between international and regional public sector accounting harmonization, such as the one emerging in Europe (Aggestam and Brusca 2016), where region-specific reporting requirements within the EU call for a different type of accountability, including considering the link to the National Accounts (Caruana et al. 2019).

Finally, different users' needs nowadays go beyond the traditional financial and budgetary information, and require accountability concerning different issues (Manes-Rossi 2019), hence extending public sector entities' and governments' reporting to embrace other types of (nonfinancial) information. A few examples concern performance reporting (Steccolini 2004; Cunningham and Harris 2005; Marcuccio and Steccolini 2009), sustainability reporting, integrated reporting, and popular reporting (Marcuccio and Steccolini 2005; Yusuf et al. 2013; Cohen and Karatzimas 2015; Oprisor et al. 2016; Cohen et al. 2017; Guthrie et al. 2017; Biondi and Bracci 2018). The concept of public value accounting, which is still developing, seems to call for yet another reporting type, as governments and public sector organizations need to make visible how they create/destroy public value for public interest (Moore 2014; Bracci et al. 2019).

Henceforth, this chapter addresses the aforementioned perspectives as complementary to the traditional accounting reporting which are expected to enhance the discharge of accountability by public sector entities towards citizens and other stakeholders. Section 2 refers to budgetary reporting, followed by performance reporting in Sect. 3; sustainability, popular, and integrated reporting are discussed in Sect. 4, and finally public value accounting and the potential for a new reporting type are briefly presented in Sect. 5. The chapter concludes with final remarks concerning how the combinations of these perspectives in public sector entities' reporting may foster accountability.

2 Budgetary Reporting and the Link to the National Accounts—EU Context

Reforms in public sector accounting in the last decades have, among other things, introduced accrual business-type accounting and financial statements, thus allowing for increased accountability, as financial reporting has become more informative than when including only cash-based information. However, these improvements in accountability in the public sector setting can be questioned when the accounting and reporting system comes too close to business accounting (Dorn et al. 2019).

Accrual-based accounting has developed in the business context, where organizations are profit- and market-oriented and there are no public budgets. Accountability is needed from managers to investors on the use of investor money and on how income is generated. In the public sector realm, entities seek social well-being instead; hence it is paramount to show citizens, taxpayers and their representatives (politicians), oversighting bodies, and international organizations how public moneys are used to accomplish those purposes. Investors in markets, donors, and other funders may also require information on the profitability of their financial investments, but reporting on the accomplishment of public policies and sustainability of public services, as well as consequences in taxes, seems to be a prevailing purpose of GPFR of public sector entities and governments overall.

Therefore, even if accrual-based information is recognized as important, most business accounting principles and standards may constrain accountability outcomes in the public sector, as there are specific activities and dimensions to report about, for example, grants, transfers, taxes, and public domain assets (see other chapters in this book), for which market-based recognition and measurement criteria are not adequate, hence often leading to arbitrary estimations.

> *"Accrual accounting balance sheets ... show the entire intertemporal resource formation and consumption of the government and reflect the scope and quality of the public capital stock more transparently. Accrual accounting reveals the allocation of public resources over time, which may give rise to greater intergenerational equity and sustainable budgeting because under- and overinvestment is reduced."* But *"while accrual accounting may provide more information, the information may not be reliable"*. (Dorn et al. 2019)

Reporting on the accomplishment of public policies implies budgetary reporting, as budgets are, *par excellence*, instruments authorizing spending in implementation of legally approved public policies. The cases where budgets are accrual-based are rare (e.g., in Europe, UK, Austria, and Finland in central government; and in Germany in some local governments—see Jorge 2019), as most countries still use cash-based budgets and budgetary reporting (Brusca et al. 2015; Reichard and van Helden 2016). Therefore, accountability, especially towards citizens and their representatives, makes budgetary cash-based reporting perhaps the most important part within the GPFR of public sector entities and governments at large. Despite the introduction of accrual-based financial statements, roots of traditional public sector accounting remain in most jurisdictions. Moreover, the GPFR in each country, even if possibly moving towards the adoption of international standards, tends to reflect different accounting and reporting national traditions and priority purposes (Oulasvirta 2014; Manes-Rossi et al. 2016).

One example of this regards Finland, where the national tradition in accruals in business accounting, imported to public sector accounting, has made the country resist the adoption of the IPSAS (Oulasvirta 2014). The Finish Governmental Accounting Board has not accepted most of the pronouncements of the IPSASB CF, given the national priority to the purpose of accountability (instead of decision-making), prudence and historical cost (instead of market value), as well as the prevalence of the revenue/

expense model, whereby the operating statement is a more important financial statement within the public sector financial reporting than the balance sheet.

Another example is the case of Portugal—while adopting an IPSAS-based accrual accounting and reporting system (even if accrual-based accounting has been existent since 20 years), complementary statements were found important to include in the GPFR, intending, among other purposes, to improve accountability: budgetary reporting and management/cost accounting reporting (Jorge 2019). The former comprises the following cash-based budgetary reporting statements, where expenditure and revenue are displayed mainly according to their nature:

- Budgetary performance statement (reports on the way the budget execution is performed, leading to a budgetary deficit or surplus)
- Revenue budgetary execution statement
- Expenditure budgetary execution statement
- Statement of the execution of the Multiannual Investment Plan
- Notes to the budgetary statements

Cash-based budgetary information and budgetary reporting indeed continue to assume crucial importance (Ramkumar and Shapiro 2010), despite an era of accrual-based financial reporting. Reichard and van Helden (2016) note that, in several countries, budgetary reporting and financial reporting coexist and are decoupled, as the former follows the organization and rules as in the budget, while the latter does not actually report on the budget accomplishment. The authors further explain that *"a PSO* [public sector organization] *may need different accounting systems—cash- and accrual-based—serving different purposes and related stakeholders"* (Reichard and van Helden 2016).

Whereas creditors and other financiers may have primary interest in accrual-based information about the financial health of an entity or a government, public sector managers and politicians (and eventually citizens they represent) are more interested in cash-based budgetary information (Reichard and van Helden 2016; Jorge et al. 2019a). Several reasons seem to justify this (Reichard and van Helden 2016):

- Cash movements and language are easier and less ambiguous to understand and communicate—several nonexpert users, such as poli-

ticians, lack skills to properly interpret more advanced accrual information (e.g., depreciation, provisions, and deferrals).
- Main actors have longer and major expertise with cash-based budgetary reporting than with accrual-based financial reporting—not only politicians and public managers in understanding, but also civil servants in preparing; parliamentarians also better understand cash language when authorizing budget appropriations to be spent by government and when requiring accountability on those.
- Cash-based budgetary reporting is closely related to medium- and long-term fiscal policy, which politicians are more concerned with.

"Politicians are mainly interested in budgetary affairs including appropriations and comparing actual and budgeted appropriations; … accrual information in reports only receives little attention, irrespective of whether budgeting is cash- or accrual-based" (Reichard and van Helden 2016). Fundamental budgeting logic also explains that cash-based budgetary reporting continues to be seen as a fundamental instrument for accountability, especially from governments to parliaments, as it allows comparing cash-based appropriations with actual cash outflows, hence being an easy and straightforward control mode (Reichard and van Helden 2016). The value-added of accrual-based budgets and accrual-based financial reporting are yet to be explained and understood by the main users, especially by politicians and public managers, and even by those who assist them in preparing financial information for their use (Jorge et al. 2016, 2019a).

In the international reporting sphere, budgetary information, regardless of whether it is cash-based or accrual-based, is also the one used for international accountability purposes (Ramkumar and Shapiro 2010). Within the European Union (EU) context, Member States have to report on the accomplishment of convergent fiscal policies. While this reporting is based on the European System of Regional and National Accounts framework (ESA 2010), which allows preparing of the National Accounts (financial statistics), these are based on information that comes from public sector and governmental accounting, notably essentially from budgetary reporting, for most EU members, and is still cash-based. Because the National Accounts endorse an accrual-based reporting system, year-end adjustments need to be made when translating data from governmental accounting to the National Accounts, which may allow creativity/discretion and raises questions about the reliability of the data finally reported (Jesus and Jorge 2015). These data are the basis for monitoring Member

States' fiscal policy, such as the convergence criteria (public deficit and public debt) underlying the Euro currency.

Nevertheless, within the EU, mainly for supranational accountability reasons, there is a need for an 'integrated' reporting, linking accrual-based financial statements, cash-based budgetary reporting, and financial statistics reporting (Dabbicco 2018; Jorge et al. 2018; Montesinos et al. 2019).

Since 2013 the EU has embarked on a project to develop European Public Sector Accounting Standards (EPSAS), addressing more technical issues starting from 2016. EPSAS, when they come to exist, are supposed to allow not only regional harmonization among EU Member States' public sector accrual-based accounting and financial reporting (Aggestam and Brusca 2016), but also convergence with the reporting under the National Accounts and the ESA (EC, Eurostat 2013). EPSAS aim at more reliable reporting by EU Member States, regarding the debt and deficit levels as required by the Maastricht Treaty (EC, Eurostat 2017). However, these standards are not expected to address budgeting or budgetary reporting, given that this follows budget laws often specific to each country.

> *In order for the EPSAS to achieve the ambitious target of being viewed as building blocks that could bridge the gap between micro- and macro-reporting levels, the input of various disciplines is required.*
>
> *The EPSAS might be seen as a multi-disciplinary project, in which actors from different fields* [accountants, auditors, lawyers/public administrators and policy-makers, economists, statisticians, ...] *work together, each drawing on their disciplinary knowledge and methods, using a real synthesis of approaches.* (Jorge et al. 2019b)

Therefore, it can be said that EPSAS targets the improvement of public sector financial accountability within the EU. But, to fulfill this purpose, as underlined by Caruana et al. (2019), several issues need to be considered:

- A proper development of EPSAS requires a "concerted multidisciplinary approach" to bridge the gap between conceptual differences that are likely to remain between financial public sector or governmental accounting, budgeting, and National Accounting; this would benefit from increased collaboration between professionals and academics in these three fields, combining their knowledge in a holistic involvement.

- Specific and particular characteristics of the public sector need to be attended to, namely the central role of budgets and budgetary accounting (rather than the balance sheet).
- Reliability of whatever reports are to be considered points to an increased role of auditing and proper audit procedures that secure the required public oversight.

3 Performance Reporting

The concept of accountability in the public sector has changed over the last decades. The notion of accountability towards the parliament regarding the budget accomplishment has changed to include accountability of public management performance (namely efficiency and effectiveness) towards the customers/citizens. This has implied changes in the way public sector entities' performance is evaluated, including nonfinancial measures and new ways of reporting and communicating these to stakeholders (Steccolini 2004; Oprisor et al. 2016).

Brusca and Montesinos (2016) explain that the financial information provided in the accounting and budgetary statements of many public entities is insufficient to achieve public sector accounting objectives and needs to be supplemented with performance information. Performance is measured and reported by means of performance indicators that account for the economy, efficiency, and effectiveness of public resources. Performance reporting is a means to disseminate information to stakeholders on public sector entities' performance for accountability purposes.

Therefore, performance reporting has been claimed worldwide as a means to achieve increased public accountability by public sector organizations and governments, leading to greater efficiency and effectiveness in delivering public services (Cunningham and Harris 2005). Performance reporting is also often associated with enhancing the entity's reputation and legitimacy and external support next to citizens and other stakeholders. Nevertheless, its implementation often results from external coercive and political pressures (Gomes 2018).

The existence of a uniform statewide (management) accounting system, as well as political-level support, are key issues for the implementation of performance reporting (Cunningham and Harris 2005).

The relationship between performance reporting and accountability in the public sector is based on the idea that the former, being externally oriented, supports monitoring the actions of politicians and public managers, helps learning and improving, namely by comparing actual performance with expected results, and can be used as a benchmark (Gomes 2018).

Cunningham and Harris (2005) evidenced several functions and benefits of performance reporting in public sector entities:

- It contributes to the (internal) management process—it requires clear definitions of responsibilities and of the relationship of the performance to the entity's objectives; it is integrated in the strategic and business plans system, being closely linked to the budget activity.
- It has (external) control function, though with some flexibility, given that the report tends to focus on end-line indicators (regardless of the policies to reach them); still, the reporting of performance to the parliament and central government or to the public motivates public managers or (local) politicians to pay attention to those indicators.
- It allows improving and communicating the results of the governmental activity and therefore enhancing accountability.
- The visibility of the performance reporting process is viewed as causing public sector entities to be more accountable, allowing for better monitoring of public policies and of the budget.
- It includes performance indicators that may be centrally defined as a homogeneous and standardized framework, allowing for comparability between entities and local governments, as well as for auditing the results; these are also easy to be externally communicated, for example, using the *media*.
- The performance indicators to be considered in performance reporting may be defined by the public, especially in the context of local governments, increasing public engagement in the entities' management.
- It allows for enhancing communication, performance information being used in the budget and other legislative processes and by legislative committees.

"Top-level control combined with incentives to use performance measures in local management, and the flexibility of local managers to manage on their own," is favorable to performance reporting being seen as an accountability tool. But, if there are reasons for accepting the ability of performance reporting systems to achieve accountability and effectiveness in government entities, *"performance reporting systems per se are not sufficient*

to achieve the desired accountability and effectiveness and (…) the ability of the system to foster communication is more important than performance indicators themselves" (Cunningham and Harris 2005).

Performance evaluation and reporting in government organizations are considered complicated tasks given the multiplicity of actions and objectives to which they are subjected, adding to the existing political pressures. Nevertheless, the systematic monitoring and evaluating of public sector activities, and communicating the results via performance reporting, have been pushed by the increased overall request for accountability, transparency, efficiency, and responsiveness (Gomes 2018).

Accordingly, performance reporting of accountability is strongly associated with the need to measure, report, and manage public sector organizations' performance (Gomes 2018). Performance measures, namely indicators, are therefore important components of performance reporting (Cunningham and Harris 2005; Van Helden and Reichard 2018).

There are several types of performance indicators of a public sector organization that can possibly be included in the performance reporting, which embraces the whole of the transformation process of the organization: single indicators of inputs, throughputs, outputs and outcomes, and efficiency and effectiveness indicators resulting from combining the former performance indicators. *"The organization often defines objectives with regard to its transformation process. An objective is translated into measurable aspects through performance indicators (PIs), and subsequently targeted (ex ante) and realized (ex post) figures about these PIs are compared, both for accountability reasons and for considering corrective actions"* (Van Helden and Reichard 2018). The users of this performance information, while they may be internal to the organization (managers for decision-making and management purposes), are to a large extent external, inasmuch as public sector organizations report on performance for the purposes of external control and accountability, for example, to inform oversight authorities, the parliament, *media*, or citizens (Van Helden and Reichard 2018).

In the performance reporting process, there is a risk of too much concentration on the definition of indicators, targets, and monitoring, more than in the reporting itself, namely for accountability towards citizens and customers. Additionally, output measures tend to be used instead of outcome measures, because the latter are often difficult to define and sometimes not controllable by the organizations. Yet, most of the time, output measures are not so important to the public, who pay better attention to qualitative factors (Cunningham and Harris 2005). Moreover, public sector organizations need to report on the accomplishment of societally relevant goals (Van Helden and Reichard 2018).

The literature has shown that, for accountability, as for decision-making purposes, often, several stakeholders do not appreciate financial information. Technical complexity inherent to financial information, especially if accrual-based, makes nonfinancial performance information the preferred type, namely by politicians (e.g., Askim 2007; Liguori et al. 2012; Jorge et al. 2019a) and also by those they represent, that is, citizens. Except for some rare experts (e.g., the *media* or public commentators), citizens do not use public sector financial information directly, but resort to 'information brokers' (e.g., journalists) in order to understand such information (Lourenço et al. 2016).

Steccolini (2004) evidenced that the annual financial reporting, often seen as a medium to discharge external accountability, may not be enough for that purpose in the local government. Financial reporting seems to be used essentially by internal users to the organizations, if read at all. Therefore, if local authorities merely comply with legal pronouncements and report financial information, sometimes not even accrual-based yet, they do not discharge enough accountability to external stakeholders, namely citizens. Without performance reporting, or with a type of financial reporting where service performance evaluation is not given enough importance, the role of annual reporting as a tool for accountability is questionable. This reporting should provide *"comprehensive, understandable and reliable (financial and non-financial) information"* to be the *"basis for the evaluation of the public organisation's actions and results"* (Steccolini 2004). It should also allow stakeholders to monitor governmental activities and results, and to be involved in the definition of governmental objectives.

The IPSASB has also acknowledged the need to complete GPFR with performance information, issuing Recommended Practice Guidance (RPG) 3 for reporting service performance information (IPSASB 2015). Performance information is regarded as important as long as it meets financial reporting objectives and qualitative characteristics. The boundary and period of performance reporting is the same as the one for financial reporting. Performance indicators (both quantitative and qualitative) are recognized as the main important tools to assess and report on service performance objectives; total costs of the services are also included in the information to be displayed. It should be considered planned and actual information for the reporting period, as well as actual information for the previous reporting period. Performance information reports are also to include cross-references to the financial statements where appropriate, contributing to a more comprehensive GPFR (IPSASB 2015, §§38–40). Professional judgment may be required in deciding what service performance information should be disclosed to users, so that they understand the basis of the information disclosed, and receive a concise overview of the entity's service performance.

RPG 3 establishes principles for reporting service performance information which are important to understand the purposes of performance reporting (IPSASB 2015, §§32–37):

- An entity should present service performance information that is useful to users for accountability and decision-making purposes, so this information should allow users to assess the extent, efficiency, and effectiveness of the entity's service performance.
- When used in combination with the information in an entity's financial statements, service performance information should enable users to assess the entity's finances in the context of its achievement of service performance objectives and vice versa.
- Service performance information presented should take into account the entity's specific circumstances, namely the services that the entity provides, the nature of the entity, and the regulatory environment in which the entity operates.
- Aggregation or disaggregation of service performance information should be at a level that conveys a meaningful understanding of the entity's service performance achievements; and the information reported should be sufficiently detailed for users to hold the entity accountable for its service performance, particularly its performance with respect to its service performance objectives.
- Comparability to other entities can be difficult to achieve in the context of service performance information, since diverse services are provided. Inter-entity comparability may need to be traded off against relevance, so that service performance objectives and their related performance indicators are chosen to be relevant to the service performance situation of the entity.

Regarding the organization of service performance information, RPG 3 suggests the elaboration of the *"statement of service performance,"* which involves organizing information into a tabular or statement form (IPSASB

2015, §78). This statement will support understandability and comparability of (quantitative and qualitative) performance indicators, which are the basis for the success of performance evaluation and reporting. However, in cases where service performance information is provided in narrative form, a mixture of these case studies with tables has to be considered (IPSASB 2015, §79).

Performance management systems have been developed since several years in many countries, with a special predominance in local government. Therefore, one may say that there is already some experience with performance reporting practices (Van Helden and Reichard 2018). Brusca and Montesinos (2016) compared the state of performance reporting practice in several countries, showing different states of development, with countries like Australia, Canada, and the United States being in a more advanced situation than France, Italy, Portugal, and Spain. Gomes (2018) also explains that many countries started including performance reporting as a complement to financial reporting, and the development of performance reporting systems has been influenced by different contexts and by the successful introduction of the New Public Management (NPM). In some jurisdictions, public sector entities' performance reporting is required by law, while in others it is voluntary, hence depending on the public sector entities' will to enhance accountability and inform decision-makers on nonfinancial performance matters.

Marcuccio and Steccolini (2009) showed how, in the context of local authorities, voluntary extended performance reporting practices emerged, while only financial reporting (namely budgetary accounting and accrual-based financial statements) had been extensively regulated. This voluntary behavior seems to have signaled the weakness of existing compulsory legal reports. Performance reporting appears as an additional effort for organizations to communicate performance to external stakeholders, hence reinforcing accountability; it was noted as a specific reference to the results achieved in social and economic development areas. A clear link was evidenced between the content of voluntary performance reports and the local authorities' type of activities performed and strategic priorities.

Overall, organizations seem to resort to voluntary performance reporting to disclose strengths of specificities of their governance and management, to overcome the fact that traditional accounting and reporting systems are not always effective communication tools. Accordingly, there is no standardized model of performance reporting. If performance reporting is to also serve as a benchmark across comparable organizations, it seems desirable that a general model should exist, given that a variety of models may put accountability into question (Marcuccio and Steccolini 2009). A legally imposed performance reporting model would perhaps be desirable, at least at a national level, as there is evidence that, in this way, it would lead to a wider implementation (Cunningham and Harris 2005). However, undesirable behaviors could raise resistance to such coercion. Maybe because of this, several performance reporting practices in the public sector have been issued in the form of non-legally binding recommendations (IPSASB 2015; Brusca and Montesinos 2016; Gomes 2018).

4 Sustainability, Popular and Integrated Reporting

Pressures towards greater accountability by public sector organizations and governments overall have increased under the NPM stream, whereby informing external stakeholders, especially citizens, about the use of public resources should contribute to increase engagement in public policies and management. However, nowadays, as discussed in this chapter, it is generally accepted that the annual financial reporting (either in single format or consolidated) hardly responds to the needs of most users of information of public sector organizations. If it can satisfy needs of users such as internal managers and financial directors, or external financial analysts, investors, and oversighting bodies, it clearly does not meet information needs of external stakeholders, such as citizens (taxpayers or public service consumers) or companies located in a certain territory (Manes-Rossi 2019).

Traditional financial reporting is considered capable neither of depicting the real impact of public resources on outcomes (Steccolini 2004) nor of fulfilling the accountability needs of the wider nonexpert citizenry. Financial accounts present only one standpoint of the organizations' reality, and are too complex, requiring accounting-specific knowledge to be understood (Biondi and Bracci 2018). *"Consequently, there is a need for accessible, timely, objective and clear information, which can be understood by non-specialists"* (Manes-Rossi 2019). Therefore, new accountability tools have been proposed, namely sustainability reporting, integrated reporting, and popular (financial) reporting. Another additional concept seems to be emerging—an integrated popular reporting (Manes-Rossi 2019). None of these frameworks of external reporting to stakeholders has, so far, binding standards for public sector organizations (Biondi and Bracci 2018).

Sustainability reporting, popular financial reporting, and integrated reporting have been seen as different accountability innovations. However, Biondi and Bracci (2018) underline that they *"may end up just in a fad or fashion uptake,"* not leading to the intended effects of increasing accountability, but merely constituting a managerial fashion. All these reporting tools seem to be more shaped by the preparers (international bodies and the organizations adopting them, for political legitimacy) than customized for the users' perspective. The authors also alert us to the fact that, due to more commonalities than differences between these types of reporting, the improvements in effective public accountability when passing from one to another may not be significant, as they may appear as similar concepts with new labels.

4.1 Sustainability Reporting

NPM reforms and United Nations pressures for attaining sustainable development goals have brought to the public sector realm concerns about reporting on social and environmental matters, especially since the 1990s (Giacomini et al. 2018; Manes-Rossi 2019). Social and environmental reporting (focusing on performance of social and environmental policies), today more commonly known as sustainability reporting, started to be introduced in public sector organizations inspired by the search of increased sustainability and democratic accountability (Marcuccio and Steccolini 2005; Biondi and Bracci 2018). It has to report in the impact of the output produced by public sector organizations on the community and on the environment (Manes-Rossi 2019).

As a separate report or part of the annual report, sustainability reporting started to be seen as a way to complete the GPFR, enhancing organizations' external communication, increasing their legitimacy, and allowing them to deal with the emergence of environmental and sustainability issues. It may be seen *"as a response to the ... weaknesses of accounting and management control systems in responding to internal and external users' needs, to the ambiguity and complexity of methods of measuring the performance of public organizations, and to the absence of performance evaluation guidelines"* (Marcuccio and Steccolini 2005).

Several overall reasons for public sector organizations to adopt sustainability reporting may be leadership, accountability (legitimacy), stakeholder engagement (building trust), and financial benefit in accessing capital (Farneti and Guthrie 2009; Manes-Rossi 2019). Marcuccio and Steccolini (2005) classify the reasons for adopting sustainability reporting in public sector organizations (namely local authorities) into those associated to a rational/technical perspective (economic forces) and/or those within an institutional perspective (sociopsychological forces). The first group includes reasons such as to acquire management tools designed to measure costs and evaluate performance at the organizational and individual levels; to obtain funding; and to acquire management tools designed to govern relations with external partners. In the second group the following reasons can be found: to emulate other entities that have already implemented such reporting; to be seen, internally and externally, as innovative and progressive/pioneer; and to anticipate mandatory practices of sustainability reporting. The latter relate to *"willingness to signal the innovativeness and progressiveness of the management techniques,"* whereas the former concern *"the search for improvements in financial and nonfinancial performance through better accounting, reporting and management systems."*

While both groups of reasons can be combined for the adoption of sustainability reporting, Marcuccio and Steccolini (2005) evidenced that sociopsychological forces often prevail. Accordingly, sustainability reporting may become a management 'fashion,' being influenced by ongoing processes of public sector reforms, and not reflecting real sustainability concerns. When reform processes pressure for public managers and politicians to demonstrate conformity to norms of rationality, efficiency, and effectiveness, and to show improvements in financial and service performance, sustainability reporting may not lead to enhanced accountability to the society. It may instead be adopted as a management technique believed as rational and progressive, to show those who scrutinize public managers' activity about how they perform on conformity with more rational norms and practices.

The Global Reporting Initiative (GRI)[1] is the international framework acknowledged to support the preparation of sustainability reporting (Farneti and Guthrie 2009). But its comprehensiveness makes it difficult to organizations, including those in the public sector, to gather all the necessary information (Manes-Rossi 2019). Therefore, organizations

[1] https://www.globalreporting.org/Pages/default.aspx.

adopting it cherry-pick parts of the standards they wish to apply (Biondi and Bracci 2018).

Some other constraints have been presented to the adoption of sustainability reporting by public sector organizations: lack of political and management commitment with sustainability matters, reporting on sustainability information not being legally compulsory, lack of resources for implementation (cost issues), and lack of organizational capability overall, namely in small-size entities (Giacomini et al. 2018).

In some jurisdictions (e.g., Italian local government), the enthusiasm about sustainability reporting seems to be fading. Initially it was seen as a 'bait' to meet citizens' expectations and increase stakeholders' engagement. However, as it has become a mere description of tendencies of some indicators, it has lost attractiveness to the public and its role as an accountability tool is diminishing (Giacomini et al. 2018). One way of overcoming this problem may be by promoting the role of this type of report *"as a tool to legitimize the local politician's actions given its provision in political and electoral programs as the result of a sustainable development commitment. This could enhance accountability in the social and environmental aspects."* Furthermore, because entities tend to focus on mandatory financial reporting obligations, especially when resources are scarce, perhaps if sustainability reporting comes to be legally compulsory (recognized standards), its intended accountability effects may become effective (Giacomini et al. 2018). Moreover, a binding regulatory framework could also allow for a more standardized reporting model, allowing for comparability and benchmarking of sustainable development practices.

Governments and public sector organizations overall have a central role in implementing sustainable development goals, ensuring a socially responsible society and a more sustainable future. Becoming a widespread practice in the public sector, sustainability reporting can increase the interest of public opinion in social and environmental issues. The interest of sustainability reporting in the public sector may also be enhanced if reporting and sustainability accounting models that more adequately suit the public sector are developed and disseminated (Marcuccio and Steccolini 2005).

4.2 *Popular Reporting*

As it has been made clear in this chapter, constant pressures for more accountability have required public sector organizations to adopt new forms of reporting. Another of these alternative tools for communicating effectively to the stakeholders has been popular reporting (Steccolini 2004; Biondi and Bracci 2018), which can therefore be presented as a document supposed to facilitate communication between governments and citizens (Manes-Rossi 2019). Compared to sustainability reporting (and integrated reporting), popular reporting addresses mainly the citizens, while the other types of reporting address several stakeholders (Biondi and Bracci 2018). It started as *"a movement targeting [] the preparation and publication of reports especially addressing citizens' profile"* (Cohen and Karatzimas 2015), acknowledging that poor financial reporting and budgeting tools could impair democratic accountability.

Popular (financial) reporting can be defined as a simplified (not simplistic) report that provides financial information concerning government entities and governmental activities in a comprehensive and simple manner, in order to be understood by users who are not familiar with accounting and financial management issues (Yusuf et al. 2013; Cohen et al. 2017; Manes-Rossi 2019). Targeted users of popular reporting include typically citizens, businesses, the *media*, and community groups interested in understanding the dynamics of government finance. Average citizens find typical governmental financial statements too long, complicated, and confusing. Therefore, it is important to provide such information and improved transparency and accountability by delivering more user-friendly financial reports, helping non-accounting experts understanding traditional financial reports (Cohen et al. 2017; Biondi and Bracci 2018). Still, people with a lower level of instruction tend to have more difficulties in understanding the information provided by popular reports, which points to a need of giving privilege to more qualitative (not so technical) data (Biancone et al. 2016).

Popular reporting is believed as *"important for facilitating communication pathways between government and citizens, and fulfilling the democratic goals of accountability and transparency in governance"* (Yusuf et al. 2013). It aims at sustaining citizens' trust on government, and encourages citizen engagement in the decision-making of public organizations (Biondi and Bracci 2018). Popular reports are tools governments can resort to for developing informed, invested public participation (Jordan et al. 2016). One of the objectives of popular reporting is also to contribute to the construction of a democratic political system, through equality in access to governmental financial information among all citizens (Oliveira et al. 2018)

This type of reporting started in the 1990s and is quite widespread in the USA, Canada, and Australia, at local government level (Yusuf et al. 2013; Biondi and Bracci 2018; Manes-Rossi 2019); to a lesser extent, a similar type of information is also distributed to citizens in some European jurisdictions, for example, the UK (Manes-Rossi 2019). But, in principle, popular reports can be developed regardless of the accounting regulations and principles applied (e.g., national standards, IPSAS, or EPSAS), the time frame (budget and/or end of the year report), and the level of government (central, regional, or local) (Biondi and Bracci 2018).

The North American professional organizations—Governmental Accounting Standards Board and Government Finance Officers Association—started developing popular reporting in an effort to unite the concepts of financial reporting and of municipal communication (Oliveira et al. 2018). These organizations, together with the Association of Government Accountants, developed different types of popular reports—Popular Annual Financial Reports, Service Effort and Accomplishment Reports, and Citizen-centric Reporting—and agreed on some general principles to be followed when preparing popular reports (Jordan et al. 2016). Mostly relying on information of official financial statements, popular reports should be visually appealing (e.g., with graphic presentations, diagrams, and charts), clear and understandable (avoiding complicated and technical terms), with fewer pages, and including relevant community-oriented information, such as population figures, regional characteristics and government goals for the community, performance report on key missions and service, and detailed expenses and revenues (e.g., investments, expenses per areas, taxes) (Jordan et al. 2016; Cohen et al. 2017). The information should be future-oriented, namely looking at the year ahead. Biancone et al. (2016) evidenced suggestions citizens themselves made of nonfinancial information to be included in popular reporting, referring to cities' work policies, architectural barriers, policies in favor of victims of violence, policies for the new hires, names of sector managers, and councils with financial capacity.

Despite general common guiding principles, popular reports do not follow binding standards; they are not comparable either, as cities and organizations tend to develop their own model/contents, disclosed on voluntary basis, leading to large diversity. This also creates limits to the auditability, hence reducing the validity of the information included in these reports (Yusuf et al. 2013; Biancone et al. 2016; Biondi and Bracci 2018).

As to the possible actors within public sector organizations involved in the preparation of such reports, Yusuf et al. (2013) evidenced finance and budget departments as the most frequently implicated. However, other actors are city/county managers, communication and public relations staff, executive officers such as the mayor or council members, and the auditing department. The technology department and the department of management services may also participate, though with reduced contribution. This reveals that often organizations' concerns go beyond financial information, seeking to show *"the 'big picture' conveyed by the numerical data"* (Yusuf et al. 2013).

As interesting example is the popular report of the city of Turin (Italy) (Biancone et al. 2016), started through a collaboration with the local university, which provided the knowledge and expertise needed, evidencing how the academics provided the legitimation for the development of the project (Biondi and Bracci 2018).

Several reasons have been identified for local governments issuing popular financial reports, including informing citizens of their government's finances (transparency), addressing citizens' needs for financial information (accountability), and increasing citizen engagement and public participation (supporting governments and involving in public policies decision-making). Additionally, evidence was found that *"local governments' decisions regarding the adoption and practicing of popular reporting may be driven by specific management and local constituency factors not measured (e.g., responding to government scandals, citizen trust concerns, performance management emphasis, etc.) instead of sociodemographic and political factors"* (Yusuf et al. 2013).

In other words, popular (financial) reports are important to inform common citizens about government's finances, for reasons related to accountability to taxpayers and voters, transparency, and knowing where and how government resources are used, as well as the contributions of information and knowledge being better engaged (Oliveira et al. 2018). However, to be effective, they need to include information that is relevant to citizens—*"to be of value to citizens, the information provided must be in context and relevant to issues that citizens care about. Information also needs to be provided that allows a basis for understanding the impacts on citizens"* (Jordan et al. 2016). Also, popular reports have to be made accessible to the general public, using formats and mediums to easily reach their target addressees. Preferable dissemination means have been displaying the reports online, on the organizations' official websites, or making them available in printed format in city halls and other administrative buildings, and in public libraries (Yusuf et al. 2013; Biancone et al. 2016; Cohen et al. 2017). However, these means of dissemination assume that constituents are interested enough to actively look for the information. Mailing to citizens, namely in a printed format, and distributing in selected events (e.g., local conferences, meetings, and fairs) and as press releases, are less preferred, perhaps due to the high costs involved, compared to possible low effectiveness in attaining the intended effects (Yusuf et al. 2013).

Other experiences have been considered (Biancone et al. 2016): sharing popular reports on social networks, namely the institutional Facebook profile of the city, recording comments about contents obtained by the social media interactions; making annual public presentations where printed copies are distributed, this distribution being also done to professional associations and unions in the city; distributed directly to citizens using iPhone applications; publicized in a specific banner at bus stops and in buses themselves; developing a specific website dedicated to the city's popular reporting; and disseminating leaflets in hairdressers'.

Despite the undisputed usefulness of popular reporting as an accountability medium, international experience reveals a lack of active dissemination of popular reports from reporting entities to citizens. Some (local) governments do not seem to see popular reports as *"an avenue for gaining active citizen involvement. Whether this is because the majority of local governments simply are not interested in or concerned with involving citizens in the decision making process, or because they believe there are better avenues than popular reporting for gaining this involvement, is not clear"* (Yusuf et al. 2013).

On the other hand, citizens do not seem to be so interested either. Alternative ways of disseminating (e.g., Internet, social media), as well as certain presentation formats, can be used to attract citizens' interest, making them more aware of popular financial reporting contents, hence enhancing its use. Compared to the paper-based traditional format, the Internet is seen as a more efficient medium to increase reporting frequency, and improve visibility via better presentation and format (Cohen and Karatzimas 2015; Cohen et al. 2017).

Even if citizens may value information disclosing regardless of the format, the presentation format of a given popular report has indeed different value to users, and this can be boosted by using modern technologies such as the Internet, which therefore appears as a potent mean to support accountability and citizens' engagement in government strategic decision processes (Lourenço et al. 2015; Cohen et al. 2017). The format of popular reporting that better satisfies citizens' needs (in terms of usefulness and ease of use) can be analyzed by considering several dimensions: information quality (scope, completeness, and clarity), visual appearance, website navigability and usability, overall citizen satisfaction, and the effect of each format to the municipality image (Cohen et al. 2017). Among different possible formats of popular reports, the preference for websites specifically developed for that purpose (over PDF reports or flipping books, for example) evidences that new technologies can be strategically used by public sector organizations, namely in the local government context, to enhance democratic accountability in what concerns disclosing financial information to effectively reach citizens overall. Moreover, new technologies combined with the Internet allow overcoming dependence on other means (e.g., *media*) for this, also reducing printing costs and maintaining mailing lists, *"permitting data merging and processing, linking to additional sources,* [and] *real-time open data updates"* (Cohen et al. 2017).

Apart from content and dissemination issues, several other challenges to the preparation of popular reporting have been evidenced, namely by those who do not (yet) use this tool: lack of knowledge about it; the use of other means to provide such information; rarity of use by the public (more interest in the budget); not believing that this reporting is the adequate method to communicate with citizens; and lack of financial and personnel resources to prepare it, as it is also very time-consuming. Therefore, mainly due to resource constraints, popular reporting is often not a priority (Yusuf et al. 2013).

4.3 Integrated Reporting

A more recent concept of reporting coming from the business companies' context is that of integrated reporting (Manes-Rossi 2019), which seems to have derived from extending the concept of sustainability reporting, hence also endorsing sustainable development matters (Guthrie et al. 2017; Biondi and Bracci 2018). Integrated reporting has been seen as a new accountability enhancement tool for public sector entities (Oprisor et al. 2016).

Integrated reporting is one single document prepared by an organization, including financial and nonfinancial information, embracing information about all forms of (tangible and intangible) resources that are considered important for the organization's long-lasting prosperity (IIRC

2013; Cohen and Karatzimas 2015; Biondi and Bracci 2018). According to the International Integrated Reporting Council (IIRC),[2] it is a strategic and future-oriented communication tool between the entity and its stakeholders. The IR Framework[3] explains that *"an integrated report is a concise communication about how an organization's strategy, governance, performance and prospects, in the context of its external environment, lead to the creation of value in the short, medium and long term."* The underlining idea is that an organization uses resources of different natures—the so-called six capitals (financial, manufactured, intellectual, human, social and relationship, and natural) (IIRC 2013)—which should interact to *"create value* [for stakeholders], *thus augmenting all the various capitals"* (Manes-Rossi 2019).

> *The intent of integrated reporting is to ensure that organizations report on their building or depletion of any of the capital sources.* (Adams and Simnett 2011)

Preparing and implementing integrated reporting in not only about information disclosure. It compels organizations to think holistically about their strategy and plans, analyzing the impacts of their activities on the different capitals. 'Integrated thinking' (Adams and Simnett 2011; Guthrie et al. 2017) *"implies that all actors inside an organization share a common vision and values and that strategies, programmes and operations are designed coherently"* towards integrated decision-making and value creation over time (Manes-Rossi 2019). But these internal dynamics are not easily attained in many organizations. Moreover, the implementation of integrated reporting depends on adequate (management) accounting technologies (e.g., XBRL), political and economic contexts, and internal engagement processes (Guthrie et al. 2017). An integrated reporting approach emphasizes a commitment of the organization to transparency, reducing the level of detail in a report and focusing on a concise representation of the most strategically (qualitative) material issues for the organization (Adams and Simnett 2011; Guthrie et al. 2017).

[2] https://integratedreporting.org/the-iirc-2/.

[3] https://integratedreporting.org/what-the-tool-for-better-reporting/. https://integratedreporting.org/.

The following are presented as benefits of integrated reporting for (private sector) organizations (Oprisor et al. 2016)[4]: endorsement of a long-term vision and decision-making, leading to more informed decision-making and improved risk management; better assessment of the organization overall and of its prospects by investors and other stakeholders; better resource allocation, according to the long-term objectives of the organization and of the society, contributing to building trust and creating value.

The adoption of integrated reporting in the private sector is still mostly voluntary, being addressed by several *"market-driven initiatives,"* such as the aforementioned IIRC Framework, and the OECD Guidelines for Multinational Enterprises. The EU Directive on disclosure of nonfinancial and diversity information (2014/95/EU) is one of the rare cases that is *"legislation-driven"* where the adoption of integrated reporting is mandatory for certain companies (Biondi and Bracci 2018).

Integrated reporting has recently been encouraged in the public sector too, namely via the Public Sector Pioneer Network developed in 2014 by the IIRC (with partners such as CIPFA, the World Bank, and others). One important publication of the Network was IIRC (2016),[5] *"an introductory guide with the aim of encouraging public sector leaders and their staff to implement <IR> to improve governance, accountability, trust and transparency regarding the use of resources and the value creation process for stakeholders"* (Biondi and Bracci 2018). Nevertheless, cases of public sector organizations in the world following an integral reporting approach are still scarce; despite its increasing importance, *"there has been more discussion than actual diffusion"* (Biondi and Bracci 2018). Proper implementation in the public sector has raised some doubts, namely by academics and some professionals, given that the integrated reporting framework has been designed considering the needs of investors in the context of listed companies, and requires adjustments to be properly adapted to the public administrations setting (Cohen and Karatzimas 2015; Oprisor et al. 2016; Manes-Rossi 2019).

Oprisor et al. (2016) explain that the key dimensions of the integrated reporting framework could be addressed to the public sector organizations, as they are not constrained to the private businesses realm:

[4] https://www.youtube.com/watch?v=EFm0sKeBLh0.

[5] https://integratedreporting.org/resource/focusing-on-value-creation-in-the-public-sector/.

- The value creation process is based on flows and elements that are similar in the public sector (such as capitals, activities, inputs, outputs, outcomes); concepts such as value preservation and capital maintenance also suit well.
- The content elements are not restrictive towards public sector entities; there is also strategic planning (e.g., public institutions' master plans for 5–7 years), connectivity of information (both horizontally, between agencies on the same level, and vertically, between agencies on different levels), as well as stakeholder inclusiveness.
- Certain adjustments can be made, for example, more/fewer capitals, resource limitations addressed, and political dimension inserted in the model.
- The main principles are paramount for the public sector as well, namely those of materiality, conciseness, and which are the stakeholders who need to be engaged.

Integrated reporting is believed to offer the opportunity for public sector organizations to produce a more flexible and meaningful reporting (Adams and Simnett 2011). Considering that NPM pressures to adopt businesslike approaches to delivering public services continue to require new information and measurement criteria, public sector financial reporting must adapt. *"Integrated reporting is a new approach to reporting that may represent the next evolution of accounting,"* ensuring *"reporting is more holistic, strategic, responsive, material and relevant across multiple time frames."* It can become a more widespread practice in public sector organizations, which would *"benefit from moving beyond compliance-based reporting to a report that emphasises trust and transparency"* (Adams and Simnett 2011).

The core construct behind integrated reporting reveals the matching of several dimensions of public accountability, *"thus enabling the reporting system as an accountability tool for public sector entities (allowing users to understand and judge the most important aspects of an organization's activity)"* (Oprisor et al. 2016).

However, several challenges need to be considered, even if the international framework is further adapted and becomes overall acceptable by the public sector (Adams and Simnett 2011):

- Some organizations may not have available the information required to prepare such a report.

- The preparation involves costs that may be difficult to bear by some organizations—size and capability issues need to be taken into account.
- Auditing integrated reports are likely to require material assessment of qualitative elements (e.g., related to social and environmental matters) with which auditors are not so familiar.

Management accounting assumes particular importance in supporting the implementation of integrated reporting in public sector organizations as well, inasmuch as it allows for linking financial and nonfinancial information and facilitates the identification of strategic material areas in the organization (which have to consider public value issues), hence endorsing an integrated reporting logic. Changes in management accounting may therefore stimulate internal reporting and internal thinking (Guthrie et al. 2017).

4.4 *Integrated Popular Reporting*

From the previous section, integrated reporting appears to be the most attractive tool to promote accountability of public sector organizations, inasmuch as it reports on how they create value over time in the context of each one's activity/business model. However, it is also clear that implementing integrated reporting within the public sector may be quite challenging, even if an overarching framework is internationally agreed. Moreover, *"the length of an IR report may become an obstacle for ordinary people"* (Manes-Rossi 2019), so that democratic accountability towards 'not-informed' citizens can continue to be quite compromised.

The solution to get the best from this reporting format so that it reaches all citizens may be achieved by combining integrated and popular reporting in a hybrid format—an integrated popular reporting—as suggested by Cohen and Karatzimas (2015) and Biancone et al. (2016). Combining these two reporting perspectives, however, may be found strange, as they point to opposite directions: while popular reporting tries to present financial information in a simplified way, integrated reporting engages additional, not necessarily financial-oriented, material, to the traditional financial reports, making it more complicated to be understood (Cohen and Karatzimas 2015). But, according to Biancone et al. (2016), *"the popular financial reporting is a new integrated reporting frontier,"* limiting the complexity of the latter.

Integrated popular reporting appears as a *"meaningful reporting with potential strategic advantages,"* offering *"the adequate information matrix for citizens and other* [nonexpert] *user groups (e.g., politicians, public executives), that are interested to understand the 'whole picture' of public sector entities"* (Cohen and Karatzimas 2015). Integrated popular reports can be used to intrigue citizens' interest in governmental (financial) information, hence increasing the possibility of further engagement with public sector organizations, and of participation in collective decision-making. They can be used for definitely changing the role of citizens—*"from spectators of changes to influencing players"* (Cohen and Karatzimas 2015). Furthermore, these types of reports would allow for the necessary flexibility in the communication process between public sector organizations and the society, enhanced by the use of social media, which could further promote those reports to the general public. Standardization in terms of content and format would not be desirable, as these reports should consider countries'/entities' specifics in what regards communication needs.

Although not yet applied in practice, integrated popular reporting in public sector organizations, while allowing fulfillment of reporting obligations, provides a holistic overview of the entity with a simplified disclosure approach (Manes-Rossi 2019). But, reporting in this twofold way requires a balance that is not easy to strike—extensive and pluralistic versus concise and easily comprehensive content (Cohen and Karatzimas 2015). Additionally, it is not simple to explain the creation of public value to ordinary citizens.

Another problem with integrated popular reports is related to the objectivity and reliability of their content. Neither popular nor integrated reporting are externally audited, so only financial information included in integrated financial reports can be assured as bias-free and nonselected, as financial statements are the only ones externally audited. The quality of integral popular reporting as a whole would therefore have to rely on internal auditing (Cohen and Karatzimas 2015).

Still, integrated popular reporting can be seen as a way to empower populations and other stakeholders by providing results in different perspectives, but not excessively constraining public managers' decisions, even if seen as unpopular, taking into account collective well-being and long-term value creation (Biancone et al. 2016).

5 Public Value Accounting and Reporting

The notion of 'public value,' adapted to the context of public administration and management, comes from the idea of 'firm value' in the private sector, thereby enabling managers to use their knowledge to create value to shareholders using private assets. This idea was adapted to the public and government sectors by Moore (1995). 'Public value' is *"defined in terms of the many dimensions of value that a democratic public might want to see produced by and reflected in the performance of government"* (Moore 2014). A simple definition can be as follows: it is the value created by a government through all its actions, to the society overall, this value being determined by citizens' preferences. Therefore, citizens must believe that governments produce something of value to them as citizens, becoming arbiters of public value.

Public value may be said to provide a benchmark against which to gauge the public organizations and government policies. Because the public value notion emerges in democratic regimes, accountability requirements impel public sector organizations and governments, at different levels, to (be able to) assess and report on their performance concerning the value contributed to the public or the society. However, the intangible and contextual nature of public value creates difficulties in this assessment.

Moore (2014) develops the basics for a public value accounting scheme, deriving from conventional financial accounting. The underlining idea is that, in public value, there are costs (money spent in inputs, and the use of state authority) and results of the actions of public sector organizations and governments. *"Net value is created when the valued results are greater than costs used in producing the desired results."* This scheme reflects on how to account for the value created by public services and collectively owned assets used in the process. Money (to purchase labor and other materials needed to produce the desired results) and authority to make individual actors engage in activities that could improve (or refrain from activities that would harm) overall social welfare are assets transformed as costs (Moore 2014).

However, the revenue side becomes complicated to establish in public value accounting, as *"assigning value to the results of government action is ... problematic"* (Moore 2014). It is difficult to develop an accounting model that captures the (intangible) value of what governments produce.

Somehow, this problem resembles those of performance measurement overall in public sector organizations, namely questions related to get to the adequate outcome indicators.

"The term public value accounting implies a focus on the definition, justification and measurement of public value generated through the production of public services, from both a theoretical and practical point of view" (Bracci et al. 2019). But public value accounting does not seem to be a settled concept yet. It is acknowledged that further research is needed, as public value accounting has not attracted much research, especially coming from the public sector accounting perspective. There is *"lack of theoretical contributions by accounting scholars on what public value accounting is and how it can be accounted for"*; there are very few studies, mainly on the public management field, regarding methods to account for public value (related to performance measurement and management accounting).

Additional theoretical and practical contributions may come from studies on accountability/external reporting, given that traditional financial reporting methods, as well as other alternative reporting models such as those addressed in this chapter, do not seem to be able to account for public value. Further knowledge needs to be gained about the producers, users, and uses of public value information (Bracci et al. 2019). As external reporting has to attend to these, a new reporting model may emerge, other than performance, sustainability, or integrated, or perhaps extending and combining these previous concepts. For this, it will also be important to understand how public value is perceived by accountants, who most likely will be preparers of this new form of public sector reporting.

> *If someone wants to govern, or at least manage, the production of public value for public interests, it should at least be able to be accounted for, thereby making "visible" the capacity (or lack of capacity) to deliver and create value through public services and/or public policies. Citizens and other stakeholders will be the main beneficiaries.* (Bracci et al. 2019)

Moore (2014) himself claims that progress is needed *"in developing accounting schemes that can recognize public value in useful ways"*; *"improving the philosophy and practice of public value accounting provides a path forward toward enhanced government accountability, improved collective decision making, and continuous learning about what is valuable and possible to do through government action."*

6 Final Remarks

The importance of the GPFR as an accountability medium in public sector organizations is undeniable, just as is the effort that has gone into bringing this closer to stakeholders', namely citizens', information needs. In fact, given the inherent accountability obligations of these organizations, namely towards the general public, this purpose has been evidenced in the GPFR in relation to the purpose of supporting decision-making.

It has been overall acknowledged that, nowadays, the addressees of the public sector organizations' financial reporting are diverse: investors in markets; central governments and parliaments; Courts of Auditors and other national oversight bodies; international oversight and statistics bodies; national statistics authorities; taxpayers and citizens at large; and other, for example, rating agencies and the *media* (IPSASB 2014; Jorge 2019).

Given that those potential users of public sector organizations and governmental reports present a large variety of information needs and requirements, terms of education, maturity, and expertise, the efforts of improving the GPFR towards the satisfaction of the information needs of all of them have not been enough. These differences are not always compatible and are hard to mitigate, especially considering that stakeholders may change their disclosure requirements. So, accountability obligations, namely towards the general public, are often not completely accomplished, considering that the 'message' does not properly reach the relevant 'audience.' Especially nonexpert users, such as politicians and citizens at large, are still lost amid the complexity of financial information, often preferring and giving importance to nonfinancial and qualitative matters about public resources management and service delivery.

On the other hand, public sector organizations tend to adopt accounting and reporting innovations for technical and efficiency reasons (e.g., for better management and decision-making support; for making funding easier), but also for legitimation-related institutional reasons (because they are mandatory, or to imitate best practices).

This chapter has addressed reporting practices that, motivated by one or other reasons, have appeared in the public sector realm in order to increase accountability in practice, fulfilling the still existent gap left by traditional financial reporting. These reporting modalities have complemented financial information with other, such as budgetary, reporting, or even alternative nonfinancial information like that about organizational and service performance, sustainability, and value creation to the main stakeholders and to the society.

The one that has persisted for longer is performance (nonfinancial) reporting, which has been in practice for a while in public sector organizations. However, the fact that it endorses specificities of organizations' governance and management means that binding regulation has been difficult to establish, especially at an international level. Only general guidance exists, which may justify the fact that most public sector organizations still prepare performance reporting on a voluntary basis. Also, performance indicators to be reported are often not easy to define.

Sustainability reporting has appeared later, as a result of the need for public organizations reporting practices to embrace sustainability development concerns, namely social- and environmental-related. Its preparation is not mandatory, though strongly encouraged, but the existent international guidance, namely from the GRI, is quite demanding, requiring very comprehensive information, hence creating difficulties and making this type of reporting not so attractive for preparers in technical terms. However, as it happens with the integrated reporting, it is quite attractive for legitimation reasons.

Popular reporting has been applied mostly at local level in the USA and in South Africa, and offers an almost natural appeal to reach full accountability—transforming the recognized complex financial information into a simpler and concise reporting model, addressed fundamentally to citizens. This report has the great advantage of deeply considering questions of financial information understandability, highlighting how this is important for effective accountability. It allows considering citizens as true accountees and coproducers in the public decision-making process. But it requires citizens to have interest in such information, to understand that they have these roles to play, and to be willing to engage in a communication process with public sector and governmental organizations. Moreover, its focus on citizens may lead to neglect other stakeholders' information needs.

Integrated reporting has been considered only recently for public sector organizations. In spite of some guiding principles that have started to be developed internationally (in a project led by the IIRC), questions still arise about its relevance in the public sector, as the concept was initially developed taking into account the context of listed business corporations. But it appears attractive in the public sector too, as it is able to tell the 'whole story' about how public organizations create value for their different stakeholders. Going beyond sustainability issues and combining financial and nonfinancial information, it comes forward as a more developed form of previous modalities, namely performance and sustainability reporting. However, its comprehensive scope also makes its preparation an exhaustive task. Additionally, complexity and extension lead to an overall lack of understanding (and even interest) by citizens, so again it is not so effective as a new tool to improve accountability.

A new concept is emerging as a possible solution, with enough attractiveness to combine the best of existing models towards full accountability—an integral popular reporting. The underlining idea is that, with this reporting, public sector organizations will be able to provide an integrated overview of their activities and outputs (including of financial and budgetary statements), as well as of value creation, in a way simple enough to be understood by all stakeholders, and particularly by ordinary citizens. Nevertheless, the combination of holistic and simplified approaches seems a difficult balance to strike in practice. There may be a risk of this type of reporting continuing to be quite extensive and difficult to read.

In summary, despite being very well intentioned initially, the reality has revealed that most of the so-called reporting innovations discussed here have not (yet) led to the desired improved accountability. Essentially following signaling and imitation motivations, they have often become mere fashions within the management of public sector organizations, not resulting from true decision-making. As these 'new' reporting practices tend to be included in larger reform processes, they often degenerate and become diluted, reappearing later under different names, not really constituting an innovation. The exception is integrated popular reporting, which is rather new and has only started to be conceptually considered.

Also with the exception of integrated popular reporting, all types of reporting discussed in this chapter provide, at least in theory, wider disclosure on policies, strategies, and actions pursued by public sector organizations than traditional financial reporting does. However, they are *"still not enough for citizens' engagement."* As Manes-Rossi (2019) stresses, *"to be effective in terms of accountability … reports should be connected with democratic participation initiatives, such as participatory budgeting."*

Moreover, *"maybe [it] is time to think about a demand-led approach, rather than a supply-led one in the construction of accountability systems for the general public, to avoid the risk of the diffusion of the new managerial … fashion"* (Biondi and Bracci 2018).

An additional important matter to be considered for the implementation of these reporting modalities concerns the reliability of their contents. While external auditing is quite an established practice for traditional financial reporting, it does not apply to most of these new types of reporting (except for performance reporting). However, faithful and trustful information continues to be essential, which is likely to call for extending auditing practices, embracing qualitative information, and enhancing the role of internal auditing.

History tell us that some practices in public sector organizations are implemented and diffused only if they become mandatory. Therefore, without legal coercion, the reporting models addressed in this chapter may be hard to be effectively and generally implemented. On the other hand, making further reporting practices obligatory can create undesirable effects of those being seen and yet another (ineffective) reporting obligation. Still, perhaps it is possible to find a compromising solution. Biondi and Bracci (2018) refer to promotions via national governmental regulations (even if not making the practices mandatory). Manes-Rossi (2019) mentions rewording schemes to encourage such practices, so that any changes do not come to be mere cosmetic operations.

One can think of EPSAS as an example of 'new' reporting requirements to public sector organizations in Europe. If European regulations would not allow for a mandatory framework, but just point to a nonbinding guidance, EPSAS's usefulness can be at stake, or perhaps not, given that cyclic worldwide crises, as the one currently passing (COVID-19), have raised new needs for further public sector reporting improvements. Therefore, EPSAS, as a 'new' financial reporting practice, were initially seen as important by some, after the 2009 financial crisis; recently, Member States enthusiasm towards such standards clearly faded. Perhaps the current crisis creates the right context for the EPSAS project to regain prominence, given that new accountability needs arise: it becomes imperative to disclose, in an understandable manner for stakeholders and the general society, the consequences of current public policies in actual and future public resources, public services, and creation of value by public sector organizations and governments overall.

References

Adams, S., & Simnett, R. (2011). Integrated Reporting: An Opportunity for Australia's Not-for-Profit Sector. *Australian Accounting Review, 58(21)*(3), 292–301.

Aggestam, C. A., & Brusca, I. (2016). The First Steps Towards Harmonizing Public Sector Accounting for European Union Member States: Strategies and Perspectives. *Public Money and Management, 36*(3), 181–188.

Alt, E., Lassen, D., & Rose, S. (2006). The Causes of Fiscal Transparency: Evidence from the U.S. States. *IMF Staff Papers, 53*, 30–57.

Armstrong, E. (2005). *Integrity, Transparency and Accountability in Public Administration: Recent Trends, Regional and International Developments and Emerging Issues.* New York: United Nations.

Askim, J. (2007). How Do Politicians Use Performance Information? *International Review of Administrative Sciences, 73*(3), 453–472.

Behn, R. D. (2001). *Rethinking Democratic Accountability.* Washington, DC: The Brookings Institution.

Biancone, P., Secinaro, S., & Brescia, V. (2016). The Popular Financial Reporting: Focus on Stakeholders. The first European Experience. *International Journal of Business and Management, 11*(11), 115–125.

Biondi, L., & Bracci, E. (2018). Sustainability, Popular and Integrated Reporting in the Public Sector: A Fad and Fashion Perspective. *Sustainability, 10*(9), 3112.

Bovens, M. (2007). Analysing and Assessing Accountability: A Conceptual Framework. *European Law Journal, 13*(4), 447–468.

Bracci, E., Papi, L., Bigoni, M., Deidda Gagliardo, E., & Bruns, H. (2019). Public Value and Public Sector Accounting Research: A Structured Literature Review. *Journal of Public Budgeting, Accounting & Financial Management, 31*(1), 103–136.

Brusca, I., & Montesinos, V. (2016). Implementing Performance Reporting in Local Government: A Cross-Countries Comparison. *Public Performance & Management Review, 39*, 506–534.

Brusca, I., Caperchione, E., Cohen, S., & Manes-Rossi, F. (2015). *Public Sector Accounting and Auditing in Europe: The Challenge of Harmonization.* Basingstoke: Palgrave Macmillan.

Caba Pérez, C., Rodríguez Bolívar, M. P., & López Hernández, A. M. (2005). Citizens' Access to on-Line Governmental Financial Information: Practices in the European Union Countries. *Government Information Quarterly, 22*(2), 258–276.

Caba Pérez, C., Rodríguez Bolívar, M. P., & López Hernández, A. M. (2014). The Determinants of Government Financial Reports Online. *Transylvanian Review of Administrative Sciences, 42E*, 5–31.

Caruana, J., Dabbicco, G., Jorge, S., & Jesus, M. A. (2019). The Development of EPSAS: Contributions from the Literature. *Accounting in Europe, 16*(2), 146–176.

Cohen, S., & Karatzimas, S. (2015). Tracing the Future of Reporting in the Public Sector: Introducing Integrated Popular Reporting. *International Journal of Public Sector Management, 28*(6), 449–460.

Cohen, S., Mamakou, X. J., & Karatzimas, S. (2017). IT-Enhanced Popular Reports: Analyzing Citizen Preferences. *Government Information Quarterly, 34*(2), 283–295.

Cunningham, G. M., & Harris, J. E. (2005). Toward a Theory of Performance Reporting to Achieve Public Sector Accountability: A Field Study. *Public Budgeting & Finance, 25*(2), 15–42.

Dabbicco, G. (2018). A Comparison of Debt Measures in Fiscal Statistics and Public Sector Financial Statements. *Public Money & Management, 38*(7), 511–518.

Dorn, F., Gaebler, S., & Roesel, F. (2019, In Press). Ineffective Fiscal Rules? The Effect of Public Sector Accounting Standards on Budgets, Efficiency, and Accountability. *Public Choice* , Working Paper No. 312.

EC, Eurostat. (2013, March 6). *Towards Implementing Harmonised Public Sector Accounting Standards in Member States, the Suitability of IPSAS for the Member States.* Report from the Commission to the Council and the European Parliament [COM(2013) 114 final], Brussels, Belgium.

EC, Eurostat. (2017, November 3). *Collection of Additional and Updated Information Related to the Potential Impacts of EPSAS.* EPSAS WG 17/15, Luxembourg.

ESA. (2010). European System of Accounts. *Luxembourg: Publications Office of the European Union.*

Farneti, F., & Guthrie, J. (2009). Sustainability Reporting by Australian Public Sector Organisations: Why They Report. *Accounting Forum, 33*, 89–98.

Frederickson, H. G. (1996). Comparing the Reinventing Government Movement with the New Public Administration. *Public Administration Review, 56*(3), 263–270.

Giacomini, D., Rocca, L., Carin, C., & Mazzoleni, M. (2018). Overcoming the Barriers to the Diffusion of Sustainability Reporting in Italian LGOs: Better Stick or Carrot? *Sustainability, 10*(1), 131.

Gomes, P. S. (2018). Performance Evaluation and Reporting. In A. Farazmand (Ed.), *Global Encyclopedia of Public Administration, Public Policy, and Governance.* Cham: Springer.

Guthrie, J., Manes-Rossi, F., & Orelli, R. L. (2017). Integrated Reporting and Integrated Thinking in Italian Public Sector Organisations. *Meditari Accountancy Research, 25*(4), 553–573.

IIRC. (2013). *The International <IR> Framework.* International Integrated Reporting Council.
IIRC. (2016). *Integrated Thinking and Reporting: Focusing on Value Creation in the Public Sector—An Introduction for Leaders.* London: IIRC.
IPSASB. (2014). *The Conceptual Framework for General Purpose Financial Reporting by Public Sector Entities.* New York: International Public Sector Accounting Standards Board (IPSASB)—International Federation of Accountants (IFAC).
IPSASB. (2015). *RPG 3—Reporting Service Performance Information.* New York: International Public Sector Accounting Standards Board (IPSASB)—International Federation of Accountants (IFAC).
IPSASB. (2019). *Handbook of International Public Sector Accounting Pronouncements, Vols, I, II and III.* New York: International Public Sector Accounting Standards Board (IPSASB)—International Federation of Accountants (IFAC).
Jesus, M. A., & Jorge, S. (2015). Governmental Budgetary Reporting Systems in the European Union: Is the Accounting Basis Relevant for the Deficit Reliability? *International Review of Administrative Sciences, 81*(1), 110–133.
Jordan, M., Yusuf, J. E. W., Mayer, M., & Mahar, K. (2016). What Citizens Want to Know About Their Government's Finances: Closing the Information gap. *The Social Science Journal, 53*, 301–308.
Jorge, S. (2019). Reporting Components and Reliability Issues. In P. Lorson, S. Jorge, & E. Haustein (Eds.), *European Public Sector Accounting.* Coimbra: IUC—Imprensa da Universidade de Coimbra. Chapter 9, 214–250.
Jorge, S., Jesus, M. A., & Nogueira, S. (2016). Information Brokers and the Use of Budgetary and Financial Information by Politicians: The Case of Portugal. *Public Money and Management, 36*(8), 515–520.
Jorge, S., Jesus, M. A., & Laureano, R. (2018). Budgetary Balances Adjustments from Governmental Accounting to National Accounts in EU Countries: Can Deficits Be Prone to Management? *Public Budgeting & Finance, 38*(4), 97–116.
Jorge, S., Jesus, M. A., & Nogueira, S. (2019a). The Use of Budgetary and Financial Information by Politicians in Parliament: A Case Study. *Journal of Public Budgeting Accounting and Financial Management, 31*(4), 539–557.
Jorge, S., Caruana, J., & Caperchione, E. (2019b). The Challenging Task of Developing European Public Sector Accounting Standards—Editorial. *Accounting in Europe, 16*(2), 143–145.
Kopits, G., & Craig, M. (1998). *Transparency in Government Operations. International Monetary Fund.*
Liguori, M., Sicilia, M., & Steccolini, I. (2012). Some Like It Non-Financial… Politicians' and Managers' Views on the Importance of Performance Information. *Public Management Review, 14*(7), 903–922.

Lourenço, R. P., Sá, P. M., Jorge, S., & Pattaro, A. F. (2013). Online Transparency for Accountability: One Assessing Model and Two Applications. *The Electronic Journal of e-Government, 11*(1), 280–292.

Lourenço, R. P., Piotrowski, S., & Ingrams, A. (2015). *Public Accountability ICT Support: A Detailed Account of Public Accountability Process and Tasks.* International Conference on Electronic Government (pp. 105–117). Springer International Publishing.

Lourenço, R. P., Jorge, S., & Rolas, H. (2016). Towards a Transparency Ontology in the Context of Open Government. *Electronic Government, an International Journal, 12*(4), 375–394.

Manes-Rossi, F. (2019). New Development: Alternative Reporting Formats: A Panacea for Accountability Dilemmas? *Public Money & Management, 39*(7), 528–531.

Manes-Rossi, F., Cohen, S., Caperchione, E., & Brusca, I. (2016). Harmonizing Public Sector Accounting in Europe: Thinking Out of the Box. *Public Money and Management, 36*(3), 189–196.

Marcuccio, M., & Steccolini, I. (2005). Social and Environmental Reporting in Local Authorities. *Public Management Review, 7*(2), 155–176.

Marcuccio, M., & Steccolini, I. (2009). Patterns of Voluntary Extended Performance Reporting in Italian Local Authorities. *International Journal of Public Sector Management, 22*(2), 146–167.

Meijer, A. J. (2003). Transparent Government: Parliamentary and Legal Accountability in an Information Age. *Information Polity, 8*(1-2), 67–78.

Montesinos, V., Dasí, R., & Brusca, I. (2019). A Framework for Comparing Financial Sustainability in EU Countries: National Accounts, Governmental Accounting and the Challenge of Harmonization. In J. Caruana, I. Brusca, E. Caperchione, S. Cohen, & F. Manes-Rossi (Eds.), *Financial Sustainability of Public Sector Entities—The Relevance of Accounting Frameworks* (pp. 41–61). Cham: Palgrave Macmillan.

Moore, M. H. (1995). *Creating Public Value: Strategic Management in Government.* Cambridge, MA: Harvard University Press.

Moore, M. H. (2014). Public Value Accounting: Establishing the Philosophical Basis. *Public Administration Review, 74*(4), 465–477.

OECD. (2001). *OECD Best Practices for Budget Transparency.* Paris: OECD publications.

Oliveira, A., Jorge, S., & Santos, J. P. (2018). Popular reporting nos municípios portugueses? *Revista Iberoamericana de Contabilidad de Gestión, XVI*(31). Enero-Junio, 20–36.

Oprisor, T., Tiron-Tudor, A., & Silvia, N. C. (2016). The Integrated Reporting System: A New Accountability Enhancement Tool for Public Sector Entities. *Audit Financiar, XIV (7)*(139), 749–762.

Oulasvirta, L. (2014). The Reluctance of a Developed Country to Choose International Public Sector Accounting Standards of the IFAC. A Critical Case Study. *Critical Perspectives on Accounting, 25*(3), 272–285.

Pavan, A., & Lemme, F. (2006). Central Government Financial Information and User-Orientation on the Internet in Italy and the USA. In E. Lande & J. C. Scheid (Eds.), *Accounting Reform in the Public Sector: Mimicry, Fad or Necessity?* (pp. 115–129). Paris: Expert Comptable Media.

Piotrowski, S. J., & van Ryzin, G. G. (2007). Citizen Attitudes Toward Transparency in Local Government. *The American Review of Public Administration, 37*, 306–323.

Pollitt, C. (2000). Is the Emperor in His Underwear? An Analysis of the Impact of Public Management Reform. *Public Management, 2*(2), 181–199.

Ramkumar, V., & Shapiro, I. (2010). Guide to Transparency in Government Budget Reports: Why Are Budget Reports Important, and What Should They Include? *International Budget Partnership*. Retrieved from https://www.internationalbudget.org/publications/guide-to-transparency-in-government-budget-reports-why-are-budget-reports-important-and-what-should-they-include/.

Reichard, C., & van Helden, J. (2016). Why Cash-Based Budgeting Still Prevails in an Era of Accrual-Based Reporting in the Public Sector. *Accounting, Finance & Governance Review, 23*(1–2), 43–65.

Steccolini, I. (2004). Is the Annual Report an Accountability Medium? An Empirical Investigation into Italian Local Governments. *Financial Accountability & Management, 20*(3), 327–350.

Van Helden, J., & Reichard, C. (2018). Performance Management. In A. Farazmand (Ed.), *Global Encyclopedia of Public Administration, Public Policy, and Governance*. Cham: Springer.

Wong, W., & Welch, E. (2004). Does E-Government Promote Accountability? A Comparative Analysis of Website Openness and Government Accountability. *Governance, 17*(2), 275–297.

Yusuf, J.-E., Jordan, M. M., Neill, K. A., & Hackbart, M. (2013). For the People: Popular Financial Reporting Practices of Local Government. *Public Budgeting & Finance, 33*(1), 95–113.

CHAPTER 5

A Sustainable Accounting Approach for Reporting on Long-Term Fiscal Sustainability

1 Introduction

Public sector fiscal sustainability is necessary for encouraging economic growth needed for the well-being of current and future generations (Chapman 2008; Dabbicco 2019). Fiscal sustainability is defined as the ability of the government to meet its current and future financial obligations and can be expressed with respect to the government living within its budget constraint over time. In other words, it is the ability of the government to cover its expenditures from its own revenues, while reducing its dependence on borrowing and lending (Bird 2003). Fiscal sustainability aims to assure that current taxpayers are paying for the services that they receive and not passing these costs on to future generations. The main concern of fiscal sustainability is that governments have accumulated long-term liabilities that do not appear in current balance sheets but may hurt future generations when they are due. If the accumulated long-term liabilities do not appear in the balance sheet, this does not mean that the government has a healthy fiscal position but it shows the lack of an accounting system to provide an adequate picture of the financial health of a government (Schick 2005). The concept of fiscal sustainability should be grounded on the norm that responsible government should not do harm that will appear decades after the relevant policies were adopted (Buiter 1990; Schick 2005; Gooptu 2005; Rodríguez and López-Subires 2017).

H. Ouda, *Practice-Relevant Accrual Accounting for the Public Sector*, Public Sector Financial Management,
https://doi.org/10.1007/978-3-030-51595-9_5

Traditionally, public sector accounting has been based on a cash basis. The key reason for the use of cash accounting by the government is to focus on the public debt as the key fiscal sustainability measure. The main problem with debt as a measure of the financial position of the government is that it ignores a whole range of other assets and liabilities—including fixed assets, land, and liabilities such as public service superannuation—which are an important part of government finances (Robinson 1996; Dabbicco 2018). Thus, focusing only on debt without taking the other assets and liabilities into consideration will create a false picture of government finances. However, traditional indicators of fiscal activity like public debt and public deficit fail to measure the sustainability of the government's policy because they only capture the short-term effects of current political decisions. Recent attempts have been made to extend these measures in order to get a longer-term view of fiscal sustainability as a solution to this problem by using accrual accounting to report the financial position of the government sector. This has led to replacing debt as the fundamental indicator of the financial position of the government with what is known as "net worth/public equity." Accordingly, a new type of deficit measure might have come into play, which would indicate changes in net worth rather than changes in debt alone (Robinson 1996; Buiter 2004; Yeyati and Sturzenegger 2007; Rodríguez et al. 2016; Carini and Teodori 2019).

In addition, the use of accrual accounting will also assist in measuring intergenerational equity, which is also considered to be a measure of fiscal sustainability. Intergenerational equity means the capacity of the government to pay its current obligations from its current revenues without shifting the costs to future generations. The supporters of using accrual accounting see that it offers better indicators of how past and present fiscal policies will affect future governments and taxpayers. Unlike cash accounting, if an asset is sold, accrual accounts would show up the impact of this upon the net worth, which would take into account the disposal of the asset as well as debt reduction from the asset sale proceeds (when the latter is used to pay off the debt). Similarly, the difference between capital and current expenditure would be brought out clearly, because the assets created by capital expenditure would be highlighted in the net worth measure (Robinson 1996; IPSASB 2013).

While the notion of using accrual accounting in the government sector is to assist in measuring long-term fiscal sustainability, the accrual-based balance sheet has inherent limitations that greatly reduce its utility as a measure of long-term fiscal sustainability. One problem is that the balance sheet recognizes liabilities arising out of past activity, not future obligations arising out of current policy (Schick 2005; Silvia 2011; Aquino and Cardoso 2019). In addition, the accrual-based balance sheet does not include future commitments and contingent liabilities. In assessing long-term fiscal sustainability, undisclosed commitments and future obligations weigh far more heavily than those that are disclosed or have already been incurred (Schick 2005; Silvia 2011; Carini and Teodori 2019). Consequently, this situation can raise the following questions:

- ***Are accrual-based financial statements providing practice-relevant accounting information required for reporting on the government's long-term fiscal sustainability?***
- ***Can the net worth and intergenerational equity provide the best measures of long-term fiscal sustainability?***
- ***To what extent can the public sector accounting go beyond the traditional accounting reporting and provide information for reporting on long-term fiscal sustainability?***
- ***Should the scope of public sector financial reporting be expanded to include both backward- looking (past) activity and forward-looking (future) activity?***
- ***Do accounting bases need to be developed to be able to report on long-term fiscal sustainability?***

These crucial questions have not received the attention they deserve. Supporting our questions, Dabbicco (2019) assured that a research gap remains in the current literature on the role of accounting frameworks for fiscal sustainability reporting. This offers new areas for research, notably on the role of public sector accounting in the provision of information that would assist fiscally sustainable policy-making as well as the relevance of accounting frameworks in this process. Therefore, the main purpose of this chapter is to investigate if the public sector accounting financial statements can provide an adequate picture of the long-term fiscal sustainability of a public sector entity. If not, it will attempt to propose a sustainable accounting approach that provides practice-relevant accounting information, which assists in measuring and reporting on long-term fiscal sustainability. This will be based on the development of accounting bases and the expansion of the scope of public sector general purpose financial reporting. Thus, the public sector accountants, standard-setters, and academics are required to take the initiative and think outside the box and innovate additional accounting bases and financial reporting systems (which may not be guided by current accounting policies and regulations) that are basically directed to the provision of accounting information needs of long-term fiscal sustainability. This is, of course, without sacrificing the traditional form of accrual accounting which leads to preparing the cost-based financial statements.

2 Current Accounting Bases and Long-Term Fiscal Sustainability

The indicators of and reporting on long-term fiscal sustainability will differ according to the accounting bases/systems used. The accounting bases determine the elements to be recognized in the financial statements. It is mentioned by IFAC (1991) that there is a spectrum of accounting bases that ranges from the cash basis of accounting, at one extreme, to the full accrual basis, at the other end of the spectrum. In between, there are many variations that are, in effect, modifications of either the cash or the full accrual bases. Conceptually, there are four accounting bases in practice: cash basis, modified cash basis, modified accrual basis, and full accrual basis. Therefore, this section focuses on these four accounting bases and their role in providing the accounting information required for measuring and reporting on long-term fiscal sustainability.

2.1 Cash and Modified Cash

Cash basis of accounting is a method of recording transactions by which revenues and expenditures are reflected in the accounts in the period in which the related cash receipts or disbursements occur. Accordingly, the financial statements are usually prepared to disclose information about cash receipts, cash disbursements, and cash balances. The cash balance is the only available cash at the end of the period and it is considered as the cash that past taxpayers leave to future taxpayers (Ouda 2006).

According to the modified cash basis, the financial statements can disclose, in addition to the cash flows and cash balances, the short-term liabilities and short-term account receivables. Consequently, the modified cash basis can provide information about cash flows during the period, those liabilities that must be met within a short period from reporting date and current cash balances, and receivables available to meet those liabilities. The measurement focus according to the modified cash basis is on current financial resources and changes therein.

So the net assets are the difference between cash and accounts receivable in short term and accounts payable in short term. Positive net assets means that present taxpayers have contributed current financial resources for payments in the future and negative net assets means that the current generation leaves more debt to future generations (Cortes 2004; Ouda 2005). The bottom line of Table 5.1 can be either **Cash Balance** (if the balance is positive) or **Net Debt** (if the balance is negative).

The traditional public sector accounting (based on the cash or modified cash bases) confines its coverage on the future implications of fiscal decisions to debt (Robinson 1996). The main indicator of the long-term fiscal sustainability under cash accounting is the debt and the changes in debt. The net debt measure under cash and modified cash accounting is the result of subtracting the cash balances from debt obligations (debt obligations minus cash balances). The use of net debt as indicator for fiscal sustainability tends to give the view that increases in debt leave the future worse off, and reductions in debt leave the future better off. The main problem of using the net debt as a measure of fiscal sustainability is that, on the one hand, the conventional debt is not the only type of future obligation into which the government enters, and, on the other hand, the interest earned by monetary assets held by the government is not the only type of future benefit which accrues as a result of past fiscal actions (Robinson 1996; Cortes 2004; Ouda 2005).

The traditional net debt measure (based on cash and modified cash accounting) has serious problems on both liabilities side and assets side. On the liabilities side, it fails to include current and long-term liabilities

Table 5.1 Assets and liabilities reported under the cash and modified cash bases and indicator of fiscal sustainability

Assets	*Liabilities*
Cash balance	Short-term accounts payable
Short-term accounts receivable	Transfer payments payable within specified number of days
	Borrowings

Source: Author

such as pensions and compensated absences, social security commitments, and future commitments related to service contracts for the provision of contracted-out goods and services. Under the use of debt as indicator of fiscal sustainability, most liabilities are hidden, and this gives the government the opportunity to manipulate the debt and deficit amounts (Ouda 2006). Similar problems can be found on the assets side, as it also fails to include assets other than monetary assets. It does not take into account the total assets (financial and physical). For example, there is no information provided about the investment in materials, supplies, equipment, and other assets, which are available for future use in carrying out the government unit's work. In addition, Robinson (1996) argued that the traditional net debt measure fails to register the increase or decrease in future flows and/or social benefits which occurs when assets are acquired or sold. Instead, all it registers is any increase in debt when an asset is acquired and any reduction in debt when an asset is sold. This leads to misunderstanding of the impact of capital expenditure and capital revenue upon fiscal sustainability and intergenerational equity. Consequently, the focus on net debt in isolation without taking all other assets and liabilities (which are relevant for measuring long-term fiscal sustainability) into consideration will reduce the importance of the debt as a measure for long-term fiscal sustainability. Thus, the net debt only shows half the picture, so we need to look at what the public sector entity *owns* as well as what it *owes* (Dennis 2018).

2.2 *Modified Accrual Accounting*

The modified accrual basis recognizes transactions and events when the transactions or events occur rather than when cash is paid or received. The main difference between modified accrual and full accrual bases is that under the modified accrual basis physical assets are expensed at the time of purchase (IFAC 1998). Under the modified accrual basis, the measurement focus is on total financial resources and changes therein. This means that this basis can provide the users with information about liabilities, the total financial assets available to meet those liabilities, and the amount and sources of the period's revenues and expenditures.

Accordingly, the modified accrual basis provides users with information on the sources, allocations, and uses of financial resources (IFAC 1998). It provides information about how the government financed its activities and met its cash requirements. This information, in turn, provides a basis to evaluate the government's ability to finance its activities and meet its liabilities and commitments (IFAC 1991). Therefore, it can be concluded that modified accrual accounting can meet the objectives of governmental accounting and financial reporting to a great extent. On the other hand, the modified accrual basis does not provide information about the physical assets and depreciation costs. This means that under the modified accrual basis, the cost of physical assets is included in expenditures at the time of purchase rather than being depreciated over its useful life (IFAC 1996).

The bottom line of Table 5.2 can be either **Net Financial Worth (NFW)** if assets are greater than liabilities or **Net Financial Debt (NFD)** if assets are less than liabilities. Net financial worth means that past generations leave financial resources to acquire goods and provide services in the future and net financial debt means that future financial resources have been used by past generations to pay services and goods previously acquired (Cortes 2004).

Compared with the debt measure based on cash accounting, the net financial worth can be considered to be a better measure for long-term fiscal sustainability. This superiority is due to the fact that the net financial worth includes the total financial assets and total liabilities of the governmental entities which are not taken into account in the cash accounting debt measure. On the assets side, it includes the total financial assets such as investments, inventories for sale, loans outstanding, revenue receivables, cash, bank deposits, and other receivables. Furthermore, it includes the value of the government's equity in public enterprise as this is recognized as a financial asset in the general government balance sheet. On the liabilities side, it includes accounts payable, transfer payments payable, borrowings, and accrued liabilities (e.g., employee pension obligations and accrued interest) (IFAC 1993; Robinson 2009). It is argued that from a fiscal sustainability point of view, the recognition of a wider range

Table 5.2 Assets and liabilities reported under the modified accrual basis and indicator of fiscal sustainability

Assets	*Liabilities*
Total financial assets (including both liquid and illiquid)	Total liabilities accumulated to date **Net financial worth**

Source: Author

Table 5.3 Content of public sector net debt (as a National Accounts measure of fiscal sustainability)

Assets	*Liabilities*
Liquid financial assets	Total liabilities accumulated to date

Source: Author

of financial assets and liabilities is useful because of their relevance to fiscal sustainability (Robinson 2009). In addition, the net financial worth/net financial debt as a measure of fiscal sustainability is also superior to the public sector net debt (PSND) which is a National Accounts measure for fiscal sustainability. The PSND is the difference between liquid financial assets (those assets that could be readily sold) and total liabilities accumulated to date. This means that it excludes the illiquid financial assets and the public corporations' equity from analysis. One of the shortcomings of PSND as indicator of fiscal sustainability is that it does not account for future liabilities arising from past government activities, for example, the accrued rights to pension payments built up over the past by public sector workers and contracted payments to Private Finance Initiative (PFI) providers. In fact, this shortcoming would also apply to net financial worth/ net financial debt. The bottom line of Table 5.3 measures the PSND according to the National Accounts.

However, the net financial worth/net financial debt does not comprise the fixed assets, which are included in the balance sheet that is based on full accrual accounting. This can lead us to see whether the use of full accrual accounting can report on long-term fiscal sustainability and whether its bottom line (net worth) can be considered to be the right measure for long-term fiscal sustainability.

2.3 *Full Accrual Accounting*

The full accrual basis recognizes transactions and events when they occur rather than when cash is paid or received. The financial statements under the accrual basis disclose the total assets (including current and physical assets), total liabilities (including short- and long-term liabilities), net worth, revenues, and expenses. Accordingly, the measurement focus under the full accrual accounting is on total economic resources. The accrual basis provides users with information about such matters as the resources controlled by the entity, the costs of providing services, and other information useful in assessing financial position and changes in financial position, and in assessing whether the reporting entity is operating economically and efficiently (IFAC 1991). The balance sheet under full accrual accounting is a statement which seeks to identify and value all assets and liabilities. Net worth is the bottom line of a balance sheet, obtained by subtracting the total liabilities from the total assets (including both current and fixed assets). So the net assets represent the entity's net worth. The bottom line of an accrual statement of financial performance is referred to as an operating deficit/surplus. This operating deficit/surplus represents the measure of changing the net worth within the accounting period. The net worth shows the resources left by past generations to future ones. It is a measure of the government's ability to provide services in the future. If it is negative, it implies that future resources will fund services and goods consumed in the past (Cortes 2004) (Table 5.4).

As a result of the inclusion of all assets and all liabilities in the balance sheet, the supporters of the balance sheet approach believe that net worth provides the best measure for long-term fiscal sustainability. Accordingly, it has been claimed by different supporters that balance sheet and net worth are superior to the previously stated fiscal sustainability measures. Based on reviewing the literature (e.g., Rowles 1992; AARF 1995; Mellor 1996), Robinson (1996) has stated the following advantages of using the net worth as a measure for long-term fiscal sustainability:

- Net worth provides the best measure of fiscal sustainability.
- Net worth provides a means of assessing the compatibility of fiscal policy with intergenerational equity principles.
- The change in net worth (or, to be more precise, an adjusted variant of this) is a superior measure of the government's contribution to

Table 5.4 Assets and liabilities reported under the full accrual basis and indicator of fiscal sustainability

Assets	*Liabilities*
Physical assets (tangible and intangible) Total financial assets (liquid and illiquid)	Total liabilities accumulated to date
	Net worth (NW)

Source: Author

national savings because it measures net savings (i.e., savings after depreciation) rather than gross savings.
- A focus on net worth eliminates fiscal illusions associated with asset sales.
- Conversely, the focus on net worth encourages the sale of public assets (as opposed to passively holding those assets out of habit) where it is genuinely beneficial to do so.
- It removes incentives for governments to run up unfunded superannuation and similar liabilities in order to give themselves more short-term fiscal freedom.
- The valuation of the physical asset stock in a balance sheet removes the anti-capital expenditure bias of traditional cash accounting.
- The valuation of physical assets also facilitates assessments of the adequacy of the capital stock, and draws attention to future replacement costs.
- It removes the illusion, arising from the failure of traditional accounting to recognize the future implications of reduced service potential, that deferring maintenance of fixed assets across the government somehow improves the budgetary position.

Besides the net worth, it is claimed that intergenerational equity can also provide a reliable measure for the long-term fiscal sustainability of the government. In fact, intergenerational fairness is important in fiscal policy. Under this concept, each fiscal period should be accountable for the resources used to provide benefits during that period. In other words, the burden of providing current services should not be shifted to future periods or generations of taxpayers. Therefore, the provision of a comprehensive picture of government liabilities can assist in the formulation of realistic fiscal policies. One consequence of the adoption of accrual accounting by the government is that it will provide an indication of the extent of capital maintenance. In the private sector, a company achieves capital maintenance when the amount of its capital at the end of a period is unchanged from that at the beginning of the period. Any excess amount above this represents the company's profit. In the public sector, capital maintenance means that it is not eroded during the financial year and remains the same at the end of that financial year and any excess amount above this represents the surplus.

Applying the notion of capital maintenance to any part of the public sector brings intergenerational equity into consideration. In addition, a comparison of the depreciation expenses and capital expenditure on fixed assets in the reporting period and over time would give a broad indication of whether today's consumption has been made good to maintain the stock of assets constant (Mellor 1997). This means that identifying the surplus or deficit each year would over time enable a conclusion to be reached about whether a government is eroding, enhancing, or maintaining the asset base (capital maintenance) and whether each generation is bearing its burden or shifting this burden to future generations. Accordingly, the intergenerational equity can be measured from the bottom line of the statement of financial performance (income statement). If it is a surplus, this means that the current generation has borne its own burden as well as providing support to the next generations. If it is a deficit, then the current generation is shifting its burden to the next generations.

So, in addition to the net worth, intergenerational equity can also be used as a measure of long-term fiscal sustainability of the government. It is inferred that fiscal sustainability is achieved from the accrual accounting point of view when the intergenerational equity is zero or positive and the net worth is positive.

Fiscal Sustainability = Zero Intergenerational Equity + Positive Net Worth.

FS = ZIE + PNW

However, while the aforementioned claims (that net worth and intergenerational equity are best measures of fiscal sustainability) seem impressive, the balance sheet has inherent limitations and problematic issues (e.g., assets valuation issue) that greatly diminish its utility as a measure of long-term fiscal sustainability and, hence, it makes the net worth not the best indicator for long-term fiscal sustainability. These limitations and problems will be discussed further.

- **Inherent limitations of balance sheet**

At first glance, it seems that the balance sheet under full accrual accounting and its net worth can provide the best measure for long-term fiscal sustainability of governmental entities. This is due to the fact that it includes all assets and all liabilities accumulated to date and the difference between them is the net worth, which is considered as the most comprehensive accrual stock aggregate. However, the government's responsibilities, policy commitments, and contingencies are much broader than these reported balance sheet liabilities. In fact, the balance sheet includes only explicit liabilities, but it excludes implicit obligations which will affect the financial position of the government in the future. Moreover, the accrual accounting balance sheet recognizes the liabilities arising out of past activities such as accounts payable and accrued payments, but it excludes future liabilities and contingent liabilities arising out of the past and current policy which according to the Office for Budget Responsibility OBR-UK (2011) include the following:

- Future public service pension payments, where the liability to pay the pension was incurred as a result of past employment
- Capital payments to PFI providers and other payments from previous long-term contracts
- The future costs of student loans, to the extent that previous loans or the costs of servicing those loans are not fully recovered
- Provisions, contingencies, guarantees, and other risks of future costs that might materialize as a result of past activities

As further explanation, the government has entered into contractual commitments requiring the future use of financial resources and has unresolved contingencies where existing conditions, situations, or circumstances create uncertainty about future losses—contingencies and commitments that do not meet the criteria for recognition as liabilities on the balance sheets, but for which there is at least a reasonable possibility that losses have been incurred.

In assessing long-term sustainability, Schick (2005) argues that implicit commitments and future obligations weigh far more heavily than those that are explicit or have already been incurred. In fact, the exclusion of the aforementioned liabilities from the balance sheet will provide a net worth which does not present fairly the actual financial position of the government and hence diminishes its utility as a measure of long-term fiscal sustainability.

As with reported liabilities, there are other significant resources available to the government that extend beyond the assets presented in the balance sheet. These resources include community assets and heritage assets, in addition to the government's sovereign powers to tax. The government's sovereign power to tax is excluded because it is debatable whether such power can satisfy the definition of assets or not.

The inherent limitations of the balance sheet show that there was no consensus about the usefulness of the balance sheet and its net worth as a measure for long-term fiscal sustainability. For example, some accounting experts (Robinson 1996, 2009; Walker 2011; Bisogno et al. 2015; Dennis 2018) have argued that the balance sheet presents a misleading picture of the future financial condition and that the net worth is not a useful measure of a government's solvency, whereas others have argued that the balance sheet applies identical recognition rules to liabilities and assets, that net worth is a relevant measure of the government's capacity to finance incurred liabilities, and that the balance sheet is not designed to be a prognosis of future financial condition (Blejer and Cheasty 1991; Schick 2005)

- **Assets Valuation Problems**

In addition to the inherent limitations of the balance sheet, there are other challenges such as assets valuation problems. One of these problems is related to finding alternative valuation concepts for the physical assets/nonfinancial assets. The valuation problems have profound implications for the meaning and usefulness of net worth as a measure for long-term fiscal sustainability. Therefore, the question here is: shall the physical assets be included in the balance sheet according to economic value or cost-based value?

Some have argued that the economic valuation of nonfinancial assets is more appropriate for measuring long-term fiscal sustainability as the net worth based on the economic value of assets provides a measure for solvency. The term fiscal sustainability has retained its original meaning as a measure of solvency of the government, that is, the ability of the government to meet future obligations with existing tax burdens. To understand whether the economic valuation of nonfinancial assets can be more suitable for measuring long-term fiscal sustainability, we should compare the situation in the context of both the private sector and the public sector. In the public sector context, Robinson (1996) has argued that the principle meaning of the economic value of an asset is the sum of money that represents the discounted value of the future net cash receipts which the assets can be expected to generate for their owner. Herein, the accounting literature distinguishes between two variants of economic value. First, when the asset is kept to be used in the firm, the future net cash receipts refer to net receipts from the sale of the goods or services produced by the asset. The discounted sum of these receipts from the sale of goods and services is referred to as value-in-use.

Second, if the asset is sold, the future cash receipts means the market price of an asset, and this is termed as value-in-exchange. The net worth of a firm arising from preparing a balance sheet based on the economic valuation of nonfinancial assets provides a solvency measure.

However, to what extent is the economic valuation of nonfinancial assets relevant to the public sector? In fact, not all assets of the public sector earn revenue and not all are intended to do so. Most of these assets provide benefits to the community without charge or with a charge sufficient to at least fully cover costs. These assets are termed by Robinson (1996) as social assets. Social assets are mainly acquired for providing nonmonetary benefits; therefore, it is not sufficient to adopt the private sector approach to nonfinancial assets evaluation of recognizing future expected monetary returns from assets and disregarding nonmonetary benefits to consumers as both are relevant (Robinson 1996). According to the IPSAS definition of assets, assets are acquired not only for future economic benefits but also for providing service potential. Service potential is a measure of the capacity of an asset to provide services or benefits to those who use that asset. Future economic benefit is a measure of the capacity of an asset to provide monetary benefits to those who hold or own that asset.

So this leads to the extension of the economic value concept regarding social assets. If the asset concerned is a purely social asset generating no monetary returns, then it can only be valued in terms of the sum of discounted nonmonetary benefits. This requires assigning a dollar value to the nonmonetary benefits. However, assigning a dollar value for nonmonetary benefits is subjective and impractical. Consequently, including the economic value of nonfinancial assets which are considered as social assets will yield an economic net worth that does not provide the right measure of long-term fiscal sustainability. This can lead us to discuss whether the cost-based net worth can provide a better measure for long-term fiscal sustainability than the economic net worth can.

Cost-based valuation is very different from the economic valuation concept. Under cost-based valuation, most of the assets are included in the balance sheet at cost even if they have significantly increased in value over time. Furthermore, in accordance with accounting conservatism, asset depreciation must be recorded to account for wear and tear on long-living assets. On the balance sheet, annual depreciation is accumulated over time and recorded below an asset's historical cost. The subtraction of accumulated depreciation from the historical cost results in a lower net asset value, ensuring no overstatement of an asset's true value. Because the assets are included in the balance at cost and the depreciation expense is calculated at historical cost, the balance sheet produced based on the cost-based value concept indicates nothing at all about what a firm or asset is worth. Therefore, it can be inferred that cost-based net worth measures indicate precisely nothing about long-term fiscal sustainability. Consequently, the cost-based net worth is misleading and cannot be considered as the best measure of long-term fiscal sustainability. It can also be inferred that the economic net worth measures are of highly questionable value in this respect.

2.4 *Pyramid of Accounting Bases and Measures of the Long-Term Fiscal Sustainability: Discussion and Evaluation*

The previously stated analysis leads to concluding the pyramid of accounting bases currently used and their relationship with measuring and reporting on long-term fiscal sustainability. The currently used accounting bases have provided three measures of long-term fiscal sustainability which are considered the bottom line of the balance sheets prepared according to these accounting bases. They are as follows (see Fig. 5.1):

- Net debt (ND) measure based on cash accounting
- Net financial worth (NFW)/net financial debt (NFD) measure based on modified accrual accounting
- Net worth (NW) measure based on full accrual accounting

The question here is:

- ***Do these currently used accounting bases provide practice-relevant information for measuring the government's long-term fiscal sustainability?***

Based on the previous analysis provided in Sects. 2.1, 2.2, and 2.3, the answer to this question is no. This is not surprising; all current accounting bases have provided partial measures rather than comprehensive measures. Without exception, all the balance sheets and their bottom lines are partial measures which ignore more or less items that should be included in the balance sheets. Net debt measure based on conventional cash accounting is considered as a very partial measure of long-term fiscal sustainability. It is the result of subtracting the debt obligations from the cash balances neglecting all other assets (financial and nonfinancial assets) and all other liabilities (short- and long-term liabilities). While the net financial worth recognizes all the liabilities accumulated to date and all financial assets, it does not take into account the nonfinancial assets/physical assets. This means that a great part of the assets side is neglected and, hence, the net financial worth also provides a partial measure of long-term fiscal sustainability. Unlike the previous two measures, the net worth includes all assets and all liabilities arising out of past activities but it neglects the future liabilities arising out of past activities such as pensions and superannuations. The government also has resources in addition to those that might be expected to appear on the balance sheet. These additional resources include, most importantly, the government's sovereign power to tax. The latter is also not included in the balance sheet.

This is in addition to the several problems that are related to assets valuations. Due to these problems the balance sheet and its net worth do not provide the required information about whether the governmental entity is fiscally sustainable or not. Therefore, all the currently used accounting bases (see Fig. 5.1) and the accompanied financial statements and their bottom lines provide partial measures of long-term fiscal sustainability.

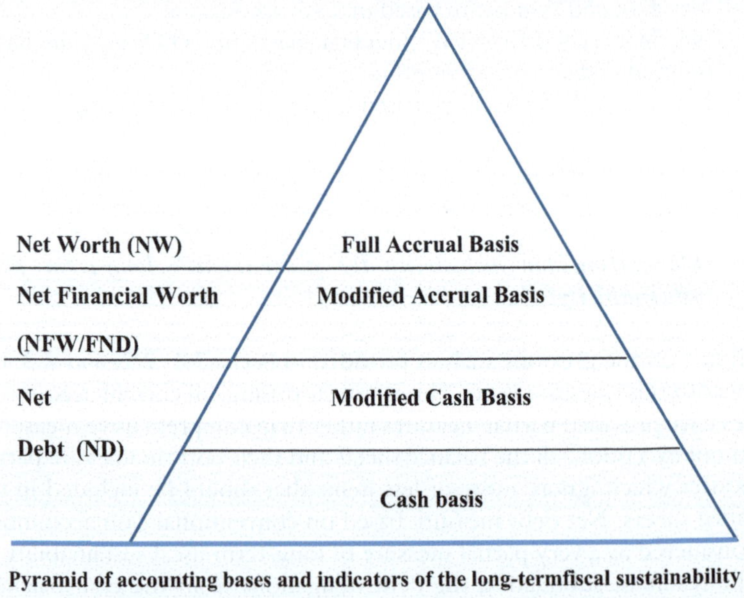

Fig. 5.1 Pyramid of accounting bases and indicators of long-term fiscal sustainability. (Source: Author)

However, in spite of the net worth in the bottom line of a balance sheet including nonfinancial assets, some argue that the net financial worth is superior to the net worth. This is because the value of physical assets/nonfinancial assets in a general government balance sheet provides little information about the government's capacity to meet its financial obligations. This is due to the following arguments suggested by Robinson (2009):

- The only unambiguously relevant measures of nonfinancial asset value from a fiscal sustainability point of view are those which reflect either the future income flows that the asset will yield or the asset's potential sale price.
- Most general government fixed assets are non-income earning (in contrast to physical assets held by for-profit corporations in the private or public enterprise sectors). This means that valuation based on future income flows (sometimes referred to as the "income approach" to valuation) is not relevant.
- Although valuation on the basis of potential sale price (sometimes referred to as "recoverable value") would, for many assets, be highly relevant to fiscal sustainability, nonfinancial assets are not generally valued in balance sheets on this basis.
- Many government nonfinancial assets would never be sold, even in an acute fiscal crisis. Many are also highly illiquid. Recoverable value in these cases would not even be, in principle, relevant to the sustainability analysis.

Therefore, the inclusion of nonfinancial assets in the net worth makes it less suitable for measuring long-term fiscal sustainability compared with the net financial worth/net financial debt.

3 Developments in the Fiscal Sustainability Reporting: Literature Review

As a result of shortcomings of the conventional accounting statements in providing information required to measure and report on long-term fiscal sustainability, different parties—standard-setters, professional bodies, practitioners, and academics—have attempted to clarify the role of accounting and accountants in how governments report on long-term fiscal sustainability. A number of standard-setters, such as the International Public Sector Accounting Standards Board (IPSASB), the Federal

Accounting Standards Advisory Board (FASAB), and the Governmental Accounting Standards Board (GASB), have worked to develop guidance and guidelines focusing on long-term fiscal sustainability reporting.

The GASB has started a project addressing fiscal sustainability in 2010. This project has dealt with whether guidance or guidelines should be provided for including additional information about fiscal sustainability as part of general purpose external financial reporting (GPEFR). The project has three objectives:

- To identify the information that users of governmental financial information need to assess a governmental entity's fiscal sustainability
- To compare those needs with the information that users receive under both current accounting and financial reporting standards and from other sources
- To consider reporting alternatives for additional information needed by users

In addition, GASB staff research attempted to identify the meaning of fiscal sustainability via a survey. The interviewees' response about the meaning of fiscal sustainability was as follows:

- The ability and willingness to maintain or improve services
- To meet financial obligations
- To achieve and maintain intergenerational equity
- To balance revenues and expenses

> In other words, financial reporting users seek to assess a public sector entity's ongoing ability to raise future revenues, to continue to deliver services, to issue debt, and to meet obligations as they become due. This means that it is important for the financial reporting users to understand a government's past and current economic conditions, in addition to assessing a government's future financial viability or fiscal sustainability.

GASB also addressed fiscal sustainability assessments, examples of which were identified, As follows:

- The assessment can be based on current fiscal policy without change.
- It can be based on reasonable assumptions about changes in tax rates or debt levels.

Some respondents prefer the assessment on current policy without change and they believe that basing the projections on currently known facts is better. Furthermore, it is hard to project fiscal policy changes in the future given the potential unreliability of assumptions. Others believe that the assessments should be made using reasonable assumptions about future fiscal policy changes. Finally, some participants said they believe that a government should make these assessments both ways. As for the time horizon, GASB did not determine a certain time horizon but the respondents did not agree about a certain period, as some respondents prefer a period of five years and other participants stated that 15–25-year projections would be better if the projections were presented on an annual basis and updated based on shorter-term information that becomes available. Unfortunately, the GASB project was stopped in 2013 and did not result in issuing guidance on reporting on long-term fiscal sustainability.

One of the important studies with respect to reporting on long-term fiscal sustainability is issued by IPSASB (2013). This study is not issued in the form of a standard but as voluntary guidance known as a Recommended Practice Guideline (RPG). The RPG aims to provide information on the impact of current policies and decisions made at the reporting date on future inflows and outflows and supplements information in the general financial statements. IPSASB (2013) has further stated that the aim of such reporting is to provide an indication of the projected long-term fiscal sustainability of an entity over a specified time horizon in accordance with stated assumptions. Similar to the GPFRs regarding the decision to adopt a certain accounting system which depends on the users and their needs, IPSASB argued that reporting on long-term fiscal sustainability depends on the existence of potential users for prospective information and their needs. IPSASB identified the potential users for long-term fiscal sustainability for entities with the following characteristics: tax and/or revenue raising power; power to incur significant debt; and power to determine the nature and level of service delivery. In addition, IPSASB supports that the assessment of long-term fiscal sustainability is to include financial and non-financial information about future economic and demographic conditions, and assumptions about country and global trends.

It is worth noting that IPSASB encourages the use of the same reporting boundary as for the financial statements to enhance the understandability of projections and increases their usefulness to the users of GPFRs. It is also possible for an entity to report long-term fiscal sustainability information using another reporting boundary such as the General

Government Sector (GGS), which can be used to enhance consistency and comparability with other jurisdictions.

IPSASB proposed the following components of long-term fiscal sustainability information: projections of future inflows and outflows and a narrative discussion explaining the projections. This is in addition to the narrative discussion of the dimensions of long-term fiscal sustainability and of the principles, assumptions, and methodology underlying the projections. It also suggested that long-term fiscal sustainability may be published as a separate report or as part of another report. Moreover, it may be published at the same time as the entity's GPFRs or at a different time.

With respect to presenting the projections of future inflows and outflows, IPSASB has advised the public sector entity to present the projections of future inflows and outflows, including the capital expenditure, and these projections should be based on current policy assumptions, and assumptions about future economic and other conditions. This information is considered as complementary to the core information in the financial statements to meet the objectives of financial reporting by including information about future inflows and outflows which do not meet the definition of and/or recognition criteria for assets and liabilities at the reporting date. IPSASB suggested reducing the costs associated with this information; the public sector entity can use the assumptions, projections, and indicators prepared by other entities such as Ministries of Finance.

Moreover, IPSASB identified three dimensions for reporting long-term fiscal sustainability information (service, revenue, and debt). The service dimension focuses on the capacity of an entity to maintain or change the volume and quality of services it provides. The revenue dimension focuses on the capacity of an entity to change the existing taxation levels or other revenue sources or to tap a new revenue source. The debt dimension concentrates on the capacity of the entity to meet its financial obligations when they are due or to refinance or increase debt as necessary. These dimensions are interrelated as the changes in one dimension affect the other dimensions. IPSASB also identified two aspects to each dimension: capacity (ability of the entity to change or influence the dimension) and vulnerability (dependence on factors outside the entity control or influence).

Moreover, IPSASB believed that reporting long-term fiscal sustainability information might not be appropriate for all entities, especially for individually controlled entities, as these entities may have limited tax-raising power and/or the cost of production of the information could likely be greater than the benefit to users. IPSASB believes that reporting long-term fiscal sustainability information is likely more relevant at the overall government level, consolidated national level, and for other entities which have tax-raising powers enabling them to generate a significant proportion of their total revenues.

While IPSASB did not determine a certain time horizon, it believed that in selecting an appropriate time horizon an entity should balance the qualitative characteristics of verifiability, faithful representation, and relevance. The majority of respondents have approved a period of five years for predicting and updating long-term fiscal sustainability information whereas others have argued that five years would be too long, suggesting a period of three years instead.

Finally, IPSAS also presented examples of indicators to assess long-term fiscal sustainability such as net debt, the difference between the gross debt and financial assets; net financial worth, total value of financial assets of an entity minus total value of its total outstanding liabilities; net worth, total value of assets minus total value of liabilities; and fiscal gap, the net present value of projected spending minus projected receipts, adjusted by the decrease (or increase) in public debt required to maintain public debt at or below the target percentage of GDP for the stated projection period.

The FASAB also published in 2008 an exposure draft of a proposed Statement of Federal Financial Accounting Standards entitled "Reporting Comprehensive Long-Term Fiscal Projections for the U.S. Government." According to this document, fiscal sustainability reporting should provide information to assist readers of Consolidated Financial Reporting (CFR) in assessing whether future budgetary resources of the U.S. government will likely be sufficient to sustain public services and to meet obligations as they become due. In other words, the users of financial reports should be provided with information that assists in assessing whether the government will continue to provide public services to the taxpayers and to assess whether financial burdens without related benefits were passed on by current-year taxpayers to future taxpayers. FASAB has required long-term fiscal projections information to be presented as required supplementary information for the first three years of implementation (2010, 2011, 2012). FASAB determined, starting from 2013, that the required information should be presented as a basic financial statement and related disclosures. The basic financial statement, long-term fiscal projections for the U.S. government, should include the following information stated in both present-value dollars and as a percentage of the present value of GDP for the projection period:

(a) Receipts, disaggregated by major programs such as Medicare, Social Security, and all other revenues, and total receipts
(b) Spending, disaggregated by major programs such as Medicare, Medicaid, Social Security, and all other non-interest spending, total non-interest spending
(c) The difference between projected receipts and projected noninterest spending

In addition, FASAB also suggested that the basic financial statement should also include comparative amounts for the current year and prior year, and the net change for each line item from the prior year and this year should be effected after the initial year of implementation.

FASAB has differentiated between financial position and financial condition (see Table 5.5). FASAB is in the view that fiscal sustainability reporting is focused on the financial condition of the federal government as a whole. Financial condition is forward-looking and multidimensional. Assessing financial condition requires financial and nonfinancial information related to the long-term fiscal outlook for the federal government. Therefore, fiscal sustainability reporting should provide information about the future to help readers assess the magnitude of future spending and receipts and the burden that any resulting deficits might place on future taxpayers.

Table 5.5 Comparison of financial position and financial condition

Financial position	*Financial condition*
Entity perspective	Broad perspective including reporting on the impact on the entity of the nation's economy and other external trends
Accrual-based or modified cash basis data	Additional, forward-based information
Financial data	Financial and nonfinancial data
Assets, liabilities, and net position	Future effects of • Current demands, risks, and uncertainties • Anticipated future events, conditions, and trends
Example: Balance sheet	Examples: • Projections of receipts, spending, and debt – In present-value dollars – As a share of GDP • Nonfinancial data, such as demographic trends

Source: FASAB (2008)

It is worth noting that FASAB agreed with IPSASB that reporting on long-term fiscal sustainability should apply to the consolidated financial report of governments but it does not apply to financial statements prepared at the entity level. Furthermore, FASAB (2016) has identified the scope and importance of long-term projections, as it is argued that long-term projections should assist the reader to understand the fiscal implications of continuing current policy without change regarding public services, and taxation along with other factors such as projected economic and demographic trends. FASAB made it clear that projections are not forecasts or predictions; they are designed to depict results that may occur under various conditions—for example, what if current policy without change regarding federal government public services and taxation are continued in the future? Projections are useful to display alternative future scenarios, but it is important to clearly explain the nature of the information being presented.

After presenting the fiscal sustainability developments by different standard-setters, it can be inferred that they have addressed almost the same points that are fundamental for measuring and reporting on long-term fiscal sustainability. However, they did not elaborate how the public sector accounting can contribute to measuring and reporting on long-term fiscal sustainability. This is not only the case of the standard-setters but also the case of public sector accounting literature, which generally does not provide a solution to how accounting for sustainability might advance. This brings us to the principal thrust of this chapter: ***To what extent can the public sector accounting go beyond the traditional accounting reporting and provide information for reporting on long-term fiscal sustainability?***

This question takes us to the next section.

4 Sustainable Accounting Approach for Reporting on Long-Term Fiscal Sustainability

Caruana et al. (2019) have argued that "while international organizations (European Commission [EC] 2013; International Public Sector Accounting Standards Board [IPSASB] 2013) and prior literature (Navarro-Galera et al. 2016; Rodríguez Bolívar et al. 2016; Drew and Dollery 2014) appreciate the usefulness of government financial statements for reporting on the financial sustainability of public sector entities,

there is no elaboration on how governmental accounting can contribute towards this objective." In other words, the current literature lacks focus on the role of accounting frameworks in the endeavor to make public sector entities financially sustainable. This means that a research gap remains in the current literature on the role of public sector accounting in assessing and reporting on long-term fiscal sustainability. This can lead to the following two questions:

- ***Do accounting bases need to be developed to be able to report on the government's long-term fiscal sustainability?***
- ***Should the scope of government financial reporting be expanded to include both backward-looking (past) activity and forward-looking (future) activity?***

In fact, public sector accountants and academics have to take the initiatives to the maximum extent possible that accounting can achieve and not stay forever on the level of traditional reporting to provide backward-looking financial information. They are now being asked to take a step further and take on a broader strategic and innovative role to develop a public sector accounting framework that can assist governments in reporting on long-term fiscal sustainability. Basically, the accountancy profession should play an important role in defining and delivering the means by which long-term fiscal sustainability is measured and reported and not leave this task to economists, statisticians, and policy analysts. While there is a clear role for the public sector accountants in fiscal sustainability reporting and in influencing how governments report on such issues, fiscal sustainability reporting also provides a number of challenges for accountants, in particular, professional development, including establishing a deeper understanding of the interdependence of social, environmental, and economic issues; long-term and future-focused accounting practices; and working alongside other professions (ACCA 2010). In addition, ACCA (2010) has recommended the following:

> There are undoubtedly a number of challenges to sustainability reporting, including difficulties of estimation and projections, materiality, understanding links between actions and impact, establishing robust indicators, verifiability and assurance and the challenge of applying the traditionally rigorous standards of accounting to sustainable development issues. *However, the accountancy profession should not shy away from the challenges presented by sustainability reporting, as it provides opportunities to develop the strengths of*

> *the profession in an important area.* The accountancy profession should seek to adapt its training support and programmes to accommodate the future needs of sustainability reporting. The experience of public sector accountants in reporting on financial indicators means they are well placed to adapt these skills and could act as leaders in the field of sustainability reporting. *Future training and development should focus on linking financial and non-financial indicators, improving accountants' understanding of how social, environmental and sustainable development issues interconnect,* ***and developing a long-term future focus alongside retrospective accounting practices.*** Also, accountants should be encouraged to work in collaboration with economists, social scientists and environmental scientists on new forms of integrated reporting.

Of course, this will require fresh thinking in terms of new accounting bases, new scope of financial reporting, and new long-term and future-focused accounting practices alongside retrospective accounting practices. As an initial step, public sector accountants and academics should develop both the accounting bases and the scope of financial reporting to start a new era in accounting. This era does not mean that the traditional form of accrual accounting financial reporting will have to be sacrificed; on the contrary, it has to be maintained, as it represents the objectivity of accounting information and is based on facts and events incurred, not projections. However, the new era means that we will evolve a forward-looking approach of accounting. In order to be able to provide practice-relevant information for measuring and reporting on long-term fiscal sustainability, the new approach (which I call ***sustainable accounting approach***) will not only comprise forward-looking information but will also include the backward-looking accounting information. In other words, the sustainable accounting approach should be based on long-term future-focused accounting practices alongside retrospective accounting practices. Accordingly, the sustainable accounting approach will include two phases:

1. Backward-looking phase: This phase is a fundamental phase that has lasted for many decades or centuries and has witnessed a lot of research work about how accountants and accounting provide objective accounting information and disclose the financial results and financial positions of both private and public sector entities. Accordingly, the backward-looking financial statement includes physical assets, financial assets (both liquid and illiquid financial assets), and all liabilities accumulated to date (see Table 5.6). In this phase,

Table 5.6 Assets and liabilities reported in backward-looking phase

Assets/inflows	*Liabilities/outflows*
Physical assets (tangible and intangible) Total financial assets (liquid and illiquid)	Total liabilities accumulated to date

Source: Author

the public sector accounting as a discipline is established on facts and events incurred and focused only on past-oriented information. We, as accountants and academics, are not ready to lose or sacrifice this phase but, on the contrary, should continue our march to improve this phase. However, accountants should not be marginalized and should not continue neglecting the new developments in the field of fiscal sustainability and keep this field only for economists, statisticians, and policy analysts, and continue arguing that accounting financial reporting should focus only on backward-looking accounting information regardless of whether this information can help in assessing and reporting on long-term fiscal sustainability or not.

2. Forward-looking phase: A forward-looking phase describes future events or results. A forward-looking financial statement predicts, projects, or uses future events as expectations or possibilities. This means that the forward-looking financial statement should include future assets, future revenues, future liabilities incurred in the future, future liabilities from the past activities, and contingent liabilities (see Table 5.7).

As is clear from the public sector accounting literature and from the aforementioned analysis, the public sector accounting standards and frameworks are focused only on the backward-looking phase. However, to move forward and to think about the government's long-term fiscal sustainability, we should take into account the impact of both past and future fiscal activities. As OBR (2011) pointed out, as a consequence of its past activity, the government has accumulated assets (physical and financial) and liabilities. Moreover, the past activity results in financial flows in the future, such as public service pensions and the government's servicing of its debt. Furthermore, the past activity has created contingent liabilities. In addition to the past activity, the forward-looking phase, that is, the government's future activity, will involve financial outflows, partly on the accumulation of future assets but mostly to pay for current spending on

Table 5.7 Assets and liabilities reported in forward-looking phase

Assets/inflows	*Liabilities/outflows*
Future assets	Future liabilities incurred in the future
	Future liabilities from past activities
Future revenues	Contingent liabilities

Source: Author

public services and transfer payments. It will also receive future revenues, mostly from taxation.

If accountants need to create a role for public sector accounting in assessing and reporting long-term fiscal sustainability, this should involve summarizing the fiscal consequences of all past and future activities. However, the current public sector accounting standards and frameworks do not allow for the inclusion of both backward-looking accounting information and forward-looking accounting information together in a financial statement such as the balance sheet. As a matter of fact, we should again ensure that we will not sacrifice the traditional form of audited financial reporting, but rather start working with the accounting approach which I call the ***sustainable accounting approach***. This approach will result in developing new accounting bases and a new scope of financial reporting. The new scope of financial reporting is not going to replace the traditional form of accounting financial reporting but will be considered as an extra/complementary or special purpose financial reporting that aims to create a new role for the public sector accounting in assessing and reporting on long-term fiscal sustainability. The following two developments will form the cornerstone of the sustainable accounting approach.

4.1 Developing the Pyramid of Accounting Bases and Measurement Focuses

The accounting bases determine the elements to be recognized in the financial statements. The earlier concluded pyramid of accounting bases (see Fig. 5.1) is based entirely on the backward-looking phase. This pyramid needs to be developed to include new accounting bases, which can allow for recognizing elements that are related to the forward-looking phase; in other words, to allow for the recognition of future elements arising out of both past and future activities. Needless to say, this is in addition to all past elements arising out of the past activities. The development of the new accounting basis will not start from scratch but rather from the point that accrual accounting has reached, which is the backward-looking phase, and complement this phase by including the forward-looking phase. Accordingly, this new basis should provide the users with information about the total assets, liabilities, revenues, expenses, and net assets arising out of past activities as well as the information about future assets, liabilities, revenues, expenses, and net assets arising from future activities. This new accounting basis is what I call ***Sustainable Full Accrual Basis***. Similar to the conventional full accrual and modified accrual, we can also have another new basis called ***Sustainable Modified Accrual Basis***, comprising all the information provided by the sustainable full accrual basis with the exception of past and future nonfinancial assets. This means that it provides the users with information about total financial assets, liabilities, revenues, expenditures, and net financial assets arising out of past activities as well as information about future financial assets, liabilities, revenues, expenditures, and net financial assets arising from future activities. While the full accrual basis and the modified accrual basis are based on different principles (matching principle, recognition principle, etc.), the sustainable full accrual basis and the sustainable modified accrual basis should also be based on some principles that enable them to reflect both past-oriented information and future-oriented information which are necessary for reporting on long-term fiscal sustainability. In fact, the information required for reporting on long-term fiscal sustainability needs to be based on new principles, which, as stated by IPSASB (2013), should include the following:

- Whether the projections should be based on current or future policy
- The approach to revenue inflows
- The approach to age-related and non-age-related programs
- The approach to sensitivity of analysis

In fact, it is too early to say whether the aforementioned principles are enough to apply the two new accounting bases or not; therefore, future research should focus on the appropriate principles for the application of both the sustainable full accrual basis and the sustainable modified accrual basis.

While the basis of accounting determines the elements to be reported or recognized in the financial statements, the measurement focus determines what is being measured. IFAC (1993) has identified four types of measurement focuses: total economic resources concept (based on full accrual basis), total financial resources concept (based on modified accrual basis), current financial resources concept (based on modified cash basis), and cash flow and cash balances concept (based on cash basis). Similarly, the two newly developed accounting bases can also result in creating two new types of measurement focuses: *Total Sustainable Economic Resources* and *Total Sustainable Financial Resources (see phase b)*. Accordingly, if we need the financial statements to measure the total sustainable economic resources, we can apply the sustainable full accrual basis, but if we need the financial statements to measure the total sustainable financial resources, we should apply the sustainable modified accrual basis. Accordingly, the relationship between the measurement focuses and the accounting bases can be shown in the following two phases:

a. **Backward-Looking Phase**: This includes the four types of measurement focuses identified by IFAC (1993) which represent the past-oriented information phase:
   - ***Total economic resources*** (and changes therein): to provide users with information about assets, liabilities, revenues, expenses, and net assets (equity) and changes therein, and whether the reporting entity is operating economically and efficiently. This means that the *total economic resources concept* is consistent with the concept of *full accrual accounting*.
   - ***Total financial resources*** (and changes therein): to provide users with information about liabilities, the financial assets available to meet those liabilities, and the amount and sources of the period's revenues and expenditures. This is consistent with the concept of *modified accrual accounting*.
   - ***Current financial resources*** (and changes therein): to provide users with information about cash flows during the period, those liabilities that must be met within a short period from reporting date, and current cash balances and receivables available to meet those liabilities. It is clear that the current financial resources concept is consistent with implications of the *modified cash basis*.
   - ***Cash flows and balances*** (and changes therein): to provide users with information about the sources and the uses of cash and cash balances at reporting date. Accordingly, this is consistent with the concept of the *cash basis*.

b. **Sustainable Forward-Looking Phase**: This is the new phase that includes the two new types of measurement focuses (total sustainable economic resources and total sustainable financial resources), which are based on the two new accounting bases (sustainable full accrual and sustainable modified accrual) and represent the information required for reporting on long-term fiscal sustainability as follows:
   - ***Total sustainable economic resources*** (and changes therein): to provide the users with information about total assets, liabilities, revenues, expenses, and net assets arising out of past activities as well as the information about future assets, liabilities, revenues, expenses, and net assets arising from future activities. This means that the total sustainable economic resources is consistent with the concept of the *sustainable full accrual basis.*
   - ***Total sustainable financial resources*** (and changes therein): to provide users with information about past and future liabilities, past and future financial assets available to meet those liabilities, and the amount and sources of the period's and future revenues and expenditures. This is consistent with the concept of the *sustainable modified accrual basis.*

Based on the aforementioned developments, the earlier developed pyramid of accounting bases and its relationship with the measurement focus shown in Fig. 5.1 can be expanded to include both the sustainable full accrual basis and the sustainable modified accrual basis and the two new measurement focuses *Total Sustainable Economic Resources* and *Total Sustainable Financial Resources* (see Fig. 5.2). In fact, the newly developed pyramid of accounting bases includes the backward-looking phase, which represents the whole march of accountants in developing the accounting discipline during the past decades and centuries and it is based on current accounting standards and frameworks. In addition, it includes the new phase, which is the sustainable forward-looking phase. This phase can be considered a fundamental phase if the accountants want to create a new role for public sector accounting to contribute to measuring the government's long-term fiscal sustainability. This phase requires the development of new accounting standards and new financial statements, either as part/supplementary of the conventional financial statements or they can be published as special purpose financial statements. They can also be published at the same time as the audited financial statements are or at another date.

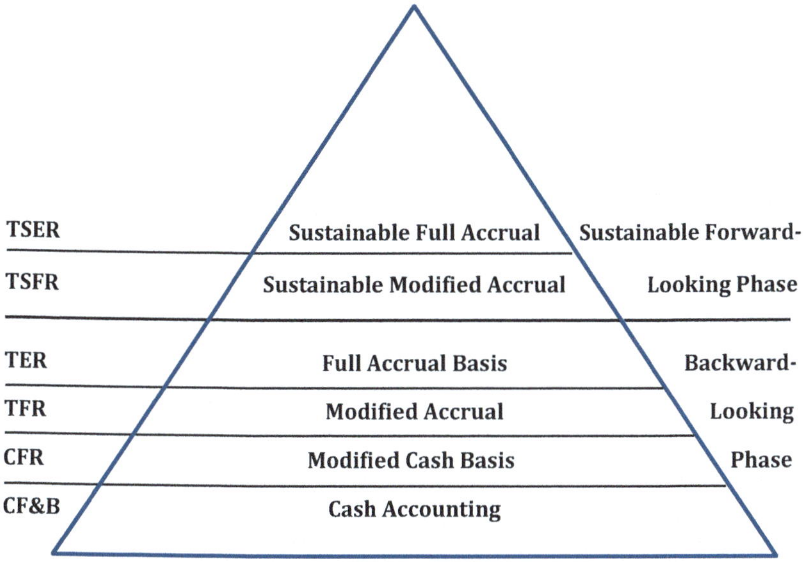

Fig. 5.2 Pyramid of accounting bases and their relationship with the measurement focuses. TSER = *Total Sustainable Economic* Resources; TSFR = *Total Sustainable Financial Resources*; TER = *Total Economic Resources*; TFR = *Total Financial Resources*; CFR = *Current Financial Resources*; CF&B = *Cash Flow and Balances*. (Source: Author)

4.2 Expanding the Scope of Government Financial Reporting and the Indictors of Long-Term Fiscal Sustainability

Accrual-based balance sheets provide a snapshot of the fiscal consequences of the government's past activity at any point of time, by providing information on its stock of assets and liabilities. Balance sheets provide interesting information, but their usefulness as an indicator of long-term fiscal sustainability is limited by their backward-looking nature (OBR 2011). They exclude the future cost of known expenditure commitments and, crucially, the present value of future revenues. The greatest financial resource of any government is, of course, its ability to levy future taxes (OBR 2011). As previously shown, the traditional balance sheets provide three measures of fiscal sustainability (ND, NFW/NFD, and NW) which capture an entirely backward-looking subset of the government's activities. These three measures have been criticized as measures of long-term fiscal sustainability because they exclude futures liabilities and contingent liabilities arising out of past activities. However, in order to assess long-term fiscal sustainability, we need to understand how future government activity might affect these balance sheets (or at least some of the summary measures based upon them).

Based on the sustainable full accrual basis, we can expand the scope of the balance sheet, naming it the ***Sustainable Balance Sheet***.

The sustainable balance sheet shall include both backward-looking and forward-looking accounting information. This means that the sustainable balance sheet will include both past-oriented accounting information and future-oriented accounting information. Transparent information on current and future assets, liabilities, revenues, expenditures, and net assets is the raw material for assessing long-term fiscal sustainability. As things stand, the existing financial statements are not, of themselves, sufficient to meet the needs of users to assess the fiscal sustainability of government. In fact, in order to provide information about long-term fiscal sustainability, we cannot prepare the financial statements based only on all assets and all liabilities accumulated to date; they should include projections of future inflows and outflows. Therefore, the sustainable balance sheet will include three types of information as follows:

- Past-oriented accounting information, which is prepared in accordance with the current accounting standards such as International Public Sector Accounting Standards (IPSAS).
- Present value/discounted value of future liabilities and contingent liabilities arising out of past activity
- Present value/discounted value of future assets, future revenues, and future liabilities arising from future activities

Obviously, the sustainable balance sheet will not start from scratch as the past-oriented accounting information which is related to the backward-looking phase can be obtained from the existing financial statements that are prepared in accordance with the IPSAS. Regarding the second type of accounting information, the sustainable balance sheet can benefit from the experience of the UK in preparing the Whole of Government Accounts (WGA). The WGA paints a broader picture of the public sector balance sheet as it includes financial and nonfinancial assets and liabilities, plus some costs incurred in the past for which the payments will occur in the future. In particular, they take account of net pension liabilities, provisions, and commitments for finance leases such as PFI. WGA also reports provisions and contingent liabilities related to risks of future costs that could, but are not certain to, materialize as a result of past activities.

While the WGA balance sheet provides a useful snapshot of the fiscal impact of past government activity, including some future cash flows, it is of limited use in assessing long-term fiscal sustainability, as it excludes the expected impact of future government activity, notably future spending and future tax raising. To assess long-term sustainability, we also need to estimate the potential fiscal impact of future government activity.

This can be done by making long-term projections for public spending, revenues, and financial transactions, and then assessing their implications for the potential path of public sector net debt, net financial worth/net financial liabilities, and net worth. This is consistent with IPSASB (2013), where it is argued that long-term fiscal sustainability information is broader than information derived from the financial statements. It includes projected inflows and outflows related to the provision of goods and services and programs providing social benefits using current policy assumptions over a specified time horizon. This means that it takes into account decisions made by the entity on or before the reporting date which will give rise to future outflows that do not meet the definition of and/or recognition criteria for liabilities at the reporting date. Similarly, it takes into account future inflows that do not meet the definition of and/or recognition criteria for assets at the reporting date.

FASAB (2008) is also in the view that long-term projections should help the reader to understand the fiscal implications of continuing current policy without change regarding public services, taxation, and other factors such as projected economic and demographic trends. This also means that the long-term projections should take into account three types of assumptions (FASAB 2008): policy assumptions, which address the factors under the direct control of the federal government concerning the taxes and other revenues to be received by the federal government and the public services to be provided by the federal government; economic assumptions, which address the economic factors that are not under the direct legislative control of the federal government (e.g., inflation and growth in GDP); and demographic assumptions, which address projected population trends (e.g., birth rates, mortality rates, and net immigration). Basically, the combination of policy, economic, and demographic assumptions will determine the future projected receipts and spending.

In addition, projections of deficits, surpluses, and debt are a central feature of the long-term fiscal sustainability reporting. FASAB made clear that projections are not forecasts or predictions; they are designed to depict results that may occur under various conditions; for example, what if current policy without change regarding federal government public services and taxation are continued in the future? Projections are useful to display alternative future scenarios, but it is important to clearly explain the nature of the information being presented (FASAB 2008, 2015). Consequently, the sustainable balance sheet, whether it is based on the sustainable full accrual basis or sustainable modified accrual basis, is shown in Tables 5.8 and 5.9 respectively.

Table 5.8 Sustainable balance sheet based on sustainable full accrual accounting

Assets	*Liabilities*
Physical assets	All liabilities accumulated to date
Liquid financial assets	Future liabilities from past activity:
Illiquid financial assets	– PV of commitments
PV of future assets	– PV social security
PV of taxes	– PV health insurance
PV other revenues	– PV other expenditures
Net worth of SOE	PV of contingent liabilities
	PV of future liabilities incurred in the future
	Sustainable net worth (SNW)

Source: Author

Table 5.9 Sustainable balance sheet based on sustainable modified accrual accounting

Assets	*Liabilities*
Liquid financial assets	All liabilities accumulated to date
Illiquid financial assets	Future liabilities from past activity:
PV of future assets	– PV of commitments
PV of taxes	– PV social security
PV other revenues	– PV health insurance
Net worth of SOE	– PV other expenditures
	PV of contingent liabilities
	PV of future liabilities incurred in the future
	Sustainable net financial worth (SNFW)

Source: Author

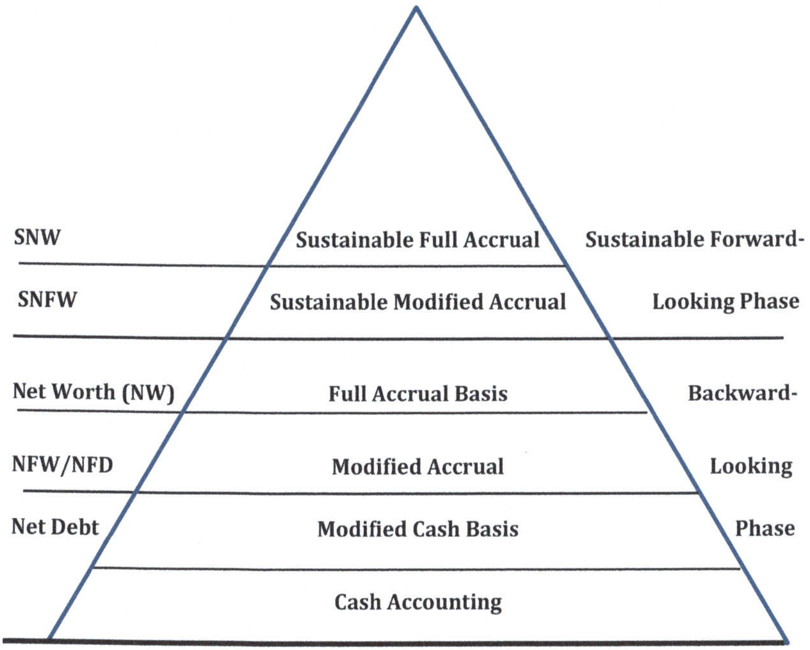

Fig. 5.3 Pyramid of accounting bases and their relationship with the long-term fiscal sustainability indicators. ND = *Net Debt*; NFD = *Net Financial Debt*; NFW = *Net Financial Worth*; NW = *Net Worth*; SNFW = *Sustainable Net Financial Worth*; SNW = *Sustainable Net Worth*. (Source: Author)

The bottom line of the sustainable balance sheet will be the sustainable net worth (SNW) in the case of using the sustainable full accrual basis and sustainable net financial worth (SNFW) in the case of using the sustainable modified accrual basis (see Fig. 5.3). As a result of including all past and future assets and all past and future liabilities in the sustainable balance sheet, the SNW gives a full picture of the fiscal impact of past government activity and the potential fiscal impact of future government activity. Accordingly, it can be inferred that the sustainable balance sheet can report on long-term fiscal sustainability and the SNW and SNFW can be used to measure long-term fiscal sustainability.

It has been argued by Robinson (2009) that net financial worth is a superior measure for fiscal sustainability than the net worth is. Nevertheless, is this superiority still valid for the SNFW? In fact, the following two capacities can, to some extent, assist in considering whether the SNFW or the SNW will be the most appropriate measure for long-term fiscal sustainability:

- *Fiscal capacity* is the government's ability and willingness to meet its financial obligations as they become due on an ongoing basis.
- *Service capacity* is the government's ability and willingness to meet its commitments to provide services on an ongoing basis.

If the financial reporting users need to assess whether a government will be able to meet its obligations as they become due, the SNFW measure is more suitable for measuring long-term fiscal sustainability and this will require the preparation of the sustainable balance sheet based on sustainable modified accrual accounting. However, if the financial reporting users need to assess whether the government will be able to continue in the future to provide services at the current levels and on an ongoing basis, the SNW is a more appropriate measure for long-term fiscal sustainability. This is due to the fact that the future services are mainly provided by the physical assets and this will require the preparation of the sustainable balance sheet based on the sustainable full accrual accounting basis.

However, the preparation of the sustainable balance sheet will raise many issues and problems which need to be addressed by the public sector accountants, academics, and standard-setting bodies such as IPSASB. These issues are as follows:

- Given that the sustainable balance sheet includes the present value of future assets and liabilities, what discount rate should be used to do such discounting?
- Should physical assets be treated as "marketable," which means that they can be used to finance the liabilities?
- Should debt be valued at face or market value?
- Should contingent liabilities be taken at their actuarial value?
- Should the tax revenue or social security be extended forward assuming today's legislation (Yeyati and Sturzenegger 2007)?
- How can public sector accountants most usefully present the sustainable balance sheet information?
- How can we improve long-term revenue and spending projections?
- How should we deal with contingent liabilities in long-term projections (OBR 2011)?

In addition to the aforementioned issues, we will face the measurement issues of each item included in both the assets side and the liabilities side. Therefore, the actual implementation of the sustainable accounting approach into practice needs a lot of work. Further research from all interested bodies such as public sector accountants, standard-setting bodies, and academics should be conducted to resolve the outstanding issues.

5 Conclusion

The contribution made in this chapter can be considered as a response to the ACCA which stated that ***"the accountancy profession should not shy away from the challenges presented by sustainability reporting, as it provides opportunities to develop the strengths of the profession in an important area."***

Until now, the long-term fiscal sustainability of governments is still a main concern of all stakeholders (taxpayers, citizens, public managers, politicians, and investors) and has become one of the main objectives of national governments. Reporting on long-term fiscal sustainability is fundamental for all these stakeholders. It gives an indication of the ability of a government to maintain both its fiscal capacity and service capacity over the long term. On the one hand, maintaining the fiscal capacity gives assurance that the government is able to meet its obligations when they are due and gives an indication that the public debt is still within affordable level. In fact, high and increasing debt levels are harmful to governments' fiscal positions and have a negative impact on economic growth. On the other hand, maintaining the government's service capacity ensures the ability of a government to continue providing its services in the future. However, ensuring long-term fiscal sustainability requires that governments should make long-term projections of future revenues and liabilities, and take into account the socioeconomic and environmental factors to adopt the long-term financial projections accordingly. This means that reporting on long-term fiscal sustainability should include both backward-looking information and forward-looking information. This has raised a debate among standard-setters who support the notion that public sector accounting should focus only on traditional general purpose financial statements (past-oriented information) and those who wish to extend the boundary of standard-setting and public sector accounting to a potentially forward-looking general purpose financial reporting (Dabbicco 2019).

While different standard-setters (e.g., IPSASB and FASAB) have issued different guidelines and guidance related to reporting on long-term fiscal sustainability, this debate is not yet resolved. In addition, the public sector accounting literature does not elaborate on how public sector accounting can report on long-term fiscal sustainability. Accordingly, the main objective of this chapter was to contribute to this debate by elaborating on how public sector accounting can report on long-term fiscal sustainability. This brings us to the principal thrust of this chapter: *To what extent can the public sector accounting go beyond the traditional accounting reporting and provide information for reporting on long-term fiscal sustainability*?

This chapter has concluded that the traditional general purpose financial reporting, based on the current accounting bases, does not provide accounting information which can assist in measuring the government long-term fiscal sustainability. Actually, all current accounting bases have provided partial measures rather than comprehensive measures. Therefore, I have attempted to elaborate the role of public sector accounting in measuring and reporting on long-term fiscal sustainability by developing the sustainable accounting approach. The development of this approach has been based on two cornerstones: (1) developing the accounting bases and measurement focus; and (2) expanding the scope of government financial reporting and the indicators of long-term fiscal sustainability.

The development of the accounting bases was required to allow for recognizing future elements arising out of both past and future activities, in addition to all elements arising from the past activity. This has resulted in developing two accounting bases, which I call the sustainable full accrual basis and the sustainable modified accrual basis. The sustainable full accrual basis provides users with information about total assets, liabilities, revenues, expenses, and net assets arising from past activities and also provides information about future assets, liabilities, revenues, expenses, and net assets arising from future activities. This basis has resulted in creating a new measurement focus, which I call the *total sustainable economic resources*. In addition, the sustainable modified accrual basis provides all information provided by the sustainable full accrual basis with the exception of the past and future nonfinancial assets. This basis has also led to creating another measurement focus, which I call *total sustainable financial resources*. In fact, accounting bases determine the elements that should be recognized in the financial statements whereas the measurement focus determines what is being measured. The development of the two accounting bases and the two measurements focuses can assist in developing a long-term future focus alongside retrospective accounting practices, and hence the role of public sector accounting can be extended to go beyond the traditional general purpose financial reporting to forward-looking general purpose financial reporting.

Based on the development of accounting bases and measurement focuses, I have expanded the scope of the balance sheet to call it the *sustainable balance sheet*. The sustainable balance sheet will include both past-oriented information and future-oriented information. Therefore, the sustainable balance sheet will include three types of information: (1) past-oriented accounting information, which is prepared in accordance with the current accounting standards such as IPSAS; (2) present value/discounted value of future liabilities and contingent liabilities arising out of past activity; and (3) present value/discounted value of future assets, future revenues, and future liabilities arising from future activities. The inclusion of these three types of information in the sustainable balance sheet is consistent with IPSASB (2013), where it is argued that long-term fiscal sustainability information is broader than information derived from the financial statements. It includes projected inflows and outflows related to the provision of goods and services and programs providing social benefits using current policy assumptions over a specified time horizon.

It is worth noting that the content of the sustainable balance sheet will differ according to which accounting basis is used. The use of the sustainable full accrual leads to the recognition of all past and future assets, liabilities, revenues, expenses whereas the use of sustainable modified accrual accounting leads to the recognition of all elements recognized under the sustainable full accrual basis with the exception of the past and future non-financial assets. The bottom line of the sustainable balance sheet will be the SNW in the case of using the sustainable full accrual basis and the SNFW in the case of using the sustainable modified accrual basis. As a result of including all past and future assets and all past and future liabilities in the sustainable balance sheet, the SNW gives a full picture of the fiscal impact of past government activity and the potential fiscal impact of future government activity. Accordingly, it can be inferred that the sustainable balance sheet can report on long-term fiscal sustainability and the SNW and SNFW can be used to measure long-term fiscal sustainability. I have also inferred that the government's two capacities (fiscal capacity and service capacity) can indicate in which case the SNW or SNFW can be considered more suitable for measuring long-term fiscal sustainability. I have suggested that when the financial reporting users need to assess whether a government will be able to meet its obligations as they become due, the SNFW measure is more suitable for measuring long-term fiscal sustainability and when the financial reporting users need to assess whether the government will be able to continue in the future to provide services at the current levels and on an ongoing basis, the SNW is more appropriate for measuring long-term fiscal sustainability.

Future research is required to investigate the practical implications for the implementation of the sustainable accounting approach in the public sector. Further, future research is needed to research its impact on the current and future accounting standards, financial statements, and auditing.

References

ACCA. (2010). *Sustainability Reporting Matters: What Are National Governments Doing About It?* The Association of Chartered Certified Accountants.

Aquino, A., & Cardoso, R. (2019). Accounting Framework (Re)Interpretation to Accommodate Tensions from Financial Sustainability Competing Concepts: Published in J. Caruana et al. (Eds.), *Financial Sustainability of Public Sector Entities, Public Sector Financial Management.* https://doi.org/10.1007/978-3-030-06037-4_5.

Australian Accounting Research Foundation (AARF). (1995, March). *Financial Reporting by Government.* Exposure Draft 62, Melbourne.

Bird, G. (2003). Restructuring the IMF's Lending Facilities. *The World Economy, 26*(2), 225–245.

Bisogno, M., Santis, S., & Tommasetti, A. (2015). Public-Sector Consolidated Financial Statements: An Analysis of the Comment Letters on IPSASB's Exposure Draft No. 49. *International Journal of Public Administration, 38*(4), 311–324.

Blejer, M., & Cheasty, A. (1991). How to Measure the Fiscal Deficit: Analytical and Methodological Issues. Washington, DC: International Monetary Fund. Retrieved from www.imf.org.

Buiter, W. (1990). *Principles of Budgetary and Financial Policy.* Cambridge, MA: MIT Press.

Buiter, W. (2004). Joys and Pains of Public Debt. In P. de Gijsel and. H. Schenk (Eds.), *Multidisciplinary Economics: The Birth of a New Economics Faculty in the Netherlands.* Kluwer Publishers.

Carini, C., & Teodori, C. (2019). Making Financial Sustainability Measurement More Relevant: An Analysis of Consolidated Financial Statements: Published in J. Caruana et al. (Eds.), *Financial Sustainability of Public Sector Entities, Public Sector Financial Management.* https://doi.org/10.1007/978-3-030-06037-4-6.

Caruana, J., Brusca, I., Caperchione, E., Cohen, S., & Manes Rossi, F, (2019). Exploring the Relevance of Accounting Frameworks in the Pursuit of Financial Sustainability of the Public Sector Entities: A Holistic Approach. Published in Caruana et al. (Eds.), *Financial Sustainability of Public Sector Entities*. https://doi.org/10.1007/978-3-030-06037-4-1.

Chapman, J. (2008). State and Local Fiscal Sustainability: The Challenges. *Public Administration Review, 68*(s1), S115–S131. https://doi.org/10.1111/j.1540-6210.2008.00983.x.

Cortes, J. (2004). The Meaning of Intergenerational Equity in Governmental Financial Statements. *Public Fund Digest, IV*(1), 58–76.

Dabbicco, G. (2018). A Comparison of Debt Measures in Fiscal Statistics and Public Sector Financial Statements. *Public Money and Management., 38*(7), 511–518.

Dabbicco, G. (2019). The Potential Role of Public Sector Accounting Frameworks Towards Financial Sustainability Reporting, Published in Caruana et al. (Eds.), *Financial Sustainability of Public Sector Entities*. https://doi.org/10.1007/978-3-030-06037-4-1.

Dennis, I. (2018). What Is a Conceptual Framework for Financial Reporting? *Accounting in Europe, 15*(3), 374–401. https://doi.org/10.1080/17449480.2018.1496269.

Drew, J., & Dollery, B. (2014). The Impact of Metropolitan Amalgamations in Sydney on Municipal Financial Sustainability. *Public Money and Management, 34*(4), 281–288.

EC. (2013). *Report from the Commission to the Council and the European Parliament—Towards Implementing Harmonized Public Sector Accounting Standards in MS—The Suitability of IPSAS for the MS*. Luxembourg: Publication Office.

Federal Accounting Standards Advisory Board (FASAB). (2008, September). *Reporting Comprehensive Long-Term Fiscal Projections for the U.S. Government*. Exposure Draft.

Federal Accounting Standards Advisory Board (FASAB). (2015). *Statement of Federal Financial Accounting Standards 36: Comprehensive Long-Term Projections for the U.S Government*. Version 14 (06/15). Retrieved from www.fasab.gov/fiscal-sustainability-reporting-sffas-36/.

Federal Accounting Standards Advisory Board (FASAB). (2016). Handbook of Federal Accounting Standards and Other Pronouncements, as Amended, Statement of Federal Financial Accounting Concepts (SFFAC) SFFAC 1: Objectives of Federal Financial Reporting FASAB Handbook. Version 15 (06/16).

Gooptu, S. (2005). Achieving Fiscal Sustainability. In *East Asia Decentralizes: Making Local Government Work* (pp. 53–65). Washington, DC: World Bank.
IFAC. (1991). *Financial Reporting by National Governments.* Issued by the International Federation of Accountants, Study 1.
IFAC. (1993). *Elements of the Financial Statements of the National Governments.* Issued by the International Federation of Accountants, Study 2.
IFAC. (1996). *Definition and Recognition of Revenues.* Study 9.
IFAC. (1998). *Guideline for Governmental Financial Reporting.* Exposure Draft.
IPSASB. (2013). *Reporting on the Long-Term Sustainability of Public Sector Entity's Finances.* Recommended Practice Guideline No. 3.
Mellor, T. (1996). Why Governments Should Produce Balance Sheets. *Australian Journal of Public Administration, 55*(1), 78–81.
Mellor, T. (1997). Why Governments Should Produce Balance Sheets. In *IFAC: Perspectives on Accrual Accounting, IFAC, 1997.*
Navarro-Galera, A., Rodríguez Bolívar, M. P., Alcaide Muñoz, L., & López Subires, M. D. (2016). Measuring the Financial Sustainability and Its Influential Factors in Local Governments. *Applied Economics, 48*(41), 3961–3975.
Office for Budget Responsibility (OBR). (2011, March). *What Should We Include in the Fiscal Sustainability Report?* Discussion paper No. 1.
Ouda, H. (2005). *Transition to Accrual Accounting in the Public Sector of Developed and Developing Countries: Problems and Requirements, with Special Focus on the Netherlands and Egypt* (p. 405). Veenendaal: Universal Press.
Ouda, H. (2006). Cash Accounting and the Backwardness of Government Accounting and Related Systems. *Public Fund Digest, 6*(1), 55–65. Washington, DC: The International Consortium on Governmental Financial Management (ICGFM).
Robinson, M. (1996). *Public Sector Net Worth: Is it Worth Measuring?* Australian Parliamentary Library—1995–96 Research paper 36.
Robinson, M. (2009). *Accrual Budgeting and Fiscal Policy.* IMF Working Paper.
Rodríguez Bolívar, M. P., Navarro Galera, A., Alcaide Muñoz, L., & López Subirés, M. D. (2016). Risk Factors and Drivers of Financial Sustainability in Local Government: An Empirical Study. *Local Government Studies, 42*(1), 29–51.
Rodríguez, M. P., & López-Subires, M. D. (2017). Financial Sustainability in Governments. A New Concept and Measure for Meeting New Information Needs. In *Financial Sustainability in Public Administration.* Cham: Palgrave Macmillan.
Rodríguez, M. P., Navarro, A., Alcaide, L., & López, M. D. (2016). Measuring the Financial Sustainability and Its Influential Factors in Local Governments. *Applied Economics, 48*(41), 3961–3975.

Rowles, T. (1992). *Financial Reporting of Infrastructure and Heritage Assets by Public Sector Entities*. AARF Discussion Paper No. 17, Melbourne.

Schick, A. (2005). Sustainable Budget Policy: Concepts and Approaches. *OECD Journal on Budgeting, 5*(1), 107–126.

Silvia, N. (2011). Sustainability of Public Resources—International Debate. *AUDCE, 7*(4), 187–198.

Walker, R. G. (2011). Issues in the Preparation of Public Sector Consolidated Statements. *Abacus, 47*(4), 477–500.

Yeyati, E., & Sturzenegger, F. (2007, October). *A Balance-Sheet Approach to Fiscal Sustainability*. Working Paper-Center for International Development at Harvard University, No. 150.

PART II

The Users' Perspective

CHAPTER 6

A Suggested Dynamic Model for Making Public Sector Accrual Accounting and Financial Reporting More User Practice-Relevant: Using Practice-Oriented Co-Design Approach

1 Introduction

The movement towards the New Public Management (NPM) has required the reforming of public sector accounting through the adoption of accrual accounting, performance-based budgeting, and accrual budgeting in the public sector (Hood 1995; Ball and Grubnic 2008; Steccolini 2019). The NPM philosophy is based on the assumption that public sector entities regardless of prior orientation would be more efficient and effective if run like their private sector counterparts (Hooper and Kearins 2005; Guarini 2016; Neves and Gomez-Villegas 2020). However, while many scholars have exerted great efforts in the last three decades aiming at reforming and developing public sector accounting, these efforts are still of little value to the public sector accounting practice, particularly from users' perspective. This has been proven by different studies such as Lűder's case study (2013) on the adoption of accrual budgeting and accounting in the German state of Hessen. One of his conclusions was that politicians neither appreciated nor used the improved accounting information resulting from the adoption of accrual accounting and budgeting in the state of Hessen. Other researchers (e.g., Hyndman et al. 2005; Caruana and Farrugia 2018) have also reached the same conclusion, observing that

H. Ouda, *Practice-Relevant Accrual Accounting for the Public Sector*, Public Sector Financial Management,
https://doi.org/10.1007/978-3-030-51595-9_6

politicians are not interested in the accounting information provided by the accrual accounting and budgeting. In addition, Yamamoto (2014) reached similar results in Japan. In fact, Yamamoto gave some well-chosen examples of objectives that politicians are interested in, such as finding resources for new policy initiatives, trade-offs and financial cuts, avoiding overspending of budgets, resource allocation, and avoiding depreciation costs. Basically, these objectives of politicians are mainly related to carrying out the budget functions, some of which can be served by accounting and some others for which accounting plays no role. Moreover, many of the politicians' financial information needs cannot be satisfied only by general purpose financial reporting but also require a specific context-bound accounting and financial reporting system, even though it contrasts with the New Public Financial Management (NPFM) (Olson 2001). Furthermore, Christiaens (2014) argues that in the political arena the pros and cons of cash accounting and accrual accounting are not the issue; the main questions are the different users' needs. This should, in turn, make the scholars of public sector accounting exert more research efforts to develop a conceptual framework approach, which can lead to the understanding of the diverging needs of different users. Mayston (1992) argues that a central role of an adequate conceptual framework for financial reporting is then to identify user needs for accounting information and how best to satisfy them. He further states that making the right connections can be very productive in meeting the user needs. Moreover, to satisfy the politicians' and other users' needs, Van Helden (2014) asked the CIGAR community to develop a practice-oriented research agenda on the use of accounting information by politicians and other users. Current accounting literature has indicated that several highly respected accounting scholars have addressed the failure of accounting research to improve the accounting practices and to make the public sector accounting more user practice-relevant (Inanga and Schneider 2005; Demski 2001; Assad 2001; Askim 2007; Coleman 2007; Jorge et al. 2016; Van Helden and Reichard 2018). This, in turn, means that public sector accounting should start a new era that shifts its focus from attempting to fit users and their needs into the design process to challenging the design process to better fit into users' practice. Accordingly, the goal of this chapter is to explore a method for insight generation of a user practice-relevant public sector accrual accounting and financial reporting system. This method uses a practice-oriented co-design approach aiming at conceptualizing a dynamic model for designing an accrual accounting and financial reporting system that can produce practice-relevant accounting information which can take into account the diverging needs of different users and can enhance its use and appreciation by politicians and other users. Accordingly, the research questions are as follows:

- ***Why do public sector accrual accounting and financial reporting fail to be user practice-relevant?***
- ***Can the use of the practice-oriented co-design approach overcome this failure and lead to developing a dynamic model aimed at designing a practice-relevant public sector accrual accounting and financial reporting system that satisfies the diverging needs of different users, and if so, how?***

The chapter's contributions to the literature are twofold: First, to the best of my knowledge, there is no study that uses the practice-oriented co-design approach in accounting as it is mainly designed for engineering studies. Consequently, this chapter comprises the first study to develop a new version of the practice-oriented co-design approach that integrates the efforts of accounting researchers, practitioners, consultants, standard-setting bodies, and users to produce a user practice-relevant accounting and financial reporting system that considers the diverging needs of different users. The practice-oriented co-design approach is developed for applying a user-centered orientation for sustainable design which blends emerging concepts of co-design and co-creation with a practice-oriented approach. This approach is considered important because designing an accounting system without a clear focus on the user context and creating a channel for communication among accounting researchers, practitioners, consultants, users, and standard-setters often results in unintended and unsustainable outcomes.

Second, this chapter has conceptualized a dynamic model which is especially important for countries that have to follow their own method of adoption of accrual accounting and accrual budgeting in the public sector, as it can assist them in designing a user practice-relevant system from the outset and in making it more dynamic by taking into consideration the changes in the social, political, economic, regulatory, and technological environment, hence fulfilling the new information needs of current and potential users. Thus, our study contributes to a deeper understanding of the dynamics of the users' needs and provides insight into the development of a user-practice-relevant public sector accounting and financial reporting system.

The remainder of the chapter is structured as follows. Section 2 deals with a critical analysis of the reasons for the failure of public sector accounting in being user practice-relevant. Section 3 develops a practice-oriented co-design approach to be applied to public sector accounting (as it is currently applied to engineering studies). Section 4 focuses on the conceptualization of a dynamic model for making public sector accounting more user practice-relevant. Section 5 concludes the chapter.

2 Public Sector Accounting and Financial Reporting and Their Failure in Being User Practice-Relevant

In fact, the traditional accounting approach for designing a suitable public sector accounting and financial reporting system is based on the following basic hypothesis: *"The decision to adopt a certain accounting and financial reporting system in the governmental entities depends heavily on what kind of financial information we want to be provided by this system. In order to determine this information, we need to know: Who the users are of public sector accounting and financial reporting and what their needs are. Consequently, the objectives of accounting and financial reporting can be determined. Once those objectives are determined, the accounting principles and practices or procedures should follow logically from those objectives, namely, the design of the suitable public accounting and financial reporting system can consequently be determined"* (AICPA 1973; Lűder 1989; IFAC 1991; Ouda 2005). Accordingly, the suggested reference framework or the underlying basic hypothesis is depicted in Fig. 6.1.

So the traditional accounting approach (called "user needs" approach) has been widely accepted as the basis for any conceptual framework (McCartney 2004). Suggests the logic of the user needs approach which is used to construct a conceptual framework is as follows:

a. Identify the users to be served, and their decisions.
b. For each decision, identify the accounting information that can be provided.
c. In each case, compare benefits and costs and choose the alternative with the greatest net benefit.

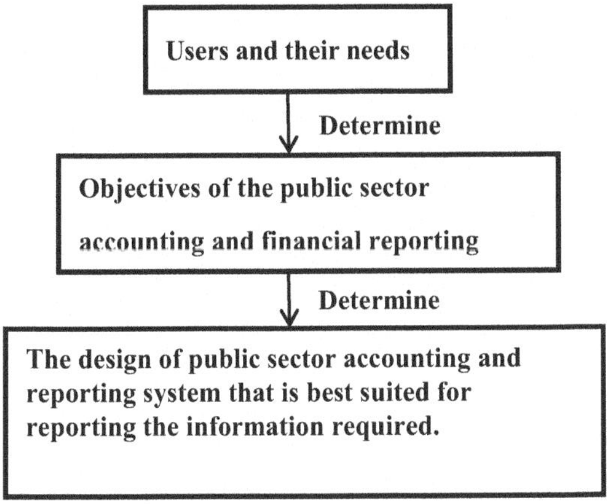

Fig. 6.1 Reference framework. (Source: (Ouda 2005))

If the objective of financial reporting is determined as the provision of the information needs specified, fundamental concepts can be derived followed by accounting standards, in a normative or deductive approach (McCartney 2004). Generally, the identification of the users of financial reporting and their needs can be carried out normatively or positively. The normative approach identifies the users' information needs by a priori theorizing, but this theorizing must be derived from empirically plausible, actual or potential, users with empirically plausible classes of the decision to be taken (Rutherford 1992). By contrast, the positive approach uses empirical methods to determine the users who use or would use the public sector financial reports and to establish either what decisions they wish to take or what information they perceive they need or both. However, conceptual frameworks themselves tend to be normative in approach and to base arguments about information needs on a priori assertions rather than rigorous empirical research (Rutherford 1992). Jones and Pendlebury (2000) also argue that public sector accounting has been based on "hypothesized users and hypothesized needs.". This, in turn, means that standard-setters have hypothesized the accounting information needs of the users without communicating or coordinating with them. McCartney (2004) assert this fact:

> The purpose of financial reporting, it is alleged, is to serve the user/consumer of financial statements. The task of the preparer/standard-setter is to find out what the consumers need/want, and give it to them. At first sight,

> this seems overwhelmingly reasonable, and indeed unarguable, which is how it is presented in the official statements. Neither FASB's Conceptual Framework Project nor the ASB's Statement of Principles attempt[s] to justify the adoption of user needs by any explicit theoretical rationale. The reader is presented with a *fait accompli*, a self-evident truth, and theoretical argument is avoided by positing the preparers of financial statements as mere suppliers of accounting goods to meet consumer demand. ***The users/consumers are not actually allowed to make demands however: they are not asked what they want, and what is prescribed is disconnected from any actual user needs, which become logically redundant.***

Moreover, the practical experiences of many countries with respect to the adoption of accrual accounting and accrual budgeting have proven the failure of accounting in providing practice-relevant information for politicians and other users (Hyndman et al. 2005; Lűder 2013; Van Helden and Northcott 2010; Van Helden and Reichard 2018). In addition, many accounting scholars have also addressed the failure of accounting research in improving accounting practices (Abrahamson and Eisenman 2001; Bazerman 2005; Inanga and Schneider 2005; Demski 2001). Furthermore, the report of the American Institute of Certified Public Accountants' (AICPA) Special Committee on Financial Reporting (Jenkin's Committee) entitled *Improving Financial Reporting—A Customer Focus* (AICPA 1994) provided the first empirical evidence that financial reporting was not effectively meeting user needs. This is in addition to the lack of appropriate and structured research to identify the ongoing and emerging needs of the users for accounting information and to develop products to meet those needs (Inanga and Schneider 2005). Basically, we see that there are several reasons underlying the failure of public sector accounting and financial reporting to be user practice-relevant.

First, the users themselves are unable to determine their information needs. This has been indicated by an earlier study (Ouda 2005) which aimed at determining the user information needs in the Dutch central government and Egyptian central government. In order to empirically identify the users' needs, the author has interviewed some high-level officials in the Dutch central government such as the Dutch Court of Audit, Central Plan Bureau, Ministry of Finance, and Central Bureau for Statistics, and some high-level officials in the Ministry of Finance, the Central Auditing Organization, and the Ministry of Planning in Egypt. When he asked them about their information needs, he found out that all of them were focusing on the information, which is currently provided in accordance with the applicable laws and regulations that specify the types and timing of financial information that they are entitled to receive. Besides, they are not able to identify the information that should be provided to them. This finding is consistent with what Sutcliffe (1985) said: "One of the biggest problems in identifying users' needs is their own inability to articulate what these are in any convincing way. They cannot assess the importance of information that has not previously been provided and, if asked, tend to ask for information that reflects the prevailing conventional wisdom." Anthony (1978) has also argued that users (e.g., managers) can neither appreciate nor judge the importance of information that has not yet been furnished. In addition, Anthony stated that, in the absence of hard evidence, therefore, one must rely on one's own judgment as to what information a user ***should*** need. This is, of course, a highly subjective and speculative process, but there seems to be no alternative (Anthony 1978). Consequently, the inability of the users to determine their financial information needs has resulted in those needs being determined by others, and this can explain why the public sector accounting and financial reporting fail to provide the practice-relevant accounting information to the users (politicians, public managers, and others).

Second, the accounting and financial reporting system in the public sector does not effectively provide or take into account the financial information required for carrying out the budget functions. Unlike the private sector, there is a very close relationship between the budget and the accounting system in the governmental sector. The budget is a financial plan and describes proposed expenditures and the means of financing them. The main task of the accounting system in the governmental sector is to execute the budget and to report on its results and performance. Jones (2003) argued that for the central government, the budgeting and accounting systems are inextricably bound with one another. Hence, most of the principles and practices of budgeting are principles and practices of accounting and vice versa. In addition, Drebin et al. (1981) stated that governmental financial reporting has a unique feature (in comparison with commercial financial reporting), which is the inclusion of budgetary information and comparisons (budgetary comparisons) in the financial reports and this information is important for the management. Furthermore, Drebin added that in a business corporation the stockholders, while technically the ownership group, do not get involved in day-to-day resources allocation decisions. On the other hand, such decisions in the government frequently require approval of the voters or their representatives. Presumably, those responsible for making these decisions need relevant financial information. “Although a budget for a commercial enterprise may be viewed as an internal management report, the budget for a governmental unit is a public document, a matter of law. The public has an interest in knowing, not only the planned allocation of financial resources, but also how these were actually utilized in comparison with the plan” (Drebin et al. 1981). Consequently, the lack of furnishing the required information for carrying out the budget functions that really matter to the top politicians can also explain the failure of public sector accounting to be practice-relevant for these top politicians and other users.

Third, the accounting literature has addressed the lack of effective communication and cooperation among accounting researchers, practitioners, consultants, standard-setters, and users (Inanga and Schneider 2005; Demski 2001; Van Helden and Northcott 2010). Frankly speaking, the lack of communication and cooperation is not only between the users and the other four groups (accounting researchers, practitioners, consultants, standard-setters) but also among these four groups themselves. This lack of communication and cooperation can have a direct and indirect impact on the public sector accounting and financial reporting not being user practice-relevant. The indirect impact can result from the lack of communication and cooperation between two or more of these four groups. For instance, the lack of communication between accounting researchers and practitioners can emerge from the fact that the issues and methods of interest to accounting researchers are of little or no value to practitioners (Inanga and Schneider 2005); in addition, there is no focus on finding practical solutions for the accounting problems that practitioners encounter in practice.

On the other hand, practitioners, because of their training and lack of experience with and interest in research, tend not to look to research findings to meet their professional needs (Inanga and Schneider 2005). In addition, the lack of communication between the accounting researchers and practitioners may also arise because both have different interests. Inanga and Schneider (2005) argue that most researchers are unconcerned with the immediate and short-term needs of practitioners. While accounting practitioners are interested in short-term research results capable of providing an immediate solution to professional problems, the focus of researchers is on academic career advancement and a professional reputation built on a publication record. Their status is determined by the quality of the journals in which their research findings are published (Brinn et al. 1996) and not necessarily by the quality of the problem or the findings.

Consequently, researchers and practitioners do not communicate with each other, and the financial statements resulting from the practitioners' efforts do not relate to users who do not effectively communicate their needs to either practitioners or academics (Inanga and Schneider 2005). Another research paper has also focused on the role that can be played by consultants, for example, in solving practical problems and creating applied knowledge that is of direct relevance to their clients. However, the situation is further exacerbated by neglecting the role of consultants and standard-setters in supporting the design of the user practice-relevant public sector accounting and financial reporting system. Consequently, this lack of communication and cooperation among researchers, practitioners, consultants, standard-setters, and users can explain the failure of the public sector accounting in furnishing practice-relevant information to the users.

Fourth, it is learned from the Norwegian, Dutch, and Japanese experiences that a great part of politicians' financial information needs are not satisfied by traditional accounting regulations and policies. In other words, they need specific accounting information that cannot be provided by an accounting system that is constrained by GAAP. They mainly need information such as finding resources for new policy initiatives, trade-offs, and financial cuts, avoiding overspending of budgets, resource allocation, and avoiding depreciation costs (Rynes et al. 2001; Hitt 2005; Olson 2001; Van Helden 2014; Yamamoto 2014). Moreover, the main focus of politicians is on cash flows—simple, understandable, and useful measures, but effective ones. The Norwegian experience has indicated that the specific information required by politicians cannot be provided by the traditional accounting system that is constrained by GAAP, as it requires a context-bound accounting system (Olson 2001). According to Olson, the context-bound accounting system is not based on overall rhetoric but is instead related to local political discourses. Generally, the main characteristic of a discourse is that it is a process of talk. Most political discourses are going on within the frames of decision procedures, and the main decision procedure of most governmental entities is the budgetary procedure. Olson (2001) further indicates that the context-bound accounting system does not require one to sacrifice the traditional form of accounting but can be considered as extra work and innovation from the accountants' side to help the politicians in their decision-making through designing accounting systems where they can translate the accounting information into a form that can be understood by politicians. Accordingly, there should be a connection between the political discourse and the design of accounting and financial reporting to satisfy politicians' information needs.

Consequently, the disconnect between the design of accounting and financial reporting and the political discourse can explain the failure of public sector accounting and financial reporting to provide practice-relevant information to politicians and other users.

Fifth, while accounting is considered as a branch of social sciences, meaning that it is social and accordingly dynamic, the design process of public sector accounting and financial reporting system considers the accounting system, and hence the users and their needs, as hermetic and static, so that behaviors and needs of users are assumed not to change or interact with the changes taking place in the social, political, economic, regulatory, and technological environment. Basically, the traditional user-oriented approach fails to recognize the dynamic nature of the users and their needs (Ouda 2005). Within fast-changing socioeconomic–political systems, design approaches that prescribe certain users' needs should consider these changes. Therefore, public sector accountants should be aware of the fact that a more user practice-relevant approach requires a reorientation towards working within, rather than fighting against, the dynamics of user needs.

Sixth: Shapiro et al. (2007), writing on the perceived disconnect between research and practice in the management discipline, argue that the practical relevance of research can be lost either before or in translation. They explain that a 'knowledge production' problem arises where research fails to focus on phenomena that matter to practitioners. This leads to practical relevance being lost before translation. A different, 'knowledge transfer' problem arises where researchers fail to translate their research into publications, frameworks, and tools that managers can use in their work—that is, the relevance of their academic work is lost in translation (Rynes and Shapiro 2005; Hogye 2002; van Helden and Northcott (2010). Similarly, the user relevance of public sector accounting can be lost either before or in translation. On the one hand, it can be lost before translation when the design of public sector accounting and financial reporting system fails to focus on financial topics that really matter to users (e.g., politicians) and hence their needs are not taken into account and are not reflected into the objectives and design of the accounting and financial reporting system. This can happen either because of the ignorance of the users' needs or because those needs are contrasted with the GAAP. On the other hand, when public sector accountants take the users' needs into account but fail to translate the financial accounting information into a form that can be understood by users (e.g., politicians), the user relevance of public sector accounting and financial reporting is lost in translation. So the approach of Shapiro et al. can also explain the failure of public sector accounting and financial reporting in being user practice-relevant.

Finally, Mayston (1992) argued that the lack of satisfaction of users' needs can emerge from a poor design of the product on offer, which results from a lack of understanding of relevant principles that are used to analyze user needs and an ignorance of user needs, both of which can be traced back to a lack of commitment to meeting user needs (see Fig. 6.2).

The aforementioned gaps/shortcomings would not exist if accounting practice and actual user information needs were to be broadly conceptualized as the primary objective of designing the public sector accounting and financial reporting system. Such broad conceptualization would view public sector accounting practice not just in terms of how accounting information is prepared, but also in terms of the reaction of politicians, managers, investors, creditors, and other users to whom such information is presented. In addition, to satisfy the diverging needs of users, public sector accountants are not required to sacrifice the traditional form of accrual accounting but are instead requested to undertake some extra work and innovation to help politicians in their decision-making by designing an accounting system where they can translate the accounting information into a form that can be understood by politicians. Olson (2001) calls this accounting system a context-bound accounting system. In addition to the traditional role of public sector accounting in providing traditional users' needs and specific politicians' needs, public sector accounting

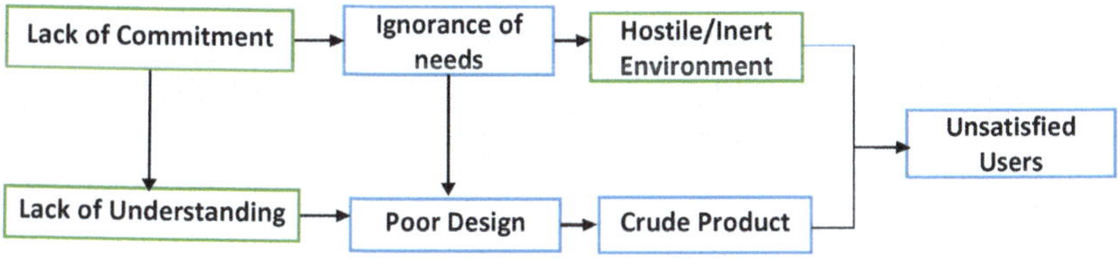

Fig. 6.2 Mode B behavior. (Source: (Mayston 1992))

is currently required to furnish information about the fiscal sustainability of governmental entities that indicates the ability of the government to meet the current and future obligations when they are due and to continue providing services to the public in current and future periods. Accordingly, to satisfy different users' needs public sector accountants are required to keep the traditional accrual accounting system which produces cost-based financial statements that are basically constrained by GAAP and directed towards satisfying the decision-making, accountability, compliance, and stewardship objectives. They must also take the initiative and to think outside the box and innovate additional accounting and financial reporting systems which may not be guided by the current accounting policies and regulations such as the following:

- Context-bound accounting and financial reporting system, which is mainly directed to satisfying the specific accounting information needs of politicians
- Economic-based accounting and financial reporting system, which is basically directed to providing the accounting information needs of fiscal sustainability.

Moreover, the previous discussion leads to several conclusions. One of these is that the designing of an accounting and financial reporting system which is constrained by GAAP inhibits rather than encourages meaningful designing of a user practice-relevant public sector accounting and financial reporting system. Therefore, the context within which public sector accounting is perceived as a discipline worthy of research must be reconceptualized to provide the extra required financial information even though the provision of this information may contrast with the GAAP. Furthermore, the institutional context within which the design of the user practice-relevant public sector accounting and financial reporting system is conducted must be understood and operationalized in a new way. Because of the cost-based accounting regulations and policies, and hence the cost-based financial statements, in addition to accounting arithmetic structure and legalistic preoccupation, both in terms of what and how to report, public sector accounting has imposed an intellectual straightjacket on accounting researchers, practitioners, consultants, and standard-setters. Moreover, the production of the user practice-relevant public sector accounting and financial reporting system is no longer confined to the efforts of accounting researchers only or practitioners only but is a product of communication and cooperation among different parties such as accounting researchers, practitioners, consultants, users, and standard-setters. This of course requires the public sector accountants/scholars to develop a new approach that blends emerging concepts of co-design and co-creation with a practice-oriented approach used in sociological studies of consumption and design. This approach is called the practice-oriented co-design approach and will be discussed in the following section.

3 Practice-Oriented Co-Design Approach

3.1 A Conceptual Framework

A practice-oriented co-design approach was proposed by Scott (2008) and used in engineering studies, especially in the field of Design for Sustainability (DfS). Researchers in DfS and related fields argue that to reach sustainability, radical innovation is required (Brezet and van Hemel 1997). To achieve this radical innovation required to shift society in a more sustainable direction, designers need to take a more systemic approach to DfS that looks beyond single products and individual users (Kuijer and de Jong 2009). In fact, this is what we, as public sector accountants, need to do. We need to look beyond the traditional role of accounting which is constrained by GAAP and to put in extra work to provide the required information by politicians and other users even though it may contrast with accounting regulations and policies. Wever et al. (2008) argue that experience has learned that when aiming for a specific (radical) effect of products during the use phase, like reduced resource consumption, involving a user perspective in the design process is essential. When aiming to achieve practice level innovation, it is therefore particularly important to integrate users' perspectives and researchers' perspectives in the design process. Similarly, when aiming to design a user practice-relevant public sector accounting and financial reporting system, it is important to integrate the users', researchers', practitioners', standard-setters', and consultants' perspectives for the identification of the users and their needs.

Based on these considerations, the practice-oriented co-design approach was developed and is given for applying a user-centered orientation for sustainable design which blends emerging concepts of co-design and co-creation with a 'practice-oriented' approach. Notions like co-creation and co-design are beginning to turn design on its head by increasingly putting the tools of design into the hands of end-users. Co-creation is already appearing in emerging trends of social innovation, user-generated content, and open-source design, providing real-life examples from which the design profession is beginning to learn some valuable lessons (Sanders and Stappers 2008). Co-design can be defined as a cooperative, continuous process bringing everyday people together with design professionals to find new and better ideas for daily life. Scott further argued that the idea of a practice-oriented approach in design comes from an ongoing discussion about the conceptual and practical relevance between practice theory, studies of consumption, and product design (Julier 2007; Shove et al. 2008; Ingram et al. 2007; Fisher and Hielscher 2008).

The argument is that practice theory can provide a better framework for understanding issues of consumption (including both purchase and use), and this learning can be applied in design approaches in order to establish more sustainable and effective modes of consumption. A practice-oriented approach is intended to guide the design process to look more broadly, beyond individual products and users, to the integrated routines, materials, bodies, meanings, functions, and abilities that make up everyday practices. The practice-oriented co-design approach is useful for understanding the dynamics of practice as it is. Design is specialized in thinking about the potential scenarios and ways of satisfying the accounting information needs through designing suitable public sector accounting and financial reporting. The practice-oriented co-design approach has been tested by Scott (2008); Kuijer, and de Jong (2009) and it was indicated that this approach has its benefits and limitations. One of its benefits is that it empowers and aligns teams: Co-design not only creates a safe space for cross-disciplinary teams to build on one another's perspectives but also creates more buy-in into the overall direction and priority of a project. Each party knows the logic and rationale behind the design decision and can move forward knowing how they plan to satisfy the practice-relevant users' needs. Another benefit is that it reveals blind spots: Co-design creates a more unified view of user needs by bringing disparate insights into users' needs into a more cohesive view.

The limitations of the practice-oriented co-design approach are summed up by Scott (2008) as follows: it sends a warning that not only can design enable people to do things they could not do before, it can also disable people by reducing their options for practical behavior, making them passive users and locking them into patterns of consumptions which they might be happier to change. Finally, I see that while the consumer might have clear preferences about experience goods, I doubt that accounting information users can articulate in the same way their preferences about an accounting framework (as an information good). However, in order to make the practice-oriented co-design approach applicable to accounting, I will rely on the core concept developed by Scott (2008) and develop a new version that will be suitable for designing a user practice-relevant public sector accounting and financial reporting system. I will start by developing the principles that frame the new version of the practice-oriented co-design approach.

3.2 *Developing the Principles of a Practice-Oriented Co-Design Approach to Be Applied to Public Sector Accounting*

While the traditional accounting approach for designing a suitable government accounting and financial reporting system is based on a basic hypothesis that attempts to fit users and their needs into the design process, both co-design and practice-orientation challenge the design process to better fit into users' practice. In order to achieve this, according to the recommendation of the American Institute of Certified Public Accountants' (AICPA) Special Committee on Financial Reporting (Jenkin's Committee) entitled *Improving Financial Reporting—A Customer Focus* (AICPA 1994), the design process should see the users, including politicians, as the customer and the focus must move away from the final product of accounting, which is the financial statements that are constrained by GAAP, towards thinking about the design of public sector accounting and financial reporting as a starting point or tool, and should take into account the information needs of the politicians and other users, whether this information is consistent with GAAP or in contrast to it. According to the practice-oriented co-design approach the information needs of users are part of the design process and not only its outcome, and the design process is a dialogue, not just a performance. Basically, the merging of co-design with a practice orientation approach is meant to explore how politicians, internal managers, other users, accounting researchers, practitioners, consultants, and standard-setters can be co-operatively engaged in the formation of more user practice-relevant public sector accounting and financial reporting and how the design of the accounting and financial reporting system can be reoriented towards enabling these changes.

So this chapter is driven by the following research question: *Whether and how the practice-oriented co-design approach could lead to designing a user practice-relevant public sector accounting and financial reporting system that can satisfy the diverging needs of different users?*

For this to happen, the following principles were developed to make the practice-oriented co-design approach applicable to public sector accounting:

1. *Intervention*: Relying only on users to determine their needs has proven to be insufficient in itself as the users are unable to articulate what their needs are in any convincing way (Sutcliffe 1985). This has resulted in those needs being determined by others (e.g., standard-setters), hence leading to designing a public sector accounting and financial reporting system that does not fulfill users' information needs. Moreover, the conceptual frameworks themselves tend to use the normative approach and to determine the information needs on a priori assertions rather than rigorous empirical research (Rutherford 1992). This can clearly explain why the public sector accounting and financial reporting system is not user practice-relevant. Therefore, the intervention of standard-setters with the users can assist in determining the practice-relevant accounting information needs and this can happen, for instance, by holding a roundtable meeting including both of them. Scapens (2008) also notes that accounting researchers can seek to make their research relevant by 'intervening' in various ways that range from direct intervention within individual organizations to the production of critical writings that draw out the social and political consequences of accounting in modern organizations, and in society more generally.
2. *Communication and combination*: *users + researchers + practitioners + consultants + standard-setters*: The communications among these parties and the combination of their efforts reflect a common format in the co-design and practice-orientation approach. It is important that the co-design approach brings together diverse roles and perspectives to get the maximum value, as each party brings a different set of expertise and constraints applicable to the discussion and each party approaches the problem from a different perspective. For example, accounting researchers can assist in developing new methods or approaches and can formulate theoretically informed answers to questions raised by other parties, in addition to providing analytical skills to guide the parties in designing the accounting and finan-

cial reporting system. Practitioners are the producers of the financial statements and their working on the ground enables them to be familiar with the practical problems. Therefore, they can play a significant and positive role in helping the other parties in determining the practical users' needs and designing a user practice-relevant public sector accounting and financial reporting system. Consultants gather knowledge initiated by problems stemming from practice that has to be customized for application in practice. Therefore, they help in solving the practical problems and providing solutions for the users' needs and demands that stem from practice. Finally, the accounting standard-setting bodies can play a significant role in tackling specific accounting issues and designing the user practice-relevant accounting and financial reporting system. Consequently, the communication among these participants and the combination of their efforts (e.g., through holding a roundtable) will assist in determining the objectives of and hence designing a user practice-relevant public sector accounting and financial reporting system. The main motive for this to happen is to have a real impact on improving the practice and practically satisfying the different users' needs.

3. *Dynamic*: Within fast-changing socioeconomic–political and technological systems, design approaches that prescribe certain user needs should consider these changes and do not treat these systems as being somewhat hermetic and static. This reflects the idea of co-creation as a continuous process of discovery and invention, and the dynamic nature of practices in terms of persistence and changes over time. In addition, there should be appropriate and structured research to identify the ongoing and emerging needs of users of accounting information and to develop products to meet those needs (Inanga and Schneider 2005). Therefore, public sector accountants should be aware of the fact that a more user practice-relevant approach requires a reorientation towards working within, rather than fighting against, the dynamics of user needs and accounting as a social science.
4. *Do not sacrifice the traditional form and role of accounting but consider extra work and innovation*: The traditional role of accounting which only served the traditional users' needs that are constrained by GAAP is no longer sufficient to provide the specific needs of politicians as it requires a context-bound accounting system (Olson

2001), which requires extra work and innovation from the accountants' side. Furthermore, nowadays, users' needs extend beyond the traditional users' needs and specific politicians' needs to include information about long-term fiscal sustainability where the users need to have information about the ability of a governmental entity to meet service delivery and financial commitments both now and in the future. Accordingly, public sector accounting should also serve the fiscal sustainability information needs although it may be contrasted with the accounting regulations and policies. So in order for public sector accounting to serve different users' needs, the objectives of public sector accounting and financial reporting should be broadened to include the specific information needs of the politicians and the fiscal sustainability information needs, without sacrificing the traditional form of accounting and traditional information needs.

5. *Budget functions and their needs*: Based on the specific relationship between the budgeting and accounting system in the governmental entities, in addition to the users and their needs, the budget functions and their information needs are important to the point that they can be taken into consideration in designing the public sector accounting and financial reporting system. Basically, public sector accounting and financial reporting are valid only to the extent that they reflect the users' information needs and the required information for carrying out the budget functions efficiently and effectively. It is assumed that provision of information required for carrying out the budget functions, which really matter to top politicians, can assist in making public sector accounting more user practice-relevant.
6. *Creativity in doing + innovations in practice*: These are two overlapping and complementary ideas from co-design and practice orientation (Scott et al. 2009). If the public sector accounting and financial reporting system exists primarily to enable practice, then the innovative practice-relevant accounting system, which is based on the dynamics of user needs and not constrained by the GAAP, should be designed to enable innovative practices. The goal is to help accounting researchers, users, practitioners, consultants, and standard-setters reinvent ordinary practices to become more user practice-relevant and effective.

7. *Information needs of users are part of the design process and not only their outcome, and the design process is a dialogue, not just a performance*: The information needs of the users need not necessarily be the ultimate goal of the design process, but rather stepping stones or building blocks for accountants to design more effective practices and hence a more user practice-relevant public sector accounting and financial reporting system.
8. *Blurring of roles*: This reflects an effort towards the 'democratization' of co-design and to reduce the distance between participants (Scott et al. 2009). Users are treated as equal participants rather than as mere 'subjects' (Sanders and Stappers 2008), and are involved in determining both their accounting information needs and budget functions needs. Researchers, consultants, standard-setters, and practitioners take on user roles in their personal practices to recognize the practical consciousness at work in real life.

3.3 Co-Design Framework and Conceptualization of Dynamic Model

In addition to the previously developed principles, the conceptualization of the dynamic model should be based on the following co-design framework where the accounting researchers, practitioners, consultants, standard-setters, and primary users such as politicians and public managers can work together to co-discover the users. After that, they can, together with the users, co-define the users' needs. In addition, the accounting researchers, practitioners, consultants, users, and standard-setters should co-determine the objectives and co-design the public sector accounting and financial reporting system (Fig. 6.3).

Together with the co-design framework, the following eight essential elements derived from the principles of practice-oriented co-design approach are essential for the conceptualization of the dynamic model:

1. Public sector accounting should start a new era that shifts its focus on attempting to fit users and their needs into the design process to challenging the design process to better fit into users' practice by using the practice-oriented co-design approach.

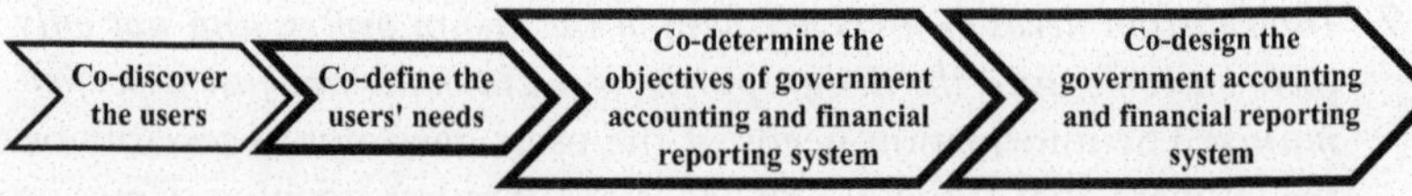

Fig. 6.3 Co-design framework. (Source: Author)

2. Users and budget functions and their needs are both the driving forces behind the design of user practice-relevant public sector accounting and financial reporting.
3. Co-design makes users act as experts of their own experience by actively involving them in all design decisions and these decisions should be taken within the context of the users, their needs, and their environment.
4. Intervention of and communication among accounting researchers, practitioners, consultants, users, and standard-setters at all phases are essential.
5. Not all information needs can be provided by the accounting system that is constrained by GAAP and hence public sector accountants are required to consider extra work and innovation to provide the specific needs of the politicians and fiscal sustainability needs.
6. Users and their needs are not hermetic and static, but dynamic. Therefore, there should be appropriate and structured research to identify the ongoing and emerging needs of users of accounting information and to develop products to meet those needs.
7. Public sector accounting is required to broaden its objectives to satisfy the emerging users' needs and hence develop a new set of public sector accounting and financial reporting systems.
8. Producing a user practice-relevant public sector accounting and financial reporting system does not automatically guarantee that the politicians and other users will use it; therefore, we should add to the dynamic model the determinants of accounting information use as machinery that will make politicians and other users use the accounting information (Fig. 6.4).

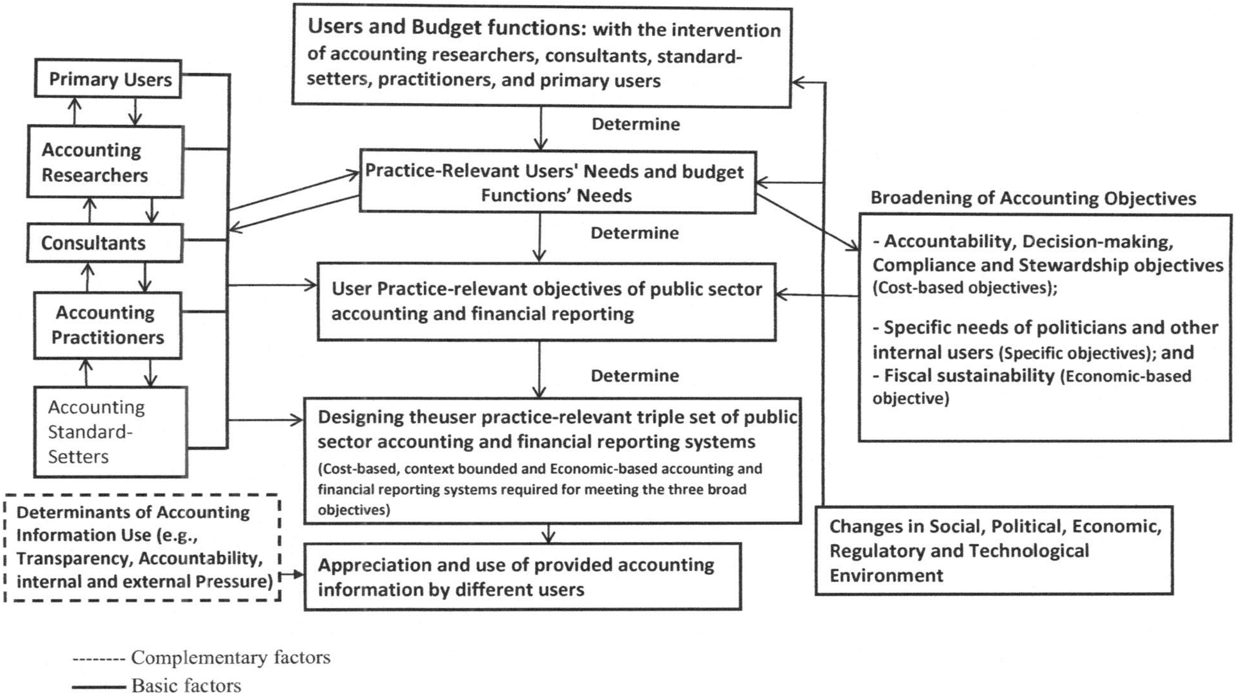

Fig. 6.4 A suggested dynamic model for making public sector accrual accounting and financial reporting more user practice-relevant. Spaced line: Complementary factors; Solid line: Basic factors. (Source: Author)

4 A Suggested Dynamic Model for Making Public Sector Accrual Accounting and Financial Reporting More User Practice-Relevant

4.1 Description of the Model

This section deals with the suggested dynamic model from two perspectives: basic factors and complementary factors. Basic factors are considered important for co-designing the user practice-relevant public sector accounting and financial reporting system. Complementary factors are required to increase the use of accounting information provided by the user practice-relevant public sector accounting and financial reporting system.

4.1.1 The Dynamic Model: Basic Factors

Users of Accounting Information and Budget Functions: With the Intervention of Accounting Researchers, Consultants, Standard-Setters, Practitioners, and Primary Users

We, as public sector accounting scholars, should admit that identification of the users of accounting information and budget functions is the cornerstone and starting point for designing a user practice-relevant government accounting and financial reporting system. In the second half of the last century, various studies were undertaken to identify the users of government financial information (e.g., NCGA 1968; AICPA 1973; Drebin et al. 1981; CICA 1977; Anthony 1978; Ferguson and Drebin 1981; IFAC 1991). After a deliberate study it was concluded (Ouda 2005) that there is no unanimity about who the users of governmental financial information are. Some studies found that some users are important enough to be included in the users' list of financial information and other studies found that it does not seem necessary to include certain users as principal users of financial information. It is also noticed that most of these studies focused more on the external users of governmental financial reporting than on internal users. Their opinion was based on the fact that those users have limited authority, ability, or resources to obtain the information they want. On the other hand, there are among external users mentioned by these studies some users who have the authority and ability to obtain whatever financial information they need such as the legislative and oversight bodies. Accordingly, argues that the identification of user groups of governmental financial information should be approached from the context of the unique nature of the government (in comparison with business), as well as the significant characteristics of the environment within which it operates. One of the primary characteristics of the government environment is that the government is a representative of its citizens. This also means that the citizens delegate the power to the government in order to be able to make decisions about the allocation and management of public resources. This delegation of powers is usually accompanied by "separation of power" between executive, legislative, and judicial bodies of government. This, in turn, means that legislative, executive, and oversight bodies are responsible for the financial management of governmental entity resources to the citizens. Thus, those who argue that legislative and oversight bodies are external users cannot be justified. This is because it is not logical that bodies that have the power (delegated to them by the citizens) and are accountable to the citizens for the management of the public resources can be considered as external users (Ouda 2005). These bodies cannot wait until the financial reporting is promulgated at the end of the fiscal year to carry out their responsibilities efficiently and effectively. In addition, these bodies have the power, ability, and authority to obtain whatever financial information they want and can be considered as semi- external/internal users.

Therefore, the use of the practice-oriented co-design approach through the intervention and collaboration of accounting researchers, consultants, standard-setters, practitioners, and the primary users such as politicians and public managers can assist in co-discovering and identifying the right users and the right classification of user groups. This intervention can be based on the practical-differential approach (Ouda 2005). This approach will not limit the user groups to the extent that it emphasizes the commonalities or expand the user groups to the extent that it makes the number of such groups unmanageable. This approach also emphasizes the complexity of public sector accounting, but it produces manageable user groups. Consequently, the identification of users should be reconsidered in a way that takes into account the unique nature of the government as well as the significant characteristics of the environment within which it operates. This means that we should not give more weight only to external users as the principal users of governmental financial information but also to politicians, internal managers, policy-makers, and administrators as primary users of public sector accounting financial information.

In addition to the identification of users, the identification of budget functions is essential for politicians, internal managers, and policy-makers on the one hand and because, on the other hand, public sector accounting can serve in some functions whereas it plays no role in others. Therefore, it is important to determine which functions can be served by the public sector accounting system and which cannot. Bac (1994, 2003) has mentioned the following budget functions and the relationship of the accounting role with these functions:

- Allocation function: this function is concerned with the allocation of resources to different purposes and choosing or determining the plans that should or should not be executed. Herein, Bac (2003) argues that the allocation function does not apply to accounting and reporting, because allocation plays a role in the budget preparation phase, except for choices that have to be made after windfalls have delivered unexpected resources during the year of budget execution.
- Authorization function: once the amounts have been allocated in the budget, this provides the authorization to incur expenditure or levy charges that have been agreed. In fact, there is a relationship between the role of accounting and reporting and the authorization function, as accounting plays a continuous role during the year of budget execution in order to prevent budget overruns (Bac 2003).
- Management function: this function is concerned with the execution of tasks related to the decision-making process and carrying out the management responsibility efficiently and effectively. Herein, accounting and reporting play an essential role in supporting day-to-day management.
- Control function: this can be exercised by comparing budgeted results with actual results to ensure that expenditure levels are not exceeded and that planned activities are achieved. Bac (1994) mentioned that this function is concerned with discharging accountability. He also added that accounting does play a real role in the control function (Bac 2003).
- Macroeconomic function: this function indicates the degree to which the budget process has affected economic variables such as

purchase power, work opportunities, and development of interest. With respect to the macroeconomic function no direct role for accounting and reporting can be identified (Bac 2003).

Consequently, the identification of users, taking into consideration the unique nature of the government and the significant characteristics of the environment within which it operates, and the budget functions in which public sector accounting can play a role are essential in facilitating the design of a user practice-relevant public sector accounting and financial reporting system.

Practice-Relevant Users' Needs and Budget Functions' Needs
Due to the fact that users are, on the one hand, not precisely able to determine their needs and, on the other hand, do not communicate effectively their needs to either standard-setters or practitioners because these needs are assumed to be known, the use of a practice-oriented co-design approach is fundamental. The practice-oriented co-design approach firstly makes users act as experts of their own experience by actively involving them in generating their needs and, secondly, requires the intervention of and communication among accounting researchers, practitioners, consultants, and standard-setters with the users as this can assist in and facilitate the identification of the practice-relevant information needs. Both the intervention and communication should consider the users' needs that are constrained by accounting regulations and policies, as well as the specific needs of politicians which need extra work from the accountants' side; this is in addition to users' needs that are related to fiscal sustainability and carrying out budget functions. The original idea underlying the intervention of the participants and communication with the users is to solve problems that users face, and the users are consulted and their inputs seriously taken into account.

Based on an earlier study (Ouda 2005) regarding the identification of users' needs, it has been concluded that users' needs are ***no longer confined to*** information constrained by GAAP and to compliance with legislation, rules, and regulations. On the contrary, those needs are extended to comprise more significant and valuable information where some of this information is related to the specific needs of politicians as well as carrying out the budget functions, and some other is related to serving fiscal sustainability. For example, reporting long-term fiscal sustainability information provides information on the impact of current policies and decisions made at the reporting date on future inflows and outflows and financial statements. Long-term fiscal sustainability is broader than information derived from financial statements; therefore, it takes into account the future outflows that do not meet the recognition criteria of liabilities, and the future inflows which do not meet the criteria of recognition of an asset. Another example is of politicians who need specific information related to finding resources for new policy initiatives; trade-offs and financial cuts; and avoiding overspending of budgets; resource allocation and avoiding depreciation costs; the cost of governmental programs and activities.

In addition, based on the specific relationship between the budgeting and accounting systems in the public sector, budget functions and their information needs are important to the point that they can be taken into consideration when designing a user practice-relevant public sector accounting and financial reporting system. The following are budget functions and their information needs:

- *Planning and allocation functions*: In order for the resources to be efficiently and effectively planned and allocated, policy-makers require information on the programs assumed to be implemented, their costs, and the costs of alternatives, and on whether these resources have been directed towards current expenditure or capital expenditure. In case these resources have been directed towards capital expenditure, they need information about whether it will be used to maintain the existing structure or to carry out new constructions. They need information on whether these resources will be used to redeem short- or long-term liabilities; hence, they need information about commitments, and short- and long-term liabilities.
- *Authorization function*: Before the legislative bodies provide authorization to incur expenditure or to levy charges, they need information on how resources will be obtained, how they will be used, and whether the sources and uses conform to budget requirements. They need information over whether services and costs are distributed equitably and whether physical resources are properly maintained. They also need to assess the extent to which revenues are sufficient to cover the costs of operations. They need information to help them assess the government's stewardship of resources and information on whether the current and long-term liabilities are met.

- *Management function*: After the resources have been allocated and authorized, the management function of the budget starts, namely, the carrying out of the management responsibility concerning the execution of the budget. This includes translating the objectives into certain projects and activities; designing the management units that will embark on the implementation of programs; and employing the staff that is required to implement these programs. In short, it involves organizing, staffing, and directing necessary units to carry out the selected programs. Herein, the management function requires necessary information about government programs and activities that have to be carried out. The management also needs information to help predict the relationship between units of input and units of output. In order to improve efficiency, the management may require information on existing costs per unit of output; information helpful in predicting the cost of alternative programs would also be useful to management in making implementation decisions. In general, management needs information for managing the allocated and authorized resources.
- *Control function*: Control is the process by which activity is compared with expected results, and deviations from intended results are located and corrected. The function of control implies measuring performance to see whether objectives are being achieved and constraints are being observed. It involves detecting departure from the budgeted position and taking action to correct deviations. Thus, relevant, accurate, and timely information of actual and budgeted positions needs to be provided to all levels of management to enable performance to be monitored against budget (Jones and Pendlebury 1984). Thus, the control function of the budget requires information regarding regularity, efficiency, and effectiveness in order to be able to confront it with realized figures in the financial report (Bac 2001).
- *Macroeconomic functions*: In fact, this function has been considered in the literature as a consequence of the Keynesian notion that fiscal policy can be planned and utilized to achieve economic objectives. Many believed that macroeconomics could transform the budget process into a vehicle for attaining both efficient and effective policy ends. Thus, the budget process could be directed towards reducing inflation rates, improving the standard of living, increasing work

opportunities, decreasing interest rates and redemption of external debts. Herein, the fiscal policy-makers require information to evaluate the economic impact of the government on the economy as a whole and to evaluate government spending options and priorities. Thus, they need information that assists them to understand the full nature, scope, and extent of government financial activities in the overall economy.

Broadening the Objectives of Government Accounting and Financial Reporting

Having identified the users and budget functions and their needs, the objectives of accounting and financial reporting should support those users' needs and budget functions' needs. Namely, the objectives should reflect the information needs of those users, otherwise they are deemed to be useless. IFAC (1991) stated that "as a general principle, financial reports should communicate information that is relevant to the decision-making and accountability needs of users." The NCGA in April 1982 promulgated its statement No. 1: Objectives of Accounting and Financial Reporting for Governmental Units. The statement has identified the overall objective of public sector accounting and financial reporting as follows:

The overall goal of accounting and financial reporting for governmental units is to provide the following:

1. Financial information useful for making economic, political, and social decisions, and demonstrating accountability and stewardship
2. Information useful for evaluating managerial and organizational performance

However, the overall objective of the public sector accounting and financial reporting focused on the external and semi-external users' needs which are constrained by GAAP and did not focus on the specific needs of politicians, policy-makers, and top management, as well as fiscal sustainability information needs. In fact, the public sector accounting system exists not only to serve the external and semi-external users' needs, but presumably, its basic function is to facilitate the work of politicians, aid management in planning, control, and day-to-day decision-making process, as well as help policy-makers, in addition to fiscal sustainability; hence, the following could complement the overall objective:

3. Information useful for the specific needs of politicians and carrying out the budget functions
4. Information useful for serving fiscal sustainability

Accordingly, the objectives of public sector accounting and financial reporting should be broadened to serve the three objectives shown in Fig. 6.5.

Similar to the identification of users' needs, the users' practice-relevant objectives of public sector accounting and financial reporting require the intervention and communication of accounting researchers, practitioners, consultants, users, and standard-setters. Basically, the broadening of public sector accounting and financial reporting objectives and the intervention of and communications among all participants are essential for determining these user practice-relevant objectives. So it can be concluded that objectives of public sector accounting and financial reporting are valid only to the extent that they reflect the traditional users' information needs that are constrained by GAAP, specific needs of politicians, fiscal sustainability, and the required information for carrying out the budget functions efficiently and effectively.

Designing the User Practice-Relevant Public Sector Accounting and Financial Reporting

Similarly, the accounting system in the governmental entities is valid only to the extent that it reflects the objectives of the public sector accounting and financial reporting system. Thus, the accounting standards and

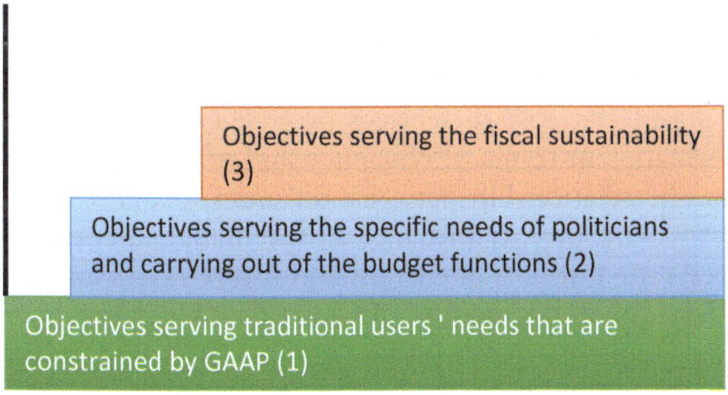

Fig. 6.5 Broadening the objectives of public sector accounting and financial reporting system. (Source: Author)

procedures or practices have to follow logically from those objectives and design the public sector accounting and financial reporting system so that it reflects these objectives. Herein, the main benefit of using the practice-oriented co-design approach is that the accounting researchers, practitioners, consultants, users, and standard-setters should challenge the design process to better fit into users' practice. The design process should see users including politicians as the customer and the focus must move away from the final product of accounting, which comprises the financial statements that are constrained by GAAP, to thinking about the design of public sector accounting and financial reporting as a starting point or tool, and should take into account the information needs of the users, whether this information is consistent with or in contrast to GAAP. Basically, the merging of co-design with the practice-oriented approach is meant to explore how the politicians, internal managers, other users, accounting researchers, practitioners, consultants, and standard-setters can be co-operatively engaged in designing user practice-relevant public sector accounting and financial reporting and how the design of an accounting and financial reporting system can be reoriented towards enabling these changes. Consequently, serving of the broadened objectives stated earlier will require a triple set of public sector accounting and financial reporting systems as follows:

a. ***Cost-based public sector accounting and financial reporting***, which will serve the users' needs that are constrained by accounting regulations and policies (GAAP), such as how the financial and economic resources have been obtained and used; whether these resources have been used in an efficient and effective way and in the interest of both current and future generations; information about assets, liabilities, revenues, and expenses; information about the cost of services provided, cost-effectiveness, and performance in terms of efficiency and effectiveness; information about the relationship between revenues, expenses, and changes in net worth; the performance of the management; the trade-off between the burdens of current and future taxpayers; and the cost of governmental programs and activities. However, there are significant limits to what public sector cost-based balance sheets alone can tell us about fiscal sustainability or the specific needs of politicians. In particular, balance sheet measures, which are based on GAAP, look only at the impact of past government activity.

They do not include the present value of future spending, for example, on health, education, and pension provision. And, just as importantly, they exclude the public sector's most valuable financial assets—its ability to levy future taxes. Accordingly, the cost-based balance sheet indicates absolutely nothing about fiscal sustainability (Robinson 1995) as the cost of fixed assets bear no necessary relationship to future returns (either in use or through sale) from that asset. In addition, it does not provide the specific needs of politicians which are mainly related to carrying out the budget functions. Therefore, the public sector accountants should do extra work to cover these deficiencies through developing two more sets of public sector accounting and financial reporting systems as follows:

b. ***Context-bound accounting and financial reporting system***, which can serve the specific needs of top politicians and top managers in carrying out the budget functions. Olson (2001) argues that a context-bound accounting system was defined as a system constructed upon the ideas of the actors in the organization and their discourses related to the organization. This should be viewed in contrast to a situation when an accounting system is based on general discourses of external actors, that is, a contextual discourse. If we, as public sector accountants, provide the needed information by politicians, we shall not follow NPFM but rather the political discourse, which is not guided by existing accounting theories and contrasts with the NPFM. The main focus of politicians is on the cash flows—simple, understandable, and useful measures, but effective ones. Olson further notes that existing accounting theories are not guidelines in the construction of context-bound accounting practice. This is also in very sharp contrast to NPFM, which almost totally has existing accounting procedures and control arrangements as a point of departure. This means that the context-bound practice gives politicians the information they want to include in their political discourses, while NPFM gives politicians the information to which they have to adapt their political discourses.
c. ***Economic-based accounting and financial reporting system***, which can serve the fiscal sustainability information needs. In fact, the cost-based balance sheet (GAAP-based balance sheet) is mainly backward-looking and does not include future liabilities and contingent

liabilities arising out of past activity such as future pension payments to past and existing public sector workers. To serve the fiscal sustainability objectives, economic-based balance sheets should estimate the present value of future public service pension payments. So, the economic-based balance sheet is forward-looking and includes the economic valuation of fixed assets and the present value of future revenues and future expenditures, and is used only for serving fiscal sustainability purposes (see Chap. 5 on the sustainable balance sheet).

In conclusion, we can say the following:

- Different information needs for different users
- Different financial reporting objectives for different information needs
- *Different accounting systems for different financial reporting objectives*

Recognizing the Changes in the Social, Political, Economic, Regulatory, and Technological Environment

Basically, the user practice-relevant public sector accounting and financial reporting system must be considered in complex environments (social, economic, political, etc.) of many constituencies with diverse interests and information needs. Each has its unique cognitive sets and world contexts. The accounting system, if it is to be user practice-relevant, must be tailored to a specific context, but not excluding appropriate interrelationships and interdependencies. As a result of the fact that accounting is a social science, and is therefore dynamic, the users and their needs are also dynamic. Accordingly, the triple set of the public sector accounting and financial reporting systems should reflect the changes in the social, political, economic, regulatory, and technological environments because these changes would result in changing the users' needs. Of course, if the public sector accountants need to maintain the public sector accounting and financial reporting as user practice-relevant, then public sector accounting must reflect these changes. The notion of considering the accounting system and the users' needs as hermetic and static is no longer valid in the context of the dynamic social world. On the contrary, the design decision of a user practice-relevant accounting system should be taken within the context of the users, and changes in their needs and their environment.

4.1.2 *The Dynamic Model: Complementary Factors*

Determinants of Accounting Information Use

However, the experiences of earlier reformer countries have indicated that designing a user practice-relevant public sector accounting and financial reporting system does not automatically mean that the politicians and other users will use the information provided by this system (Lűder 2013; Hyndman et al. 2005). Therefore, there should be some machinery that can make politicians and other users avail this practice-relevant information. Thus, to complement the dynamic model, we should add the determinants of accounting information use. The public sector accounting literature has addressed the determinants which affect the use of accounting information from different perspectives (Kurunmaki et al. 2003; Mkasiwa 2011; Vyas and Souchon 2003; Assad and Goddard 2006; Mzenzi 2013). Some of these studies have focused on the external environment and thus consider it a crucial element in the emergence of the legitimizing behavior of using accounting information and activities in public sector budgeting decision-making that does not necessarily increase efficiency (Kurunmaki et al. 2003). Other studies (Raudla 2012; Askim 2008) have focused on both institutional elements (e.g., the power and the role of the legislature in the budget process, the budget format) and individual characteristics (e.g., length of politicians' tenure; political experience) as the most likely factors that can influence the use of performance information. Furthermore, other studies have addressed this issue from different dimensions such as those related to external institutional factors, internal organizational factors, individual actor factors, and processing of accounting information factors (Mbelwa 2014, 2015). Based on the extant literature (theoretical and empirical), I will focus only on the factors that are most likely to influence the use of accounting information by the politicians as an example of the primary users of accounting information. These factors are as follows:

- *Political competition and conflict*

The public sector accounting literature has indicated from both theoretical and empirical perspectives that the degree of political competition can affect the degree of accounting information use by politicians. Moynihan and Ingraham (2004) assumed that the greater the degree of political competition, the higher will be the expected use of accounting information by the politicians. The political competition can be enhanced by strengthening the role of the opposition parties against the ruling parties. Askim (2008) argued that political competition is high when there is a balance between the politicians who belong to the governing parties and the members of the opposition parties. A Norwegian study conducted by Askim and his colleagues (2008) supports this assumption. This study found that municipalities were most likely to consider benchmarking experiences when many parties competed to affect policies.

Moreover, an empirical study (Mbelwa 2014) has explored that the greater the balance between the ruling and opposition parties, the higher the competition, which, in turn, enhances the use of accounting information by the politicians. In addition to political competition, the degree of political conflict can also influence the degree of accounting information use. As stated by Giacomini and his colleagues (2016), political conflict can affect the three levels of decisions which are low, moderate, and high. Each level will, in turn, affect the degree of accounting information use and the type of accounting information use. Askim (2008) also argued that high-conflict environments increase the opportunities for opposition parties to employ performance information in their efforts to embarrass the governing parties in power, in particular, when the performance of the governing parties is poor. Accordingly, one of the most important driving forces that enhance the use of accounting information by politicians is political competition and conflict; therefore, strengthening the opposition parties can contribute to forcing the governing bodies to increase the use of accounting information.

– *Laws and regulations*

Some of the practical problems that decrease the use of accounting information by politicians are legal in origin (Ouda 2005). Namely, when there are no regulations, rules, and laws that require politicians to use the accounting information in all stages of policy decision- making processes, this will lead to a lack of legal pressure and, hence, reduce the commitment of politicians to using such information. In reality, the lack of legal pressure could in part account for the governing body's lack of enthusiasm to pursue the development of the public sector accounting system, which can enhance the financial accounting information provided to politicians and increase chances for the use of accounting information. Empirical results support this notion, as Mbelwa (2014) argued that the availability and enforcement of updated financial rules, procedures, regulations, and by-laws generally constitute coercive factors that influence the use of accounting information and contribute to influencing the instrumental-conceptual use of accounting information in budget decision-making processes. Thus, legal pressure can be the vehicle for compelling recalcitrant bureaucratic politicians and other users to be committed to using the accounting information resulting from the developed public sector accounting and financial reporting system.

– *Accountability framework and transparency*

Transparency and accountability are interrelated concepts that are mutually enhancing. Without transparency there cannot be any accountability. Unless there is accountability, transparency will be of no value. In fact, transparency is built on a free flow of information and requires that the governments be explicit about their fiscal objectives and report on a wide range of economic and fiscal information (Ouda 2005). The empirical results of Mbelwa's study (2014) indicate that the culture of transparency in local governments can affect instrumental-conceptual use and reduce symbolic nonuse of accounting information. Vyas and Souchon (2003) defined the symbolic nonuse of information in decision-making as the lack of export information use owing to either lack of information availability or avoidance of information that is readily available. However, it was indicated that the lack of transparency leads to the symbolic nonuse of accounting information whereas its availability leads to instrumental-conceptual use of accounting information (Mbelwa 2014).

In addition to the existence of transparency, accountability requires a system to monitor and control the performance of government officers and organizations, particularly with respect to quality, inefficiency, and the abuse of resources. Hence, open and rigorous systems of financial management, accounting and auditing, and revenue collection are also necessary. Therefore, there should be an accountability framework that renders politicians responsible for their decisions and actions and makes them accountable for the consequences of their decisions. This will assist in enabling politicians to make the best use of available information.

– *Challenges and problems*

Generally, politicians do not seriously tackle the root cause of their problems until the situation approaches crisis conditions and the need for remedial action becomes evident and broadly accepted by the unions and the population at large. The political commitment for the use of accounting information is obtained, either through politicians becoming aware of a problem (awareness of a problem can occur either by a disaster or by the persistent efforts of actors proactively raising attention to an issue) or through a change of administration which alters the political priorities (Kingdon 1984, p. 92).

It is also assumed that when there are severe challenges and problems that politicians face, this makes them strive for the best use of accounting information. Accounting information can be used not only to solve problems and challenges but also to justify or interpret them. It can also be used to find rational reasons for the emergence of these problems and challenges. This means that, in such cases, politicians will do their best to use the accounting information to justify their failure in achieving the targeted objectives because they have faced severe problems and challenges, especially if the accounting information can support their interpretation. Furthermore, they can use accounting information to alleviate the consequences of these problems and challenges.

– *Training, experience, and qualifications of politicians*

In reality, the training, experience, and qualifications of the staff that is going to use the accounting information in all policy decision-making processes are essential and they should be taken into consideration while researching the use of accounting information. However, neglecting or not recognizing the training, experience, and qualification of the politicians has been persistently mentioned as a constraint in using accounting information in the public sector (Ouda 2005). Generally, based on their popularity, politicians are elected, not appointed or recruited like administrators. Mbelwa (2014) argues that the election of the councilors in Tanzania is based more on their political capability than on their educational level, let alone professional credentials. She gives the example of the legal framework, which governs election in Tanzania and allows any citizen to contest for councillorship as long as he/she has a sound mind and can read and write (Mbelwa 2014). A similar situation takes place in most of the developing countries. For instance, in Egypt, according to the

Egyptian constitution, 50% of the parliament members should be elected from workers and farmers as long as they can read and write. So you can imagine a parliament member whose qualifications are defined by his/her capability to read and write. It is fruitless to talk here about the usefulness of accounting information and how it should be used in all stages in the policy decision-making processes.

Accordingly, the need for training politicians should be considered as part of the decision to increase the use of accounting information in the public sector. Thus, the training, qualification, and experience of politicians are of great importance for enhancing the use of accounting information. Moynihan and Ingraham (2004) argued that highly educated staff members are more likely to use accounting information than staffers who are less educated. The rationale behind this assumption is that politicians with advanced degrees and training are skilled at handling large amounts of formal, numerical, and technical information. These skills are required to collect, analyze, and use accounting information (Askim 2008). Some developing countries have solved these problems by offering specific training to politicians, such as in Tanzania. Mbelwa (2014) argued that the political actors and administrators have revealed that their knowledge was enhanced by participating in training offered within and outside the organization, such as workshops and employee transfers. Others have attempted to train and educate the party's members, whether they belong to governing parties or opposition parties. This can enhance the party members' capability of understanding the financial statements and financial matters, which in turn can increase the opportunity for using accounting information.

- *External pressure from donors and other parties*

External pressure does not only mean here the pressure that comes from outside the country such as that exerted by international organizations (such as the IMF and the World Bank). What we really mean is the pressure that can be exerted by the following three parties:

- Pressure from international organizations such as the IMF and the World Bank
- Pressure from outside the government, for example, from civil society and taxpayers

- Pressure from legislative and oversight bodies on the politicians/governmental entities to use the accounting information

The first pressure is exerted by donors/international financial institutions, such as the International Monetary Fund (IMF) and the World Bank (WB), on most countries to make the required economic reform, including the public sector accounting reform. This pressure is termed coercive pressure according to the New Institutional Theory and can be observed more widely in underdeveloped and transitional economies where international organizations require particular accounting innovations to be effected as a sine qua non of assistance being provided. However, the donors usually follow up on what the funded government did with the money. They also set difficult conditions for accessing the funds. In order for politicians to be able to have access to the funds, they must use the accounting information to legitimize the funds. This is consistent with the empirical results obtained by Mbelwa (2014) that the existence of the coercive donor pressure increases symbolic-legitimating use more than instrumental use of accounting information in the budget decision-making process.

The second can be operationalized when civil societies have reached a degree of consciousness that enables them to measure and evaluate the performance of the government. This is in addition to the opportunity available to civil societies to elect their real representatives, especially those who will undertake financial responsibilities and be accountable to citizen and taxpayers. Moynihan and Ingraham (2004) found a positive relationship between the direct use of performance information and strong citizen pressure in the public sector. Another study also indicated that the lack of this kind of pressure is assumed to be a barrier for the use of accounting information, especially in developing countries (Ouda 2005). However, the empirical results have indicated that citizen pressure can be used to influence both the symbolic-legitimating use of accounting information such as in the mass media and the instrumental-conceptual use of accounting information in decisions related to introducing and collecting new fees or charges as own sources of revenues of local government (Mbelwa 2014, 2015). Finally, it is assumed that the pressure from the legislative and oversight bodies on the executive politicians is considered to be a real enhancing factor for increasing the actual use of accounting information. However, this kind of pressure can really occur when real structural reforms of government activities and tasks are taking place. Structural reforms aim at improving the quality of policy and management, improving information flows, and strengthening incentives for performance; shaping the accountability relationships between politicians, civil servants, and managers of public institutions. Accordingly, the structural reforms of the government can exert real pressure on the politicians/governmental entities to use the accounting information (Ouda 2005). Consequently, the inclusion of determinants of accounting information use in the dynamic model is essential to complement the intervention of and communication among the accounting researchers, consultants, practitioners, users, and standard-setters.

5 Conclusion

This study examines how the public sector accounting and financial reporting can be made more user practice-relevant. It has attempted to adopt a new approach that has already been used in engineering studies but which needs to be developed in order to be applicable to public sector accounting. This is the practice-oriented co-design approach. Unlike the traditional accounting approach which focuses on attempting to fit users and their needs into the design process, the newly developed practice-oriented co-design approach focuses on challenging the design process to better fit into users' practice. The new developed approach is used in this chapter to suggest a dynamic model that aims at making the public sector accounting and financial reporting more user practice-relevant. The dynamic model requires the accounting researchers, consultants, practitioners, primary users, and standard-setter to cooperate in order to co-discover the users, co-identify the users' needs, co-determine the objectives of the public sector accounting and financial reporting system, and co-design the public sector accounting and financial reporting system that is best suited for reporting the information required. The user practice-relevant public sector accounting requires the use of the practice-oriented co-design approach and the suggested dynamic model to reconsider the users' list and consider the politicians, top managers, and policy-makers as the principal users, and hence consider their needs and deal with them as experts by involving them in determining their needs. If the accounting system that is constrained by

GAAP does not provide their needs, the public sector accountants should do extra work and innovation to help politicians and other users in their decision-making by designing an accounting system where they can translate the accounting information into a form that can be understood by the politicians. In addition, the dynamic model considers the information required for serving fiscal sustainability purposes. It also deals with increasing the usability of accounting information provided by the public sector accounting and financial reporting system by adding complementary factors, which are the determinants of accounting information use. It may be useful for future research to extend the work of this chapter by testing the plausibility and workability of the suggested dynamic model.

References

Abrahamson, E., & Eisenman, M. (2001). Why Management Scholars Must Intervene Strategically in the Management Knowledge Market. *Human Relations, 54*(1), 67–75.

American Institute of Certified Public Accountants. (1973, October). *Report of Study Group on the Objectives of Financial Statements.* New York: AICPA. Report of Trueblood Committee.

American Institute of Certified Public Accountants. (1994). *Improving Financial Reporting—A Customer Focus.* New York: AICPA-Report of Jenkin's Committee.

Anthony, R. (1978). *Financial Accounting in Non-Business Organizations.* FASB Study.

Askim, J. (2007). How Do Politicians Use Performance Information? An Analysis of the Norwegian Local Government Experience. *International Review of Administrative Sciences, 73*(3), 453–472.

Askim, J. (2008). The Demand Side of Performance Measurement. *International Public Management Journal, 12*(1), 24–47.

Assad, M., (2001). *Accounting in Non-Government Organizations: Towards Theory of Navigating Legitimacy.* PhD Thesis, University of Southampton.

Assad, M., & Goddard, A. (2006). Accounting and Navigating Legitimacy in Tanzanian NGOs. *Accounting, Auditing & Accountability Journal, 19*(3), 377–404.

Bac, A. (1994). Performance Measurement in the Dutch National, Provincial and Local Government. In E. Buschor & K. Schedler (Eds.), *Perspectives in Performance Measurement. Berne Haupt* (pp. 309–324).

Bac, A. (2001). *International Comparative Issues in Government Accounting: The Similarities and Differences Between Central Government Accounting and Local Government Accounting Within or Between Countries.* Boston, MA: Kluwer Academic Publishers.

Bac, A. (2003). The Netherlands. In K. Lűder & R. Jones (Eds.), *Reforming Governmental Accounting and Budgeting in Europe.* Frankfurt: Fachverlag Moderene Wirtschaft.

Ball, A., & Grubnic, S. (2008). Sustainability Accounting and Accountability in the Public Sector. In J. Unerman, J. Bebbington, & B. O'Dwyer (Eds.), *Sustainability Accounting and Accountability* (pp. 243–265). Abingdon: Routledge.

Bazerman, M. H. (2005). Conducting Influential Research: The Need for Prescriptive Implications. *Academy of Management Journal, 30*, 25–31.

Brezet, J., & van Hemel, C. (1997). *Ecodesign, A Promising Approach to Sustainable Production and Consumption.* Paris: UNEP.

Brinn, T., Jones, M., & Pendlebury, M. (1996). UK Accountants' Perception of Research Journal Quality. *Acc Bus Res, 26*(3), 265–277.

Canadian Institute of Charted Accountants. (1977, December 31). *Accounting for Non-Profit Organization.* Discussion Draft.

Caruana, J., & Farrugia, B. (2018). The Use and Non-Use of the Government Financial Report by Maltese Members of Parliament. *Accounting, Auditing and Accountability Journal, 31*(4), 1124–1144.

Christiaens, J. (2014, July). Politicians Also Use Accounting Information, But of Different Kind. *CIGAR Newsletter, 5*(3), p. 1.

Coleman, H. (2007). New Development: Connecting Public Service Researchers and Practitioners. *Public Money & Management, 27*(4), 281–283.

Demski, J. (2001). Some Thoughts on Accounting Scholarship. In Presidential Address. Annual American Accounting Association Meeting. Atlanta, GA, August 22. Reprinted in Accounting Education News, 5, 1–3.

Drebin, A., et al. (1981). *Objectives of Accounting and Financial Reporting for Governmental Units: A Research Study* (Vol. I, pp. 59–74). Glen Ellyn, IL: National Council on Governmental Accounting.

Ferguson, L., & Drebin, A. (1981). *Decision and Information Needs of Management, NCGA Research Study, Objectives of Accounting and Financial Reporting for Governmental Units: A Research Study.* A. Drebin, J. Chan, & L. Ferguson, vol. II.

Fisher, T., & Hielscher, S. (2008). *Are You Worth It? Can You Fix It? Investigating the Sustainability of Mundane Activities Using Theories of Everyday Practice and Human/Object Interaction.* Paper for Changing the Change Conference. Turin.

Guarini, E. (2016). The Day After: Newly-Elected Politicians and the Use of Accounting Information. *Public Money & Management, 36*(7), 499–506.

Hitt, M. A. (2005). Management Theory and Research: Potential Contribution to Public Policy and Public Organizations. *Academy of Management Journal, 48*(6), 963–966.

Hogye, M. (2002). *Theoretical Approaches to Public Budgeting: Local Government Budgeting*. Budapest: Open Society Institute.

Hood, C. (1995). The 'New Public Management' in the 1980's: Variations on a Theme. *Accounting, Organizations and Society, 20*(2/3), 93–109.

Hooper, K. C., & Kearins, K. N. (2005). Knowing the Price of Everything and the Value of Nothing: Accounting for Heritage Assets. *Accounting, Auditing and Accountability Journal, 62*(4), 181–184.

Hyndman, N., Ezzamel, M., Johnsen, A., Lapsley, I., & Pallot, J. (2005). Conflict and Rationality: Accounting in Northern Ireland's Devolved Assembly. *Financial Accountability & Management, 21*(1), 33–55.

IFAC. (1991). *Financial Reporting by National Governments*. Issued by the International federation of Accountants, Study 1.

Inanga, E., & Schneider, W. (2005). The Failure of Accounting Research to Improve Accounting Practice: A Problem of Theory and Lack of Communication. *Critical Perspectives on Accounting, 16*(2005), 227–248.

Ingram, J., Shove, E., & Watson, M. (2007). Products and Practices: Selected Concepts from Science and Technology Studies and from Social Theories of Consumption and Practice. *MIT Design Issues, 23*(2, Spring), 3–16.

Jones, R. (2003). United Kingdom. In K. Lűder & R. Jones (Eds.), *Reforming Governmental Accounting and Budgeting in Europe*. Frankfurt: Fachverlag Moderene Wirtschaft.

Jones, R., & Pendlebury, M. (1984). *Public Sector Accounting*. London: Pitman.

Jones, R., & Pendlebury, M. (2000). *Public Sector Accounting* (5th ed.). New York, NY: Prentice Hall.

Jorge, S., Jorge de Jesus, M. A., & Nogueira, S. (2016). Information Brokers and the Use of Budgetary and Financial Information by Politicians: The Case of Portugal. *Public Money & Management, 36*(7), 515–520.

Julier, G. (2007). Design Practice within a Theory of Practice,' in Design Principles & Practices. *An International Journal, 1*(2), 43–50.

Kingdon, J. W. (1984). *Agendas, Alternatives, and Public Policies*. Ann Arbor: The University of Michigan.

Kuijer, L., & de Jong, A. (2009). *A Practice Oriented Approach to User Centered Sustainable Design*. Sapporo: Japan Society of Mechanical Engineering.

Kurunmaki, L., Melia, K., & Lapsley, I. (2003). Accountingization v. Legitimation: A Comparative Study of the Use of Accounting Information in Intensive Care. *Management Accounting Research, 14*(2), 112–139.

Lűder, K. (1989, August). *Comparative Government Accounting Study—Interim Summary Report*. Forschungsinstitut Fur Offentliche Verwaltung.

Lűder, K. (2013, September 2–3). *Accrual Accounting and Budgeting in Government—A History of the Hessian "New Administrative Management (NVS)" Project.* Paper Presented at 14th Comparative International Governmental Accounting Research (CIGAR) Conference, Birmingham University, Birmingham.

Mayston, D. (1992). Developing a Conceptual Framework for Public Sector Financial Reporting. *Financial Accountability and Management, 8*(4).

McCartney, S. (2004). The Use of Usefulness: An Examination of the User Needs Approach to the Financial Reporting Conceptual Framework. *Journal of Applied Accounting Research, 7*(2), 52–79.

Mbelwa, L. (2014). *Determinants of the Use of Accounting Information in the Public Sector Budgetary Decision-making Processes: The Case of Tanzanian Local Government Authorities (LGAs).* PhD Thesis, Umea University, Sweden.

Mbelwa, L. (2015). Factors Influencing the Use of Accounting Information in Tanzanian Local Government Authorizes (LGAS): An Institutional Theory Approach. *Research in Accounting in Emerging Economies, 15*, 143–177.

Mkasiwa, T (2011). *Accounting Changes and Budgeting Practices in the Tanzanian Central Government: A Theory of Struggling for Conformance.* PhD Thesis, University of Southampton.

Moynihan, D., & Ingraham, P. (2004). Integrative Leadership in the Public Sector: A Model of Performance-Information Use. *Administration & Society, 36*(4), 427–453.

Mzenzi, S. (2013). *Accounting Practices in the Tanzanian Local Government Authorities (LGAs): The Grounded Theory of Manipulating Legitimacy.* PhD Thesis, University of Southampton.

National Committee on Governmental Accounting, Governmental Accounting, Auditing and Financial Reporting. (1968). Chicago: Municipal Finance Officers Association.

Neves, F., & Gomez-Villegas, N. (2020). Public Sector Accounting Reform in Latin America and Epistemic Communities: An Institutional Approach. *Journal of Public Administration, 54*(1), 11–31.

Olson, O. (2001) *Context Bounded Accounting.* Retrieved from http://citeseerx.ist.psu.edu/viewdoc/download?doi=10.1.1.201.2907&rep=rep1&type=pdf.

Ouda, H. (2005). *Transition to Accrual Accounting in the Public Sector of Developed and Developing Countries: Problems and Requirements, with special focus on the Netherlands and Egypt* (p. 405). Veenendaal: Universal Press.

Raudla, R. (2012). The Use of Performance Information in Budgetary Decision-Making by Legislators. *Public Administration, 90*(4), 1000–1015.

Robinson, M. (1995). *Public Sector Net Worth: Is It Worth Measuring?* Australian Parliament Library, Research Paper.

Rutherford, D. (1992). Developing a Conceptual Framework for Central Government Financial Reporting, Intermediate Users and Indirect Control. *Financial Accountability and Management, 8*(4, Winter), 265–280.

Rynes, S. L., & Shapiro, d. (2005). Academy of Management Journal Editors' Forum: Public Policy and the Public Interest: What If We Mattered More? *Academy of Management Journal, 48*(6), 925–927.

Rynes, S. L., Bartunek, J. M., & Daft, R. L. (2001). Across the Great Divide: Knowledge Creation and Transfer Between Practitioners and Academics. *Academy of Management Journal, 44*(2), 340–355.

Sanders, E., & Stappers, P. (2008). Co-creation and the New Landscapes of Design. *Co Design, 4*(1), 5–18.

Scapens, R. (2008). Seeking the Relevance of Interpretive Research: A Contribution to the Polyphonic Debate. *Critical Perspectives on Accounting, 19*(6), 915–919.

Scott, K. (2008). *Co-Designing Sustainable User Practices.* Thesis in Industrial Ecology Master's Program. TU Delft, Erasmus University, Leiden University.

Scott, K., Bakker, C., & Quist, J. (2009, June 8–10). *Co-Design, Social Practices and Sustainable Innovation: Involving Users in a Living Lab Exploratory Study on Bathing, Joint Actions.* Paper Presented at Climate Change Conference, Aalborg, Denmark.

Shapiro, D., Kirkman, B., & Courtney, H. (2007). Perceived Causes and Solutions of the Translation Problem in Management Research. *Academy of Management Journal, 50*(2), 249–266.

Shove, E., Matthew, Watson, M., Ingram, J., & Hand, M. (2008). The Design of Everyday Life. *Berg, 134*, p. 192.

Steccolini, I. (2019). Public Sector Accounting and the Post-NPM: Out of the Golden (C) Age? Re-Considering the Public Side of (Public Sector) Accounting Research. *Accounting, Auditing and Accountability Journal, 32*(1), 255–279.

Sutcliffe, P. (1985). *Financial Reporting in the Public Sector—A Framework for Analysis and Identification of Issues.* Australian Accounting Research Foundation: Melbourne.

Van Helden, J. (2014). What Are the Financial Topics Which Make Politicians Lose Sleep? *CIGAR Newsletter, 5*(1), p. 1.

Van Helden, J., & Northcott, D. (2010). Examining the Practical Relevance of Public Sector Management Accounting Research. *Financial Accountability & Management, 26*(2), 0267–4424.

Van Helden, G. J., & Reichard, C. (2018). Cash or Accruals for Budgeting: Why Some Countries Changed Their Budgeting Mode and Others Not. *OECD Journal on Budgeting, 18*(1), 89–113.

Vyas, R., & Souchon, L. (2003). Symbolic Use of Export Information: A Multidisciplinary Approach to Conceptual Development and Key Consequences. *International Marketing Review, 20*(1), 67–94.

Wever, R., van Kuijk, J., & Boks, C. (2008). User-Centered Design for Sustainable Behavior. *International Journal of Sustainable Engineering, 1*(1), 9–20.

Yamamoto, K. (2014). Why and When Do Politicians Use Accounting Information? *CIGAR Newsletter, 5*(2), p. 1.

CHAPTER 7

Accounting and Politicians: A Theory of Accounting Information Usefulness

1 Introduction

While Chap. 6 focused on making public sector accounting and financial reporting more user practice-relevant by using the practice-oriented co-design approach, which integrates the efforts of accounting researchers, practitioners, consultants, standard-setting bodies, and users together to produce a public sector accounting and financial reporting system that considers the diverging accounting information needs of different users, Chap. 7 focuses on developing a theory that aims at producing practice-relevant accounting information for the governing politicians by making such accounting information more specific to the task to be performed, to the problem to be solved, to the challenges to be coped with, and/or to the matter at hand *('task fit')*.

Although governments have made radical reforms in their public management and public financial management systems which aim at creating a more informative accounting system, they have largely neglected the question of how to foster accounting information use (Van Dooren and Van de

This chapter is based on my earlier published paper together with Professor Ralf Klischewski: Ouda, H., and Klischewski, R, (2019), "Accounting and Politicians: A Theory of Accounting Information Usefulness", *Journal of Public Budgeting, Accounting and Financial Management*, Vol. 31, Issue, 4, pp. 496–517.

H. Ouda, *Practice-Relevant Accrual Accounting for the Public Sector*, Public Sector Financial Management,
https://doi.org/10.1007/978-3-030-51595-9_7

Walle 2008; Raudla 2012; Pollitt 2007). The experience of earlier reforming countries, such as the UK and New Zealand, indicates that many users, especially politicians, do not use the improved accounting information that has resulted from revamping the public sector accounting. Different studies (Lűder 2013; Hyndman et al. 2005; Parry and Hughes 2018) indicate that politicians neither appreciate nor use the improved accounting information resulting from the adoption of accrual accounting and budgeting. Only recently the use of accounting information has become a central issue in the public sector literature (Moynihan and Pandey 2010; Hammerschmid et al. 2013; Kroll 2013, 2014; Taylor 2011). The following are among other, important questions (Van Helden 2014): Is it mere stupidity or ignorance of politicians to underestimate the value of accrual accounting? Or do we, as accounting scholars, fail to understand what financial topics really matter to politicians?

The two questions indicate that the use of accounting information by the users depends on two actors: producers (supply side) and users (demand side). To date, however, whether, how, and under what circumstances the politicians actually use accounting information is significantly under-researched (Pollitt 2006; Van Helden 2015).

Scholars have mainly focused on the demand side (Mbelwa 2014; Van Helden 2016; Giacomini et al. 2016), which is the use of information by users, and have neglected the supply side, which is the provision of information by the producers. Very few studies (e.g., Mimba et al. 2007; Van Dooren and Van de Walle 2008) have focused on both the supply and demand sides. The main advantage of concentrating on both supply and demand sides is to understand the clear distinction between the production of information and the use of information (Hatry 1999; Van Dooren 2005). However, different studies have indicated that, in spite of increasing the usefulness and relevance of accounting information, politicians' use of accounting information is still low (Hatry 1999; Van Dooren 2005; Ter Bogt 2004; Ouda 2017). Another literature review study conducted by Van Helden (2016) has shown that a low level of accounting information use was found in studies conducted at the central government level in the UK (Johnson and Tabot 2007); at the state level (Bourdeaux 2008) and at the federal level (Stalebrink and Frisco 2011) in the USA; in Estonia's central government (Raudla 2012); and in German and Italian local governments (Grossi et al. 2016). In addition, other studies have indicated different results of the appreciation and use of accounting information by politicians. While Aldermen in Italy highly appreciate budgetary cash-based accounting information and approve of accrual accounting information (Liguori et al. 2012), in Belgium, however, the actual use of this information by Flemish councilors is very low for budgetary items and almost absent for accrual items (Buylen 2014; Buylen and Christiaens 2016; Van Helden 2016). Based on Liguori et al. (2012) and Buylen (2014), Van Helden (2016) has inferred that the appreciation or usefulness of a certain type of accounting information by politicians does not automatically lead to its use; and politicians' appreciation or perceived usefulness of accounting information is much higher than their actual use.

Most of the previous accounting studies (Mimba et al. 2007; Van Dooren and Van de Walle 2008; Liguori et al. 2012; Buylen 2014; Ouda 2015, 2017) have been based on rationality and objectivity without considering the production and use of the accounting information as an act of human and social agency. In fact, the producers of accounting information are human and so are the users of accounting information. Individual and collective psychological aspects do not vanish while producing or using accounting information. While we still need the traditional accounting models and theories (e.g., decision-usefulness theory of accounting, Staubus 2000), our understanding of this issue needs to be enriched by adding insights from other social sciences. Incorporating human behavior into traditional accounting models and theories improves our explanation and predictions of producers' and users' behavior, including the issue in focus, which is the scarcity of actual use of accounting information by politicians. Although the production and use of accounting information have received considerable attention in the public sector literature, researching the production and actual use of accounting information in relation to the human and social agency involved has always constituted a negligible part of the research agenda (Raudla 2012). Therefore, the research question is:

- How do cognitive aspects influence the use/nonuse of accounting information by politicians?

This research aims to fill this gap by conceptualizing and theorizing the readiness to use and the actual use of accounting information in relation to the human and social agency involved. This emphasizes our interest in explaining how and why politicians do not use what the accountants make available to them. To achieve the research aim, we propose to build on the concept of fit in several dimensions while assuming that all actors involved follow their own context-bound rationality:

1. The first level of analysis is *the individual and his/her cognitions/intentions*. We build on the Cognitive Fit Theory (CFT) to understand the formation of mental representations adequately to solve the tasks at hand. Due to the different tasks of producers and users of accounting information, different mental representations leading to divergent observable behavior are developed and maintained.
2. The next level of analysis takes into account the duality caused by the *independency of the supply side (accounting) and demand side (policy/politicians)*: Each side constitutes the environment for the other. Social Cognitive Theory (SCT) is helpful to further explain how cognitive learning and behavioral change can emerge from interacting with the environment. The perception of social agency—that is, the behavior and its outcomes—as a match (fit) or mismatch (misfit) is an important source of learning and development. Notably the unit of analysis is extended from the individual towards the group, organization, and/or (professional) community.
3. Generalizing a coherence of rationality and assuming a degree of alignment within the supply side (accounting) and the demand side (policy/politicians), we can explain why and how cognition on each side is divergent (misfit) while at the same time *a significant degree of cognitive match (fit) is a prerequisite for producing accounting information that matches (fits) the need of the consumers*, that is, a prerequisite for its usefulness.
4. Finally, in search of collective learning and change management, we assume a common professional and organizational frame on the supply side (accounting) and the demand side (policy/politicians) so that *individual learning processes may be treated as aligned. In addition, individual mental representations may be altered collectively.* This develops an appropriate cognitive fit on each side and a sufficient cognitive match between both sides that is more supportive towards producing useful accounting information that can actually be used.

Aiming to integrate both technical and cognitive aspects of the producers and the users of accounting information and to explain the divergence of (rational) behavior, we combine all of these levels of analysis into a

Theory of Accounting Information Usefulness. Such a theory explains the relation of production and consumption of accounting information, including prediction for change management. As the accounting literature does not currently provide such a theory, we consider our contribution as a stepping stone towards enhancing the accounting discipline for more behavioral accounting (Strong 1999; Strong and Portz 2003; Bourmistrov 2017). Yet, the conceptualization as such is only a milestone, and empirical research to follow will bring evidence about the utility of such a theory and its further development.

The structure of the chapter follows the methodology indicated earlier. Sections 2 and 3 identify how we use CFT and SCT to explain how the cognition of accounting information producers and users relates to their tasks and their environment, respectively. Then, Sect. 4 takes the argument further and analyzes cognitive match and accounting information usefulness, building on the literature related to behavioral accounting. Here, we introduce our core proposition indicating that accounting information usefulness is a function of cognitive match between producers and users. Section 5 extends this conceptualization even further to align individual and collective learning on both sides and to introduce information use audit as an instrument for empirically supporting collective learning. Section 6 is dedicated to the application of the theory into practice using the public policy decision-making process and its five stages and it identifies how the learning alignment can be operationalized and institutionalized. Section 7 finally summarizes our contribution to the public sector accounting domain and the practical implications of the theory as well as future research.

2 Cognition and Behavior in Accounting Information Production and Use

To better understand the scarcity of actual use of accounting information by politicians, incorporating the human behavior into traditional accounting models and theories is fundamental. The first level of analysis is *the individual and his/her cognition/intentions*. We build on the CFT to understand the formation of mental representations adequate to solve the tasks at hand. Due to the different tasks of producers and users of accounting information, different mental representations leading to divergent observable behavior are developed and maintained.

2.1 *Cognition and Actors*

Cognition definition can assist to some extent in determining the cognitive factors (Williams and Thayer 2009). Cognition refers to internal mental representations that result from different mental processes and operations including knowledge, awareness, perception, reasoning, attitude, and judgment. In addition, Hartono (2007) and Abdillah (2013) argue that "cognition is a term used in cognitive psychology to describe a form of thought or perception of the individual or the tendency to use perceptual and information events in solving problems." Hartono (2007) indicates that cognitive psychology explains how people think, learn, feel, remember, make decisions, and process (perceive, interpret, store retrieve) data in the memory of the brain.

The concept of cognition may embrace both process and product, and this duality has been already discussed in the literature. Cognition as a process (learning process) refers to the mental process by which external or internal input is transformed, reduced, elaborated, stored, recovered, and used (Neisser 1967). Such mental processes involve the generation and use of internal representations to varying degrees, and may operate independently (or not) at different stages of processing (Brandimonte et al. 2006). Cognition as product is considered to be a mental representation that surfaces to consciousness when we perceive, reason, or form mental images (Brandimonte et al. 2006). Cognition can perform a governance task that assists in creating and forming the mental representation which governs, with reference to our interests, the production and use of accounting information by politicians. For understanding and following up cognition in our domain, we need to identify the relevant actors in accounting information production and use.

Producers of accounting information: To understand who the producers of accounting information are, we distinguish between the following:

1. An inner circle of practitioners/preparers of financial statements such as the employees in accounting departments and controllers
2. An intermediate circle of employees in an internal audit office or corporate controllers, technical units, and advisory bodies
3. An outer circle of standard-setters, professional bodies, and academics

Our study focuses only on the internal accounting information *(special-purpose financial statement/specific user interests)* provided to the governing politicians. Accordingly, producers will only include the inner and intermediate circles and exclude the outer circle because the people of the inner and intermediate circles not only apply accounting standards and prepare the financial statements but also enrich and summarize the accounting information or present it in a user-friendly way. Moreover, they are involved in generating, interpreting, organizing, or communicating accounting information for a particular purpose to specific groups (Wolfe 2006). They necessarily play a significant role in preparing a summary of budgetary and financial information, making it more understandable to politicians. Production of accounting information is the process by which the producers follow the accounting standards and practices to generate accounting information assumed to satisfy the demands of users (decision-makers/ politicians). Accounting information includes budgetary and financial information which comprises cash and accrual information.

Users of accounting information: Accounting literature has identified several users of the accounting information in the public sector (e.g., Anthony 1978; IFAC 1991) such as legislative and other governing bodies; the public, investors and creditors, economic and financial analysts, and public managers. However, as representatives of citizens and decision-makers, governing politicians are assumed to be the main users of public sector budgeting and financial information. It is therefore important to clearly understand what accounting information the governing politicians need and what role the producers have to undertake to provide useful accounting information that fits the governing politicians' needs. Generally, consumption/use of accounting information is the extent to which accounting information is taken into consideration when decisions are made (Diamantopoulos and Souchon 1999). However, some studies address the use of accounting information based on the purposes of use. For example, the instrumental use of accounting information is mainly related to relevant information of decision-making that can affect the efficiency of an organization and enhance its performance. Kurunmaki et al. (2003) argue that the instrumental use treats accounting information as a technical aspect which increases efficiency in the decision-making process. In addition, Mbelwa (2014) argue that the symbolic use of accounting information is all about using the accounting information for legitimizing and confirming decisions. For our study, the accounting information use means both the instrumental and symbolic use as the governing politicians mainly need accounting information that improves the efficiency of the decision-making process and also to legitimize and confirm their decisions.

As scientific inquiries should be guided by solid theoretical underpinnings, we build on the CFT to understand the relation between solving the aforementioned tasks and related cognitive formation.

2.2 Cognitive Fit Theory (CFT)

The CFT (Vessey 1991) is based on the information-processing theory, which argues that human problem solvers will look for ways to reduce their problem-solving efforts (Newell and Simon 1972; Hubona et al. 1998). Vessey and Galletta (1991) indicate that one of the ways to reduce processing effort is to facilitate the problem-solving processes that human problem solvers use in completing the task. The CFT has contributed to this by matching the problem representation to the task as it asserts that problem-solving performance is affected by a fit between a task and a problem representation. Task in the CFT refers to the problem-solving task that the user has to perform, while problem representation refers to the way in which the information pertaining to the task is presented to the user (Collier 2003; Chan et al. 2012). The task and the problem representation emphasize certain information, which leads to the creation of mental representation. The mental representation is the way the problem is presented in human working memory (Vessey 1991). The mental representation is formed using the characteristics of both the problem representation and the task. It is determined by the information required by the task and the information emphasized by the problem representation. Figure 7.1 presents the general model of problem solving on which the CFT is based.

According to the CFT, fit is explained as a match between the information emphasized in the problem representation and the information requirements of the task. Consequently, matching problem representation to task leads to the use of similar, and therefore consistent, problem-solving processes and hence to the formation of a consistent mental representation that emphasizes the same type of information (Vessey 1991). This means that when the cognitive processes used to act on the problem representation match with those used to complete the task, cognitive fit is said to exist, resulting in better problem-solving performance (Vessey 1991). When a mismatch occurs between problem representation and task, cognitive fit will not result, since similar processes cannot be used to

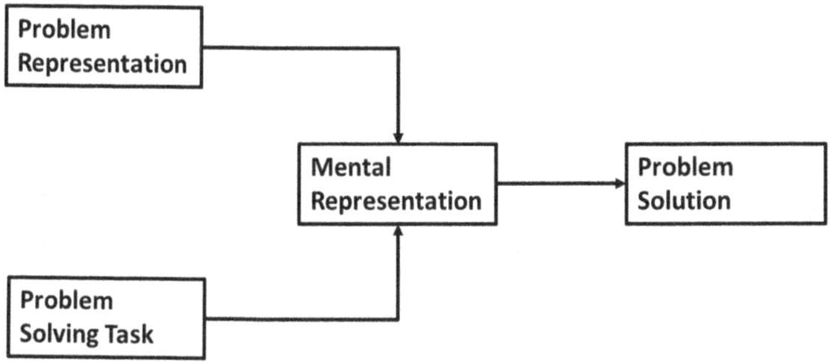

Fig. 7.1 Model of cognitive fit. (Source: Vessey (1991))

act on both the problem representation and solving the problem (Vessey and Galletta 1991).

2.3 *Cognitive Factors in Accounting*

The basic notion of cognitive fit as matching the problem representation to the task needs to be extended to incorporate the cognition in terms of individual cognition factors and characteristics of both producers and users, such as knowledge, awareness, and beliefs. These cognition factors will facilitate the formation of mental representation that governs the production and use of accounting information and, hence, may also affect the cognitive fit. Analogous to the basic cognitive fit arguments, we expect that a specific cognition (cognition factors/characteristics) will have its greatest effect on the performance when it emphasizes the same type of information as in the associated problem-solving elements (i.e., problem representation and task).

As cognition plays a significant role in determining behavior (Danili and Reid 2006; Hall 2010; Williams and Thayer 2009), the study of cognitive factors can assist in a better understanding of the processes and outcomes in the production and use of accounting information. Danili and Reid (2006) argue that cognitive factors indicate the characteristics of the individual that influence performance and learning. In the accounting field, different studies have considered the following six cognitive factors.

1. Knowledge: The behavioral accounting literature (Anderson 1993; Strong 1999; Strong and Portz 2003; Bourmistrov 2017) considers the knowledge as one of the cognitive factors that may affect the production and the use of accounting information. According to the CFT, the use of accounting information depends on the cognitive aspects of individual actors (Strong and Portz 2003). The decision-usefulness theory assumes that users who have reasonable knowledge of accounting as well as of business and economic activities will properly be able to use the accounting information. This argument is also supported by cognitive theorists such as Strong and Portz (2003), who posit that accounting knowledge and information presentation format affect the cognitive ability of individual actors to use accounting information, which can result in improving the decision-making performance (Mimba et al. 2007; Mbelwa 2014). Moreover, the cognitive induction theory posits that existing knowledge structures stored in a decision-maker's memory influence how external cues are included in information that exists in memory to form a mental model of the problem (Strong 1999). Anderson (1993) suggests that accounting knowledge consists of both declarative knowledge and procedural knowledge. Declarative accounting knowledge includes both double-entry representation for ex-post accounting events and the skeletal forms of the traditional financial statements. Procedural accounting knowledge consists of analytical judgment strategies that are developed through the problem-solving tasks in the formal accounting education process (Anderson 1993). Strong's study (1999) argues that accounting knowledge interferes with the individual's ability to form the mental representation of the problem that provides a cognitive fit with graphical information presentation. Knowledge is also empirically tested and the findings indicate that users who have a high level of accounting knowledge should perform better using tabular information presentation (Strong 1999). This may be due to the fact that high accounting knowledge interferes with the user's ability to construct an internal model (a mental representation) that assists in performing the decision-making task (Tuttle and Kershaw 1998; Strong 1999).

Knowledge not only influences the mental representation of the users but may also influence the mental representation of the producers. The extent and type of use of accounting information might depend on the policy decision-making processes where different stages can be identified (Lasswell 1956; Howlett and Ramesh 2003): agenda-setting, policy formulation, decision-making, implementation, and evaluation. When the producers have enough knowledge about each stage of the policy decision-making process, the type of information required by each stage, and the accounting standards and practices, and the most suitable way of presenting the accounting information to the users, this can facilitate the forming of consistent mental representation between the producers and the users. For example, agenda-setting: in order for politicians to create the demand required for introducing a new health policy or transportation policy, they need specific accounting information that assists them in promoting these health and transportation policies. If the producers of accounting information have enough knowledge about the type of information required for the agenda-setting stage and are able to provide the required information that allows users to bring and promote a new issue to the attention of others (public and/or other politicians) and enables them to put it into the political agenda, this will increase the opportunity of the actual use of accounting information, whether it is financial or managerial or both (Ouda 2017). Accordingly, accounting information knowledge can be considered as one of the cognition factors that governs the production and use of accounting information through forming a consistent mental representation between the producers and the users that enhances the task performance.

2. Perception: the perception of the users and the producers of accounting information is also considered a cognitive factor in the accounting literature. Most empirical studies show evidence of producers'/users' perception gap (Alves 2010; Labinot and Summermatter 2012). This gap explains why the accounting information provided by the producers will be used or not by the users. Alves' study (2010) argues that accounting information is not used in the same way in all decision process phases, as producers and users have different perceptions with respect to which phase the accounting information will be used in. The user perception is that accounting information is most used in the phases of identifying the problem, and listing and analyzing the alternatives, whereas the producer perception is that accounting information has greater impact on the phases of listing and analyzing the alternatives (Alves 2010). Labinot and Summermatter (2012) argue that attempts to understand the use, nonuse, or even misuse of accounting information therefore need to address how politicians perceive the decision situations they face, what questions they try to answer therein, and elaborate on the goals these actors try to achieve by using accounting information. The perception of politicians regarding the significance of financial statements and to what extent they perceive them as a reliable source of accounting information will also affect the user cognition with respect to the use or nonuse of the accounting information. Moreover, the perceived risk associated with the task to be completed can also affect the cognitive ability of the users: if the risk is perceived to be high, this may increase the opportunity of using the accounting information compared with if the risk is low. Romolini et al. (2015) have conducted an empirical study about the different perceptions of politicians and managers regarding the use of accounting information in the local utilities. The findings indicated that the perceptions of politicians and managers differ with regard to the importance and the use of accounting information. The main interest lies in the insight gained into the different perceptions of the actors regarding using accounting information from local utilities. Politicians and managers differ in their attention to and use of governance information. This difference of perception among politicians and managers has influenced the use or nonuse of accounting information. Moreover, the producers' perception regarding the situation faced by the users and the nature of information required for such situations will have implications for the design and format of financial reporting and the type of information provided to the users. The producers and the users should exert more effort to provide consistent indicators as to how these gaps can be narrowed. So the perception of the producers and the users regarding the nature of the task to be performed and what kind of information is required for that task, the reliability of the source of the information, as well as the risk associated with the task will all influence the behavior of the users and the producers of the accounting information.

3. Expectations: When the expectations of the producers and those of the users about what the special-purpose financial statements should contain match, this can positively influence the decision-making performance. However, the accounting literature has ensured that there is a gap between the expected accounting information of producers and users. Liggio (1974) and Aljaaidi and Salamen (2009) have defined the accounting information expectation gap as the difference between the levels of expected performance as envisioned by the independent accounting producer and by the user of the financial statements. In addition, the expectation gap is not only related to the content of accounting information but also to the expectation of producers about the level of accounting knowledge of the user. Accounting information producers have an expectation that the users of accounting information should have a 'reasonable knowledge' of accounting. For example, the IASB Framework argues that "users are expected to have a reasonable knowledge of business and economic activities and accounting and a willingness to study the information with reasonable diligence." Hence, there is an expectation that financial statements are not tailored to meet the needs of users who have not, in some way, studied financial accounting. In fact, public sector entities have multiple groups of users who often have differing and competing accounting information needs, as well as expectations and desired outcomes (Lawrence and Weber 2016). The complexity of the expectation may be attributed to misalignment of the users' expectations with the producers' expectations. To narrow the expectation gap, there should be alignment between the users and the producers of accounting information as this will have an impact on operating and disclosure policies of the public sector entities. Alignment can make a difference to decisions by improving decision-makers' capacities to predict expectations or by providing feedback on earlier ones. In the light of this feedback, the producers can reconsider their expectations and hence the way of presenting the accounting information (format and content of financial reporting).

4. Beliefs: Bandura (1997) asserts that individuals' level of motivation and actions are based more on what they believe than on what is objectively the case. This is consistent with the Bamber study (1993), which argued that users assume that the information confirming their judgments and decisions is more valuable than the information that did not confirm their decisions and judgments. Therefore, they may favor or even seek information that confirms their beliefs and expectations. The beliefs of the users may also influence the information selection, as argues, such as the beliefs that the recently received accounting information influences the decisions more profoundly than the previously obtained accounting information, which may affect the selection of the accounting information presented in the financial reports. While the production of accounting information is governed by the public sector accounting standards and practices, the producers may present the accounting information to the users based on their beliefs rather than the users' beliefs. Also the users, especially politicians, need specific information that serves their political discourse and their beliefs. They need a context-bound accounting system that is constructed upon their ideas and beliefs and their discourses related to their organizations (Olson 2001). This should be viewed in contrast to a situation in which an accounting system is based on general discourses of external actors, that is, a-contextual discourses, where the accounting information is produced using the traditional accounting standards and presented in a standard financial reporting format (Olson 2001; Ouda 2015, 2017). So the existence of different beliefs between the producers and the users may influence both the production and the use of accounting information.

5. Awareness: To increase the use of accounting information by politicians, the producers of accounting information should be aware of the antecedents of accounting information use. The producers' awareness tends to influence the users' perception towards the use of accounting information. Lack of the users' awareness concerning their accounting information needs has proved to be one of the hurdles for users in using the accounting information. The awareness about produced accounting information is essential for users because it influences their decision-making process. Accordingly, we can assume that increasing the users' and the producers' awareness of accounting information demanded and supplied can be considered to be an important part of a holistic cognition approach to manage the accounting information production and use. Parsons et al. (2014) emphasizes the importance of building awareness in accounting information at the levels of both the users and the producers. Building appropriate awareness is primarily aimed at increasing the users' understanding of what type of situation they face and what type of accounting information they need to enable them to make the right judgment and decision. In the same vein, increasing the awareness of the producers of the previous information needs of users will assist them in providing the relevant accounting information. Kagan proposed the concept of information need as a "cognitive representation of a future goal that is desired." Awareness of accounting information is capable of making a difference in a decision by helping users to form predictions about the outcomes of past, present, and future events or to confirm or correct prior expectations. In addition, awareness can improve users' capacities to predict or provide feedback on earlier expectations.

Without awareness of antecedents of accounting information use, producers lack the ability to predict information needs. Without an interest in the future, awareness of the antecedents of accounting information use is sterile. However, the question is: how can we build and create proper awareness? The answer is: Learning is one of the basic elements for creating accounting information awareness (see Sect. 5).

6. Interpretation: Hawkins and Mothersbaugh (2010) argue that interpretation can be described as the way users understand information based on the particular stimulus, the situation, and themselves. Past research has suggested that interpretation of accounting information is affected by previous knowledge and experience of users, users' goals, users' awareness, users' perception, and the context of the decision-making process (Fogg 2003). This means that the aforementioned cognition factors all play an essential role in forming the interpretation ability of the users. For example, if the users do not have enough knowledge of accounting as well as of business and economic activities, this will affect the way the users understand the accounting information and, consequently, their ability of considering whether information is relevant and credible for use. Accordingly, producers can affect the interpretation ability of the users through the content of accounting information, the way of presentation, and the format of financial reporting. Analysis and interpretation can assist in turning the raw data into usable information. Increasing the interpretation ability of the users requires interaction between technical and cognition factors as well as cooperation at the producers' and users' levels.

While understanding cognition on the individual level is essential, we need to extend our scope to professional communities and to how cognitive processes are related to their social agency and interaction.

3 Independency of Accounting and Policy

The next level of analysis takes into account the duality caused by the ***independency of the supply side and demand side***: Each side constitutes the environment for the other, and the SCT can explain how cognitive learning and behavioral change can emerge from interacting with the environment. The perception of social agency—that is, the behavior and its outcomes—as a match (fit) or mismatch (misfit) is an important source of learning and development. Notably the unit of analysis is extended from the individual towards the group, organization, and/or (professional) community.

Lack of communication between accounting information production and use creates the duality problem. Production of accounting information takes place as an independent process from the use of accounting information. To illustrate how the independency of the supply and demand affects the intersection of the behavior of both producers and users of accounting information and its outcome (match/mismatch), we will consider the policy decision-making process and its five stages identified by Lasswell (1956) and Howlett and Ramesh (2003): agenda-setting, policy formulation, decision-making, implementation, and evaluation. It is assumed that the usefulness of accounting information and its actual use will be enhanced when it is specific to the problems the users face in each stage (Ouda 2017). When the producers do not learn about the policy decision-making process and its five stages and what kind of information should be provided to each stage, then the produced information will not match the users' information needs. When the users (governing politicians) do not learn and increase their knowledge about accounting, and economic and business activities, they will not be able to use the accounting information.

To explain how the duality problem affects the intersection of the behavior of both producers and users of accounting information and how to overcome this problem, we build on the SCT.

3.1 Social Cognitive Theory (SCT)

SCT (Bandura 1986) has attempted to provide a comprehensive framework for understanding human behavior. It postulates that individual behavior is formed by a model of a triadic reciprocal causation relationship including cognition (personal factors), environment, and behavior. These three factors operate as interacting determinants that influence one another bidirectionally (Bandura 1986; see Fig. 7.2).

The reciprocal causation does not mean that the different sources of influence are of equal strength. Some may be stronger than others. Nor do the reciprocal influences all occur simultaneously. It takes time for a causal

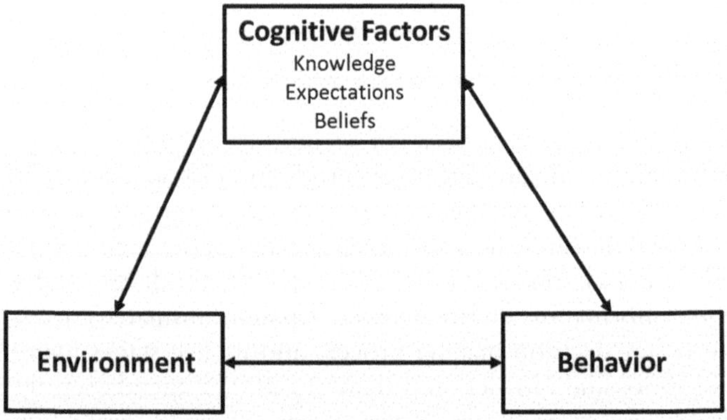

Fig. 7.2 Triadic reciprocal determination of human behavior. (Source: Bandura (1986))

factor to exert its influence and activate reciprocal influences (Bandura 1989).

SCT states that personal behaviors are shaped and affected by variations of cognitive factors and the conditions of associated social environment (Bandura 1986). SCT proposes that the cognitive factors such as expectations, beliefs, knowledge, self-perceptions, goals, and intentions give shape and direction to behavior. What people think, believe, and feel affects how they behave (Bandura 1986). Personal behavior is also affected by environmental factors; for example, peer behavior acts as an environmental factor for an individual behavior. Bandura (1986) argues that the social environment which the individual resides in can affect his/her behavior. In addition, SCT offers important insight into the reciprocal causation that is concerned with the interactive relation between personal characteristics (cognition) and environmental influences. Human expectations, beliefs, and cognitive competencies are developed and modified by social influences that convey information and activate emotional reactions through modeling, instruction, and social persuasion (Bandura 1986). The interactive relationship between cognition and the environment is an important factor for our theory as the behavior is learned from the environment through the process of observational learning. Bandura (1986) believes that observational learning could not occur unless cognitive processes were at work. These mental factors mediate (i.e., intervene) learning to determine whether a new response is acquired. We will build on this concept to propose a learning alignment between the producers and the users of accounting information in order to enable a more consistent behavior between both. This can increase the consistency of processes related to the production and use of accounting information.

3.2 *Learning in Accounting Information Production and Use*

The accounting literature (Anthony 1978; Sutcliffe 1985; Inanga and Schneider 2005; Ouda 2015, 2017) has indicated that there is a lack of communication between the accounting information production and use in the public sector. On the one hand, accounting information producers learn to have enough knowledge and information about accounting regulations, practices, and preparing financial reports. On the other hand, public sector entities are governed by the governing politicians who have different educational background and may have insufficient or no knowledge about accounting, and economic and business activities. Insufficient accounting and business knowledge leads users to be unable to determine their accounting information needs (Ouda 2015). This result is consistent with the finding of Sutcliffe (1985), who said: "One of the biggest problems in identifying users' needs is their own inability to articulate what these are in any convincing way. They cannot assess the importance of information that has not previously been provided and, if asked, tend to ask for information that reflects the prevailing conventional wisdom." In addition, Anthony (1978) indicates that users can neither appreciate nor judge the importance of information that has not been furnished yet. In absence of hard evidence, therefore, one must rely on one's own judgment as to what information a user should need. This is, of course, a highly subjective and speculative process, but there seems to be no alternative (Anthony 1978). Consequently, the inability of the users to determine their financial information needs has led to those needs being determined by others (the producers). The traditional accounting theories propose that the accounting system and the format of financial reporting are considered hermetic and static. Hence, the behaviors and needs of users are assumed not to change or interact with the changes taking place in the social, political, economic, regulatory, and technological environment (Ouda 2017). Therefore, the producers should be aware of the fact that production of useful accounting information for the users' needs requires a reorientation towards working within, rather than fighting against the dynamics of user needs. It also requires that the producers should continuously learn about the changes in the users' environment and this should be reflected in the production process of accounting information. In addition, due to their different tasks, both the producers and the users of accounting information develop different cognitions. These differences can be considered to be the main hurdle in matching between the producers' cognition and the users' cognition (Fig. 7.3).

Therefore, it is important for producers to learn as much as possible about the mindset of the users. After all, if the producers cannot figure out what is driving the users' motive, they may not be able to get on the road to actual use of accounting information. In the same vein, it is important for the users to learn as much as possible about the mindset of the producers and how the accounting information production takes place. Based on the SCT, we consider the cognition and behavior of the users as the environment of the producers and vice versa (see Figs. 7.3 and 7.4).

The interactive relationship between cognition and the environment is an important factor, as the behavior of producers and users is learned from

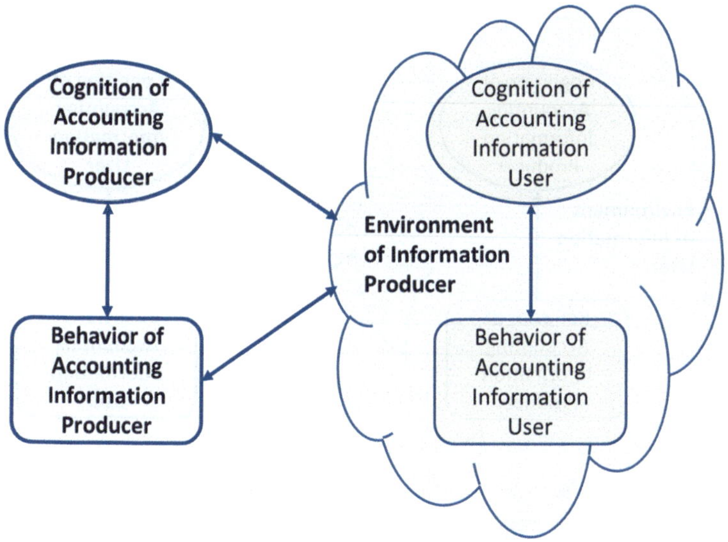

Fig. 7.3 Triadic reciprocal determination of the producers' behavior. (Source: Ouda and Klischewski (2019))

the environment through the process of observational learning (Bandura 1986). Behavior of the producers (which is the production of accounting information) is shaped and directed by the producers' cognition and social environment (which includes the cognition and behavior of the users). Similarly, the behavior of the users (which is the use of accounting information) is shaped and directed by the cognition of the users and the social environment (which includes the cognition and behavior of the producers).

Due to the independency of actors, producers' learning about the users and their mindset or vice versa does not solely create the match between the cognitions of the accounting information producers and users. The next step is to conceptualize the match of cognitive factors, on the basis of which we can consider the interrelation of learning and increasing the degree of cognitive match between the accounting information producers and users.

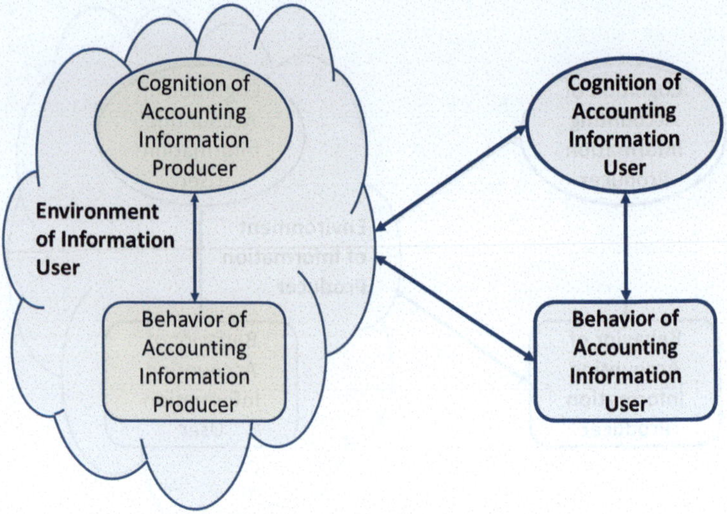

Fig. 7.4 Triadic reciprocal determination of the users' behavior. (Source: Ouda and Klischewski (2019))

4 Cognitive Match and Accounting Information Usefulness

Basically, we assume that both accounting information producers and accounting information users perform their tasks on the basis of specific rationales with specific cognitive elements, structures, and processes ("cognition"); that is, the performance of their task is governed by specific mental representations and other cognitive elements. For our theory development, we adapt the following concepts from CFT and SCT:

- **Cognitive fit**: the formulation of a consistent mental representation adequate to solve the task at hand (Vessey 1991; Shaft and Vessey 2006); due to their different tasks, the producers and the users of accounting information develop and maintain different mental representations.
- **Task governance**: the determining influence of mental representations (as per CFT) and other cognitive elements on observable task performance.

- **Learning**: a cognitive process that takes place in a social context as conceptualized within social cognitive/learning theory.

For the interrelation of constructs, we additionally define the following:

- **Match**: the degree of congruence of cognitive elements, structures, and processes (e.g., schemas, mental representations—in short, "cognition") which are in effect when producing and using accounting information.
- **Alignment**: the coordination of learning processes with the aim of sharing cognitive elements, structures, and processes to build a common task understanding.

Generalizing a coherence of rationality and assuming a degree of alignment within the supply side and the demand side, we can now explain why and how cognition on each side is divergent (misfit) while at the same time *a significant degree of cognitive match (fit) is a prerequisite for producing accounting information that matches (fits) the need of the consumers*, that is, a prerequisite for its usefulness.

The accounting literature has already distinguished between accounting information use and usefulness. Van Helden (2016) argued that the information usefulness is assumed to be driven by the user needs. However, in some cases, the producers provide accounting information which is generally considered useful by the users but is not useful for a matter at hand or the task to be performed. Based on the CFT, increasing the probability of using accounting information means to make it more specific to the task to be performed, to the problem to be solved, to the challenges to be coped with, and/or to the matter at hand *('task fit')*.

Meanwhile, numerous scholars have acknowledged that behavioral and cognitive aspects do have an influence on the use of accounting information, but so far no framework has emerged to explain the nexus of all these aspects. In the following, we review cognitive factors identified in the extant accounting literature and propose the construct of cognitive match as a prerequisite for accounting information usefulness.

4.1 *Cognitive Processes in Accounting Information Production, and Use*

Different studies have inferred that lack of actual use of accounting information is due not only to rational and technical reasons but to a great extent to behavioral reasons (Hall 2016; Grossi et al. 2016; Bourmistrov 2017). In addition, it is argued that shifting from the traditional accounting and economic theories to the psychological and sociological theories provides insight into how people, individually or in combination, actually use and are affected by accounting information, rather than how people should use or be affected by such information if they behave according to "rational man" economic and accounting theories (Maines 1994). Bourmistrov (2017) argued that public servants were reluctant to use the new accounting information because it contradicted their mental models (mental representation) and these mental models can constitute a barrier for the use of accounting information. He further indicated that to make real use of the new accounting information, all training should properly address users' mental models. This is due to the fact that change in use first requires changes in users' mental models. Therefore, Hall (2016) and Bourmistrov (2017) call for using the cognitive theories which can assist in identifying the nuances of how psychological (cognitive) processes influence the production and use of accounting information in the public sector entities.

To be able to understand how the cognitive processes can influence the accounting information producers' and users' behavior, and since 'cognition' itself is not testable, we need to address and explore the cognitive factors that can play an essential role in both producing and using the accounting information processes (see Sect. 2.3). Table 7.1 aims to summarize factors that contribute to the development of the theory and what accounting studies may contribute to the framing, in particular when comparing concepts and proposed relationships addressed within the public sector as a specific research field. For that purpose, the header of Table 7.1 exhibits concepts as introduced by the basic frame (e.g., performance, problem solution, cognitive fit, problem representation) whereas the first column exhibits the distinct areas of research (e.g., accounting, public sector accounting). Hence, each table field indicates a research domain that may contribute to a more detailed development of the theory. In this sense, the table may be read as an evidence of the particular contribution of a research area or domain, which also illustrates why a research

Table 7.1 Cognitive factors identified in accounting information production and use

	Performance (refers to match/ mismatch as observed by studies)	*Problem solution (refers to behavior as observed by studies) – expectation*	*Cognitive fit/ mental representation, refers to – awareness – interpretation – beliefs*	*Problem representation, refers to – knowledge – perception*
Accounting studies	Bourmistrov (2017), Van Dooren and Van de Walle (2008)	Liggio (1974), Aljaaidi and Salamen (2009)	Parsons et al. (2014), Hawkins and Mothersbaugh (2010)	Strong (1999), Strong and Portz (2003), Alves (2010)
Public sector accounting studies	Askim (2007, 2009)	Taylor (2011), Hammerschmid et al. (2013)	Hall (2016), Olson (2001)	Caruana and Farrugia (2018), Romolini et al. (2015)
Policy, politicians studies	Pollitt (2007), Raudla (2012)	Lawrence and Weber (2016)		Lasswell (1956), Howlett and Ramesh (2003)
Behavioral economics	Thaler (1985)	Thaler (1985)	Thaler (1985)	
Others			Danile and Reid (2006), Bandura (1997)	Vessey (1991)

Source: Ouda and Klischewski (2019)

area or domain may become interesting because it contributes to the development of the theory.

According to SCT, personal behaviors are shaped and influenced by variations of cognitive factors as well as by conditions of the associated social environments/network (Bandura 1986). The interactive relationship between the cognitive factors (see Table 7.1) and the environment is important for theory development because the behavior is learned from the environment through the process of observational learning. In addition, the CFT argues that performance on a task will be enhanced when there is cognitive fit or match between the information emphasized in the problem representation and that required by the task to be completed. While the CFT suggests that cognitive fit is only influenced by the task and problem representation, our theory assumes that the cognition of producers and users of accounting information also has a significant effect on task performance. The cognition/cognitive factors (e.g., knowledge, awareness, belief, expectations, interpretation, and perception) interfere with the task and problem representation to form the mental representations (models) that govern the production and the use of accounting information. Inclusion of the cognition factors into the theory is supported by other earlier studies, as Frownfelter (1998) suggests a need for looking at other variables, in addition to the problem representation and decision-making task, which may influence this relationship. Goodhue and Thompson (1995) argue that problem representation and the task characteristics are not the only variables that influence the cognitive fit. They propose that individuals' characteristics, such as experience, motivations, and training, may also affect the cognitive fit. Therefore, the Accounting Information Usefulness Theory (AIUT) posits that cognitive fit is said to exist when the cognition of the accounting information producers matches with the cognition of the accounting information users. When a mismatch occurs between the cognitions of the producers and the users, the cognitive fit will not result, since the producers emphasize different cognitive processes than the users should use to solve the problem.

4.2 *Cognitive Match as Prerequisite for Accounting Information Usefulness*

We have argued that divergent cognition factors and context-bound rationality can have a significant impact on the use or nonuse of accounting information. Differences in the cognition of the producers and the users of accounting information mean that both of them do not emphasize the same type of information, which leads to forming inconsistent mental representation. Inconsistent mental representation will generate less useful accounting information, which will ultimately lead to mismatch between the accounting information production and use. This, in turn, will impede better problem-solving performance. Therefore, the usefulness of accounting information and its actual use will be enhanced when the cognition of accounting information producers matches with the cognition of accounting information users.

Based on this analysis, the following proposition is stated (see also Fig. 7.5).

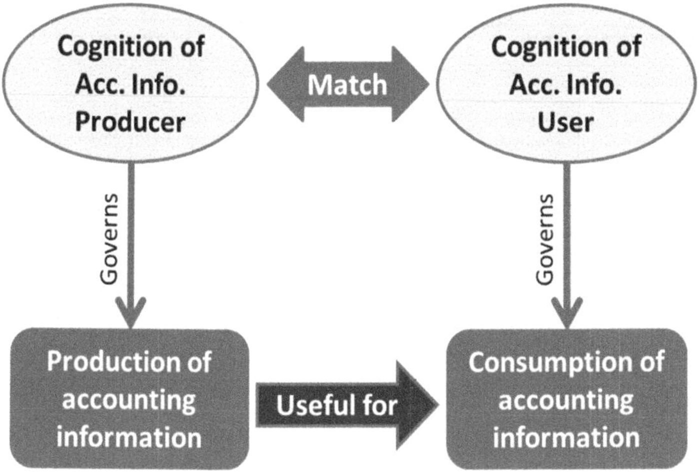

Fig. 7.5 Accounting information usefulness as a function of cognitive match of producers and users. (Source: Ouda and Klischewski (2019))

Proposition 7.1 Production of accounting information is useful for consumption of accounting information when the cognition of the accounting information producers matches with the cognition of the accounting information users.

The proposition reflects our research aim, which is to conceptualize and theorize the readiness to use and the actual use of accounting information in relation to the human and social agency involved. However, the concept of cognition is difficult for hypotheses generation and operationalizing data collection. To this end, we have to unfold again the underlying concepts of CFT and SCT, the cognitive factors involved, and the different dimensions of matching that play a role for the usefulness of accounting information. In the center of the cognition of the actors on each side of production and use is the cognitive fit, that is, the degree to how well the mental representations are governing the actual problem solution behavior. This includes several cognitive factors, namely problem knowledge, expectations regarding problem solving and awareness, beliefs, and interpretation guiding the actual task handling. The core hypothesis is that the (mis)match of cognitive factors between the producers and the

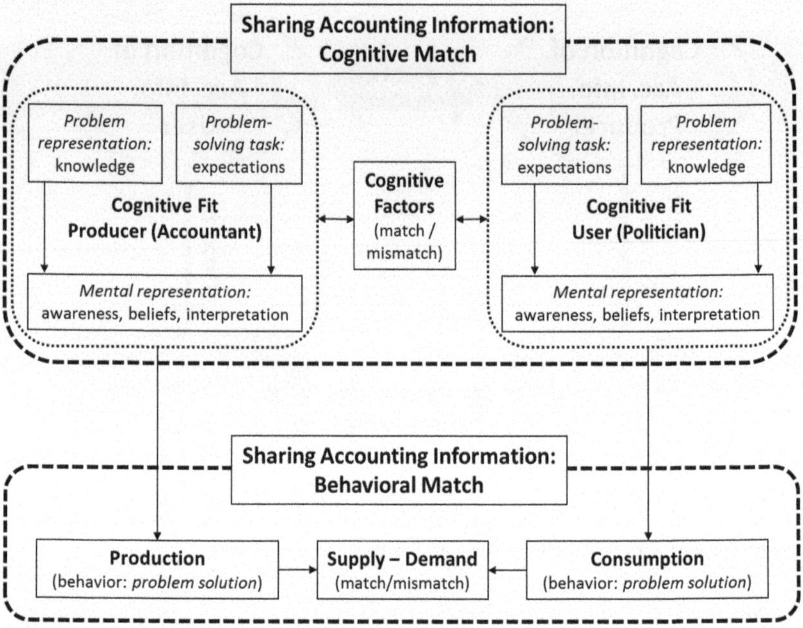

Fig. 7.6 Cognitive fit, cognitive match, and behavioral match in accounting information sharing. (Note: Original CFT concepts denoted in italics. Source: Ouda and Klischewski (2019))

users predicts the match of supply and demand in accounting information sharing (see Fig. 7.6).

Accordingly, we propose the usefulness of accounting information (i.e., match of supply and demand) as a function of the match of cognitive factors of the actors involved. However, the relative importance of various cognitive factors and their degree of matching as a predictor of accounting information usefulness remains as an open question for future empirical research. The separation of cognitive aspects from observable behavioral aspects and the focus on 'match' on the cognitive level pave the way not only for newly explaining and predicting accounting information usefulness and actual use but also for predicting how collective learning and change management can be successful. To that end, the next section unfolds the necessary extension of our theoretical model.

5 Collective Learning and Change Management

Finally, in the search for collective learning and change management, we assume a common professional and organizational frame on the supply side and demand side so that *individual learning processes may be treated as aligned and individual mental representations may be altered collectively.* This collective alignment is expected to foster an appropriate cognitive fit on each side and sufficient cognitive match between both sides, which will be more supportive towards producing useful accounting information that can actually be used. To that end, we extend our conceptualization by the following propositions (see Fig. 7.7).

Proposition 7.2 The cognition of accounting information producers matches with the cognition of accounting information users when the processes of learning how to produce and use the accounting information are aligned.

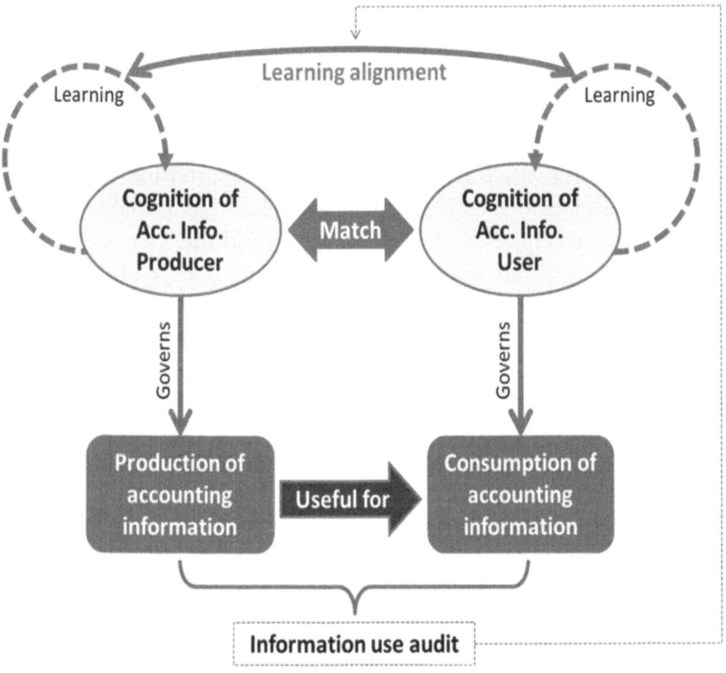

Fig. 7.7 Learning alignment and information use audit to improve accounting information usefulness. (Source: Ouda and Klischewski (2019))

Proposition 7.3 Aligning processes of learning how to produce and use the accounting information is effective when based on continuous audit of accounting information usefulness.

Learning alignment is fundamental for creating the match between the cognition of producers and the cognition of users. We describe alignment as the coordination of learning processes with the aim to share cognitive elements, structures, and processes to build common task understanding. While building a strong alignment between information technology (IT) and organizational objectives has been consistently considered as a key concern in the information technology field (Reich and Benbasat 2000), the learning alignment between the accounting information producers and users has not been of interest in the recent accounting literature. Hence, we see that building a shared understanding between the accounting information producers and users is one way of strengthening this alignment.

It is therefore essential to develop common task understanding between both the producers and the users within the government, taking into consideration that both producers (the inner and intermediate circles) and the governing politicians are part of the government. The development of the common task understanding between the two actors will rely on the strategic vision and strategic learning approaches, the latter based on integrating the views and visions of the two actors. The operationalization of the learning alignment entails both the producers and the users to exert more effort in learning about each other's mindset. The producers need to understand how the politicians perceive the decision situations they face as well as what questions they should answer therein. The producers and the users should also exert more effort to narrow the expectation gaps and to increase their awareness of the production and use of the accounting information process. Therefore, the producers should learn more about the accounting information needed in each stage of the policy decision-making process (see Sect. 6.1) as shown in Table 7.2.

On the other hand, the governing politicians should learn and increase their knowledge about accounting, and economic and business activities. When politicians are elected they should be invited to an educational session regarding the accounting information that can be provided by the producers and identify the accounting information that they would find useful for their decision-making. Some empirical studies (e.g., Strong 1999) have confirmed that users' accounting knowledge has a significant

Table 7.2 Accounting information needed by stage

Stage	*Accounting Information Needed To*
Agenda-setting	Address new issues
Policy formation	Help evaluate proposed alternatives and predict the potential effectiveness of alternative programs
Decision-making	Serve the politicians in making such decisions
Implementation	Assist in predicting the relationship between the units of input and output as well as improving the efficiency of public sector entities
Evaluation	Assist, evaluate, and monitor the results of the decisions made, as well as follow up and correct the variances

Source: Ouda and Klischewski (2019)

effect on the task and problem representation and hence on the decision-making process. In addition, the producers assume that the special-purpose financial reporting is directed to a user who possesses a good accounting knowledge and a willingness to study the information with reasonable diligence.

While the learning alignment is fundamental for building a shared understanding between the accounting information producers and users, it is considered to be effective when it is based on *continuous audit of accounting information usefulness*. Whatever the information provided to the users by the producers, there is no guarantee that the provided information will satisfy the users' needs. As stated by Van Helden (2016), "it is never absolutely clear in advance which accounting information will be helpful; politicians have to determine what they want to know and what information is available. Only then can the information be helpful in framing relatively complex problems."

Learning and learning alignment are long-term processes that always need orientation, often correction, and continuous improvement. While direct and continuous interaction between the producers and users of accounting information is and will remain the exception, other mechanisms of orientation and control are needed. We suggest the learning alignment (and hence the learning) to be informed by adequate forms of *information use audit* (Ouda 2017). Seeking to match the cognition of information producers and users is a means of improving accounting information usefulness. Such audit shall be based on the concepts implied in the mental task representations in order to provide feedback regarding which aspects of cognition matching are effective for improving usefulness and which not. Understanding the effectiveness of cognitive matching is the key to successful learning and learning alignment.

For adequately informing and guiding the learning alignment, empirically justified evidence regarding usefulness is needed. As both actor groups involved perceive the usefulness from their perspectives, this evidence can be provided by an independent/trusted third party to perform the usefulness audit on a regular basis. Such information use audit also has other effects in building a healthy culture of accounting information use, as it allows independent and/or public auditors to play active roles in scrutinizing accounting information production and use to reduce unintended use and even misuse of accounting information (Guarini 2016).

6 Application of the Accounting Information Usefulness Theory (AIUT) In the Practice of Public Sector Accounting

The theory of accounting information usefulness presented here posits that cognitive fit is said to exist when the cognition of accounting information producers matches with the cognition of accounting information users, and this results in increasing the usefulness of accounting information and hence their actual use. This, in turn, leads to improving the decision-making performance. This section discusses how the developed theory can be applied in practice. In order to fulfill this purpose, I will consider the policy decision-making process and its five stages identified by Lasswell (1956) and Howlett and Ramesh (2003): agenda-setting; policy formulation; decision-making; implementation; and evaluation. It is assumed that the usefulness of accounting information and its actual use will be enhanced when this information is specific to the problems the users face in each stage (Ouda 2017). Therefore, this theory will show that matching of cognition of the producers and users, through the learning alignment and continuous information use audit and hence the formation of consistent mental representations that emphasize the same type of information, will enhance the usefulness of accounting information and its actual use by making the accounting information more specific to the problems the users face in each stage. Accordingly, I see that practice-relevant accounting information from the users' perspective means to make it more specific to the task to be performed, to the problem to be solved, to the challenges to be coped with, and/or to the matter at hand *('task fit')*.

6.1 The Production and Use of Accounting Information and the Policy Decision-Making Process

6.1.1 Agenda-Setting

This stage includes politicians' actions to bring a new issue to the attention of their fellow politicians, such as introducing performance budget (Van Helden 2016). In this stage the politicians can raise and advocate ideas in a particular policy domain and promote a particular line of change (Ryan 1998). They can also raise awareness of the issue early in its life and soften up other issues (Kingdon 1984). However, bringing an issue into the politicians' agenda needs to create demand for this issue. The process of conversion from a "demand" to an "issue" tends to mobilize the interest of actors not previously involved in the issue (Cobb and Elder 1972). Moreover, the process of creating an issue and placing it on the political agenda means that the politicians and other influential actors in the policy community are made aware of a particular problem (Cobb and Elder 1972; Kingdon 1984; Ryan 1998). For instance, Australia introduced accrual accounting financial reporting due to the lack of accountability of government agencies while experiencing a fiscal crisis and growing public concern about the spending of the government. The process of converting a "demand" for changes to accrual financial reporting into an "issue" mobilized the accounting producers (e.g., profession) who had hitherto not taken an active interest in this stage (Ryan 1998). Insufficient accounting information about the spending of the government, accountability of government agencies, and inefficiency of measuring government performance have been used to create the change to accrual financial reporting into an issue and make other actors such as accounting producers aware of the issue. The awareness of this issue of the producers can lead to providing the required accounting information that can assist politicians to place the new issue in the political agenda. This awareness as one of the cognition factors tends to influence the user' perception towards the use of accounting information that is specific to the problem they face. This also means that when the awareness of producers matches with the awareness of users, this can emphasize the same type of information and hence the formation of consistent mental representations that govern both the accounting information production and use. This results in the accounting information being more specific to the problems the users face in the agenda-setting stage.

Another example: in order for politicians to create the demand required for introducing a new insurance policy or health policy, they need specific accounting information that assists them in promoting these policies. If the producers of accounting information are aware of these policies and the type of accounting information required to enable the users to promote and bring these policies to the attention of others (public and/or other politicians) and to put them into the political agenda, this will increase the opportunity of the actual use of accounting information, whether it is financial or managerial or both. The accounting information will be used to convince the others by the raised issue through reducing or removing uncertainty (Burchell et al. 1980; Giacomini et al. 2016). The learning alignment between the producers and the users of accounting information will likely make the producers more aware about the type of accounting information that is needed by the users for the agenda-setting stage. Due to the fact that the politicians face different new issues that entail inclusion in the agenda-setting, this will need different types of accounting information to fit with different types of new issues. Therefore, the information use audit will result in a dynamic interplay between the producers and the users, whether directly or through an independent third party that ensures the provision of specific accounting information for specific issues.

*6.1.2 **Policy Formulation**: (Identification of Alternatives for Action)*

After the issue has been created and placed on the policy agenda, policy formulation is the development of effective and acceptable courses of action for addressing what has been placed on the policy agenda. The scope of the policy formulated by the government depends on the area that such policy is going to cover (Kingdon 1984). Policies are formulated by the government in order to provide a guideline in attaining certain objectives for the benefit of the people. In this stage, politicians are required to identify and assess the alternatives. The various alternatives that are available to the politicians need to be evaluated to consider how these alternatives can contribute towards the achievement of the targeted objectives. The available alternatives can be assessed by the help of relevant accounting information. Accounting information like resource requirements, costs, and benefits related to each alternative are assumed to be helpful in evaluating the alternatives. In addition, there is a need for information to help in predicting the potential effectiveness of alternative programs and costs of alternatives and whether these resources have been directed towards current expenditure or capital expenditure (Ouda 2005). This information may also include internal data on past costs of activities and effectiveness of existing programs. Politicians will also need information on the potential impact of different programs on the various sources of government revenue (Ferguson and Drebin 1981). In fact, politicians usually have different alternatives to achieve the desired outcomes. Linking the politicians' expectations with the producers' expectations requires common understanding of purposes and goals of the various alternatives. The AIUT can assist here when the expectations of the producers of accounting information about the required information for assessing the alternatives are matched with the expectations of the politicians regarding the content of information required to evaluate these alternatives. However, matching the expectations of the producers and the users of accounting information will entail the alignment between the producers and the politicians. This alignment enables the producers to know what to do, the politicians know what to expect, and vice versa. In other words, the producers need to have a clear understanding of what they are being asked to do, what they are responsible for, and who they should consult with and report to. The alignment of expectations can achieve this objective. However, we should take into account that the alignment is not an easy task and it is unlikely that any public sector entity will completely eliminate the problem of misaligned expectations, and the higher the number of producers and users involved in the public sector entities, the greater is chance that these expectations will not be met. But if the aligned expectations are based on a continuous information use audit and the public sector entities take steps to manage, develop, and communicate the producers' and users' expectations, then the matching of their expectations is said to exist. This of course will increase the degree of usefulness and the opportunity of actual use of accounting information. Accounting information can be used in the policy formulation stage to provide answers to improve understanding (Giacomini et al. 2016). Therefore, the use of accounting information will be increased when the accounting information provided in the policy formulation stage is matched with that demanded by the users for this stage.

6.1.3 Decision-Making: *(The Formal Decision to Take on the Policy)*

Several studies make a distinction between various stages of the decision-making process (Askim 2007; Giacomini et al. 2016), Ter Bogt et al. 2015). This is due to the fact that nature, extent, and type of information required for decision-making will be differed according to each stage of the decision-making process. Also the degree of ambiguity of/disagreement on goals, that is, the level of conflict over decisions, is also affecting the accounting information use. Some authors argue that contextualization of the political decisions entails that two factors should be taken into account (Giacomini et al. 2016): the different policy stages at which decision take place and the degree of political conflict over goals. Giacomini et al. (2016) have identified two policy stages: policy formulation, which is presented in the aforementioned section (this stage takes place when the alderman of the council's executive board drafts, discusses, and approves the budget proposals to be submitted to the council), and decision-making (this takes place when the whole council approves the budget). This study has concluded that the level of conflict affects the quantity of information used as well as the type of use. The role of accounting information is also affected by the degree of conflict over goals. For instance, when conflict increases in the policy formulation stage, accounting information is used to answer questions, and in the decision-making stage it will be used in terms of rational economic considerations (Giacomini et al. 2016).

Furthermore, the accounting information will differ according to the budgeting decision process, which involves three basic stages: budget preparation, budget approval, and budget execution. These three basic stages will require different accounting information. However, Melkers and Willoughby (2005) find that accounting information is most useful to decision-making during the budget preparation. In addition, Halachmi (2005) argues that accounting information can be useful not only in determining whether things are done correctly, but also for exploratory deliberations over what to do. Moreover, Askim (2007) argues that the degree of accounting information use will also differ according to whether the decision is related to hard-core tasks or soft-core tasks. For example, Johansson (1995) expects high use of accounting information when dealing with 'hard-core' tasks like technical services, and low use when dealing with 'soft-core' tasks like social services. However, all these studies do not fully account for why the decision-makers deviate from the rational approach. Since the decisions are ultimately made by an individual decision-maker or a group, it is almost inevitable that their decisions are affected by several cognitive factors such as beliefs, knowledge, perception, experience, and expectations. Therefore, it is fundamentally important that the producers of accounting information understand how politicians make decisions and recognize the influence of cognitive factors on the decision-making process. Accordingly, I can assume that the level of conflict over the decisions, the degree of disagreement on goals, the budgeting decision process, and whether the decision is related to hard-core tasks or soft-core tasks are affected by different cognitive factors. Strong (1999) argues that politicians with a high level of accounting knowledge will perform better in the decision-making stage compared with politicians who have a low level of or no accounting knowledge.

Moreover, the degree of perception gap between the producers and the users affects the decision-making stage. The decision-making stage will be influenced by how politicians perceive the decision situation they face, what type of questions they try to answer therein, and what kind of accounting information they need. The politicians' perceptions of other actors involved in the decision-making and the perceived consequences of the decision can also affect the decision-making process. If the producers' perception matches the politicians' perception, the perception gap will be narrowed and both will emphasize the same type of information required for decision-making.

It is also assumed that politicians make their decisions based more on what they believe than on what is objectively the case (Bandura 1997). In other words, politicians tend to reject and distrust accounting information or solutions that seem to be in conflict with their beliefs while embracing those that are not. Differences of the beliefs between the producers and the users will affect the decision-making stage. The convergence of the beliefs between the producers and the users will entail a holistic cognition approach to manage the production and use of accounting information through by common beliefs within the public sector entities through learning alignment. Accordingly, the learning alignment and the continuous information use audit will, to a great extent, achieve the matching between the producers and the users and hence assist in developing the holistic cognition approach that can help in sharing the same cognition within the public sector entities. Furthermore, the producers can influence the interpretation ability of the users through ways of presenting the accounting information and framing the problems that face the users in the decision-making stage, as it is assumed that the way a problem is framed can significantly affect the interpretation ability of the politicians and hence the decision that is made. Moreover, politicians tend to accept the frame as it is presented to them rather than restating the problem in their own terms. So when the interpretation of the producers matches with the interpretation of the users, only then the accounting information can be helpful in framing relatively complex problems that are usually faced by politicians in the decision-making stage.

6.1.4 *Implementation*

Having identified the policy formulation and deciding the alternative to be implemented, the implementation stage starts with putting the decision into action with conviction and the intention of delivering the services required. Services delivery can be viewed as a three-stage process, namely, inputs, outputs, and impacts (Washnis 1980). The use of accounting information can be increased by providing the information required to the implementation process. Herein, the management needs information to help in predicting the relationship between units of input and units of output. In order to improve efficiency, public managers and politicians may require information of existing costs per unit of output. Information that can help in predicting the cost of alternative programs would also be useful to politicians in making implementation decisions. In addition, Lohrey (2018) argues that "this stage consists of creating policy statements with clear parameters, including whom the policy applies to, the circumstances under which policy statements and directives apply and important conditions or restrictions." Thus, when the producers are aware of the accounting information that can help the users to predict the relationship between the units of input and units of output, this can increase the opportunity of using the accounting information in the implementation stage. On the other hand, if the producers are not aware of the accounting information that should be provided in this stage, this will result in a mismatch between the accounting information provided and the task that should be performed by the politicians. This, in turn, results in the mental representation formed by the problem representation being inconsistent with the mental representation formulated by the task representation. This can lead to impeding the improvement of problem-solving performance.

Further, when the expectation of the producers about the content of accounting information required in the implementation stage is matched with the expectation of the politicians about what kind of information should be used in this stage, this can improve the decision-making performance. If there is an increased expectation gap between the producers and the users, this will also lead to mismatching. It is therefore important to align the learning between both the producers and the users to narrow this gap.

6.1.5 Evaluation

This stage involves ongoing evaluation and monitoring of the results of the decisions made and includes follow-up and measurement of actual performance, comparing actual performance with planned performance, determining of variances, analyzing of variances, and determining the cause for variances. In short, this involves measuring performance to see whether objectives are being accomplished and constraints are being observed, and taking remedial actions whenever unfavorable results are indicated (Ferguson and Drebin 1981). In reality, politicians need financial information, which provides measures for the evaluation stage. For example, comparison of appropriations with expenditures indicates how short-term flows of resources have been handled; and comparison of future commitments with future projected resource inflows indicates whether the long-term financial status of the government is being adequately protected (Ferguson and Drebin 1981). Similarly, the evaluation stage needs specific accounting information that can assist public managers and politicians in monitoring and evaluating the results of the decisions made. In short, politicians need accounting information to assess and measure performance. However, the literature of public sector accounting has confirmed that the accounting information has not been used by politicians (Ter Bogt 2004; van Dooren 2008). Ter Bogt (2004) infers that little importance is given by councilors to accounting information while the use of qualitative information on processes and activities predominate. Pollitt (2006) also indicates a rare direct and instrumental use of accounting information on the reformulation of policy or on the better management of programs. In addition, another empirical study has indicated that the problem of use or nonuse of the accounting information is related not only to the users but also to the producers. As Caruana and Farrugia (2018) argue, the cause for nonuse of information and its effects are important considerations for preparers of financial information (producers), if they wish to make their production relevant for decision-makers.

This also means that the use or nonuse of accounting information is a common responsibility for both the producers and the users, and there is no guarantee that once the accounting information is provided and considered relevant, it will be used by the politicians. This is due to the fact that there are many cognitive factors that can influence the use or nonuse of accounting information. For example, the level of accounting knowledge of the politicians, their beliefs and perception of the significance of the performance information provided, and the situations they face will certainly influence the use or nonuse of this information. This can also be considered as another evidence for the importance of the learning alignment between the producers and the users. Table 7.3 summarizes the impact of matching the cognition aspects on the production and usefulness of accounting information.

6.2 *Institutionalization of the Learning Alignment*

It is inferred in Sect. 5 that learning alignment is fundamental for creating the match between the cognition of producers and the cognition of users. While the AIUT considers the learning and learning alignment as a cornerstone for achieving that matching, it did not explain how the learning alignment can be operationalized and institutionalized. Basically, the operationalization of learning alignment requires both ***short-term alignment*** (the degree of mutual understanding of current information needs) and ***long-term alignment*** (the congruence of strategic vision and strategic learning approaches between the producers and the users). In addition, Crossan et al. (1999) defined the institutionalization as the process through which the "learning that has occurred by individuals and groups is embedded in the design of the systems, structures, strategy and procedures of the organization." It is through institutionalization that individual and group learning is leveraged and capitalized on in an organization (Crossan et al. 1999). The institutionalization of learning alignment will entail the following procedures.

1. Professional awareness development: Herein, governmental agencies/entities and public sector accounting experts should align the professional awareness development for both the producers and the users through training sessions, workshops, and conferences with the aim of sharing cognitive elements, structures, and processes to build a common task understanding. For example, governmental entities may provide training sessions for politicians to help them understand and read the budget and financial reporting. This happened in Egypt in 2017 when the Committee of Planning and Budgeting of Egyptian Parliament organized training sessions for the parliament members on how to read, understand,

Table 7.3 Impact of matching the cognition aspects on the production and usefulness of accounting information

Policy decision-making process stage	*Matching aspect of cognition*	*New way(s) of accounting information production*	*Improvement of accounting information usefulness*
1. Agenda-setting	Awareness	Production of accounting information that is specific to place the new issue into the political agenda. For example, accounting information required to place the adoption of accrual accounting in the public sector into the agenda (Australian case), such as accounting information about the spending of the government, accountability of government agencies, and inefficiency of measuring the government performance	The accounting information will be used to convince the others by the raised issue through reducing or removing uncertainty
2. Policy formulation	Expectations	Production of accounting information that can assist in evaluation of the alternatives, such as resource requirements, costs and benefits related to each alternative, in addition to production of accounting information to help in predicting the potential effectiveness of alternative programs and costs of alternatives and on whether these resources have been directed towards current expenditure or capital expenditure. This information may also include internal data on past costs of activities and effectiveness of existing programs	The accounting information assists the politicians in proposing the alternatives to achieve the desired outcomes with reasonable costs

(*continued*)

Table 7.3 (continued)

Policy decision-making process stage	*Matching aspect of cognition*	*New way(s) of accounting information production*	*Improvement of accounting information usefulness*
3. Decision-making	Knowledge, beliefs, perception, interpretation, and expectations	Production of accounting information that facilitates the decision-making process, as this process will differ according to the budgeting decision process (which involves three basic stages: budget preparation, budget approval, and budget execution), and according to whether the decision is related to hard-core tasks or soft-core tasks	Accounting information will reduce the uncertainty and the degree of disagreement on goals and alternatives, and assist in determining the future course of actions
4. Implementation	Awareness and expectation	Providing the accounting information required for the implementation stage, such as information that can help in predicting the relationship between units of input and units of output. In order to improve efficiency, the public managers and politicians may require information of existing costs per unit of output. Information helpful in predicting the cost of alternative programs would also be useful to politicians in making implementation decisions	The accounting information assists politicians in improving the efficiency of the government

(*continued*)

Table 7.3 (continued)

Policy decision-making process stage	*Matching aspect of cognition*	*New way(s) of accounting information production*	*Improvement of accounting information usefulness*
5. Evaluation	Knowledge, beliefs, and perception	Provision of information that is required for evaluation and monitoring of the results of decisions made, such as comparison of appropriation with expenditures indicates how short-term flows of resources have been handled, and comparison of future commitments with future projected resources inflows indicates whether the long-tern financial status of the government is being adequately protected	Accounting information is useful for assessing the performance to see whether objectives are being accomplished and constraints are being observed and taking remedial actions whenever unfavorable results are indicated

Source: Author

and interpret the general budget of the country to be able to approve the budget. In addition, it held sessions on how they can understand the figures stated in the year-end account of the government. Consequently, the parliament members gained more accounting and budgeting knowledge, which assisted them in discussing the budget sections with the government and enabled them to understand and approve the budget. In the same vein, governmental entities should hold training sessions, workshops, and conferences for the producers on the policy decision-making processes and on how politicians perceive the decision situations they face, what questions they should answer therein, and what their expectations are regarding the content of accounting information and the format of financial reporting. This should be done because the politicians need specific accounting information that serves their political discourse and their beliefs. In this case, the alignment process might entail that governmental entities contract with experts and outside organizations to help in coordinating the learning process and hence in building the common task understanding.

2. Linking the accounting information production and use: It was earlier inferred that users are unable to determine their information needs and there is a lack of communication between the producers and the users. Therefore, there is a need for an independent third party to perform this linking process. Similar to marketing research, governments should establish and maintain an *Accounting Information Research Department (AIRD)*. The AIRD should represent a link between what the politicians' think they need, what the politicians really need, and what is economically feasible. The main task of the AIRD is to link accounting information production with the accounting information use through the following:

– ***Forecasting accounting information needs***: One of the main tasks of the AIRD is to forecast and discover the accounting information needs of different users for different policy decision-making stages. It can use different ways to forecast and discover the accounting information needs such as interviewing the users, survey research, observational research, designing questionnaires, or collecting secondary data from documents that are related to the antecedent use of accounting information. For example, a questionnaire for forecasting and determining the accounting information needs can include the following useful set of questions:

- What types of decisions are politicians regularly called upon to make?
- What types of information do they need to make these decisions?
- What type of information do politicians regularly get?
- What types of information would politicians like to get that they are not getting now?
- What information would politicians want weekly? Monthly? Yearly?
- What specific topics would politicians like to be kept informed of?
- What specific accounting information serves their political discourse?
- What specific financial reporting format and design would politicians prefer to receive?

– ***Validation of accounting information needs***: The production of information needs is not free of charge. It is a costly process and will require several changes, such as a change of financial reporting format and design, or new recruitment of more skilled accountants. Therefore, the forecasted and discovered accounting information needs should be validated by the AIRD to justify their production. Accounting information needs' validation is intended to provide certain well-defined guarantees for the usefulness, consistency, and relevance of accounting information that are intended to be produced. In other words, the validation is epitomized by the following question: Are we producing what we think we are producing? In a broader concept, it pertains to the extent that the producers provide what they are intended to provide and the users receive what they are intended to receive. However, it is important to note that there is no single set of validation methods that would apply every time to every situation. Accordingly, different accounting information needs will entail different validation methods, for example, interviewing different users.

– ***Communicating the validated accounting information needs to the producers***: After the validation of the accounting information needs, the AIRD should communicate these to the producers and discuss these needs with them. This also aims to survey the producers' opinion and to explore whether they are convinced by the necessity and importance of producing these information needs, as this is a costly process and the producers should be convinced by their significance. This may also require the AIRD to go back to the users to reevaluate the necessity of their accounting information needs. Therefore, we see the role of AIRD as fundamental.

– ***Information use audit***: The AIRD should also include some independent auditors to perform the information use audit. Auditors are going to play an essential role in scrutinizing the accounting information use and production to reduce the unintended use and even misuse of accounting information and to determine the new accounting information needs required.

Finally, before the alignment of learning there is a gap between the producers' cognition and the users' cognition; therefore, the main objective of the learning alignment and its institutionalization is to create joint cognition for the perception of a common task understanding.

7 Conclusion and Future Research

This chapter aims at producing practice-relevant information for the governing politicians by developing the AIUT, which seeks to explain how cognitive aspects influence the use/nonuse of accounting information by the politicians. Given the scarcity of extant research related to this question, we seek to conceptualize and theorize the readiness to use and the actual use of accounting information in relation to the human and social agencies involved. Based on the CFT and SCT, we analyze individuals and their cognitions/intentions, the independency of the supply side (accounting) and demand side (policy/politicians), the cognitive match (fit) as a prerequisite for producing accounting information that matches (fits) the need of the consumers, and individual learning processes that may be treated as aligned. Based on the combination of these four levels, we propose the AIUT to explain how cognition influences the behavior of both the producers and the users of accounting information and may lead to unexpected and/or unintended behavior. The AIUT posits that cognitive fit increases with the degree of match between the cognition of accounting information producers and the cognition of accounting information users. It proposes that enriching and matching the various cognitive factors (as empirically measurable components of cognition) lead to the formation of more aligned mental representations (i.e., practically, to a more common understanding) that can govern the processes of accounting information production and use. It realizes the importance of the interactive relationship between cognition and the environment, as the behavior of the producers and the users of accounting information is shaped and directed by their cognitions and environments.

In terms of practical implications, our research interest is to increase the degree of usefulness of accounting information, that is, to make it more specific to the task to be performed, to the problem to be solved, to the challenges to be coped with, and/or to the matter at hand ('task fit'). For example, the application of the theory into practice based on matching the cognitive aspects is expected to

- Actuate an increase in the use of specific accounting information in each of the stages of the political decision-making process
- Guide the learning alignment to create a common task understanding between both the producers and the users of accounting information, based on the professional awareness development including mutual learning about each other's perception of problems, tasks, and solutions
- Stimulate the continuous audit of information use to continuously improve the learning alignment while also addressing changes in the social, political, economic, regulatory, and technological environment

The limitations of our theory-building process are strongly related to our choice of theoretical foundation and our assumptions. The CFT and SCT set the analytical focus on certain cognitive phenomena while disregarding others that might be of importance. Furthermore, our assumptions may not hold in all settings, that is, assuming a degree of alignment within the supply side (accounting) and the demand side (policy/politicians), as well as a common professional and organizational frame for both sides. Considering the application of the theory, we must acknowledge further limitations:

- Theory application is restricted to internal users such as politicians and public managers and, similarly, to inner and intermediate circles of producers as we exclude the outer circle of producers (standard-setters, professional bodies, academics).
- The individual cognitive factors influencing behavioral intention might not be exhaustive. For example, we do not consider past experience of the users and the producers.
- As it stands, the theory does not consider the time dimension, for example, the time lapse between "cognitive match" and "behavior" for both producers and users.
- The theory does not consider any differences in relative importance of various cognitive factors and in their degree of matching as predictors of accounting information usefulness.
- The terms cognitive match and behavioral match are seemingly treated as binary (i.e., match or not), and do not yet unfold a continuum in order to discuss how a certain degree of cognitive matching may predict a comparable degree of behavioral matching.

Accordingly, applied future research should study each stage of the policy decision-making from the producers' and users' perspectives and determine what accounting information should be provided by the producers to the users and what the key cognitive matching aspects are for each stage. Similarly, future research can address what the best options are to operationalize the learning alignment in different public sector entities and how operationalization may differ depending on the type of public sector entity (e.g., central vs. local).

In terms of contribution to research, we are keen to incorporate conceptualizations of human cognition, behavior, and learning into traditional accounting models and theories in order to contribute to the explanation and prediction of behavior related to accounting information production and use. Yet, the proposed AIUT needs to be challenged and further developed, in particular, concerning the following aspects:

- The role of cognitive processes in forming and shaping the mental representation (mental models)
- How effectively the mental representation governs the production and use processes of accounting information
- The relative importance of the various cognitive factors (knowledge, awareness, perception, beliefs, expectation, and interpretation) in task governance and their degree of matching as a predictor of accounting information usefulness
- Possibly missing concepts, constructs, and/or relations to explain the phenomena
- The relationship of the learning alignment and matching between the cognition of accounting information producers and the cognition of accounting information users.

In addition, the institutionalization of the learning alignment suggests that the government should establish and maintain an AIRD, determine the tasks of this department and future research needs to address these tasks, test it empirically, and research other tasks that can be added to this department. Research should also be conducted to assess whether its establishment and maintenance within the government can be justified and is worthy.

It is inferred that there is no single validation method for accounting information needs that would apply every time to every situation; hence, future research needs to address the best methods for validation of the accounting information needs and whether to use a single method or combine two or more methods. Additional research is required to consider whether the validation methods will be different between the central government and the local governments.

In our view, it is only a first step to conceptualize and theorize the readiness to use and the actual use of accounting information in relation to the human and social agencies involved. Empirical investigations have to follow, based on measurable variables and testable relations, in order to bring evidence regarding the explanatory and predictive power of the proposed theory.

References

Abdillah, W. (2013). Personality and Cognitive Factors in information System Migration Process. *Journal of Indonesian Economy and Business, 28*(2), 269–285.

Aljaaidi, Y., & Salamen, K. (2009). Reviewing the Audit Expectations Gap Literature from 1974 to 2007. *International Postgraduate Business Journal, 1*(1), 41–75.

Alves, M. (2010). *Information Needs and the Decision Process: Perceptions of Managers and Accountants.* 2nd IEEE International Conference on Information and Financial Engineering.

Anderson, A. (1993). *Successful Training Practice: A Manager's Guide to Personnel Development.* Oxford: Blackwell Business Publishers.

Anthony, N. R. (1978). *Financial Accounting in Non-business Organizations. An Exploratory Study of Conceptual Issues.* Research Report, Financial Accounting Standards Board, Norwalk, CT.

Askim, J. (2007). How Do Politicians Use Performance Information? An Analysis of the Norwegian Local Government Experience. *International Review of Administrative Sciences, 73*(3), 453–472.

Askim, J. (2009). The Demand Side of Performance Measurement. *International Public Management Journal, 12*(1), 24–47.

Bamber, E. (1993). Opportunities in Behavioural Accounting Research. *Behavioural Research in Accounting, 5*, 1–29.

Bandura, A. (1986). *Social Foundations of Thought and Action: A Social Cognitive Theory.* Englewood Cliffs, NJ: Prentice-Hall.

Bandura, A. (1989). Social Cognitive Theory. *Annals of Child Development, 6*(1), 1–60.

Bandura, A. (1997). Self-efficacy: The Exercise of Control. New York: W. H. Freeman.

Bourmistrov, A. (2017). Mental Models and Cognitive Discomfort: Why Do Users Reject Even a Small Change in a Financial Accounting Report. *Pacific Accounting Review, 29*(4), 490–511.

Bourdeaux, C. (2008). Integrating Performance Information into legislative Budget Processes. *Public Performance Management Review, 31*(4), 547–569.

Brandimonte, M., Bruno, N., & Collina, S. (2006). Cognition. In P. Pawlik & G. d'Ydewalle (Eds.), *Psychological Concepts: An International Historical Perspective.* Hove: Psychology Press.

Burchell, S., Clubb, S., Hopwood, A., Hughes, J., & Nahapiet, J. (1980). The Roles of Accounting in Organizations and Society. *Accounting, Organizations and Society, 5*(1), 5–27.

Buylen, B. (2014). *Politics by Numbers.* Ghent: University of Ghent.

Buylen, B., & Chistiaens, J. (2016). Talking Numbers? Analysing the Presence of Financial Information in Councillors' Speech the Budget Debate in Flemish Municipal Councils. *International Public Management Journal, 19*(4), 453–475.

Caruana, j., & Farrugia, B. (2018). The Use and Non-Use of the Government Financial Report by Maltese Members of Parliament. *Accounting, Auditing & Accountability Journal, 31*(4), 1124–1144.

Chan, H., Goswami, S., & Kim, H. (2012). An Alternative Fit through Problem Representation in Cognitive Fit Theory. *Journal of Database Management, 23*(2), 22–43.

Cobb, R., & Elder, C. (1972). *Participation in American Politics: The Dynamics of Agenda Building*. Boston: Allyn and Bacon.

Collier, P. (2003). *Accounting for Managers: Interpreting Accounting Information for Decision-Making*. Chichester: John Wiley & Sons Ltd.

Crossan, M., Lane, H., & White, R. (1999). An Organizational Learning Framework: From Intuition to Institution. *Academy of Management Review, 24*, 522–537.

Danili, E., & Reid, N. (2006). Cognitive Factors that can Potentially Affect Pupils' Test Performance. *Chemistry Education Research and Practice, 7*(2), 64–83.

Diamantopoulos, A., & Souchon, A. (1999). Measuring Export Information Use: Scale Development and Validation. *Business Research, 46*(1), 1–14.

Ferguson, L., & Drebin, A. (1981). In A. Drebin, J. Chan, & L. Ferguson (Eds.), *Decision and Information Needs of Management, NCGA Research Study, Objectives of Accounting and financial Reporting for Governmental Units: A Research Study* (vol. II).

Fogg, B. (2003). Prominence-Interpretation Theory: Explaining How People Assess Credibility Online. In *Proceedings of CHI'03, Extended Abstracts on Human Factors in Computing Systems* (pp. 722–723).

Frownfelter, C. (1998). The Effects of Differing Information Presentation of General Purpose Financial Statements on Users' Decisions. *Journal of Information Systems, 12*(2), 99–107.

Giacomini, D., Sicilia, M., & Steccolini, I. (2016). Contextualizing Politicians' Uses of Accounting Information: Reassurance and Ammunition. *Public Money & Management, November, 36*(7), 483–490.

Goodhue, D., & Thompson, R. (1995). Task-Technology Fit and Individual Performance. *MIS Quarterly, 19*(2), 213–236.

Grossi, G., Reichard, C., & Ruggiero, P. (2016). Appropriateness and Use of Performance Information in the Budgeting Process: Some Experiences from German and Italian Municipalities. *Public Performance & Management Review, 39*(3), 581–606.

Guarini, E. (2016). The Day After: Newly-Elected Politicians and the Use of Accounting Information. *Public Money & Management, November, 36*(7), 499–506.

Halachmi, A. (2005). Performance Measurement: Test the Water Before You Dive In. *International Review of Administrative Sciences, 71*(2), 255–266.

Hall, M. (2010). Accounting Information and Managerial Work. *Accounting, Organizations and Society, 35*(3), 301–315.

Hall, M. (2016). Realizing the Richness of Psychology Theory in Contingency-Based Management Accounting Research. *Management Accounting Research, 31*, 63–74.

Hammerschmid, G., Walle, S., & Stimac, V. (2013). Internal and External Use of Performance Information in Public Organisations: Results from an International Survey. *Public Money & Management, 33*(4), 261–268.

Hartono, J. (2007). *Sistem Informasi Keperilakuan [Behavioral Information System]*. Yogyakarta: Andi Offset.

Hatry, H. P. (1999). *Performance Measurement: Getting Results*. Washington, DC: Urban Institute Press.

Hawkins, D., & Mothersbaugh, D. (2010). *Consumer Behavior: Building Marketing Strategy*. Boston: McGraw-Hill Irwin.

Howlett, M., & Ramesh, M. (2003). *Studying Public Policy: Policy Cycles and Policy Subsystems*. Toronto: Oxford University Press.

Hubona, G. S., Everett, S., Marsh, E., & Wauchope, K. (1998). Mental representations of spatial language. *International Journal of Human-Computer Studies*, 48, 705–728.

Hyndman, N., Ezzamel, M., Johnsen, A., Lapsley, I., & Pallot, J. (2005). Conflict and Rationality: Accounting in Northern Ireland's Devolved Assembly. *Financial Accountability & Management, 21*(1), 33–55.

IFAC. (1991). *Financial Reporting by National Governments*. Issued by the International federation of Accountants, Study 1.

Inanga, E., & Schneider, W. (2005). The Failure of Accounting Research to Improve Accounting Practice: A Problem of Theory and Lack of Communication. *Critical Perspectives on Accounting, 16*, 227–248.

Johansson, S. (1995). *Verksamhetsbedömming i mjuka organisasjoner. Om kommunala ledares verksamhetsinformation och försök att finna mätt på effektivitet inom social service [Performance Assessment in Soft Organizations]*. Stockholm: CEFOS.

Johnson, C., & Talbot, C. (2007). The UK Parliamentary Performance; Challenging or Challenged? *International Review of Administrative Sciences, 73*(1), 113–131.

Kingdon, J. W. (1984). *Agendas, Alternatives, and Public Policies*. Ann Arbor: The University of Michigan.

Kroll, A. (2013). The Other Type of Performance Information: Non-Routine Feedback, Its Relevance and Use. *Public Administration Review, 73*(2), 265–276.

Kroll, A. (2014). Drivers of Performance Information Use: Systematic Literature Review and Directions for Future Research. *Public Performance & Management Review, 38*(3), 459–486.

Kurunmaki, L., Melia, K., & Lapsley, I. (2003). Accountingization v. Legitimation: A Comparative Study of the Use of Accounting Information in Intensive Care. *Management Accounting Research, 14*(2), 112–139.

Labinot, D., & Summermatter, L. (2012). What Should We Know About Politicians' Performance Information Need and Use? *International Public Management Review, 13*(2), 85–111.

Lasswell, H. D. (1956). The Political Science of Science. *American Political Science Review, 50*(4), 961–979.

Lawrence, A., & Weber, J. (2016). *Business and Society: Stakeholder, Ethics, Public Policy* (14th ed.). New York: McGraw-Hill publishing.

Liggio, D. (1974). The Expectation Gap: The Accountants Waterloo. *Journal of Contemporary Business, 3*(3), 27–44.

Liguori, M., Sicilia, M., & Steccolini, I. (2012). Some Like It Non-Financial…Politicians' and Managers' Views on the Importance of Performance Information. *Public Management Review, 14*(7), 903–922.

Lohrey, J. (2018). *The Five Stages of the Policy Making*. Retrieved from https://bizfluent.com/info-10040221-five-stages-policymaking-process.html.

Lűder, K. (2013, September 2–3). *Accrual Accounting and Budgeting in Government –A History of the Hessian New Administrative Management (NVS) Project*. Paper Presented at 14th Comparative International Governmental Accounting Research (CIGAR) Conference, Birmingham University, Birmingham.

Maines, L. (1994). *The Role of Behavioral Accounting Research in Financial Accounting Standards Setting*. Working Paper, Duke University.

Mbelwa, L. (2014). *Determinants of the Use of Accounting Information in the Public Sector Budgetary Decision-Making Processes: The Case of Tanzanian Local Government Authorities (LGAs)*. Licentiate Thesis, Umea University.

Melkers, J., & Willoughby, G. (2005). Models of Performance-measurement Use in Local Governments: Understanding Budgeting, Communication, and Lasting Effects. *Public Administration Review, 65*(2), 180–190.

Mimba, N., van Helden, J., & Tillem, S. (2007). Public Sector Performance Measurement in Developing Countries: A Literature Review and Research Agenda. *Journal of Accounting &Organizational Change, 3*(3), 192–208.

Moynihan, D., & Pandey, S. K. (2010). The Big Question for Performance Management: Why Do Managers Use Performance Information? *Public Administration Research and Theory, 20*(4), 849–866.

Neisser, U. (1976). Cognition and Reality. New York: Freeman.

Newell, A., & Simon, H. (1972). *Human Problem Solving*. Englewood Cliffs, NJ: Prentice Hall.

Olson, O. (2001). *Context Bounded Accounting*. Retrieved from http://citeseerx.ist.psu.edu/viewdoc/download?doi=10.1.1.201.2907&rep=rep1&type=pdf.

Ouda, H. (2005). *Transition to Accrual Accounting in the Public Sector of Developed and Developing Countries: Problems and Requirements, with special focus on the Netherlands and Egypt* (p. 405). Veenendaal: Universal Press.

Ouda, H. (2015). Making Governmental Accounting More Practice-Relevant: Practitioner's Perspective. *International Journal on Governmental Financial Management, XV*(1), 9.

Ouda, H. (2017, June 8–9). *Towards Information Fit Theory Based on Accounting Information Matching Between the Producers and Users*. Paper Presented at 16th Comparative International Governmental Accounting Research (CIGAR) Conference, Porto.

Ouda, H., & Klischewski, R. (2019). Accounting and Politicians: A Theory of Accounting Information Usefulness. *Journal of Public Budgeting, Accounting and Financial Management, 31*(4), 496–517.

Parry, M., & Hughes, J. (2018). The Musings of Frustrated Government Accountants. *International Journal on Governmental Financial Management*, 43–49.

Parsons, K., McCormac, A., Butavicius, M., Pattinson, M., & Jerram, C. (2014). Determining Employee Awareness Using the Human Aspects of Information Security Questionnaire (HAIS-Q). *Computers & Security, 42*, 165–176. https://doi.org/10.1016/j.cose.2013.12.003.

Pollitt, C. (2006). Performance Information for Democracy: The Missing Link? *Evaluation, 12*(1), 38–55.

Pollitt, C. (2007). The New Public Management: An Overview of Its Current Status. *Administration of Management Review, 8*, 110–115.

Raudla, R. (2012). The Use of Performance Information in Budgetary Decision-Making by Legislators. *Public Administration, 90*(4), 1000–1015.

Reich, B., & Benbasat, I. (2000). Factors That Influence the Social Dimension of Alignment between Business and Information Technology Objectives. *MIS Quarterly, 24*(1), 81–113.

Romolini, A., Gori, E., & Fissi, S. (2015). Public Corporate Governance and Performance Information in Local Utilities: The Different Perceptions of Politicians and Managers. *Administration and Public Management, 25*(1), 55–77.

Ryan, C. (1998). The Introduction of Accrual Reporting Policy in the Australian Public Sector. *Accounting Auditing & Accountability Journal, 11*(5), 518–539.

Shaft, T., & Vessey, I. (2006). The Role of Cognitive Fit in the Relationship between Software Comprehension and Modification. *MIS Quarterly, 30*(1), 29–55.

Stalebrink, O., & Frisco, V. (2011). PART in Retrospect: An Examination of Legislators' Attitudes Toward PART. *Journal of Public Budgeting and Finance, 32*(2), 1–21.

Staubus, G. (2000). The Decision Usefulness Theory of Accounting: A Limited History. Routledge.

Strong, J. (1999). *The Effect of Accounting Knowledge and Information Presentation Format on Performance in a Multi-attribute decision-Making Task*. PhD Thesis, University of Nebraska, USA.

Strong, J., & Portz, K. (2003). A Further Investigation of Tables Versus Graphs for Decision-Making: Does Accounting Knowledge Make a Difference? *The Review of Business Information Systems, 7*(2), 39–48.

Sutcliffe, P. (1985). *Financial Reporting in the Public Sector—A Framework for Analysis and Identification of Issues.* Australian Accounting Research Foundation: Melbourne.

Taylor, J. (2011). Factors influencing the use of performance information for decision making in Australian state agencies. *Public Administration, 89*(4), 1316–1334.

Ter Bogt, H. (2004). Politicians in Search of Performance Information? Survey Research on Dutch Aldermen's Use of Performance Information. *Financial Accountability and Management, 20*(3), 221–252.

Ter Bogt, H. J., van Helden, G. J., & van der Kolk, B. (2015). Challenging the NPM Ideas About Performance Management—Selectivity and Differentiation in Outcome-Oriented Performance Budgeting. *Financial Accountability & Management, 31*(3), 287–315.

Thaler, R. H. (1985). Mental Accounting and Consumer Choice. *Marketing Science, 4*, 199–214.

Tuttle, B. M., & Kershaw, R. (1998). Information Presentation and Judgment Strategy from a Cognitive Fit Perspective. *Journal of Information Systems, 12*(1), 1–17.

Van Dooren, W. (2005). What makes organizations measure? *Financial Accountability & Management, 21*(3), 363–383.

Van Dooren, W. (2008). Nothing New Under the Sun? Change and Continuity in the Twentieth Century Performance Movements. In Van Dooren, W., & Van de Walle, S (Eds.). Performance Information in the Public Sector, (pp. 11–23), Palgrave Macmillan, a division of Macmillan Publishers Limited.

Van Dooren, W., & Van de Walle, S. (Eds.). (2008). *Performance Information in the Public Sector: How It Is Used*. Houndmills: Palgrave.

Van Helden, J., (2014), What Are the Financial Topics Which Make Politicians Lose Sleep? *CIGAR Newsletter, 5*(1). p. 1.

Van Helden, J. (2015). *A critical Literature Review and a Challenging Research Agenda on Politicians' Use of Accounting Information*. Paper Presented at the CIGAR Conference (Malta).

Van Helden, J. (2016). Literature Review and Challenging Research Agenda on Politicians' Use of Accounting Information. *Public Money & Management, 36*(7), 531–538.

Vessey, I. (1991). Cognitive Fit: A Theory-Based Analysis of Graphs Versus Tables Literature. *Decision Sciences, 22*, 219–240.

Vessey, I., & Galletta, D. (1991). Cognitive Fit: An Empirical Study of Information Acquisition. *Information Systems Research, 2*(1), 63–84.

Washnis, J. (1980). *Vocational and Technical Education*. Washington, DC: United States Department of Health Education and Welfare.

Williams, P., & Thayer, J. (2009). Executive Functioning and Health: Introduction to the Special Series. *Ann Behav Med, 37*, 101–105.

Wolfe, P. (2006). The Role of Meaning and Emotion in Learning. *New Direction for Adult and Continuing Education, 110*(Summer), 35–41.

CHAPTER 8

Conclusion

While the available public sector accounting books are either textbooks for teaching (such as Jones and Pendlebury 2010; Bandy 2011; Budding et al. 2014; Van Helden and Hodges 2015) or collections of mainly descriptive country studies (such as Lüder and Jones 2003; Brusca et al. 2015), this book is undoubtedly unique in its approach and goal, which is especially challenging. Its main goal is to tackle the necessary developments and adjustments, which can be considered as a starting point for making accrual accounting more practice-relevant for the public sector entities. Specifically, the main focus is on reshaping the application of accrual accounting principles and assumptions to fit the context of public sector entities; developing a practice-relevant holistic accounting approach for governmental capital assets that has been based on developing and reshaping the assets recognition criteria; suggesting a sustainable accounting approach for reporting on long-term fiscal sustainability; reconsidering the scope of general-purpose financial reporting from an accountability perspective; developing a dynamic model for making public sector accrual accounting more user practice-relevant; and, finally, developing a theory of accounting information usefulness, which explains how cognitive aspects influence the use/nonuse of accounting information by politicians. Fundamentally, the book tackles these necessary developments and adjustments from both the producers' and users' perspectives. Moreover, this book puts practice relevance as its main viewpoint for developing a public sector–specific form of accrual accounting. This is especially visible

H. Ouda, *Practice-Relevant Accrual Accounting for the Public Sector*, Public Sector Financial Management,
https://doi.org/10.1007/978-3-030-51595-9_8

in the fact that user needs are taken as the major starting point and it is then considered how to match these with interests of producers of accounting information. Therefore, we can assume that our work will have several implications for academics, standard-setters, practitioners, and users of accounting information.

1 Accrual Accounting Principles and Assumptions, and Their Practice Relevance for the Public Sector

Chapter 2 addressed the accrual accounting principles and assumptions (postulations) and it was found that some accrual accounting principles and assumptions could be applied equally to both public and private sectors. However, given public sector specificities, some others could only be applied to the public sector after making some modifications; and yet others need total reshaping to suit the public sector. The focus was on the challenging issues that may cause problems for the practitioners and represent an essential departure from a commercial framework.

First, I started by discussing and reshaping the matching principle. While the application of the matching principle in the private sector is based on a cause-and-effect relationship (exchange relationship) between the reported expenses and reported revenues, the findings have shown that this relationship is often missing in the public sector (Monsen & Nasi 1997). This is because the revenues, mainly from taxes, are generated through a political process, not as a result of expenditures made by the public sector entities. It is suggested by the conceptual model (Ouda 2003) that the matching principle can be applied to the public sector not to measure the net income but to measure the efficiency of governments in using the available public resources by matching resources consumed with services and goods provided during the same accounting period or by matching outputs with the associated costs. However, this fails to recognize the reality that accounting statements are themselves focused on the inputs rather than the outputs and they indicate neither the level nor the quality of goods and services provided. Thus, the conceptual approach did not provide a practical solution to how the matching principle can properly be applied to the public sector, but rather, it made the situation more complicated for the practitioners. Due to the inherent difficulties in operationalizing the conceptual approach into practice, I developed the practical approach, which takes into consideration the specific nature of the public sector activities in comparison with the private sector activities, and proposes that matching of revenues with expenses of a certain fiscal year in the public sector should be ***based on a Timing Relationship instead of an Exchange Relationship*** (Ouda 2007). This is because governments generally use resources from a variety of sources to pay for a variety of services. The matching relationship that normally exists between resources provided and services received is a timing relationship (i.e., both occur during the fiscal year) rather than an exchange relationship. Therefore, the practitioners can apply the matching principle to the public sector based on the timing relationship—not to measure the net income, but to measure the accrual-based surplus or deficit. If it is a surplus, then the government has enhanced the net worth and the current generation has borne its own burden as well as providing support to the next generations. If it is a deficit, then the current generation is shifting its burden to the next generations and the government has eroded the net worth.

Therefore, there is an urgent need for *future academic research* to explore the extent to which the practical approach can solve the dilemma of applying the matching principle to the public sector. It is also important for future research to explore whether the conceptual approach can be developed further in order to be applied to the public sector.

Second, I argued that in the light of the specificities of public sector entities, reshaping the application of the **recognition** principle is inevitable, since the recognition of revenues, resulting from exchange transactions is different from that of non-exchange transactions. To facilitate the matter for the practitioners, a practice-relevant approach for revenue recognition for both exchange and nonexchange transactions was suggested based on different approaches and models. I made it clear that the performance obligation approach used in private sector businesses can be used for exchange transactions in the public sector but only after making some amendments, which are required to simplify it and to remove the complexities highlighted in IFRS 15. This means that the development of the public sector performance obligation approach for exchange transactions should be based on the following:

1. Identifying which goods or services are distinct and hence should be accounted for as a separate performance obligation. This can be facilitated by focusing on

   a. Transactions with performance obligations stipulated in both IFRS 15 and AASB 15 such as sales and service provision
   b. Transactions with performance obligations but not included in IFRS 15 and AASB 15, such as interest, royalties, and so on
2. When considering the large volume of customers of public sector entities, it is envisaged that the use of a control-based model would be onerous to the point of becoming impracticable; therefore, the satisfaction of the performance obligation should be based on the transference of significant risks and rewards of promised goods or services to a customer.
3. Enforceability should be considered as a key aspect of the public sector performance obligation approach for legal and equivalent binding arrangements.

However, ***additional research*** is needed to investigate whether these amendments are really required to make the performance obligation approach more suitable for the public sector. Moreover, future research should go deeper and explore which model (control-based model or risk and rewards model) is more applicable to the public sector and whether the risk and rewards model can be considered as a subset of the control-based model.

Moreover, non-exchange transactions require a different approach to the recognition of revenues, which is the assets–liabilities approach that is based on the control-based model. However, it is argued that, based on the experiences of some countries (such as Australia and the USA), the control-based model alone is not enough to cover the recognition of all revenues resulting from the non-exchange transactions. For example, Australian AASB 15 distinguishes between two non-exchange transfers: ***(a) voluntary transfers*** including items such as donations, grants, and appropriations, where the recognition of revenues arising from these transactions should be based on the use of the control-based model; and ***(b) compulsory transfers*** such as taxes, rates, and fines, where the revenues would be recognized when the public sector entity has an enforceable legal claim to receive funds and the underlying taxable event occurs. Hence, it could be inferred that, in addition to the control-based model, the enforceable legal claim and the occurrence of taxable event are also essential elements for the recognition of the revenue resulting from the non-exchange transactions.

However, there is very little research on the recognition of revenues in the public sector. It is important that *future research* explores whether the application of assets–liabilities should be based only on the control-based model or should also be based on the enforceable legal claim and the occurrence of taxable event.

Third, I highlighted that for the government to provide a true and fair view of the government deficit, the development of consistent accounting policies and their use on a consistent basis (**consistency** principle) by the government as a whole is an essential step. It is also clarified that the main problem with consolidated financial statements emerges when separate legislative powers exist within the government, especially when these powers have not resulted in uniform accounting policies for similar transactions and other events in similar circumstances. If public sector entities use accounting policies other than those adopted in the consolidated financial statements for similar transactions and events in similar circumstances, the deficit included in the consolidated accrual statements would not indicate the right meaning of the government deficit.

Future research is needed to reconsider the application of the consistency principle in the public sector entities and to explore how the accounting policies and practices are consistent on both public sector entities level and consolidated financial statements level.

Fourth, due to the fact that the public sector entity obtains its revenues (inflows) from different sources, which, in turn, require different recognition points, and because it owns different types of assets that are difficult to measure reliably and the realization of the value increases of these assets is also difficult, this requires that the application of conservatism should be reshaped to fit the context of the public sector entities. Reshaping the conservatism principle is important because in a context full of particularities as the public sector, it might sometimes not be as easy to apply the conservative principle as it is in the private sector. For example, to assess impairment losses of assets requires different criteria than in business, because there is no market value; moreover, the historical cost might not be known. As another example, most receivables might come from taxpayers, whose probability of non-receiving might be more difficult to assess than that of regular clients in a company. Furthermore, making estimates of revenue to accrue is also not as easy as in business, again due to the main type of revenue—taxes, where estimates depend on macroeconomic conditions. So, I encourage *further research* on how the conservatism principle can be reshaped to fit the context of the public sector.

Finally, I argued that the application of **going concern** postulation needs to be reshaped, as its application in the public sector cannot be based only on the economic factors but also on the political factors. However, to date we *have no research* on how the application of going concern to the public sector will be different from its application to the private sector.

So, the main lesson learned here for the academics, practitioners, and standard-setters is that where the public and private sectors differ fundamentally and conceptually, more radical alternatives may need to be considered. Therefore, instead of directing their efforts to force public sector entities' information into business-reporting frameworks, they should really be thinking about reshaping the application of accrual accounting principles, assumptions, and concepts to make them more practice-relevant for public sector entities. In Chap. 2, conceptual differences are pointed out as being particularly acute with respect to the matching, recognition, consistency, and conservatism principles and going concern assumption. It is fundamental for the standard-setters, practitioners, and academics to take into consideration the implications of reshaping these principles and assumptions on accounting standards, and hence on preparing the financial statements in the public sector.

The implication for practice: the reshaping of these principles and assumption provides guidance as to how to apply the matching, recognition, consistency, and conservatism principles and the going concern in a way that is consistent with the public sector specificities, and to show that the measure is changed from the focus on the net profit, which is based on the exchange relationship, to measure the financial performance of the government in the form of surplus or deficit, and to explore whether the government's actions have enhanced or eroded the net worth, and also to measure the intergenerational equity.

2 A Practice-Relevant Holistic Accounting Approach for Governmental Capital Assets

The good governance that coupled with the idea of making public authorities accountable to act in the best interest of the citizens with respect to the preservation, employment, and value enhancement of governmental capital assets has resulted in a growing tendency to introduce accrual accounting for central and local governments, and hence, to produce annual financial reports prepared on an equivalent basis to the private sector model.

In Chap. 3, it is argued that the reporting framework for private sector entities based on GAAP is inappropriate for the public sector entities that hold specific assets such as heritage and defense, as those entities and assets are differentiated in purpose and essence. The use of the private sector reporting model in the public sector entities has led to proposing accounting approaches that don't take into consideration whether there are or not legal, cultural, social, and/or national security restrictions on the disposal of the heritage and defense assets. Besides, they don't recognize the consequences of capitalization and non-capitalization of heritage assets on both the net worth and the statement of financial performance. This could lead to the exaggeration of the net worth if a country like Egypt, which possesses two-thirds of worldwide heritage assets, has capitalized all its heritage assets. It can also lead to distortion of the statement of financial performance if the Egyptian government has not capitalized the heritage assets and expensed them in the account of revenue and expenditures.

Moreover, despite the fact that public sector accounting literature has debated the recognition of governmental capital assets for more than three decades, there is no consensus about which governmental capital assets should be reported in the financial statements and which ones should not. To overcome this dilemma, Chap. 3 has attempted to propose the practice-relevant holistic accounting approach for governmental capital assets.

First, it is highlighted that while the issue of accounting for specific assets (e.g., heritage assets) has received considerable critical attention, to date there has been little discussion about the recognition of governmental capital assets from a general perspective. Christiaens et al. (2012) have proposed a holistic approach that addresses the recognition of public sector capital goods from a general perspective. However, application of the holistic approach has focused mainly on the type of status (economic or social/cultural status) given to the assets without recognizing that the status type alone is not enough to decide whether a capital asset can be recognized in the financial statements or not. Moreover, it did not resolve the problem from the practitioners' perspective because the practitioners will find that the holistic approach is inconsistent with the two assets recognition criteria determined by IPSAS 16, 17 and IPSASB-CF (2014). These two assets recognition criteria do not focus on the type of status given to the assets but only on the flow of future economic benefits or service potential associated with the asset to the entity; and the cost or fair value of the asset to the entity can be measured reliably (IPSASB 2010). These two criteria have led to the following question: *If a capital asset has been given a social/cultural status and, on the other hand, the information on cost or value of this asset is available, should this asset be recognized?*

If the governmental capital assets are given a social/cultural status (such as heritage assets) and the information on cost or value is available and there are cultural/social or legal restrictions on the disposal of such assets, then the capitalization of heritage assets will be misleading to the management and creditors because they are not legally accessible by them. Therefore, I have argued that the current assets recognition criteria are not sufficient for determining which governmental capital assets should be capitalized and which ones should not. This requires public sector accountants to reshape/innovate the assets recognition criteria in a way that maintains the reliability of financial statements and at the same time reflects the specific nature and characteristics of the specific governmental capital assets such as heritage and defense assets.

Second, it is argued that reshaping the assets recognition criteria will be based on developing the recognition attributes. Accordingly, the following five recognition attributes have been developed: (1) status assigned to the assets; (2) type of benefits (whether economic, social/cultural, or defense/security); (3) matching (whether or not the assets can be matched against the liabilities); (4) unrestricted assets—where there are no legal/social/cultural or defense and security restrictions on those assets and, hence, they can be disposed of/sold; and (5) restricted assets—where there are legal/social/cultural or defense and security restrictions on those assets and, hence, they cannot be disposed of/sold.

Further future research is needed to examine whether the five suggested recognition attributes are all important for the capitalization of governmental assets. It is also important for future research to investigate the significance of these recognition attributes and explore to what extent they are sufficient and whether they require additional recognition attributes.

Third, I argued that the development of the recognition attributes could assist in developing the assets recognition criteria. This has resulted in developing ***two new recognition criteria***; this is besides the ***two recognition criteria stated*** *by IPSAS 16, 17 and IPSASB*-CF. The following are the two new recognition criteria:

- *There are no legal, cultural/social, and national security/defense restrictions on the disposal of the asset.*

– *Recognized assets should be matched against the liabilities to avoid misleading.*

The core of newly developed criteria is to recognize the governmental capital goods as assets in the balance sheet where the information is available on the cost or value of assets and these assets are unrestricted assets and, hence, can be disposed of and matched against the liabilities.

We encourage future research to go deeper and explore whether the two newly developed recognition criteria are needed and whether they have really contributed towards the solution of the dilemma of which governmental capital assets should be capitalized. Moreover, future research is needed to test to what extent the two new recognition criteria are appropriate for the public sector entities and to investigate whether we need additional recognition criteria that can facilitate the capitalization of governmental capital assets.

Fourth, based on the combination of the five recognition attributes, the original recognition criteria stated by IPSAS 16,17 and IPSASB-CF (2014), the two newly developed recognition criteria, Ouda's practical accounting approach for heritage assets, and Christiaens's holistic approach, I developed the *practice-relevant holistic accounting approach for governmental capital assets.* This approach is based on the following ***three sub-approaches:***

(a) **Economic businesslike assets**—under this approach, any capital asset is given the economic businesslike status and gives rise to economic benefits; it should be capitalized in the balance sheet. Similar to the businesslike assets, its expenses should be included in the statement of financial performance.

(b) **Assets–liabilities matching approach (unrestricted assets)**—under this approach, when any capital asset is given the social/cultural or defense status and this gives rise to social/cultural or defense/security benefits, and the information on cost or value is available and there are no restrictions and, hence, it can be disposed of and matched against the liabilities, then it should be capitalized in the balance sheet (Ouda 2014, 2016).

Regarding the revenues and expenses of heritage assets, they should be included in the statement of financial performance and we should differentiate between the indefinite and definite assets as we should calculate impairment for indefinite assets and depreciation for definite assets.

Regarding the defense assets, their expenses are included in the statement of financial performance.

(c) Non-assets–liabilities matching approach (restricted assets)— under this approach, the asset should not be capitalized if the information on cost or value is not available or is available but the heritage assets and defense assets cannot be disposed of and, hence, they cannot be matched against the liabilities (Ouda 2014, 2016). According to this approach, heritage assets are considered legally, culturally, and socially restricted assets and defense assets are also considered as legal and national security restricted assets. Therefore, they should not be capitalized in the balance sheet. But both assets are treated differently: heritage assets are treated as **agent assets**, **trust assets**, or **custodial assets**. Accordingly, each country should create an **agent/trust assets statement** where heritage assets are stated in this statement ***in physical units, not in financial values*** (Ouda 2014). The statement of trust assets should include a description of major categories (types), physical units added and withdrawn during the year, and a description of the methods of acquisition and withdrawal. In addition, an explanatory note (note disclosure) should supplement the statement of trust assets.

Regarding the revenues and expenses related to the restricted heritage assets, each county should create a **trust fund (agent fund)** (Ouda 2014, 2016). This fund will include all the revenues and costs related to heritage assets in a country. The balance of the trust fund would be reported as either a liability or an asset in the balance sheet. If this balance is positive (fund surplus), then it will be considered as an asset and the increase of the net worth will be called **heritage net worth**. If it is negative (fund deficit), then it will be considered as a liability and the decrease in the net worth will be called **negative heritage net worth** (Ouda 2014, 2016).

Concerning the defense assets, each country can create statements or specific reports and disclose these defense assets either in physical units (number of systems or items) or in financial value. The disclosure can include the following information: the number of units of defense assets in each category of assets (this could be a number of aircraft etc.); the number of units added or withdrawn during the fiscal period; the description of the methods of acquisition and withdrawal; the condition of the defense assets; and information on deferred maintenance on defense assets (SFFAS#8, 50, 68, 80, SFFAS#11, 10). In addition, their cost will be included in the statement of financial performance.

I encourage future research to test the suitability and workability of the three sub-approaches in practice. It is important for future research to explore whether these three sub-approaches can be extended or complemented by other sub-approaches.

The practical implication of the development of the practice-relevant holistic accounting approach for governmental capital assets is that it provides practical guidance for the academics and practitioners on how to account for different governmental capital assets in a practical way. Moreover, the current accounting approaches for heritage assets require all reporting entities, including central and local government agencies, to account for heritage assets as they would any other item of property, plant, and equipment, and to depreciate such assets based on estimates of useful life without taking into consideration the impact of this capitalization on the exaggeration of the net worth and distortion of the statement of financial performance. The developed approach has attempted to avoid both the exaggeration of the net worth and the distortion of the statement of financial performance.

Similar to Chap. 2, the first main *lesson learned* here for the academics, practitioners, and standards-setters is that where the public and private sectors differ fundamentally and conceptually, more radical alternatives may need to be considered. In this chapter, it is obvious that there are different assets in the public sector such as heritage and defense assets that need to be differently treated in comparison with the private sector. Therefore, the main message here is that more work needs to be done if the public sector accounting researchers are to claim to have an impact on the practice; therefore, they should work together with the practitioners to find practical solutions for the outstanding public sector accounting issues and stop spending their entire career just talking to other accounting researchers about their work through conferences and journals (Laughlin 2011). Otherwise, the practitioners will see accounting research as a pointless exercise unless the research is deemed to be practice-relevant.

One of the most important lessons learned is the recommendation of Weers (2016): "Future research should attempt to develop an alternative accounting system that categorizes government assets in a manner similar to Ouda's framework (2016). He makes a very convincing case for at least four types of assets. Of these, only one type completely conforms to the corporate GAAP definition of an asset. The treatment of DOD (Department of Defense) property is a central point of contention and before a new reporting format can be considered, the issue of assets must be adequately addressed. ***It is fruitless to continue attempting to fit the government's many different types of property into a private sector accounting system and expect a new outcome.*"** ***(This is the second main lesson.)***

3 Scope of General-Purpose Financial Reporting: An Accountability Perspective

The current diversity of stakeholders of public sector organizations' and governments' reporting makes it more difficult for traditional GPFR to satisfy such a variety of information needs. Moreover, NPM practices and concerns have brought to the public sector realm new matters in terms of reporting contents. In the last 40 years, several reporting models have been developed, often presented as public accountability innovations: (nonfinancial) performance reporting, sustainability reporting, popular reporting, integrated reporting, and popular integrated reporting.

However, despite initially being very well intentioned, the reality has revealed that most of these reporting innovations have not (yet) led to the desired improved accountability in practice. Essentially following signaling and imitation motivations, they have frequently become mere fashions within the management of public sector organizations, not resulting from true decision-making. As these 'new' reporting practices tend to be included in larger reform processes, they often degenerate and become diluted, reappearing later under different names, not really constituting an innovation. The exception goes for integrated popular reporting, which is rather new, and has only started to be conceptually considered. Moreover, these reports are not yet acknowledged as being capable of properly disclosing how public sector organizations and governments overall create value for society; therefore, yet another reporting model may appear—public value reporting. *It is important for future research* to investigate the developed reporting models and address the necessary adjustments for these models to make them more practice-relevant for the public sector entities.

4 Role of Public Sector Accounting in Reporting on Long-Term Fiscal Sustainability

While sustainable development is development that meets the needs of the present without compromising the ability of future generations to meet their own needs (Brundtland 1987), fiscal sustainability aims to assure that current taxpayers are paying for the services that they receive and not passing those costs on to the future generations. Therefore, the long-term fiscal sustainability of governments was and actually still is a top concern for all stakeholders (taxpayers, citizens, public managers, politicians, and investors) and has become one of the main objectives of national governments. Reporting on long-term fiscal sustainability is fundamental for all these stakeholders as it gives an indication of the ability of a government to maintain both its fiscal capacity and service capacity over the long term. However, ensuring long-term fiscal sustainability requires that governments should make long-term projections of future revenues and liabilities, and take into account the socioeconomic and environmental factors to adopt the long-term financial projections accordingly. This means that reporting on long-term fiscal sustainability should include both backward-looking and forward-looking information. In fact, this has raised a debate between standard-setters who are in the view that public sector accounting should focus only on traditional general-purpose financial statements (past-oriented information) and those who wish to extend the boundary of standard-setting and public sector accounting to a potentially forward-looking general-purpose financial reporting (Dabbicco 2019).

In Chap. 5, I have focused on how public sector accounting can report on long-term fiscal sustainability. In other words, I have attempted to answer the following question: *To what extent can the public sector accounting go beyond the traditional accounting reporting and provide information for reporting on long-term fiscal sustainability?*

First, I started by studying the current accounting bases and their role in reporting on long-term fiscal sustainability. However, it has been inferred that all current accounting bases have provided partial measures rather than comprehensive measures. Without exception, all the balance sheets and their bottom lines are partial measures which more or less ignore items that should be included in the balance sheets. The net debt measure based on conventional cash accounting is considered as a very partial measure for long-term fiscal sustainability. It is the result of subtracting the debt obligations from the cash balances neglecting all other assets (financial and nonfinancial assets) and all other liabilities (short-term and long-term). While the net financial worth (NFW)/net financial debt (NFD) recognizes all the liabilities accumulated to date and all financial assets, it does not take into account the nonfinancial assets/physical assets. This means that a great part of the assets side is neglected and, hence, the NFW also provides a partial measure of long-term fiscal sustainability. Unlike the previous two measures, the net worth (NW) includes all assets and all liabilities arising out of past activities but it neglects the future liabilities arising out of the past activities such as pensions and superannuations, and also does not include the future assets such as the government's sovereign power to tax. Therefore, all the currently used accounting bases and the accompanying financial statements and their bottom lines provide only partial measures for long-term fiscal sustainability. I expect that the relationship of currently used accounting bases with the measuring and reporting on long-term fiscal sustainability will receive significant scholarly attention in the future.

Second, based on the aforementioned conclusion, I made an attempt to elaborate the role of public sector accounting in measuring and reporting on long-term fiscal sustainability through developing the **sustainable accounting approach**. The development of this approach is based on two cornerstones: (1) developing the accounting bases and measurement focus; and (2) expanding the scope of government financial reporting and the indicators of long-term fiscal sustainability.

The development of the accounting bases was necessary to allow for recognizing future elements arising out of both past and future activities, in addition to all elements arising from past activities. This development has resulted in creating two new accounting bases, which I call the ***sustainable full accrual basis*** and the ***sustainable modified accrual basis***. The sustainable full accrual basis provides users with information about total assets, liabilities, revenues, expenses, and net assets arising from past activities and also provides information about future assets, liabilities, revenues, expenses, and net assets arising from future activities. This basis has resulted in creating a new measurement focus, which I call the ***total sustainable economic resources***. In addition, the *sustainable modified accrual basis* provides all information provided by the sustainable full accrual basis with the exception of past and future nonfinancial assets. This basis has also led to creating another measurement focus, which I call the ***total sustainable financial resources***. In fact, accounting bases determine the elements that should be recognized in the financial statements whereas the measurement focus determines what is being measured. The development of the two accounting bases and the two measurements focuses can assist in developing a long-term future focus alongside retrospective accounting practices, and hence the role of public sector accounting can be extended to go beyond the traditional general-purpose financial reporting to forward-looking general-purpose financial reporting.

It is important that future research explore to what extent the two newly developed accounting bases and their measurement focuses can really help in reporting on long-term fiscal sustainability. Moreover, future research can address the accounting standards that are required to report on future revenues and expenses.

The newly developed accounting bases and measurement focuses have facilitated the expansion of the scope of the balance sheet which I call the ***sustainable balance sheet***. The sustainable balance sheet will include both past-oriented information and future-oriented information. This means that the sustainable balance sheet includes three types of information: past-oriented accounting information, which is prepared in accordance with the current accounting standards such as International Public Sector Accounting Standards (IPSAS); present value/discounted value of future liabilities and contingent liabilities arising out of past activity; and present value/discounted value of future assets, future revenues, and future liabilities arising from future activities. The inclusion of these three types of information in the sustainable balance sheet is consistent with IPSASB (2013) and FSASB where it is argued that long-term fiscal sustainability information is broader than information derived from financial statements. It includes projected inflows and outflows (FSASB requires the inclusion of this information in present-value dollars) related to the provision of goods and services and programs providing social benefits using current policy assumptions over a specified time horizon.

We encourage further research on how the sustainable balance sheet can include both past-oriented information and future-oriented information together. Future research is also required to explore what the right content of the sustainable balance sheet should be. In addition, it is important to determine whether or not to include the future assets and future liabilities in present-value (PV) dollars and what discount rate should be used to do such discounting, as well as how we can improve long-term revenue and spending projections.

Third, I highlighted that the content of the sustainable balance sheet will differ according to the accounting basis used. The use of the sustainable full accrual basis leads to the recognition of all past and future assets, liabilities, revenues, and expenses whereas the use of the sustainable modified accrual accounting leads to the recognition of all elements recognized under the sustainable full accrual with the exception of past and future nonfinancial assets. The bottom line of the sustainable balance sheet will be the sustainable net worth (SNW) in case of using the sustainable full accrual basis and the sustainable net financial worth (SNFW) in case of using the sustainable modified accrual basis. As a result of including all past and future assets and all past and future liabilities in the sustainable balance sheet, the SNW gives a full picture of the fiscal impact of past government activity and the potential fiscal impact of future government activity. It can therefore be inferred that the sustainable balance sheet can report on long-term fiscal sustainability and the SNW and SNFW can be used to measure long-term fiscal sustainability.

I encourage *future research* to investigate the extent to which both SNW and SNFW can be considered as reliable measures for long-term fiscal sustainability.

Fourth, I argued that the two government capacities (fiscal capacity and service capacity) can indicate the case in which the SNW or SNFW can be considered more suitable for measuring long-term fiscal sustainability. I suggested that when the financial reporting users need to assess whether a government will be able to meet its obligations as they become due, the SNFW is more suitable for measuring long-term fiscal sustainability and when the financial reporting users need to assess whether the government will be able to continue to provide services at the current levels in the future and on an ongoing basis, the SNW is more appropriate for measuring long-term fiscal sustainability.

More research is needed to study the relationship between the fiscal capacity and the SNFW, and the service capacity and the SNW.

Implications for academics: standard-setters, public sector accountants, and professional bodies: The current literature has consistently assured that a research gap remains on the role of accounting frameworks for fiscal sustainability reporting. Moreover, it is argued in public sector accounting literature that while international organizations (European Commission [EC], International Public Sector Accounting Standards Board [IPSASB]) and prior literature appreciate the usefulness of government financial statements for reporting on financial sustainability of public sector entities, *"there is no elaboration on how governmental accounting can contribute towards this objective"* Caruana et al. (2019). This chapter has shown how the academics, standard-setters, public sector accountants, and professional bodies can, for the first time, develop a long-term future focus alongside retrospective accounting practices, and has responded to the public sector accounting literature through the elaboration on how public sector accounting can contribute to measuring and reporting on long-term fiscal sustainability.

In addition, the contribution made in this chapter can be considered as a response to one of the professional bodies called the ACCA, which stated that ***"the accountancy profession should not shy away from the challenges presented by sustainability reporting, as it provides opportunities to develop the strengths of the profession in an important area."***

Implications for practice: this chapter provides guidance on and a framework for how public sector accountants can report on long-term fiscal sustainability. The developed sustainable accounting approach can enhance the usefulness of accounting information by providing practice-relevant information on measuring and reporting on long-term fiscal sustainability.

Lessons learned: the impression that accounting is a profession that focuses only on past-oriented information is not acceptable now as this chapter proves that it can also include forward-looking information by developing a long-term future focus alongside retrospective accounting practices. So the accountancy profession should seek to adapt its training support and programs to accommodate the future needs of long-term fiscal sustainability reporting. In addition, public sector accountants should not accept being marginalized but be encouraged to work in collaboration with economists, social scientists, and environmental scientists on new forms of fiscal sustainability reporting.

5 Making Public Sector Accrual Accounting and Financial Reporting More User Practice-Relevant

While the previous chapters dealt with the practice relevance of accrual accounting from the producers' perspective, Chaps. 6 and 7 addressed the practice relevance of accrual accounting from the users' perspective. Practice-relevant accounting from the users' perspective requires the public sector accounting scholars to use the practice-oriented co-design approach, which integrates the efforts of accounting researchers, practitioners, consultants, standard-setting bodies, and users to produce a user practice-relevant public sector accounting and financial reporting system that can consider the diverging needs of different users. In addition, co-design makes users act as experts of their own experience by actively involving them in all design decisions and these decisions should be taken within the context of the users, their needs, and their environment. The users' perspective also requires that public sector accounting should start a new era that shifts its focus on attempting to fit users and their needs into the design process to challenging the design process to better fit into users' practice.

In Chap. 6, I focused on how the public sector accrual accounting and financial reporting can be made more user practice-relevant.

First, I elaborated on the reasons underlying the failure of public sector accounting and financial reporting to be user practice-relevant. I found that there are several reasons behind this failure: the users themselves are in fact unable to determine their information needs; the accounting and financial reporting system in the public sector does not effectively provide or take into account the financial information required for carrying out the budget functions; there is a lack of effective communication and cooperation among accounting researchers, practitioners, consultants, standard-setters, and users; a great part of the politicians' financial information needs are not satisfied by traditional accounting regulations and policies, as they need specific accounting information that cannot be provided by an accounting system that is constrained by GAAP; the design process of the public sector accounting and financial reporting system considers the accounting system and hence the users and their needs as hermetic and static; and finally, lack of satisfaction of user needs can emerge from the poor design of the product on offer, which results from a lack of understanding of relevant principles that are used to analyze user needs and ignorance of user needs, both of which can be traced back to a lack of commitment to meeting user needs.

Future research should go deeper and explore how these reasons have made public sector accounting and financial reporting not user practice-relevant. Furthermore, future research can empirically test these reasons and explore new reasons behind this failure.

Second, the findings suggest that the production of the user practice-relevant public sector accounting and financial reporting system is no longer confined to the efforts of accounting researchers or practitioners alone but is a product of the communication and cooperation among different parties such as accounting researchers, practitioners, consultants, users, and standard-setters. This of course requires the public sector accountants/scholars to develop a new approach which blends emerging concepts of co-design and co-creation with a practice-oriented approach used in sociological studies of consumption and design (Ouda 2015). Therefore, I have attempted to adopt a new approach that has already been used in engineering studies but which needs to be developed in order to be applied to public sector accounting. This is the practice-oriented co-design approach. Unlike the traditional accounting approach which focuses on attempting to fit users and their needs into the design process, the new developed practice-oriented co-design approach focuses on challenging the design process to better fit into users' practice.

Future research can investigate and test the workability of the newly developed practice-oriented co-design approach in practice.

Third, based on the newly developed approach, I suggested a dynamic model that aims at making the public sector accounting and financial reporting more user practice-relevant. This dynamic model requires the accounting researchers, consultants, practitioners, primary users, and standard-setters to cooperate with each other in order to co-discover the users, co-identify the users' needs, co-determine the objectives of the public sector accounting and financial reporting system, and co-design the public sector accounting and financial reporting system that is best suited for reporting the information required. User practice-relevant public sector accounting requires the use of the dynamic model to reconsider the users list and consider the politicians, top managers, and policy-makers as the principal users and hence consider their needs and deal with them as experts, involving them in determining their needs. If the accounting system that is constrained by GAAP does not provide their needs, the public sector accountants should do extra work and innovation to help politicians and other users in their decision-making by designing an accounting system where they can translate the accounting information into a form that can be understood by the politicians. Moreover, the dynamic model has also considered the information required for serving the fiscal sustainability purposes.

It is important that *future studies* explore to what extent the use of the dynamic model can produce a more user practice-relevant public sector accrual accounting and financial reporting system.

Finally, the dynamic model has also dealt with increasing the usability of accounting information provided by the public sector accounting and financial reporting system by adding complementary factors, which are the determinants of accounting information use. One of the most significant driving forces to enhance the use of accounting information by politicians is political competition and conflict; therefore, strengthening the opposition parties can contribute to forcing the governing bodies to increase the use of accounting information. Furthermore, the availability and enforcement of updated financial rules, procedures, regulations, and by-laws constitute generally coercive factors that influence the use of accounting information. Another driving force that can increase the usability of accounting information is the existence of an accountability framework that can hold the politicians responsible for their decisions and actions, and make them accountable for the consequences of their decisions. Moreover, training, experience, and qualifications of politicians can play a fundamental role in increasing the usability of accounting information.

It may be useful for *future research* to extend the work of this chapter by testing the plausibility and workability of the suggested dynamic model including both the basic and the complementary factors.

Lessons learned: it is learned from this chapter that the specific information required by the politicians cannot be provided by the traditional accounting system that is constrained by GAAP; it requires a context-bound accounting system which is related to local political discourses. This lesson can indicate why the accounting information constrained by GAAP does not satisfy the information needs of the politicians. Accordingly, there should be a connection between the political discourse and the design of accounting and financial reporting to satisfy the politicians' information needs.

It is also learned that we can apply approaches used in engineering studies to accounting systems such as co-design, co-creation, and practice-oriented approach. So, the merging of co-design with a practice-oriented approach is meant to explore how politicians, internal managers, other users, accounting researchers, practitioners, consultants, and standard-setters can be cooperatively engaged in the formation of a more user practice-relevant public sector accounting and financial reporting system and how the design of an accounting and financial reporting system can be reoriented towards enabling these changes.

Implications for academics: This chapter can have an impact on the academics and public sector accountants by redirecting their efforts to challenging the accounting system design process to better fit into users' practice by using the practice-oriented co-design approach.

Implication for practice: This chapter has developed a dynamic model that can assist in making the public sector accounting more practice-relevant and satisfying different information needs by recognizing the politicians' discourse and the information required for fiscal sustainability reporting, in addition to the traditional information needs that are constrained by GAAP.

6 Cognitive Aspects and the Use/NonUse of Accounting Information by the Politicians

While the main focus of Chap. 6 was on how the public sector accrual accounting and financial reporting can be made more user practice-relevant, Chap. 7 focused on the following question: How do cognitive aspects influence the use/nonuse of accounting information by the politicians? Given the scarcity of extant research related to this question, we conceptualized and theorized the readiness to use and the actual use of accounting information in relation to the human and social agencies involved (Ouda and Klischewski 2019).

First, we focused on the individuals and their cognition/intentions. Herein, the Cognitive Fit Theory (CFT) assisted in understanding the formation of adequate mental representations to solve the tasks at hand. Cognition can perform a governance task that assists in creating and forming the mental representation, which governs the production and use of accounting information by the politicians. Thus, it has been inferred that the cognitive processes used to act on the problem representation match with those used to complete the task; thus, cognitive fit is said to exist, resulting in better problem-solving performance (Vessey 1991). When a mismatch occurs between problem representation and task, cognitive fit will not result, since similar processes cannot be used to act on both the problem representation and the solving of the problem (Vessey and Galletta 1991). Moreover, we highlighted six cognitive factors in the accounting field (knowledge, perception, expectation, beliefs, awareness, and interpretation) that can facilitate the formation of mental representation that governs the production and use of accounting information and may, hence, also affect the cognitive fit.

Future research is needed to explore other cognitive factors that can govern the production and use of accounting information; the role of cognitive processes in forming and shaping the mental representation (mental models); how effectively the mental representation governs the production and use processes of accounting information; and, finally, to explore the relative importance of the various cognitive factors (knowledge, awareness, perception, beliefs, expectation, and interpretation) in task governance and their degree of match as a predictor of accounting information usefulness.

Second, we highlighted the duality caused by the *independency of the supply side and demand side*: Each side constitutes the environment for the other, and Social Cognitive Theory (SCT) can explain how cognitive learning and behavioral change can emerge from interacting with the environment (Bandura 1986). The perception of social agency—that is, the behavior and its outcomes—as a match (fit) or mismatch (misfit) is an important source of learning and development (Ouda and Klischewski 2019). Notably, the unit of analysis is extended from the individual towards the group, organization, and/or (professional) community. SCT states that personal behaviors are shaped and affected by variations of cognitive factors and the conditions of the associated social environment (Bandura 1986). Based on the SCT, we proposed a learning alignment between the producers and the users of accounting information in order to enable a more consistent behavior between both. Behavior of the producers (which is the production of accounting information) is shaped and directed by the producers' cognition and social environment (which includes the cognition and behavior of the users). Similarly, the behavior of the users (which is the use of accounting information) is shaped and directed by the cognition of users and the social environment (which includes the cognition and behavior of the producers).

Future research can go deeper and guide the learning alignment to create a common task understanding between the producers and the users of accounting information, based on the professional awareness development including mutual learning about each other's perception of problems, tasks, and solutions.

Third, we argued that generalizing a coherence of rationality and assuming a degree of alignment within the supply side and the demand side can lead to explaining why and how cognition on each side is divergent (misfit) while at the same time *a significant degree of cognitive match (fit) is a prerequisite for producing accounting information that matches (fits) the need of the consumers*, that is, a prerequisite for its usefulness. Based on the CFT and SCT, the Accounting Information Usefulness Theory (AIUT) is proposed to explain how cognition influences the behavior of both the producers and the users of accounting information and may lead to unexpected and/or unintended behavior (Ouda and Klischewski 2019). The AIUT posits that cognitive fit increases with the degree of match between the cognition of accounting information producers and the cognition of accounting information users. It proposes that enriching and matching the various cognitive factors (as empirically measurable components of cognition) lead to formation of more aligned mental representations (i.e., practically, to a more common understanding) to govern the processes of accounting information production and use. It realizes the importance of the interactive relationship between cognition and the environment, as the behavior of the producers and the users of accounting information is shaped and directed by their cognitions and environments.

Future research is needed to empirically test the AIUT and to explore to what extent the cognitive factors can have an impact on the use/nonuse of accounting information by the politicians.

Fourth, the institutionalization of the learning alignment suggests that governments should establish and maintain an Accounting Information Research Department (AIRD) and determine the tasks of this department. *Future research* needs to address these tasks and to test it empirically, and to identify other tasks that can be added to this department, in addition to determining whether its establishment and maintenance within the government can be justified and is worthwhile. It is inferred that there is no single validation method for accounting information needs that would apply every time to every situation; *future research* needs to address the best methods for validation of the accounting information needs and whether to use a single method or to combine two or more methods. Research must also be conducted on whether the validation methods will be different between the central government and the local governments.

In terms of practical implications, the main objective of this chapter was to increase the degree of usefulness of accounting information, that is, to make it more specific to the task to be performed, to the problem to be solved, and to the challenges to be coped with and/or to the matter at hand ('task fit'). For example, the application of the theory into practice based on matching the cognitive aspects is expected to actuate an increasing use of accounting information in political decision-making when specific accounting information is provided to each of the specific stages of the policy decision-making process; guide the learning alignment to create a common task understanding between the producers and the users of accounting information, based on the professional awareness development including mutual learning about each other's perceptions of problems, tasks, and solutions; and stimulate the continuous audit of information use to continuously improve the learning alignment while also addressing changes in the social, political, economic, regulatory, and technological environment.

Accordingly, *applied future research* should study each stage of the policy decision-making from the producers' and users' perspectives and determine what accounting information should be provided by the producers to the users and what the key cognitive matching aspects are for each stage. Similarly, future research can address what the best options are to operationalize the learning alignment in different public sector entities and how operationalization may differ depending on the type of public sector entities (e.g. central vs. local).

Implications for academics: it has been found that cognitive psychology has great potential in explaining the lack of actual use of accounting information by the politicians, and that this explanatory power extends the currently prevailing rationality, objectivity, and traditional accounting theories of our field. Based on this, the chapter has conceptualized and theorized the readiness to use and the actual use of accounting information in relation to the human and social agencies involved. However, this is only a first step and there is a long way to go for academics as empirical investigations have to follow, based on measurable variables and testable relations, in order to bring evidence regarding the explanatory and predictive power of the proposed theory.

Lessons learned: The most important lesson is that the lack of actual use of accounting information by the politicians and other users cannot be explained only by the traditional accounting theories which neglect the impact of social science on the use or nonuse of accounting information; understanding the way the users approach the decision-making process is at the heart of the practice of cognitive psychology.

7 Conclusion

In conclusion, the implementation of accrual accounting in the public sector and its practice relevance for the public sector entities is a fascinating topic that has triggered our interest and inspired our research for more than two decades. While scholars have made progress in studying this topic, it has been shown in this chapter that there is indeed a lot of work that needs to be done to make the public sector accrual accounting more practice-relevant from both the producer's and user's perspectives. Every research question addressed in this chapter has opened up further questions towards making accrual accounting fit the context of the public sector. The goal of this book was to open the door for developing a new version of accrual accounting that is specifically designed for the public sector entities and not just a modified version of commercial accrual accounting, and to identify the opportunities for future research that will continue to proceed towards achieving this goal.

Therefore, this book can be considered as a starting point for tracking the necessary developments and adjustments that are required for making accrual accounting more practice-relevant for the public sector entities. We hope you enjoyed our book and were able to glean some new insights into technical and behavioral issues related to the adoption of accrual accounting in the public sector.

References

Bandura, A. (1986). *Social Foundations of Thought and Action: A Social Cognitive Theory*. Englewood Cliffs, NJ: Prentice-Hall.

Bandy, G. (2011). *Financial Management and Accounting in the Public Sector*. Abingdon: Routledge.

Brundtland, (1987). *The World Commission on Environment and Development (WCED)*. United Nations 1987.

Brusca, I., Caperchione, E., Cohen, S., & Manes Rossi, F. (Eds.). (2015). *Public Sector Accounting and Auditing in Europe; The Challenge of Harmonization*. Houndmills, Basingstoke, Hampshire: Palgrave MacMillan.

Budding, G., Grossi, G., & Tagesson, T. (2014). *Public Sector Accounting*. London: Taylor and Francis.

Caruana, J., Brusca, I., Caperchione, E., Cohen, S., & Manes Rossi, F (2019). Exploring the Relevance of Accounting Frameworks in the Pursuit of Financial Sustainability of the Public Sector Entities: A Holistic Approach. In Caruana et al. (Eds.), *Published in Financial Sustainability of Public Sector Entities*. https://doi.org/10.1007/978-3-030-06037-4-1.

Christiaens, J., Rommel, J., Barton, A., & Everaert, P. (2012). Should All Capital Goods of Governments be Recognized as Assets in Financial Accounting? *Baltic Journal of Management, 7*(4), 429–443.

Dabbicco, G. (2019). The Potential Role of Public Sector Accounting Frameworks Towards Financial Sustainability Reporting. In Caruana et al. (Eds.), *Published in Financial Sustainability of Public Sector entities*. https://doi.org/10.1007/978-3-030-06037-4-1.

IPSASB. (2010). *IPSAS 17: "Property, Plant and Equipment"*. New York.
IPSASB. (2013). *Reporting on the Long-Term Sustainability of Public Sector Entity's Finances.* Recommended Practice Guideline No. 3.
IPSASB. (2014, October). *The Conceptual Framework for General Purpose Financial Reporting by Public Sector Entities.* IFAC.
IPSASB. *IPSAS 16: Investment Property.* New York.
Jones, R., & Pendlebury, M. (2010). *Public sector accounting* (6th ed.). Harlow: Prentice Hall Pearson.
Laughlin, R. (2011). Accounting Research, Policy and Practice: Worlds Together or Worlds Apart? In E. Evans, R. Burritt, & J. Guthrie (Eds.), *Bridging the Gap between Academic Accounting Research and Professional Practice* (pp. 21–30). Sydney: The Institute of Chartered Accountants in Australia.
Lüder, K., & Jones, R. (Eds.). (2003). *Reforming Governmental Accounting and Budgeting in Europe.* Frankfurt am Main: Fachverlag Moderne Wirtschaft.
Monsen, N., & Nasi, S. (1997). *The Contingency Model Reconsidered: On the Definition of Government Accounting Innovations.* Paper Published at the 6th Biennial CIGAR Conference, Milan.
Ouda, H. (2003). Accrual Accounting in the Government Sector: Background, Concepts, Benefits and Costs. *ICGFM-Public Fund Digest, 11*(2), 52–73.
Ouda, H. (2007, February). Accrual Accounting Principles and Postulations in the Public Sector: Rhetoric or Reality. *Public Fund Digest, 7*(1), 39–52. Washington, DC: The International Consortium on Governmental Financial Management (ICGFM).
Ouda, H. (2014). Towards a Practical Accounting Approach for Heritage Assets: An Alternative Reporting Model for the NPM Practices. *Journal of Finance and Accounting, 2*(2), 19–33.
Ouda, H. (2015). Making Governmental Accounting More Practice-Relevant: Practitioner's Perspective. *International Journal on Governmental Financial Management, XV*(1), 9.
Ouda, H. (2016). Governmental Capital assets: How Far Should the Accounting Recognition of These Assets Go? *International Journal on Governmental Financial Management, XVI*(1), 24.
Ouda, H., & Klischewski, R. (2019). Accounting and Politicians: A Theory of Accounting Information Usefulness. *Journal of Public Budgeting, Accounting and Financial Management, 31*(4), 496–517.
Van Helden, J., & Hodges, R. (2015). *Public Sector Accounting and Budgeting for Non-Specialists.* London: Palgrave McMillan.
Vessey, I. (1991). Cognitive Fit: A Theory-Based Analysis of Graphs Versus Tables Literature. *Decision Sciences, 22*, 219–240.
Vessey, I., & Galletta, D. (1991). Cognitive Fit: An Empirical Study of Information Acquisition. *Information Systems Research, 2*(1), 63–84.
Weers, G. (2016). *The Charitable Trust Model: An Alternative Approach for Department of Defense Accounting.* Monterey, CA: Naval Postgraduate School.

Index

H. Ouda, *Practice-Relevant Accrual Accounting for the Public Sector*, Public Sector Financial Management,
https://doi.org/10.1007/978-3-030-51595-9

The manufacturer's authorised representative in the EU is Springer Nature Customer Service Centre GmbH, Europaplatz 3, 69115 Heidelberg, Germany. If you have any concerns regarding our products, please contact ProductSafety@springernature.com

Printed and bound by CPI Group (UK) Ltd, Croydon, CR0 4YY
30/09/2026
02225452-0003